D1526285

Sounds of the Metropolis

ML
3470
.S38
2008

Sounds of the Metropolis

The Nineteenth-Century
Popular Music Revolution in
London, New York, Paris, and Vienna

Derek B. Scott

OXFORD
UNIVERSITY PRESS

2008

Oxford University Press, Inc., publishes works that further
Oxford University's objective of excellence
in research, scholarship, and education.

Oxford   New York
Auckland   Cape Town   Dar es Salaam   Hong Kong   Karachi
Kuala Lumpur   Madrid   Melbourne   Mexico City   Nairobi
New Delhi   Shanghai   Taipei   Toronto

With offices in
Argentina   Austria   Brazil   Chile   Czech Republic   France   Greece
Guatemala   Hungary   Italy   Japan   Poland   Portugal   Singapore
South Korea   Switzerland   Thailand   Turkey   Ukraine   Vietnam

Copyright © 2008 by Oxford University Press

Published by Oxford University Press, Inc.
198 Madison Avenue, New York, New York 10016

www.oup.com

Oxford is a registered trademark of Oxford University Press

All rights reserved. No part of this publication may be reproduced,
stored in a retrieval system, or transmitted, in any form or by any means,
electronic, mechanical, photocopying, recording, or otherwise,
without the prior permission of Oxford University Press.

Library of Congress Cataloging-in-Publication Data
Scott, Derek B.
Sounds of the metropolis : the nineteenth-century popular music revolution
in London, New York, Paris, and Vienna / Derek B. Scott.
p.   cm.
Includes bibliographical references and index.
ISBN 978-0-19-530946-1
1. Popular music—Europe—To 1901—History and
criticism. 2. Popular music—New York (State)—New
York—To 1901—History and criticism.   I. Title.
ML3470.S38 2008
781.6409'034—dc22   2007025321

1   3   5   7   9   8   6   4   2
Printed in the United States of America
on acid-free paper

Acknowledgments

The ten years of research that culminate in the production of this book may never have begun had not Helen Greenwald given me such warm encouragement after hearing a couple of my early conference presentations on this topic. I make this statement to express my gratitude, of course, and not to hold her responsible for any failings in the end product. Earlier versions of chapters 6 and 7 appeared, respectively, in Julian Rushton and Rachel Cowgill, eds, *Europe, Empire and Spectacle in 19th-Century British Music* (Aldershot, England: Ashgate, 2006), 265–80, and *Music and Letters* 83, no. 2 (May 2002), 237–58. I am indebted in my Strauss research to the help given to me by Eduard Strauss and Thomas Aigner of the Wiener Institut für Strauss-Forschung (WISF), and I benefited much from being able to consult the comprehensive Strauss-Sammlung housed at Bartensteingasse 9 in Vienna. I am indebted to Mireille Ribière for informative advice on various aspects of French culture, and also for being so helpful whenever I had queries or translation problems with French texts. Beate Peter performed a similar service whenever I encountered difficulty with German texts. I am grateful to Bill Weber for allowing me to peruse his forthcoming book on the transformation of musical taste in the nineteenth century—especially given that the current academic climate tends to put scholars in a competitive relation to each other rather than encouraging mutual endeavor. I wish to thank the British Academy for financial help, and the University of Leeds and the UK's Arts and Humanities Research Council for financing a period of research leave that covered the writing-up of this study.

I am grateful to the American Musicological Society Publications Committee for awarding a subvention grant from the Gustave Reese Publication Endowment Fund, and I much value the support given to me during the production process by Suzanne Ryan, Norman Hirschy, and Robert Milks at OUP, New York. Finally, thanks go to my wife, Sara, and the many friends, colleagues, and students who have helped me to clarify in my mind the ideas and arguments presented in the pages that follow.

Contents

Sounds of the Metropolis

Introduction

On hearing the words "popular music revolution," thoughts are likely to turn to the decade of the 1950s when rock 'n' roll overturned established ideas about the character and style of popular music. Alternatively, one might assume that the topic was the jazz of New Orleans and its legacy in the syncopated dance styles that preceded rock 'n' roll. However, the nineteenth century witnessed the first cultural upheaval of this kind, as popular styles began to assert their independence and distinct values. No longer was the popular style something that offered a more easily digested concoction of the techniques and cultural values found in high-status music; it had its own characteristic techniques, forms, and devices. By the end of the century, as a result of the growth of the music market and the increased professionalism in the musical world, there was a variety of popular genres, each with its own peculiar characteristics. London, New York, Paris, and Vienna feature prominently as cities in which the challenge to the classical tradition was strongest, and in which original and influential forms of popular music arose. Indeed, these metropolises were home to four distinct revolutions in popular style: London was the birthplace of music hall, New York of minstrelsy, Paris of cabaret, and Vienna of popular dance music for couples—genres that endured well into the twentieth century.

The reader may wonder what I mean by writing of a popular music *revolution*. I hope the succeeding chapters will demonstrate that such a term is not inappropriate, and also make clear that I am referring to a revolution in musical style as well as genre. This revolution was driven by social changes and the incorporation of music into a system of capitalist enterprise: it resulted in a polarization between the style of musical entertainment (or "commercial" music) and that of "serious" art. Nobody doubts that this fissure between art and entertainment was created in the nineteenth century. Henry Raynor speaks of the "great schism," and Theodor Adorno of the "scars" (*Narben*) left on Western music culture as a consequence of nineteenth-century commercialism.[1] I wanted, in this book, to select the key genres and styles that precipitated musical change at that time, and continued to affect popular music in the next century. Indeed, one might argue that popular music had become a different musical language, and one that might be spoken in different dialects and with different accents. New art worlds were being created, with the establishment of new musical conventions, new techniques, new organizations, and new networks of distribution. An art world, in Howard Becker's theorization, exists in cooperative activity rather than as a structure, and requires those who participate in it to understand its conventions and be skilled in its routines.[2] The popular music revolution in the nineteenth century meant that the understanding of certain conventions and routines was to become out of bounds for some musicians. One consequence was that the seamless incorporation of popular styles, as found in a work like *Die Zauberflöte*, was no longer a possibility. Nobody in the twentieth century would expect someone who could play Rodrigo's Guitar Concerto to be equally adept at playing a twelve-bar blues. In the nineteenth century, nobody would expect an opera singer to perform convincingly a *chanson réaliste*, or assume that a musician skilled in the classical symphonic repertoire would automatically be capable of giving a characteristic lilt to a Viennese waltz. Becker speaks of revolutionary innovations as those that involve changes of certain conventions, since every existing convention "implies an aesthetic which makes what is conventional the standard of artistic beauty and effectiveness."[3] The popular music revolution brought forth musical idioms whose difference in both style and meaning from the classical repertoire created insuperable problems for those who were unfamiliar with the new conventions and lacked the particular skills demanded by the new styles.

The legacy is with us still. As I walked into the Volksoper in Vienna in September 2006, the usher saw that behind my ticket for *Der Zigeunerbaron* was another for *Lohengrin* at the Staatsoper. He raised his eyes and declared that they were two different worlds. Indeed, a case could be made that they are two different art worlds in Becker's sense, though they overlap, as art worlds frequently do. It would be wrong to think of art worlds as homogeneous entities; often one or more practitioners within an art world find competitive coexistence is not an option, and break away to form a new organization and new distribution network, an action usually accompanied by a loss of status. Yet the usher's comment left me thinking about what it was that made opera and operetta distinct aesthetically. I did not have to wait long for clari-fication. Almost immediately on the opening of act 1, Barinkay sings an aria that shouts *Unterhaltungsmusik* at the audience—an irresistible, swinging waltz tune with a rhythmic zest that makes it almost impos-sible to keep the body still. Then I noticed the costumes; they were garish and theatrical, some containing deliberate clashes of color. Soon, Zsupán the swineherd made his entrance accompanied by ten "Miss Piggies" all wearing bespangled tutus and, during the course of Zsupán's song, linking arms to perform a parody of *Swan Lake*. After this, I began to no-tice the unusual range of physical activity taking place—acrobatics and juggling, for example—but that was not the most significant feature. What I saw was that up-to-date movements associated with the most recent pop and dance performers were perfectly acceptable. It was equally permissible to alter the original lyrics in order to incorporate topical al-lusions. All this told me two things: (1) deliberate vulgarity was relished as a means of giving high culture a cheeky slap; and (2) the popular rev-olution in the nineteenth century turned out to be a permanent one. Popular culture of the past enjoys a living relationship with popular culture of today: it retains (and continues to reach out to retain) an au-dience. High culture slowly lost its continuity with the past and, in its modernist manifestations, lost most of its audience, too.

Most accounts of the popularity of the dance music of nineteenth-century Vienna tend to concentrate on the social history of the period and on providing autobiographical information about the Strauss fam-ily. While acknowledging the importance of social and cultural context, I want, in this study, to analyze the musical features that made up the new popular style. My contention is that "popular" refers for the first time not only to the music's reception but also to the presence of these specific features of style. In Vienna the terms "entertainment music" (*Unterhaltungsmusik*) and "light music" (*leichte Musik*) were soon coined to act as descriptors of this particular musical character. It is important to realize that these cultural changes mean that "popular music" can-not be directly translated into French as "musique populaire" or into German as "populäre Musik." In French and German, the adjective "popular" retained different nuances of meaning (associated with the working class or the folk). French popular music of the commercial type would eventually come to be described as *variétés françaises*.

This new categorization of music production was inextricably linked to the industrial production of sheet music and the growth of the music entertainment business; yet, significantly, it meant that it be-came possible for a composition to be popular in style without neces-sarily being popular in terms of commercial success. Thus, the shift in meaning of "popular" provided critics with a means of condemning music that bore the signs of the popular—which they regarded as fash-ionable and facile (*leicht* in German means "easy") rather than progres-sive and serious—whether or not such music enjoyed success in the market place. Some Anglo-American critics have wished to make a distinction between light music and popular music, but there is no substantial differentiation worth pursuing: the meaning of each may be defined sociologically as music produced for a commercial market. Adorno gives the title "Leichte Musik" to the second chapter of his *Einleitung in die Musiksoziologie* (1962), and E. B. Ashton translated it, without controversy, as "popular music."[4] For Adorno, music had become carved up into just two categories, "light" and "classical"—the "classical" forming an arbitrary category that exists only in contrast to the "light."[5] Adorno is no fonder of "official" classical music than he is of popular music; in fact, he holds that they both stand apart from that "serious" music that is not given over to consumption, and he regards the differences in their reception as no longer having any real meaning.[6] It was the nineteenth-century popular music revolution that colored his views: "From the middle of the nineteenth century on, good music has renounced commercialism altogether."[7] Thus, it became an incontrovertible truth for modernists like Pierre Boulez that music written in a popular style was tantamount to music written for sale (the creation of "objects of musical consumption") and, consequently, was anathema to the composer of "serious" or "learned" music.[8] Any apparent innovation in popular music was to be exposed as pseudo-originality. Carl Dahlhaus tied this type of false novelty to market relations, remarking that it needs to establish itself immediately as convention in order to be fashionable (and thus to sell), whereas true artistic innovation presents a challenge.[9]

My argument is that what happened in London, Paris, New York, and Vienna changed perceptions completely about the nature of popular music and its perceived value. When Mozart wrote in a popular or folk-like style, it did not contradict the aesthetic values of his other music. After the popular music revolution, new styles were developing in commercial urban environments that could not be accommodated satisfactorily within the newly fashionable term "folk music." When composers wrote in these popular commercial styles they often opposed and offended the values of those who defended high art. Yet it was no mere gimmickry or perversity that prompted the development of new musical styles and genres, and the legacy of what happened in these nineteenth-century metropolises shaped twentieth-century forms of popular music in Europe and North America in important ways. The revolution also changed attitudes to class, for popular singers, like the mercantile and industrial bourgeoisie before them, were able to buy themselves into another class by purchasing country estates. The emergence of the "pop idol" and "pop aristocracy" is already discernible in the nineteenth century.[10]

Let me very briefly (and far too simply) explain the legacy of the stylistic revolution. Dance music in Vienna provided infectious rhythms, novel orchestral timbres, and a new coloristic use of harmony (chords that took on a "free-floating" major sixth or major seventh); it also employed new melodic devices (the *wienerische Note*). It was in Vienna that what became known as "light music" was created, and the old types of *contredanses* were gradually ousted by dances for couples (the waltz and polka). Blackface minstrelsy in New York provided popular music with a percussive character, a new type of syncopation, and a three-chord model—features inherited by a range of twentieth-century styles from blues to punk. Music hall in London supplied songs with a hook or catchy chorus coupled to a less memorable, narrative-driven verse section—features inherited by Tin Pan Alley, dance bands, and stage musicals. Cabaret in Paris presented songs with hard-hitting and socially concerned texts, precursors of later protest songs (for example, those of Bob Dylan) and various later forms of "realist" song (for instance, Jacques Brel's "Amsterdam," Radiohead's "Creep"). A lot of musicological ink has been spilt on the nineteenth-century revolution in classical style (how Wagner's *Tristan* supposedly led to the dissolution of tonality, and how Brahms's "developing variations" influenced Schoenberg), but there is nothing that focuses on, or even acknowledges, the revolution in popular style in this period, despite its having created its own new musical meanings. This is, I believe, the first book to study nineteenth-century popular music in terms of a stylistic revolution, to show how and why it challenged existing practices, to show how it circulated rapidly as a commodity form, and to show how it established its own aesthetic conventions across Europe and North America.[11] Consider, for example, how the legacy of the Viennese popular style contributes a special meaning to the song "Bring Me Sunshine" (words by Sylvia Dee, music by Arthur Kent, 1966), made famous by the comedians Eric Morecambe and Ernie Wise. The melody implies a minor key, with harmonies on the tonic and subdominant (see ex. I.1). This would, of course, be bizarre and inappropriate for the words "Bring me sunshine in your smile, / Bring me laughter all the while." But we find that the tonality is actually the relative major of the key implied by the tune, and the harmonies consist of the tonic (with a free-floating sixth) and dominant ninth. Suddenly the words and music make perfect sense, the tension of the dissonances conveying the sense of an appeal for sunshine, rather than the actual presence of sunshine.

The first part of this book surveys the range of new popular music for the home, concert hall, and stage in the context of the social, eco-

Example I.1 "Bring Me Sunshine" (Sylvia Dee/Arthur Kent, 1966).

nomic, and cultural life of the chosen cities. The second part consists of particularized studies relating to the genres that represent each city's unique contribution to popular music. My intention in part I is to provide an overview of popular music in these four metropolises, but I do focus on detail whenever it illustrates the broader argument or reveals developments of particular interest. The historical emphasis falls on the second half of the nineteenth century, when features of musical life associated with a capitalist economy and the consolidation of power of a wealthy industrial bourgeoisie became firmly established. Prominent among such features were the commercialization and professionalization of music, new markets for cultural goods, the bourgeoisie's struggle for cultural domination, and a growing rift between art and entertainment.

It is important to say that the topic of this book is music in the metropolis, and what is represented here is a study of four *cities*, not four *countries*. Nevertheless, these were major commercial cities of those countries, home to the wealthiest commercial families. In each, there was rapid population growth and the creation of a diverse market for entertainment that is a key feature of metropolitan life. The power wielded by the upper class began to weaken earlier in Paris than in London, first because of the French Revolution and later by the ousting of Charles X in the 1830 revolution; his replacement by the bourgeoisie-friendly Louis-Philippe led to further mixing between aristocracy and bourgeoisie. Aristocratic power was slowest to give way in Vienna, where the nobility mingled least with the bourgeoisie. In New York, there were no inherited titles, of course, although the "upper ten" of that city were often disposed to define themselves against the European aristocracy and, at midcentury, were perceived to be not dissimilar to the upper classes of Paris's Faubourg St. Germain or London's West End.[12] Paris underwent major reconstruction in the second half of the century. Napoléon III instructed Baron Haussmann to redesign Paris following the 1848 revolution, and the result was a city of wide arterial boulevards and symmetrical layout. In Vienna, the Ring developments that replaced the city walls initiated equally important changes, and for some fifty years, property developers were continually at work. The title of Johann Strauss Jr.'s *Demolirer-Polka,* op. 269 (1862) refers to the demolition of Vienna's ramparts. In both cities, working-class communities were uprooted and displaced; Vienna also saw the construction of the tightly crowded Zinkasernen for the accommodation of immigrants from the east of the empire. In all four cities, the demarcation between private and public became increasingly rigid and their boundaries ever more strictly policed.

The nineteenth-century popular music revolution—situated in this larger context—has been strangely neglected;[13] yet the distinctness of this music did not go unrecognized at the time. A brief example: Oscar Schmitz visited London after the turn of that century and wrote about his experiences in a book entitled *Das Land ohne Musik* (the land without music). Everyone seems to know that phrase, yet perhaps very few are aware that immediately after Schmitz claims the English are "das einzige Kulturvolk ohne eigene Musik" (the only cultured people lacking their own music) he adds "Gassenhauer ausgenommen" (popular music excepted).[14]

Since a great deal of part I is concerned with general matters concerning popular music, a warning is needed about interpreting popular song as a reflection of everyday social reality. The minstrel song "The Empty Cradle" (Harry Kennedy, 1880) became less popular, not more popular, when infant mortality rose.[15] More generally, it is important to recognize that high- and low-status music cannot be mapped directly onto high- and low-class consumers. There was scarcely a European ruler who did not attend a performance of Offenbach's *La Grande-Duchesse de Gérolstein*. While arguments can be made for the effectiveness of different styles in articulating distinct class interests, it should not be forgotten that a French haut bourgeois could enjoy a café-concert chanson, and an English factory worker enjoy singing in Handel's *Messiah*. We also need to be aware of Max Weber's warning not to confuse struggles between status groups as struggles between classes; indeed, status groups "hinder the strict carrying through of the sheer market principle."[16] On the other hand, for those who argue there is no relation between musical taste and social class, the empirical data gathered by Pierre Bourdieu is disconcerting.[17] William Weber has commented on the difficulty of defining the middle class in the nineteenth century,[18] but I intend to sidestep this by inclining toward a Gramscian model in which the middle class is perceived not as a homogeneous body, but as a group composed of fractional interests.[19] The field of the popular that opened up in the nineteenth century was one in which different classes and class fractions fought over questions of intellectual and moral leadership (in Gramscian terms, hegemony). This struggle concerned matters of cultural status and legitimation, and popular culture functioned frequently as an area of compromise over values. For instance, aristocratic and bourgeois interests might come together (as they often did in Paris), but the working class might adopt evasive or resistant strategies. At other times, a bourgeois bohemian fraction might have interests that coincided with those of the working class, so that more than one class would be present in a London West End music hall or a Parisian cabaret. In short, popular culture functions as a site for the contested meanings of social experience.

In tandem with the growth of a commercial music industry, the term "popular" changed its meaning during the course of the century, moving from well known to well received to successful in terms of sheet music sales. A song described as a "favorite air" suggested one widely liked; the words "sung with tumultuous applause by . . ." indicated a song adopted by a star singer whose choice an admiring audience had endorsed; the boast "20,000 copies sold" implied that there could be no better recommendation than that so many people had bought the song. The last type of claim became the key marker of the popular song; indeed, when charts began in the twentieth century, sheet music sales (later record sales) were the sole measure of popularity: a "hit" or *Schlager* was simply a big seller. However, there is no escaping the vexations of terminology here. There is the problem of the meanings "popular music" has gathered to itself since the late nineteenth century, which often conflict with the term's actual use earlier in that century, when "popular song" meant a widely known song, but not necessarily a "lesser" kind of song (some popular songs may have been seen as lesser songs, but it was not an automatic judgment). Educationalists would condemn music hall songs as rubbish, but not condemn popular song in general as rubbish (they even liked some blackface minstrel songs). A difficulty I have with Richard Middleton's definition of popular music as, among other things, "types of music that are considered to be of lower value"[20] is that it does not specify who does the considering and why their opinion counts, and it sits uncomfortably with what we know to be the case for much of the nineteenth century. Both Queen Victoria and John Ruskin, for example, loved the song "Home, Sweet Home." Here we have a member of the social elite and a member of the critical-aesthetic elite, yet neither is prepared to condemn this popular song as music of lower value.[21] It is said that Queen Victoria made Henry Bishop the first-ever musical knight because she loved the song so much. Ruskin annoyed Charles Hallé when he remarked that he preferred his performance of Thalberg's variations on "Home Sweet, Home" to his performance of a Beethoven piano sonata.[22] Nevertheless, the tendency to see all popular music as "lesser" music increases in the 1880s, as certain artists and critics take a stand against all things easy or light, and as the label "popular" becomes associated with an undiscriminating mass public at the same time as it replaces earlier terms such as "favorite" or, in Vienna, "beliebt." Tonic Sol-fa is caught in the crossfire, too, and a scorn for this easy method of sight-singing grows. The supposedly easy instruments of the brass band also begin to attract derision: the cornet is "lesser" than the trumpet; the tenor horn is "lesser" than the French horn, and so forth.

A development related to the altered use of the term "popular music" was the reluctance in the later century to accept as folk songs anything originating in composed music—an effective means of excluding commercial popular song. Folk music came to mean national music, an ideological shift aligning it with bourgeois aspirations and identity rather than the lower class.[23] In London, during 1855–59, William Chappell felt quite comfortable publishing a collection of traditional songs under the title *Popular Music of the Olden Time*. In the 1890s, however, Frank Kidson explained that he was driven to collecting the material he published as *English Peasant Songs* by the desire to counter the accusation that England had no *national* music.[24] The concept of a national music brought with it the notion that one had to belong to a nation to understand its music: for example, Wagner began to wonder if the French could really appreciate Beethoven, even though, as Henry Raynor comments, he himself wrote uncomprehendingly of Haydn's symphonies.[25]

To understand matters relating to music and class in the nineteenth century, it is important to know how ideas of class were being reformulated. A new perception grew of classes as economic social groupings with the capacity to effect social change. From this perspective, most familiar from the writings of Karl Marx and Friedrich Engels, some groups were regarded as left over from a previous "mode of production" (the aristocracy and peasantry as residual feudal elements), while others were seen to represent a modern clash of class interests (capitalists and the working class). Ideas of "class struggle" and "class consciousness" developed in the nineteenth century.[26] John Stuart Mill and Harriet Taylor wrote in 1848 that the European working classes were "perpetually showing that they think the interests of their employers not identical with their own, but opposite to them."[27] The crucial determinants of class position in these economic terms was whether or not one had ownership of the "means of production" and whether one had the ability to purchase labor power, or needed to sell one's own. Economic relations between people were of paramount importance. Class divisions described in terms of lower class, middle class, and upper class arose in the period 1770–1840, the time of the Industrial Revolution in Britain,[28] but the new conceptualization of class saw social position as something that could be, at least partially, attained by anyone. Former ideas were based on notions of hierarchy and rank, linked to a belief that these were determined at birth: hence the term "lower orders," though it continued to be used, really belonged to earlier times.[29] Raymond Williams suggested that the term "lower middle class" was first heard of in the twentieth century;[30] but it is already named in Gilbert and Sullivan's *Iolanthe* (1882): the "March of Peers" contains the command "Bow, bow ye lower middle classes."[31]

Part II of this book consists of four case studies relating to revolutionary popular genres that arose in each metropolis. Chapter 5 analyzes the musical features that appear in the Viennese waltz, and examines the sociocultural context of its reception. Heinrich Jacob, in his biography of Johann Strauss Sr., declared, "till then no music had such demotic strength."[32] Yet the origin of the Viennese waltz is still shrouded in confusion: for example, much previous scholarship has tended to emphasize the importance of the *Ländler* and neglect the influence of the *Dreher.* Chapter 6 explores the reception of black and blackface minstrelsy outside of the United States. There has been an increase in studies of this genre in its American context, but surprisingly little research (Michael Pickering excepted) into its reception in Europe, despite Charles Hamm's calling the minstrel song "the first distinctly American genre."[33] Europeans first acquired knowledge of the music making of African Americans through the distorting medium of blackface minstrelsy. In Germany, for example, some minstrel songs were published as genuine "Negro airs." Reception could also differ significantly in the European cultural context. The Ethiopian Serenaders were hugely successful in London in 1846, and performed before Queen Victoria; yet, they were a flop in Paris the following year. The argument of chapter 7 is that the representation of the Cockney in music hall went through three successive phases. It began as a parody of working-class life; then it turned into a more complex stage type played by character actors. It ended, finally, with a confusion of the real and imaginary in which the performer was seen as a "real" Cockney and no longer acting. Once this final phase had been reached, however, performers began to derive their stage representation no longer from the flesh-and-blood Cockney but, instead, by replicating already-existing representations. Chapter 8 investigates the music of the artistic cabarets of Montmartre, especially the Chat Noir, and finds a contradictory character in its reception. Aristide Bruant's chansons, for example, have been regarded as a mouthpiece for the Parisian underclass, but evidence shows they also served as entertainment for the affluent who enjoyed "slumming" in Montmartre. I argue for an interpretation of the *chansons modernes* that locates their meaning and value in the context of debates about the modern, the popular, and the avant-garde. They need to be understood as part of a new type of artistic cabaret that engaged with the contradictions and complexities of modernity, and spread quickly throughout Europe (to the Quatre Gats, Barcelona, the Elf Scharfrichter, Munich, the Schall und Rauch, Berlin, and Die Fledermaus, Vienna).

I

THE SOCIAL CONTEXT OF THE POPULAR MUSIC REVOLUTION

1

Professionalism and Commercialism

The reasons the cities that are the focus of this study became important musical centers are to be found in the social and economic conditions that gave rise to an active concert life in each of them. William Weber says that by 1848 a commercial concert world had emerged in London, Paris, and Vienna, "over which the middle class exerted powerful, if not dominant, control."[1] Antagonisms provoked by commercial interests in music began in the same period. Richard Leppert relates the "implicit social antagonism in the ideological foundation of much nineteenth-century aesthetics" to artists' increased dependence on the cultural market capitalism was creating.[2] Leonard Meyer has commented, "even as they scorned and mocked the middle class, the artists of the nineteenth century created for it."[3] Some composers depended for their livelihood on the wealthy bourgeoisie, and some musicians played low-status music because they could not find employment playing high-status music. This was also the age of musical entrepreneurialism, when many new opportunities for professionalism arose as new markets, such as blackface minstrelsy, the café-concert, and music hall, were opened up (see chapter 2).[4] The first company of minstrels established in New York was under the management of E. P. Christy at Palmo's Opera House, but "seeing a prospect of establishing themselves permanently in the Metropolis," they moved to Mechanic's Hall. Their subsequent and rapid financial success is indicated by the following figures. In 1852, they gave 69 concerts and made $1,848; in 1853, they gave 312 concerts and made $47,972.[5] In Britain, the *Era Almanack*, an annual publication related to the music hall periodical the *Era*, listed 862 musical acts in 1868; ten years on it listed 1,896.[6] Many of these music hall performers migrated to pantomime at Christmas. In 1891, 1,010 artists were performing in 85 theatres in London and the provinces during the Christmas season.[7] While Britain's population doubled in the sixty years after 1870, the increase in musicians was sevenfold, a fact Cyril Ehrlich puts down to expanded demand "derived, in large measure, from an efflorescence of commercial entertainment."[8] In a broad sense, professionalization means that specialists arise with role-specific knowledge. It is driven by a division of labor in music that demands the possession of standardized skills suited to specific tasks.[9] When Strauss Jr. gave his promenade concerts at Covent Garden during August–October 1867, he had no need to bring an orchestra with him, as his father had done. An art world was now in place that allowed him to recruit British players who could cope adequately with the task at hand, many of them drawn from the ranks of those who usually played at the Royal Italian Opera House.

In the first half of the century, music in Britain was seen as no better than sport as a career, and even the most talented musician was thought to rank "scarcely above an ordinary artisan."[10] It would be more accurate, perhaps, to ascribe a liminal status to musicians: they existed in the undefined margins of society and might, at different times, be regarded with admiration or contempt, fond regard or fear. The great wealth amassed by certain singers, as well as instrumental virtuosos like Nicolai Paganini, had an impact on perceptions, and the increased professionalism and formation of societies also helped to establish higher social status for musicians. The Gesellschaft der Musikfreunde was formed in Vienna in 1813, for example, and the Society of British Musicians was founded in 1834 to campaign for and protect musicians' professional interests.[11] The second half of the century witnessed a massive increase in the numbers of professional musicians; Ehrlich estimates the figure in England and Wales in 1840 as around 7,000 (in a population of about 27 million) and in 1930 as 50,000 (in a Britain and Ireland population of 50 million).[12] Many of the professionals would have been music teachers, whose numbers multiplied in the 1870s. Cheap music lessons were being advertised in abundance, and in the opinion of the *Musical Standard,* the art was now "being 'professed' by persons totally incapable."[13] Professional performers for the larger part of the nineteenth century acquired their training through private lessons, despite the presence of conservatoires in Paris (from 1795) and Vienna (from 1836) and the Royal Academy of Music in London (from 1823).

There was no permanent symphony orchestra in London before the founding of the Philharmonic Society in 1813. The orchestra of the Concert of Ancient Music had a restricted membership policy and performed nothing composed within the preceding twenty-five years.[14] The Philharmonic Society was interested in new music as well as old, and famously commissioned Beethoven to compose his Ninth Symphony (though it was first performed in Vienna). It would be incorrect to imagine that the Society was launched to fight the cause of high culture against the incursions of the popular. This attitude did not develop for some time (see chapter 4). Indeed, among the Society's founders were William Shield and Henry Bishop; the former was already known for popular ballads like "The Wolf," and the latter would, in the next decade, compose the biggest hit of the age, "Home, Sweet Home." The orchestra moved to St James's Hall, Piccadilly, when it opened in 1858, occupying the larger hall, while the Moore and Burgess Minstrels (London's first permanent blackface minstrel troupe) took the smaller. Unfortunately, the Philharmonic's audience could sometimes hear the minstrels, whose hall was underneath the concert platform. Since the larger hall had a capacity of 2,000, subscription rates were reduced, and unreserved tickets could be obtained for 5 shillings and 2 shillings and sixpence.[15] These are still high prices, but they show that the Philharmonic Society had to compete with cheaper concerts given at the Crystal Palace.

The Société des concerts du conservatoire presented Paris's main high-status concerts of classical music; they began under Habaneck's direction in 1828 and were attended by subscribers drawn from the city's nobility and haute bourgeoisie. Jules Pasdeloup offered seats at a cheap price for his "Concerts populaires de musique classique" at the Cirque Napoléon, which started in 1861 and lasted into the 1880s (by which time the Cirque Napoléon had been renamed the Cirque d'Hiver). Pasdeloup regularly attracted a mixed-class audience of thousands.

In Vienna, subscription concerts began in the Hofburg Redoutensaal in 1833, given by the Kärntnertor Theater's chorus and orchestra. In the next decade, Karl Otto Nicolai formed the Vienna Philharmonic Society, and the first concert was on 28 March 1842.[16] Yet no professionalization of classical music, such as that found in London and Paris, occurred in Vienna before midcentury (popular music was a different matter); a major reason was the lack of mingling between the upper middle class and aristocracy, and the latter's fondness for salon concerts.[17] The founding of the Vienna Philharmonic helped to set change in motion in the second half of the century.[18] Before then, it was popular music that became a professional world, and so quickly that Weber maintains that it "just blew the classical scene off the map."[19] In addition to the waltz orchestras, there were the virtuosos who drew enthusiastic audiences.

The professionalization of classical music was also late developing in New York. On 7 December 1842, the Philharmonic Society of New York gave its first concert, at the Apollo Rooms.[20] In the 1840s, virtuosos, especially pianists, were appearing in America. There was such an appetite for visiting celebrities that the great showman P. T. Barnum took on the promotion of Jenny Lind in America in the 1850s. New

Orleans–born Louis Moreau Gottschalk returned from Paris to New York in 1853 and became a popular pianist and composer. His piano piece *The Dying Poet* remained a favorite for the rest of the century, and he enjoyed many other commercial successes. It was in this decade that New York established itself as the center of American professional musical life, even though in 1800 it had only fifty musicians.[21] The population during the intervening years had risen from 60,000 to over 500,000.

Ticket prices were used in London, New York, Paris, and Vienna to produce a class hierarchy of concerts. A cheap price meant much the same in each city, and did not indicate a "bargain basement" price: the norm was 1 shilling in London, 25 cents in New York, 1 franc in Paris, and 10 Kreuzer in Vienna. An innovation that spread rapidly in the 1830s was the offering of reserved seats, which were available only in the higher price range. These succeeded, partly because, as Weber remarks, they "afforded people a strong sense of social distinction."[22] They ensured a socially exclusive audience at London's Philharmonic Concerts. Cheap concerts were plentiful in the 1850s. In London, Jullien (real name Louis-Antoine Julien [sic]) had always kept a close eye on prices, ensuring that there were usually tickets available for 1 shilling. In order for August Manns to fill the large hall at the Crystal Palace for the Saturday Concerts, which began in 1855, popular programming and a small admission charge was necessary. In an endeavor to obtain the largest audience, they were held on Saturday evenings, that day being a half-day holiday for manual and clerical workers. Unfortunately, this had a bad impact on Philharmonic rehearsals, which were held on Saturdays, although eighteen members of the orchestra also played for Manns;[23] the constant deputizing that resulted from this clash became a cause of declining standards for the Philharmonic, which faced further competition when the Popular Concerts (the Monday "Pops") started at St James's Hall in 1859.[24] Saturday afternoon "Pops" began there in 1865.

Such ever-increasing professional activity may have persuaded some amateur musicians to stay out of the public arena, but that did not apply to all musical genres. Participation in choral societies and parish choirs actually increased, and public concerts were given often. However, amateur activity in areas such as chamber music, which was substantial, tended to take place in private spaces, such as drawing rooms. As the middle-class audience grew, so did middle-class domestic music making. The result of this growth together with the professionalization of music performance was that amateur music making lost status. The drawing room was never to acquire any status as a site of high-quality performance. There also developed new forms of amateur music making: for instance, the playing of instruments like the flageolet, concertina, or Northumbrian pipes, and, outside of the home, performing in brass and military bands (often in a park).[25] Public performances by amateurs were frequently competitive affairs—especially those of brass bands, which remained amateur ensembles.

The railways gave a boost to the music business: they facilitated touring, they enabled people to travel to events (especially when train travel became cheaper in the 1860s and 1870s), and they transported pianos. Trade between Britain and America increased in the 1840s with the establishment of the regular Cunard steamship crossings from Liverpool to Boston. This was also the decade in which American affluence increased as a consequence of the annexation of Texas, the discovery of gold in California, and the railroad boom.

The music hall in London provides an example of the sort of entrepreneurial initiatives, business decisions, and dealings that new forms of musical activity brought about. Music hall was without doubt by 1860 the most popular form of musical entertainment in London. The back rooms of taverns and public houses that were used for "free and easy" entertainments, in which any customer could contribute a song, had gradually become concert rooms or singing saloons in the 1840s, and some landlords had begun employing professional singers. These spaces were then developed further: for instance, the Mogul Saloon became the Middlesex Music Hall in 1851. Charles Morton is credited with having created the first music hall when he built a large extension to the Canterbury Arms in Lambeth (1850–51). The Surrey Music Hall predated it, but was really for concerts (Jullien performed there with his orchestra). Morton's initiative changed the meaning of the term "music hall," so that it now increasingly suggested a venue for a particular new type of popular entertainment. The Canterbury, as it became known, took off with such success that it was further enlarged in 1856, the same year the enormous new Surrey Music Hall opened. The Surrey could hold 10,000, and had tiers of balconies and galleries. It was destroyed by fire on 11 June 1861, but the appetite for building new halls meant that attention that year was focused on the rivalry between Weston's music hall in Holborn and Morton's grand new property the Oxford (it was in London's Oxford Street).[26] What the *Musical Standard* described as the "race for music halls" continued in this decade.[27] In the mid-1860s, there were more than thirty large music halls in London, having an average seating capacity of 1,500, and employing bands of between five and ten players.[28] By the 1890s, these bands had increased a little in size: the Metropolitan (Edgware Road) employed fifteen players; the Oxford and the Cambridge both had twelve.[29] The final expansion of the music hall business was accomplished by syndicates building chains of halls and organizing nationwide touring circuits.[30] This removed the last vestiges of the community-based aspects of music hall and replaced it with a national model.

Most of the early proprietors had been publicans, but others soon became involved, especially if they had a background in the retail and service trades.[31] The availability of alcoholic drinks remained a feature of music halls. The cheapest seats in West End halls cost sixpence, but as soon as you walked east, prices began to fall. Wilton's in Stepney, for example, had seats for fourpence, and there were plenty cheaper than that further afield. The music hall, as part of the entertainment industry, was driven by business imperatives: these included the need to maximize profit (for example, raising ticket prices with the hope of encouraging a wealthier clientele); the need to stay within the bounds of the law (for example, obeying the London County Council's demand for fire curtains in 1878); and the need to avoid moral outrage and critical censure. Sometimes events were beyond management control: business was booming in the 1860s, but competition became fierce in the 1870s, and then business slowed as the effects of national economic depression registered in the 1880s. On top of that, the economic interests of proprietors were prone to clash with the leisure interests of the audience, which in itself was not homogeneous as a social class (especially in the West End), and friction could develop between clerks putting on airs, manual laborers, and bohemian "toffs."

In music hall performer Bessie Bellwood's song "What Cheer 'Ria,"[32] a girl who has been making good money selling vegetables dresses up and pays a shilling (a "bob") to sit in the stalls, only to be mocked by her pals in the gallery.

> I am a girl what's a-doing wery well in the weagetable line,
> And as I'd saved a bob or two, I thought I'd cut a shine,
> So I goes and buys some toggery, there ere wery clothes you
>   see,
> And with the money I had left, I thought I'd have a spree:
> So I goes into a Music Hall, where I'd often been afore,
> I don't go in the gallery, but on the bottom floor;
> I sits down by the Chairman, and calls for a pot of stout,
> My pals in the gallery spotted me, and they all commenced to
>   shout—

> Chorus
> What cheer Ria! Ria's on the job,
> What cheer Ria! did you speculate a bob?
> Oh Ria she's a toff and she looks immensikoff,
> And they all shouted "What Cheer Ria!"

Inevitably, a disturbance ensues, and she is thrown out. In her patter before the final chorus, she declares, "You don't catch me going chucking my money away trying to be a toff anymore." (I discuss the meanings of "what cheer" and "immensikoff" in chapter 7.)

The use of the regulating and order-keeping chairman in music hall lasted until late in the century, when he was replaced frequently by a board at the side of the stage that contained a numbered list of "turns." Performers were all now professionalized and were hired to perform their turns at various halls, sometimes on the same evening. Indeed, performers expected to have the freedom to perform at different halls rather than be restricted to one. They were also open to propositions that they advertise products. George Leybourne recommended "Moët's vintage only" in "Champagne Charlie," while the Great Vance promoted Cliquot in a song of that name.[33] Music hall performers began to become more organized in defense of and promotion of their careers, the most significant development being the founding of the Music Hall Artistes Association in 1885.[34] Songwriting for the halls was professionalized, too, and composers and lyricists would be familiar with different types of character song (the swell song, the coster song) and the skills of particular performers. The male stars of the halls, often termed the *lions comiques* (a phrase invented by music hall manager J. J. Pole),[35] came to prominence in the 1860s.

Professionalism for women performers was, at first, mainly restricted to singing and dancing, and singing continued to be important for women looking for employment opportunities in music halls and concert halls. An article in the *Woman's World* in 1889 discusses careers for singers, and notes the importance of London's various weekly concerts in this regard.[36] In addition, women were finding professional employment as piano teachers, and women pianists, like Arabella Goddard, were also coming to prominence in the 1860s. Opinions about the unsuitability of the violin for women were much changed by Wilma Neruda's performances at the Monday Popular Concerts in the 1870s, though it should be stressed that the perception of violin playing as "unladylike" was not shared in Vienna or Paris.

A novel professional concert development was the Ladies' Orchestra. English ensembles, amateur at first, arose swiftly following the acclaimed visit by the "Viennese Lady Orchestra," which performed at the Albert Palace in Battersea, London, in 1885.[37] Bernard Shaw was among the admirers, calling them "an attraction which eclipses the late Strauss concerts at South Kensington."[38] The orchestra did contain a few men playing brass, and the timpanist was male, although women played other percussion instruments. Shaw waxes lyrical in his review, describing them as "a string of nearly sixty instrumentalists, all more or less charming, and all in crimson tunics and white skirts." Continuing in similarly gendered terms, he proclaims:

> The effect of the "lady orchestra" as a whole is novel and very pleasant. They are inferior to the Strauss band in precision and perfection of detail; but the Strauss impetuosity was forced, false, and often misplaced and vulgar: these Viennese ladies seem inspired by a feminine delight in dancing that makes them play dance music in a far more captivating fashion than their male rivals. They have grace, tenderness and moderation: qualities which are very refreshing after two months of the alternate sentimentality and self-assertion of Eduard Strauss, than whom, by the by, Madame Marie Schipek, the conductor, is a much more dashing violinist. Like him,

she conducts with her bow, and acts as leader alternately. Her conducting is not conducting in the Richterian sense: there is no reason to suppose that she could use a *bâton*, so as to produce an original interpretation of a classical work; but she marks time in the boldest and gayest Austrian spirit, and makes the dances and marches spin along irresistibly.[39]

The ladies' orchestras (*Damenkapellen*) that were formed in Austria and Germany in the mid–nineteenth century were mainly involved in playing *Unterhaltungsmusik* (overtures, marches, dances, character pieces), and their members were typically of lower-middle-class origin, many drawn from families of musicians. These orchestras would usually play at leisure resorts (like spas) and in public gardens, parks, and hotel restaurants. Their size was extremely varied, and might be anything from four to sixty strong.[40] The standard of playing was generally considered to be high. The Vienna Ladies' Orchestra had been going for many years, and had already toured New York in 1871.

The first British ladies' orchestras were amateur—the Dundee Ladies' String Orchestra and Lady Radnor's Orchestra—but that was soon to change. Much praise was given to the orchestra put together for professional engagements in England by Mrs. Hunt. One critic remarks, "Those who have had an opportunity of hearing Mrs. Hunt's capable orchestra will appreciate the fact that it is quite possible to bring together a body of lady orchestral performers who will play pieces suited to string and wood-wind instruments at least as well as musicians drawn from the other sex."[41] Mrs. Hunt, the conductor, had earlier experience as a piano soloist. She then formed a band, initially twelve strong, with the help of John Ulrich, and performed for the first time at the house of Captain Barron in Grosvenor Square, on which occasion Arthur Sullivan was present. Perhaps through Sullivan's intercession, W. S. Gilbert designed their costumes after the style associated with a French women's club of the seventeenth century called Les Merveilleuses, but as the orchestra obtained more and more engagements, the players also appeared in military costume as Les Militaires if the type of engagement seemed to warrant it (see fig. 1.1). Rosabel Watson, who formed the Aeolian Ladies' Orchestra, thought the costumes worn by Mrs. Hunt's Orchestra (in which she had performed) undermined the professional status of women musicians.[42] She may well have taken note of the kind of patronizing comments made by concert reviewers such as Shaw.

Mrs. Hunt's Orchestra performed at aristocratic country homes, as well as at venues in London (including several months at the Waterloo Panorama). They then embarked on a tour, which took in Scotland and Ireland. They also toured abroad, playing at the Paris Exhibition and the Nice Municipal Casino. On tour, the orchestra consisted normally of thirty players. Like the Viennese Ladies' Orchestra, they frequently included some men in their ranks, since heavy brass instruments were not commonly played by women—though Mrs. Hunt, herself, saw no

Figure 1.1 Mrs. Hunt's orchestra in 1897.

reason why they should not be. Women brass players were certainly to be found in Salvation Army bands, since William Booth had a policy of sexual equality, and these players would have been visible at his Crystal Palace music festivals (begun 1890), which attracted many thousands.[43] The biggest difficulty for Mrs. Hunt, however, was not in finding suitable women players but in finding continuous engagements; so by 1897, the control of her orchestra had passed into the hands of a limited company. By that time, there was little doubt that women were beginning to see possibilities of making careers as professional instrumental musicians, and a *Strand Musical Magazine* article on Mrs. Hunt concludes, "there are certainly professions open to women which are not only less lucrative, but generally offer less advantages than that of an orchestral musician."[44] Women were already playing in a mixed-sex orchestra at the triennial Handel Festival at the Crystal Palace in the 1890s.[45] Nevertheless, despite their growing numbers, they were still facing prejudice and exclusion, and were not permitted membership in the London Orchestral Association. The professional mixed orchestra was finally assured when Henry Wood gave positions to six women in the Queen's Hall Orchestra in 1913 on equal pay terms with the men. Wood remarks that the men, in fact, "took kindly to the innovation."[46] Not every city in this survey responded to social change so promptly: despite those pioneering "Vienna Ladies," women were not allowed to audition for the Vienna Philharmonic Orchestra (founded, as mentioned earlier, in 1842) until 1997.[47]

Prices were said to be "within the reach of everyone" at the first Queen's Hall promenade concert, the promenade itself being a shilling;[48] however, as we have seen from Ria's story, for the same price you could have a very good seat in a music hall. "Cheap" depends heavily on context, the venue, and its location. Victoria Cooper has provided a carefully considered analysis, drawing on a variety of sources, of the amount of disposable income, as well as leisure time, that was available for people in different occupations to spend on musical activities. At the less prosperous end of the market, a budget of between 1 and 2 percent of income "would permit the purchase of one Novello score per year in addition to limited attendance at concerts" for a schoolmaster earning £81 a year in 1851.[49] This is below the income of £150 a year that Geoffrey Best set as the threshold for membership in the middle class.[50]

The Sheet Music Trade

Alongside the promotion of public performances, music publishing was the most important musical money-making enterprise of the new commercial age. The commodification of music was at its most visible in the sheet music trade, and the purchase of sheet music was an unambiguous and conspicuous example of the consumption of musical goods. After 1775, Vienna became an important center for engraved music, stimulated by the presence there of composers such as Haydn and Mozart. Music engraved on copper plates was the normal method of printing when the Austrian Aloys Senefelder sought a cheaper method in lithography. At first he worked with etched stone, but in 1797 he invented a new lithographic method in which he no longer etched away at the stone surface but instead relied on chemical reactions, especially the mutually repelling qualities of grease and water. From the town of Offenbach, lithography spread via the music publisher André's family connections to London and Paris. Senefelder himself was responsible for its introduction in Vienna, where in the early years of the nineteenth century he founded the press Chemische Druckerei.[51] The earliest Viennese examples are not of a quality to compare with engraved music, and the same goes for the Imprimerie lithographique in Paris. Lithography in London was mainly used for pictorial work before mid-century, and gave a boost to the sheet music trade because of the increased facility of including illustrations. Some of those responsible for pictorial chromolithographic title pages in the 1860s, like Alfred Concanen (mainly music hall songs) and John Brandard (mostly dance music), created work of high quality. In 1843, the sons of Senefelder's partner in the lithographic trade moved to New York.[52]

Two rival technologies to lithography, engraving (which had switched to the use of pewter plate) and moveable music type, continued to be used into the 1860s. In the 1840s, when Novello opted for musical type, most music was being engraved on pewter plates, which was a cheaper option if small numbers were required. The problem was that the plates wore out, sometimes after only a thousand impressions. Music types were expensive to purchase, and a lot of time was taken setting them in place, but they proved cheaper if sales ran into several thousands rather than several hundreds. Spina in Vienna needed to have a hundred plates made to satisfy demand for Johann Strauss Jr.'s *Blue Danube* waltz (see chapter 5), even though each plate was deemed sufficient for 10,000 copies.[53] Though some publishers were committed to the cleaner look of engraved music, the replacement of lithographic stone by zinc and aluminum plates and the use of the rotary press made lithography an ever more attractive option. Powerful lithographic machines in the 1850s could produce prints at fifty times the rate of hand presses (3,000 impressions an hour instead of 60).[54] A number of song publishers used color lithography for title pages in London and New York, and it was very popular in the 1890s.

Boston, then Philadelphia, had taken the lead in music publishing in the United States, but New York soon began to thrive as a center of sheet music and piano production in the nineteenth century. Firth and Hall began publishing music in New York in 1827, and became one of the biggest firms within a decade; their publication of Henry Russell's "Woodman, Spare That Tree!" (1837) set the seal on this. They had already become a piano business by then, having linked up with piano maker Sylvanus Pond. Hall broke with the other partners in 1847 to form Hall and Son. The business paper the *New York Musical Review* named Firth and Pond, Hall and Son, Horace Waters, and Berry and Gordon as the biggest publishers in New York in 1855—the turnover of music books and sheet music at Firth and Pond alone was worth $70,000 that year. This firm's sales of pianos were worth $50,000, and other instruments added a further $30,000. At that time, they employed ninety-two people, forty of whom were in the piano factory (soon to double in numbers).[55] Firth published Stephen Foster's songs, the biggest hit among them being "Old Folks at Home," with 130,000 copies sold between 1851 and 1854.[56] Novello opened a New York branch in 1852, having already captured the market there with the firm's cheap oratorio editions and collections of sacred music. However, prevalent piracy and ineffective copyright legislation meant that popular song publishers remained fixed in their respective countries.

Before the Civil War, the biggest American music publisher was Oliver Ditson of Boston (who was also a silent partner of Berry and Gordon in New York). The massive sales of certain Civil War songs (for instance, George Root's "Tramp, Tramp, Tramp") seemed stimulated by the exceptionally emotional times, but the music trade continued to boom in the next decade. This was helped by the simultaneous boom in music education, especially piano lessons. Census figures are not available till 1900, but then show 92,000 full-time music teachers and musicians (compared to 43,249 in Britain).[57] Ditson remained Ameri-

ca's biggest popular song publisher until the 1880s. New York's biggest
firms in this decade were Harms (established 1881) and Witmark (established 1885). The huge economic potential of popular music was evident in the 1890s when Charles Harris's "After the Ball" (1892) demonstrated that a hit song could sell millions of copies. When Witmark
moved to 49–51 West Twenty-eighth Street in 1893, it signaled a shift
of the center of music publishing from the theater district around Union
Square to what was to become known as Tin Pan Alley (a term supposedly coined by songwriter Monroe Rosenfeld). There was a new attitude to marketing, along with new strategies for promoting songs.[58]
Song-plugging, for example, involved performances in music shops
and department stores to boost sales. In a development of the Boosey
Ballad Concert practice of paying singers royalties on performances,
New York publisher Woodward began paying singers to promote songs.
Witmark introduced the professional copy, giving it free of charge to
professional singers.[59] The song itself had to have a "punch"—something to make it stand out in a competitive market, like a memorable
group of notes, or a memorable line in the lyric.[60] Other promotional
devices included advance copies and free theater band arrangements.
On the downside, prices were being cut (10–15 cents rather than 25
cents) and a song was beginning to have shorter life span—a popular
success might be forgotten after three months. However, the arrival of
attractive new syncopated styles kept the market buoyant toward the
end of the century.

In London, Novello made successive reductions in the price of
music, and cheap music was also to be had from Charles Sheard (the
Musical Bouquet series), Davidson, and Hopwood and Crew. By the end
of the century, a popular song in Britain would frequently sell 200,000
copies. There were bigger hits, such as "The Lost Chord," which sold
half a million copies between its first publication (1877) and 1902.[61]
In 1898, the *Musical Opinion* estimated the annual sales of sheet music
in Britain at around 20 million,[62] higher than the equivalent in Austria or France, though not the United States. The major reason for this
was that the eagerness to possess a piano was greater in Britain and
America.

In the competitive business of music publishing, compromises were
often necessary. There were, for example, perils attached to trying to
obtain an exclusive contract with a composer, as the Paris agent of
Breitkopf and Härtel explains to a colleague in a letter of 1837:

> Your method of buying everything by one composer is not going to work,
> considering that it leads to the present competition and [the resulting] in-
> flation. Sometimes we should let others have the less important pieces,
> whatever suits their business. [If we did that], the others would let us have
> some good things and not invade my territory. Schott and Schlesinger are
> my tough competitors who are often much faster and more generous than
> I dare to be.[63]

He then tells how, in the next month, Schott outbid him for Thalberg's piano fantasies on "God Save the Queen" and "Rule Britannia."[64] Sometimes it was a case of backing the wrong horse. Both Joseph Mainzer and John Hullah were champions of fixed-do systems for sight singing. Hullah basing his system on that used for the Orphéon choirs in Paris, but the Rev. John Curwen's moveable-do system of Tonic Sol-fa won the day in Britain.

The well-documented dealings of the firm of Novello are an illustration of the variety of business decisions that nineteenth-century music publishers had to make. Vincent Novello, an organist, set up his business at his home in Oxford Street in 1811 when he failed to find a publisher for a collection of sacred music he had compiled.[65] His son, Alfred Novello, had the idea of publishing cheap editions of admired choral works.[66] Cheap editions of oratorios like Handel's *Messiah* and Haydn's *Creation* were crucial to the spread of choral societies throughout Britain, societies that then stimulated further demand. Novello turned next to journal production, publishing the *Musical World* from 1836. Music publishers were, from the beginning, naturally keen to encourage an interest in music and especially their own catalogues. Breitkopf and Härtel began publication of the *Allgemeine musikalische Zeitung* in 1798 in Leipzig, and it allowed them to advertise and promote their trade.[67] Maurice Schlesinger, who was speculating in railway stocks when he was not engaged in music publishing matters, founded the *Gazette musicale* to promote his wares. He then took over François-Joseph Fétis's more earnest *Revue musicale de Paris,* and created the *Revue et Gazette musicale,* catering for the musical tastes and aspirations of the bourgeoisie.[68] In the second half of the century, literature about music increased significantly—eighty-three different music periodicals appeared in New York between 1850 and 1900[69]—and music publishers often started their own journals.[70]

The great success of Joseph Mainzer's singing classes in the early 1840s led Alfred Novello to take over Mainzer's periodical, which from June 1844 became the *Musical Times and Singing Class Circular,* priced at a penny halfpenny. Difficulties in getting the octavo-size publication printed encouraged him to go into printing himself in 1847, using the method of moveable musical type that William Clowes had recently improved on for the periodical the *Harmonicon* (1823–33). This meant that Novello could now publish for other firms. Henry Littleton, who had been Alfred's assistant, took over when he retired in 1857, and eventually bought up the business in 1866. The next year, Littleton bought up the firm of Ewer, primarily to acquire the British copyright of Ewer's Mendelssohn publications, especially the oratorio *Elijah.* He began promoting oratorio concerts in 1869, ensuring that ticket prices offered the same value for money as his publications, so that he was able to stimulate demand further and ensure that the firm became "one of the largest of its kind in the world."[71]

The Piano Trade

Though choral singing was certainly important to the sheet music trade (for instance, two flourishing sacred music societies merged in 1849 to form the New York Harmonic Society), most publishers were concerned above all with music for piano. Some businesses yoked the sheet music trade and the piano trade together: when Mr. Firth of Firth and Hall, New York, died in September 1864, he was declared "the oldest and probably the best known music publisher and piano dealer in the States."[72] Piano music—particularly dances, operatic excerpts, and songs—formed the largest and most profitable area of music publishing. In Vienna, it was already an established fact in the early 1800s that waltzes for piano "were among the publishers' safest aids to staying in business, and they disliked to be short of them."[73] For the prolific production of piano music based on operas, nobody beat the Viennese composer Carl Czerny. With the increased sales of pianos as the century wore on came a demand for music that sounded difficult without actually being so. An example from later in the century that remained a drawing room favorite into the twentieth century is J. W. Turner's *Fairy Wedding Waltz* (1875), which allows the fastest of scale passages to be accomplished easily as a glissando by means of a right-hand fingernail (see ex. 1.1).

In the 1790s, a piano was a fashionable luxury in wealthy Viennese homes. The English piano was substantially different from the Viennese piano in the eighteenth century; it was a heavier instrument with thicker strings and soundboard, and a more complex action.[74] Conrad Graf was the important Viennese maker, and his pianos still sounded

Example 1.1 J. W. Turner, *The Fairy Wedding Waltz* (London, 1875), measures 9–16.

different from English models in the 1820s. John Broadwood was the most significant figure in the technological development of the English piano, and London became a center of piano making. The new working relations of the Industrial Revolution were brought to the production of pianos when Broadwood introduced a division of labor to increase efficiency and lower costs.[75]

Matthias Müller in Vienna and John Hawkins in Philadelphia, both around 1800, had made early versions of the upright piano (with strings stretching downward to the floor inside the cabinet). The population living within the Vienna's city walls was, for the most part, dwelling in houses divided into apartments; space was at a premium, so a market for upright pianos opened up. Erard was the first firm in Paris to identify the market for pianos for apartment-dwellers, and set about designing an upright model in the 1820s that would fit a smaller room.[76] Uprights were to become the norm for smaller homes in Paris, London, and Vienna—but not New York, where square pianos remained in vogue longer. In London, a six-octave Broadwood cottage piano in 1828 cost 50 guineas, exactly half the price of the firm's horizontal grand.[77] A new cottage piano could be had from Robert Wornum (Bedford Square), who had patented his upright design in 1826, for 42 guineas in 1838.[78] Uprights and squares were domesticated pianos, just as reed organs were domesticated organs. American organs, which sucked through the reeds, were thought to produce a steadier tone than French harmoniums, which blew through the reeds, and they became popular during the second half of the century.[79]

In 1843, Henri Heine complained of the impossibility of escaping the piano in Paris: "you can hear it ring in every house, in every company, both day and night."[80] While this is humorous hyperbole, it is not far wide of the mark: the *Gazette* of 10 November 1845 estimated the number of pianos in Paris at 60,000.[81] In the same year, there were 108 piano makers in Vienna, but these were small businesses, and Viennese pianos were usually cheaper and not of a high quality at this time.[82] Taste in piano tone had certainly changed by the time of the Great Exhibition of London in 1851. Of the ten countries exhibiting pianos, only makers from Austria and Canada received neither a prize nor an "honorable mention."[83] Austria reestablished its reputation soon afterward, especially with the admired pianos made by Bösendorfer in Vienna. In 1851, there were around 200 English piano firms, most of them located in London, and Broadwood still dominated, with Collard in second place. William Pole, in his catalogue *Musical Instruments in the Great Industrial Exhibition of 1851,* claimed that a million pounds worth of pianos had been made that year, while France in 1849 produced £320,000 worth.[84] The number of men playing pianos should not be regarded as insignificant: there was barely a piano in Oxford colleges in the 1820s, and there were an estimated 125 pianos and 30 concertinas by the mid-1850s.[85] $15 million (representing 25,000 instruments) was spent on pianos in the United States in 1866.[86] Steinway and Sons (the name was originally Steinweg) opened in New York in 1853 on East Fourteenth Street and soon became the preeminent American maker. Steinway's overstringing, which was perfected in 1859, was a key ingredient in the firm's success. The gold medals awarded to the firms Steinway and Chickering at the Paris Exhibition of 1867 sealed the United States' reputation in the European piano market, and by 1880 Steinway was one of the world's leading brands.

The association of domestic piano playing with young middle-class women had become ubiquitous by the mid–nineteenth century.[87] Piano playing and singing were considered important genteel accomplishments for young middle-class women. It was regarded as indicative of moral and aesthetic refinement, and not of any desire to perform professionally. Because women not only played the piano but were also the chief users of another item of modern technology, the sewing machine, an unusual business opportunity arose. Some American firms after the Civil War tried to cope with the demand for both, and for a while there was even a periodical called the *Musical and Sewing Machine Gazette*.[88] The fact that middle-class girls were obliged to learn the piano does not alone explain what Cyril Ehrlich calls the "piano mania" of late nineteenth-century Britain.[89] Prices of musical instruments were falling in the second half of the century. Pianos became available to a wider social mix, not only because of the drop in price but also because a three-year installment plan (hire purchase) was introduced in London and New York. This system had arisen in London in the 1860s, at first mainly for inferior instruments, and available only to customers with permanent employment. It became more flexible in the 1870s and helped make possible the large-scale acquisition of pianos. Pianos "for the million" were being advertised at 10 guineas in 1884.[90] On top of this, there was a growing market in secondhand instruments. The price of sheet music also fell in the 1870s, as the volume of production and number of competing firms increased. In the United Kingdom, the removal of excise duty on paper in 1861 also contributed to lowering prices.[91] Instrument technology was developing throughout the century, and not only where pianos were concerned: J. P. Oates's new piston valves for brass were on show at the Great Exhibition of 1851, as were Adolphe Sax's sax horns and saxophones.

Some piano firms built their own concert halls. In midcentury, Pleyel had two halls in Paris suitable for concerts, and Erard also had a hall with an auditorium. Pleyel and Erard were the biggest firms in Paris. The Bösendorfer-Saal, a recital room holding 500, opened in 1872 in Vienna; five years later Bösendorfer's main rival opened the Saal Ehrbar, seating the same number. In 1866, Steinway built a concert hall in New York to hold 2,500, and opened a hall adjoining their London branch in 1878 (capacity 400). Music publishers also had a similar interest: Tom Chappell of the firm of that name largely financed the building of St. James's Hall. The Viennese pianist Henri Herz provides an example of how to seize opportunities and show business versatility in the first half of the century. He first earned money as a virtuoso in Paris, then as a piano teacher and composer of piano music of *seeming* difficulty, and then as a piano maker. Muzio Clementi, renowned for his piano compositions, went similarly into business as a piano maker in London.

The size and weight of pianos meant that the import and export market was not huge, though German pianos became increasingly popular in Britain after 1875, and Queen Victoria bought a Bechstein grand in 1881.[92] Bechstein (established 1853 in Berlin) were overstrung, like Steinway, and adopted the iron frame. English firms had been suspicious of this technology, thinking the tone inferior—an impression that can, perhaps, be put down to the romanticizing of wood in a country of metal industries. Steinway was heavily into sales promotion, and engaged Anton Rubinstein to tour America publicizing their business in 1872–73.[93] They also sought testimonials from eminent musicians in Europe to be quoted in their advertisements. Steinway certainly exceeded other firms in the "hard sell" tactics they employed, though the quality of their instruments was beyond question.[94] It must have been astonishing for musicians born early in the century to see America achieve the position of being the world's largest producer of musical instruments.[95]

Copyright and Performing Rights

For Raymond Williams, copyright and royalty are the two significant indicators of the changed relations that professionalization and the capitalist market for cultural goods brought about.[96] The enforcement of copyright protection on the reproduction and performance of music was an enormous stimulus to the music market, affecting writers, performers, and publishers. In Britain, the Copyright Act of 1842 allowed the author to sell copyright and performing rights together or separately. In France, protection was offered to café-concert songwriters for the first time after a court action for an unauthorized performance in Paris in 1847. Jacques Attali maintains that the French law acknowledging a performing right in songs could not have come to pass without the existence of cafés-concerts.[97] It was there that songs were recognizably commodities for consumption and, thus, had a claim to be considered "works" alongside those already protected in the law of 1791. The reaction in *La France Musicale* was one of disbelief: "If you create operas, symphonies, in a word, works that make a mark, then royalties shall be yours; but taxing light songs and ballads, that is the height of absurdity!"[98] In 1851, however, Société des Auteurs, Compositeurs, et Editeurs de Musique was founded (SACEM) and became active in collecting performing rights and pursuing infringements. Austria launched a performing rights society in 1897, but similar societies were not founded in the United Kingdom and the United States until 1914.

The British public viewed copyright law with much suspicion because of the notorious activities of Harry Wall in the 1870s.[99] Wall's strategy was to buy up old copyrights and then find performers who were "guilty" of infringement. He issued them with a £2 demand, backed up by threats of legal action. He intimidated them further by claiming he acted for the Copyright and Performing Right Protection Office (which he had cunningly set up himself in 1875). Legislation was introduced in 1882 against "vexatious proceedings" of this kind, but it failed to stop him; only the Copyright (Musical Compositions) Act of 1888, which placed the assessment of damages for breach of copyright in the court's hands, did so.[100] As they had been doing for more than thirty years, SACEM continued to collect fees for performances in Britain, though many did not like it. After the British Copyright Acts of 1882 and 1888, publishers had to announce on their sheet music whether or not a piece could be performed in public without a fee. However, far from thinking that performers should be obliged to pay to perform a piece of music, some publishers were, instead, willing to pay performers to promote their music. That is how drawing room ballads attracted the name "royalty ballads" in the later decades of the century. The names of the singers would be printed conspicuously on the title page in order to encourage sales. Publishers and composers were, in general, much more concerned about piracy than performing rights.

One gains a general impression—albeit very difficult to substantiate with hard facts—that publishers were exploiting most British and American composers in the nineteenth century. They were glad to be published and earn anything they could, and they had no idea how to better their relations with publishers, or how to exercise any kind of intellectual property rights. Stephen Foster may have been the most commercially successful songwriter of the 1850s, but his average annual income from royalties was only $1,371.92.[101] French songwriters were in the strongest position, having the protection of SACEM. In Austria, the United Kingdom, and the United States, composers associated their income with sales of sheet music, not with performing rights. Early copyright legislation favored publishers and did not offer much protection to authors and, what is more, had to be registered separately in different countries. An attempt to establish a reciprocal copyright agreement between the United States and Britain was made in 1852, but it fell through.[102] In 1855, Hall and Son created a storm by announcing that they were discounting the price of noncopyrighted foreign music, while maintaining the price of American music. Other publishers tried to organize a boycott, but Hall's business boomed. The recently formed Board of Music Trade had to agree to an across-the-board cut of 20 percent on noncopyrighted music.[103]

Publishers had other problems besides competition and rivalry; they also had to deal with the vagaries and unpredictability of the customer. Chappell made a huge profit after acquiring the British publishing rights in Gounod's *Faust* for a meager payment of around £100, prompting Boosey to jump in immediately with an offer of £1,000 for Gounod's next opera, *Mireille*. Alas, it flopped. Nevertheless, Boosey managed to buy for £100 the rights to Lecocq's *La Fille de Madame Angot,* which proved to be one of the most popular operettas of the century.[104] Boosey acquired the British copyright of nearly all Offenbach's stage works, while Chappell owned the rights to those of Gilbert and Sullivan.

During 1878, when forty-two companies in America were staging versions of *H.M.S. Pinafore,* Gilbert and Sullivan were left to consider uncomfortably that this popularity was worth nothing to them in financial terms because of inadequate international copyright laws. They hit on the idea of taking over a company from Britain to perform their next comic opera in the United States, so that they would be ahead of the game. The world première of *The Pirates of Penzance,* therefore, took place at the Fifth Avenue Theater, New York, on 31 December 1879. The score remained in manuscript, since its publication would have allowed anyone to make use of it. However, this was not their only problem, as Sullivan explained:

> Keeping the libretto and music in manuscript did not settle the difficulty, as it was held by some judges that theatrical representation was tantamount to publication, so that any member of the audience who managed to take down the libretto in shorthand, for instance, and succeeded in memorizing the music was quite at liberty to produce his own version of it.[105]

Sullivan even found that members of the orchestra were being offered bribes to hand over band parts. An additional complication was that a performance in England prior to one in America was necessary to acquire British copyright protection. Thus, a one-night performance at the small Royal Bijou Theatre in the seaside resort of Paignton took place a few hours before the New York performance.[106] It was out of the way and poorly advertised, in order not to spoil the British launch at the Opera Comique in London a few months later.

Piracy was rife, and not just in instances such as Gilbert and Sullivan faced, or in the trade of itinerant ballad vendors out on the streets (a trade on the wane in the 1870s). The Music Publisher's Association asked the *Musical Opinion and Music Trade Review* in 1882 to warn readers that copying a copyrighted song by hand was an infringement, despite the fact that advertisements in journals "circulating primarily among ladies" offered to undertake this work.[107] The practice of making manuscript copies of music continued to cause publishers concern, especially when trade was slow in the later 1880s. Some people thought that transcribing a song into another key was perfectly acceptable.

The Berne Convention for the Protection of Literary and Artistic Works took place in 1886, and ended with an agreement that copyright protection for authors would exist in the fourteen nations that signed up for it; but the United States was not a signatory. In 1888, American copyright law was changed to give reciprocal rights to American and British composers, and the 1891 American act extended this, offering 28 years' protection to authors from countries that had reciprocal copyright relations with the United States. SACEM then opened a New York office, as did Boosey and Chappell. New York's Witmark made a co-publication arrangement with London's Charles Sheard, and Harms did likewise with Francis, Day and Hunter.

Toward the end of the century, arguments raged about cuts in the retail price of music; some wholesalers were castigated for discounting the trade price when negotiating with dealers, or when selling to schools or professional musicians. The accepted system was that the publisher produced the item at a certain cost, and added a little extra when selling to the wholesaler; then the retailer bought from the wholesaler at a trade price and sold it to the customer at the retail price.[108]

The Star System

It may well be argued that there were stars before the nineteenth century, especially in the ranks of singers, and in the first half of the nineteenth century there was certainly no shortage of instrumental virtuosos who might fit that description. The modern type of star, however, emerges with the entertainment industry and is differentiated by the way he or she is turned into a commodity: for example, Johann Strauss Sr. becomes the Waltz King and Jenny Lind the Swedish Nightingale. However, in the early days they still tended to be treated as individuals possessing unique talents, rather than being promoted as part of a system of business-driven entertainment in which they might feature almost interchangeably as "top of the bill" artists, as did the *lions comiques* in London music halls. The earlier entrepreneurial musicians usually managed themselves, but those in the second half of the century were more likely to seek the services of agents, entrusting to them the scheduling of their appearances and the bargaining over fees. Strauss Sr. planned his own tours, but by the end of the century Vienna's celebrated musicians looked to the agent Albert Gutman for help.[109] Moreover, there was an advantage from the concert promoter's point of view, in that alternatives could be considered, since agents would have a variety of musicians on their books. Some of the earliest agents were music publishers.

The first star of the café-concert (the French term is *vedette*) was Thérésa (1837–1913; real name Emma Valadon). She was a sensation at the Eldorado in 1863, and was soon offered a large increase in salary (from 200 to 300 francs a month) to tempt her to the Alcazar.[110] Popular performers could now become very wealthy, and those who offered a rags-to-riches story were, in Attali's words, "a formidable instrument of social order, of hope and submission simultaneously."[111] Paulus (Jean-Paul Habans) became the foremost French male star after developing a unique jerky style (*style gambillard*) in the 1880s.[112] The star system relies on the existence of similar performance spaces that can be visited by these artists; thus, the metropolis offers an ideal environment. The star system became an important feature of London music hall after 1860: George Leybourne, the Great MacDermott (Michael Farrell), Jenny Hill, Albert Chevalier, Gus Elen, and Marie Lloyd were among the most admired. Alexander Girardi was the preeminent Viennese star: he sang the *Wiener Fiakerlied* (Pick) in the Viennese vernacular and persuaded people, as did Gus Elen in London, that he was merely being himself rather than putting on an act (even his Italian roots didn't counter the impression of authenticity). Girardi also sang in operetta, and was much applauded in the role of Zsupán in *Der Zigeunerbaron*. The glamorous female star was a feature of operetta: Hortense Schneider became famous in the title role of *La Grande-Duchesse de Gérolstein* after its tremendous success during the Paris Exhibition of 1867.[113] Emily Soldene was Schneider's counterpart in London,[114] as Marie Geistinger was in Vienna; Vienna also had an operetta star in Josephine Gallmeyer, and New York had Lillian Russell.[115]

The European aristocracy began to find themselves unable to afford the high fees of international stars for their private concerts, and their salons were on the wane during the second half of the century. Liszt's recitals took on much of the character of the aristocratic salon, involving socializing, drinking, and smoking. He appeared at the highest-status public venues at the highest prices. Wagner, attending a recital in Paris, wrote that tickets cost 20 francs, providing Liszt with 10,000 francs for one concert.[116] Strauss Sr. achieved international stardom as a consequence of touring with his orchestra (see chapter 5). However, this course of action did not always guarantee sensational success. Josef Gung'l toured—even as far as North America in 1849— but did not attain the same individual acclaim; he became known only as the Berlin Strauss. However, his waltz *Die Hydropaten* (1858) lent its name to a group of pioneers of *cabaret artistique* in Paris (see chapter 8). Setting the trend for the emergence in the later twentieth century of a "pop aristocracy," the chansonnier Aristide Bruant and Johann Strauss Jr. both bought themselves country estates on their profits.

Among the stars of the Monday Popular Concerts in the 1860s were the pianist Arabella Goddard and the tenor Sims Reeves, for whom Balfe had composed "Come into the Garden, Maud" (Tennyson) in the previous decade. John Boosey discussed the possibility of holding ballad concerts with the singer Madame Sainton Dolby, and put on the first in 1867 at St. James's Hall. He may have been influenced by the success of ballad entertainments at the Crystal Palace the previous year, which one critic described as "far superior to those of a similar kind which have taken place in the metropolis."[117] In the 1840s and 1850s an opportunity had arisen in the drawing room ballad market for women songwriters, including those like Caroline Norton, who wrote both verse and music. In the 1860s, women had become a powerful force in this market, many of them being published by Boosey. Perhaps the most commercially successful of all nineteenth-century women songwriters was Claribel (Charlotte Alington Barnard), whose songs were favorites in British and American homes from the 1860s to the 1880s.[118] For his ballad concerts, Boosey engaged star singers who could attract a large public, such as Sims Reeves.[119] One of the greatest stars proved to be the contralto Antoinette Sterling, born in Sterlingville, New York, 1850 (see fig. 1.2). She chose this type of career quite deliberately—although her training had equipped her for a range of options—having studied with the famous singing teacher Manuel Garcia (who had trained Jenny Lind and a host of others) and his daughter Pauline Viardot. Sterling made an abundance of money from ballad singing, since she had contracted to receive a royalty for a term of years on many extremely popular ballads, such as Sullivan's "Lost Chord" and Molloy's "Love's Old Sweet Song."[120]

Figure 1.2
Antoinette Sterling.

Again we find that the music business does not always succeed in achieving its desired goals: "I used to find ballad concerts handicapped," John Boosey's nephew William lamented, "by it being necessary so very frequently to repeat the same songs over and over again."[121] If many in the audience already possessed those songs, then it meant no new business, and no additional royalty payment for the singer. A positive feature of the ballad concerts for impecunious composers was that they could witness what was going down well with the audience and try to repeat it. The consequence of this, however, was that the variety of musical forms found in ballads, as well as variety of subject matter, declined from the 1870s on, and publishers began looking out for composers who might be thought to have found a formula for commercial success.[122] In the 1880s, publishers trying to break into the New York market learnt from London practice and began paying singers a royalty of 6 to 14 cents per copy sold if they would promote their songs. The equivalent type of bourgeois popular song in Paris is represented by the *romance*.[123] It grew originally out of opera comique, and is characterized by elegant lyricism and simple strophic form (and should not to be confused with the later, more harmonically complex *mélodie*). The *romance* was associated with the bourgeois salon and was as market oriented as the drawing room ballads in London or New York. Some *romances* were published in popular periodicals—one such was actually called *La Romance*. They differed from the English and American ballads in their lack of inhibition about the subject of love.

In concluding this chapter on professionalism and commercialism in music during the nineteenth century, it should be stressed that the status of popular music changed profoundly with the development of the music market. This may be summarized as follows. In the early days of commercialization, the popular was condemned as being vulgar only if it was considered to be pandering to low taste, but as the music industry grew, the more successful music was commercially, the more it was perceived as music that appealed to a low and unrefined taste, until all music written for sale was regarded as inferior. However, music that was not thought to have originated as music for sale was still able to sell in huge numbers—as did the vocal score of *Messiah*, the songsheet of the folk song "The British Grenadiers," and the collection *Hymns Ancient and Modern* (1861)[124]—and remain popular without being despised as low in status and without its provoking critical contempt. I consider these matters in more detail in chapter 4.

2

New Markets for Cultural Goods

The critic Henry Lunn, writing in the *Musical Times* in 1866, was forced to recognize that art now had to "take its place in the market with other commodities."[1] He conjured up a nostalgic vision of a supposed single culture of former times, and yearned for "one grand association for the presentation of the greatest orchestral works, which should include all the available talent in the metropolis";[2] social reformers' ideal, too, was a single, shared culture, uniting different classes and ethnic groups. But the reality was that the economics of cultural provision in the second half of the century necessitated focusing on particular consumers. Old markets had to be developed, new ones created, and where necessary, demand stimulated. In this chapter I am using the term "markets" because it makes more sense in the context of a capitalist economy than speaking of individuals. No longer did individual patrons set the agenda for the production of the majority of cultural artifacts; rather, it was the market place. The reason markets were growing in the city was simple: this was a period of urbanization in which city populations increased rapidly as people arrived looking for work or business opportunities. Georg Simmel, in his essay "Die Grossstädte und das Geistesleben" (1902–3), notes that the form of supply in the metropolis is almost entirely by "production for the market" instead of via personal relations between producer and purchaser. The "struggle with nature for livelihood" is transformed by the metropolis into an "inter-human struggle for gain, which here is not granted by nature but by other men."[3] These markets targeted groups of consumers, setting out their stalls to attract and profit from a city's highly differentiated social strata—people of different social backgrounds, needs, and interests. The diverse markets for cultural goods were noted in London at midcentury: "The gay have their theatres—the philanthropic their Exeter Hall—the wealthy their 'ancient concerts'—the costermongers what they term their sing-song."[4] Cultural value fluctuates with the consumer's social status and power to define legitimate taste. A cultural struggle occurs when a current market's values are upset by the formation of a rival market, as shown in Gilbert and Sullivan's *Patience* (1881), when Bunthorne the fleshly poet and Grosvenor the idyllic poet compete for aesthetic status.

Urban residence was vital to entrepreneurship: it was in cities that those in the business of culture looked for profit-making opportunities, for markets that might be developed, and for art worlds that might be extended or freshly created. In the 1860s, the institutions of the café-concert in Paris and the music hall in London were the sites of new and expanding networks of stage managers, lighting experts, venue managers, poster designers, and so forth. The venture capitalist, however, needed investment to open up a market, and it was in the city, too, that financial backing was to be found. For some, there was a tendency to self-promote aggressively, or to make overblown claims for their products, and "charlatan" became a common term of abuse for those who did so.[5] As the nineteenth century wore on, an entrepreneur was seen as someone risking capital, whether in building a business or in financial speculation. As noted in chapter 1, it might be a music publisher making an investment in lithography, or raising funds to open a piano factory, or sponsoring a concert series.

The biggest and most obvious change musicians faced in the early nineteenth century, though London musicians had been prepared in advance for this and Viennese musicians did not confront it till later, was that they had to deal with markets and market relations rather than patrons and patronage. Musicians were now placed in a situation that gave rise to conflict between their need to affirm capitalist relations, in order to earn a living, and a desire to transgress them, in order to assert artistic freedom. Yet musicians were not the only ones caught up in this paradoxical situation, since music promoters were often torn between their materialist interests and those that they may have felt to be spiritual or aesthetic. The problem is that these interests are sometimes drawn together in a compromising fashion. It may be recalled that, in Gilbert and Sullivan's *Patience,* the complete transformation of the plain-speaking soldiers into aesthetes is effected for decidedly materialistic and self-serving reasons.

Aristocratic taste in the eighteenth century was for ceremony and formality; the bourgeoisie reacted against this by prizing individual character and feelings. The fondness of the bourgeoisie for virtuosos, Leonard Meyer suggests, was because virtuosos were understood to possess innate gifts that were not dependent on lineage or learning.[6] A "natural" music was preferred that did not rely on previous informed knowledge. The dislike for rules and conventions, linked to a new trust in the spontaneous verdict of the people, is found in Richard Wagner's *Meistersinger von Nürnberg* (1867) when Hans Sachs asserts that if a musician follows nature's path, it will be obvious to those who "know nothing of the tablature."[7] The subject of love was favored because it cuts across class, as Earl Tolloller acknowledges with irony in his song "Blue Blood" in *Iolanthe* (1882).

> Hearts just as pure and fair
> May beat in Belgrave Square
> As in the lowly air
> Of Seven Dials!

A way of avoiding art that relied on an education many people did not possess (such as knowledge of classical antiquity) was to choose contemporary topics and to celebrate the modern rather than the old features of everyday life. The titles given to many Viennese waltzes, and the ideas that frequently acted as inspiration, are examples of this practice. The values of novelty and individuality related to bourgeois ideology, being the virtues prized by "leaders of industry."[8] Popular forms with a working-class base were more likely to offer participation (for example, the music hall song's chorus); higher forms were more likely to be objects of aesthetic contemplation. The greater the stress on the aesthetic object, such as the priority of form over function, the more likely it was to cause confusion or attract ridicule. In Gilbert and Sullivan's *Ruddigore* (1887), it is said jokingly that the villagers are odd because they go around singing in four-part harmony. Suddenly the artificial norms of opera stand exposed.

It was assumed that audiences with a higher class of musical taste attended the Philharmonic Society's concerts, and that those with less elevated taste were more interested in oratorio. The Sacred Harmonic Society had a chorus and orchestra totaling 300 in 1836, and it had increased to 700 by the time Michael Costa became conductor in 1848. The Society met in Exeter Hall and survived until 1888.[9] The issue of taste, however, was more closely aligned to matters of respectability and class status than to questions of aesthetics. A shopkeeper, for instance, would have had no difficulty becoming a member of the Sacred Harmonic Society, but Reginald Nettel reports that a tradesman was almost rejected as a member of the Philharmonic Society until an assurance was given that "he did not serve behind the counter."[10] A similar distinction of class and taste existed in London theaters, especially before the Theatres Act of 1843, when only three theaters (Covent Garden, Drury Lane, and the Haymarket) had been allowed to produce "legitimate" drama—that is, drama without music. The minor theaters, presenting their mixtures of songs and plays, were not regarded as respectable venues, and the numbers of prostitutes in the neighborhoods of such theaters added pressing moral concerns.

New markets developed for cultural goods, but each market needed to be suitable for the different classes and class fractions that wished to acquire these goods. A Viennese aristocrat, for example, might balk at attending a concert in a bourgeois salon. Ruth Solie warns about the confusion of applying latter-day ideas of salon music—as something akin to parlor music—to the earlier days of salon concerts.[11] The key questions are "Whose salon?" and "What was its social function?" The salons of the old aristocracy in Vienna, for instance, were found by Tia DeNora to play a role in the development of the concept of "serious music."[12] All classes had to take into account the character of a performance venue before stepping inside, even though a certain amount of class mixing was normal at musical entertainments. Depending on where the entertainment was held, classes could separate themselves in various ways—by occupying differently priced seats, or reserving boxes, or booking special tables. In Paris, a *cabaret artistique* was not a place in which working-class people felt at home, but neither was it suited to the lower-middle-class clientele of the Divan Japonais. Yvette Guilbert says it was a revelation for the audience at that establishment when she began singing chansons from the most celebrated of cabarets, the Chat Noir. She then moved further upmarket to perform at the bourgeois Théâtre d'Application and, by the mid-1890s, any subversive quality Guilbert may once have possessed was dissipated (see chapter 8).

Promenade Concerts

These concerts, which began in the 1830s, were the largest kind of public concert, and during them people could display any manner of inattentive listening—walking, talking, drinking, or eating. For this reason they often took place in parks, or the Champs Elysées in Paris, although in the 1840s they were becoming more formalized and were being held in renovated or purpose-built halls during the winter months. Philippe Musard had won popularity for his promenade concerts in Paris in 1833, and a few years later they were being imitated in London—an indebtedness highlighted by the phrase "à la Musard" tacked onto advertisements. The Lyceum hosted the first in 1838, with its seats boarded over to accommodate a standing audience.[13] The next year, in one of the earliest references to music being "light," the editor of the *Musical World*, noting the hundreds attracted to the Lyceum Promenade Concerts, remarks: "when we contemplate the gratification that the lighter music seems to afford to a very large portion of the audience, it appears selfish to sneer at the means that produced it."[14] The programs consisted of overtures, quadrilles, solos, and waltzes by Joseph Lanner and Strauss Sr. At Drury Lane in 1840, "Concerts d'été" were announced, and Louis Jullien, who had fled from France to London because of insolvency, was at first an assistant conductor. The following year, he had taken over and soon began to vary the repertoire, even holding Beethoven nights. His promenade concerts at Covent Garden Theatre in 1844 were made up of a first half of classical music succeeded by a second half of popular dance music. It is evidence of contested taste, since, as the *Musical Examiner* pointed out, people could, if they so wished, attend the half of their choice.[15] Jullien was alert to the value of familiarity in appealing to a British audience, and began to include vocal music in English (songs and Handel oratorio excerpts). He was most acclaimed, however, for playing French overtures and quadrilles. He gave *concerts monstres* in the Surrey Gardens from 1845, and these contained sensational showpieces such as *The Fall of Sebastopol* of 1855, which came complete with musketry, rockets, and mortar. On these occasions he augmented his orchestra with an array of brass instruments. He was giving concerts in New York in 1853. Favorite places for mixed instrumental and vocal programs in that city were Castle Garden in the Battery, where Jenny Lind's New York debut took place in 1850, and Niblo's Garden at Broadway and Prince Street. Theodore Thomas gave orchestral concerts, 1868–75, in Central Park Garden, where there was a restaurant and seating for several hundred.

The pleasure gardens began to suffer from the competition from other places of entertainment. Vauxhall Gardens were at their zenith in the late eighteenth century; in the nineteenth, they fell steadily into decline, despite efforts to lure people in with spectacles and such. Ranelagh barely made it into the nineteenth century, but the admission price there was a hefty half-crown (2 shillings and sixpence). From 1837 on, Surrey Zoological Gardens were used for public entertainments. Vienna's Augarten, in Leopoldstadt, had concerts from 1775 on, but preference was given to a high-art repertoire, and they were held in a concert room. On the other hand, Frances Trollope, visiting Vienna in 1836, comments on a "deficiency of haut-ton" at a Volksgarten concert directed by Joseph Lanner, though she puts this down to the nobility being out of town, since it was September.[16] The Champs-Elysées were going strong until late in the nineteenth century, and not just for outdoor café music; Musard conducted military band music in which new virtuosos could be heard on new instruments (for instance, Louis Dufresne on cornet). Popular music, from the beginning, marched hand in hand with technological innovation, both being energized by the new industrial age.

An overarching theme and the presence of a celebrity conductor acted as unifying principles for promenade concerts. The programs mixed popular and classical items and, in so doing, laid some of the foundations for the rise of commercial popular styles and genres. They retained a heterogeneity that gradually disappeared from other concerts in which classical music was heard. A key feature of popular music is the interest in and emphasis on the new, and promenade concerts had far more new pieces than did the severer classical concerts. Dance music—especially waltzes, polkas, and quadrilles[17]—played an important role, and not just in Vienna, which had more promenade concerts than other cities. Promenade concerts had a petit bourgeois character, catering to a taste developed in cafés, taverns, parks, and pleasure gardens (the latter busiest in summer when the aristocracy were not in town). The people who attended the concerts, however, were not drawn from a single class. In the first half of the century, "popular" did not necessarily mean "low status": some virtuoso display pieces were popular in style but enjoyed high status at that time. As already noted, class mixing was the norm at musical entertainments: for one event it might be the working class and petite bourgeoisie, for another the haute bourgeoisie and the aristocracy. This should not be interpreted as any indication that the classes that came together at such events considered each other to share a homogeneous identity as an audience: one class was certainly capable of perceiving another as of low status even if they were both taking pleasure in the same concert. Exhibitions of social distinction were perceived in the way people separated themselves from others and in the status of the spaces they occupied. The haute bourgeoisie went only to the most prestigious of promenade concerts, such as those involving Philippe Musard in Paris, Johann Strauss Sr. in Vienna, and Louis Jullien in London and New York; but the audience was still mixed, and the repertoire the same as at less grand events.

William Weber notes that "strictly defined classical-music concerts" emerged simultaneously with promenade concerts and not as a reaction to them.[18] Weber stresses the importance of the visual element in the latter, whether it was a profusion of plants or the brilliance of the lighting. They also tended to have a historical or geographical theme. There was undoubtedly some repertoire shared between the two types of concert, but the meaning of an operatic overture, for instance, was changed by the differing contexts in which it was consumed. A change Weber notices is that from promenade concerts' international quality of the 1830s and 1840s to their increasingly national quality post-1850. However, it is important to stress that national features were not localized in their appeal and created no difficulty in reception. A function of popular music is to give identity to social groups, and that is clearly happening with the national and regional emphasis of post-1848 promenade concerts and other popular concerts, but it would be wrong to link such concerts to nationalist sentiment in a more pronounced political sense before the 1870s. There is rarely anything approaching an exclusively regional emphasis; it is more of a regional flavor. Moreover, composers could pay tributes to countries other than their own. Strauss Sr.'s *Paris,* op. 101, shows how internationalization began to affect the character of the Viennese waltz—here he interweaves references to the Marseillaise. Other examples of internationalization are found in Lanner's *Pesther-Walzer*, with its Hungarian-style first waltz, and in his *Die Osmanen*, op. 146 (1839), which was dedicated to Fethi Ahmed Pasha, a son-in-law of Sultan Mahmud II.[19] What is more, composers everywhere were feeling the influence of Viennese dance music: in the 1860s, even Sultan Abdülaziz was trying his hand at waltz composition in *Invitation à la valse*.[20]

Strauss Jr. (1825–99) appeared at the Promenade Opera Concerts at the Royal Italian Opera House, Covent Garden, in August 1867. The London correspondent of the Viennese paper *Das Fremden-Blatt* claimed that the younger Strauss's waltzes were unknown to most of the London audience, but that after just one evening he and his melodies had become "extraordinarily popular."[21] In September 1867, Strauss conducted his *Potpourri-Quadrille* (no opus number), which contained popular and traditional songs from Germany, Scotland, and France. We find here more evidence of an international market for popular music—elements of European national styles one might associate with attempts to establish musical identities contiguous with national borders actually appear to possess a wider appeal. The nineteenth-century commercial popular style managed simultaneously both to be local and to transcend the local, as did the styles marketed as "world music" in the closing decades of the twentieth century. The waltz, blackface minstrelsy, music hall, and French cabaret took almost no time to cross national boundaries once an organized means of dissemination was in place. The reason is straightforward: this music became available in a commodity form designed for exchange, and it was never so circumscribed by the local as to confuse or be unintelligible to a wider audience. At first, commercially successful music was what was popular with the middle classes, who in the nineteenth century had become a powerful and sizeable social force with sufficient disposable income to indulge regularly in the consumption of musical goods. In accounting for how rapidly such music spread, we need to be aware of the similarities these classes in different countries shared in their metropolitan experiences, and how this shaped their tastes. It might be added that Jetty Treffz, Strauss's wife at the time of his Covent Garden concerts, had little difficulty in making a success of singing songs like "Home, Sweet, Home" to her London audience. When the time came for Strauss to leave England, the *Illustrated London News* (26 October 1867) pronounced his concerts "the best promenade concerts ever given in this country."[22] They gave Strauss the idea of introducing British-style promenade concerts in Vienna, using seating at the front and a promenade area at the rear.

Dance Music

Music for dancing was much sought after, especially in Vienna. The large Sperl dance hall and garden (Zum Sperlbauer) opened in the suburb of Leopoldstadt in 1807; it was spacious and fashionable, but entrance was by ticket not invitation, thus marking it out as bourgeois. The Apollo Palace (1808) was even bigger; with five huge rooms and many smaller, it could accommodate up to 6,000. However, it needed to reduce its ticket prices on certain days in order to attract patrons. The resumption of war with Napoleon in 1809 led to a devaluation of currency in 1811 that bankrupted the Apollo's owner the following year. The mood after the Napoleonic Wars was fun seeking, all the same, and more ballrooms opened throughout Vienna. The biggest of all the Biedermeyer dance halls was the Odeon, which opened in nonaristocratic Leopoldstadt in January 1845; it was, at that time, the biggest in the world, and could hold 8,000 dancers as well as an 80-piece orchestra. It was destroyed permanently in October 1848 as the Revolution was drawing to a close. The Sofiensäle were originally constructed for swimming and for taking a Turkish bath, but the huge central hall was soon converted into a more lucrative ballroom, which became a favorite. The Sofiensaal retained its reputation for many years, being much used in the Carnival season: all the important balls of the various Viennese societies were held there.

Apart from ballrooms and restaurants, dance music would be played at promenade concerts—for example, at those held on Sundays in the Blümensaal of the Horticultural Society—and in public spaces like the Volksgarten. The popular dances were those that were popular with the bourgeoisie: the waltz, the polka (from Bohemia), which replaced the *galop* in popularity after 1840, and the quadrille (from France). The quadrille had an old country-dance structure of separate figures (in the French model that was adopted in Vienna: Pantalon, Été, Poule, Trénis, Pastourelle, Finale), whereas the other popular dances, the waltz and polka, were not figure dances. It was the public dance halls, not private balls (*Redoutes*), that now determined the prevailing character of dance music. In contrast to the days of the Vienna Congress, the large Redoutensaal at the Hofburg was no longer the fashion leader in dance music.

Strauss Sr. and Josef Lanner were each giving musical entertainments three evenings a week in the 1830s, their waltz nights proving the most successful and thus stimulating the further production of waltzes. Offenbach became interested in the waltz after hearing Strauss in Paris in 1837.[23] What became typical of the French waltz, however, was an accompaniment pattern that stressed the first two beats but not the third; it had no "pushed" note like the anticipated second beat of the typical accompaniment pattern of the Viennese waltz. Strauss and Lanner had achieved fame because not only was their music thrilling to dance to but also they were exciting to watch as violinists, with their double-stopping, wide leaps, *portamento,* and variety of bowing effects, such as *spiccato,* in which the bow bounces on the string. The idiomatic violin style is retained in waltz melodies by Strauss Jr.: consider the typical violin grace notes in the first theme of the *Blue Danube*. People from a variety of social strata attended balls. During the Fasching, the carnival season before Lent, class mixing was common at masked balls. A rose might be given as an indication that a man wished to invite a woman to dance, and disguised identities could continue if the invitation was accepted, since it was not the done thing to speak while dancing.[24] Of course, it was just this sort of thing that led some to disapprove of masked balls. In *Die Fledermaus*, the date of the masked ball was changed from Christmas Eve, its date in the original play, *Réveillon* by Meilhac and Halévy, in order not to give offense by depicting such a morally dubious event taking place at that religiously sensitive time of year. People from a wide range of class backgrounds might organize balls; location would give the best indication of status. Some balls were specially named after the professions of those attending, for example, an artists' ball or a physicians' ball. Since industrialization came late to Vienna, there was for many years a predominance of merchants, craft workers, and shopkeepers (bakers, greengrocers, etc.) attending suburban dances.

The Viennese working class found music at a cheap price in suburban dance halls, in the Tafelmusik played in local coffeehouses and restaurants, and in public parks. Zither music, which had been popularized in Vienna by Johann Petzmeyer, was a favorite in taverns. In New York, inexpensive working-class dances, called "affairs," were held in rented neighborhood halls. They offered an opportunity for immigrants to enjoy the dances of their homelands. The enduring popularity of dance in New York is indicated by the fact that *The Dance Album*, published by Enoch and Sons in 1888, sold 20,000 copies in just seven weeks.[25] Public dance halls increased rapidly in the 1890s, and attracted different classes (Carnegie Hall the middle class, Liberty Hall the working class).

Strauss Jr.'s set of waltzes composed in memory of his visit to Covent Garden (*Erinnerung an Covent Garden*, op. 329, 1868), shows that he was attentive to the latest hit songs of the music hall, since he includes an arrangement of "Champagne Charlie" (words by George Leybourne, music by Alfred Lee, 1867), then at the peak of its popularity. Raymond Williams commended music hall for presenting areas of experience that other genres neglected or despised[26]—but similarly neglected areas are also presented in operetta, for example, what Henry Raynor calls the "alcoholic goodwill" of the act 2 Finale of *Die Fledermaus* (1874).[27] Consider how a chromatic string melody with unexpected phrase endings (on the 9th and 7th of V^7) signifies a giddy recklessness as Orlofsky sings "Diese Tänzer mögen ruh'n!" (These dancers must rest! [see ex. 2.1]).

The music sounds a little drunk, rather than sensual or yearning—the more usual connotations of chromaticism and dissonance. The popular style developed other novel musical features. Hubert Parry cites as a conspicuous feature of "second-rate music," providing examples from

Example 2.1 Strauss, *Die Fledermaus* (1874), act 2, Finale.

"low-class tunes" (note how the two are conflated), "an insistence on the independence of the 'leading note' from the note to which it has been supposed to lead."[28] The falling leading note in a subdominant context (the *wienerische Note*) is a feature of Viennese waltzes. The tendency for the leading note to fall was because the sixth degree of the scale attained a new importance in this music (see chapter 5). It had clearly caught the ear of Wagner when writing for his Rhinemaidens.[29] The tonic triad with added major seventh also begins to be accepted without the need for resolution: consider the refrain of Adele's "laughing song" from *Die Fledermaus* at the words "ich die Sache, ha ha ha" (see the measure marked with an asterisk in ex. 2.2).

Peter Van der Merwe says that composers "became aware that there were certain features that stamped popular music, and either cultivated these if they were writing for the general public, or avoided them if they were writing for the elect."[30] The popular style, however, allows for considerable diversity of mood. The end of the verse of "Champagne Charlie" is an unassuming descending pattern of falling leading note and chromatically inflected descending scale; yet Strauss uses a similar pattern of notes to open one of his most beautiful refrains, that of the duet "Wer uns getraut" (from *Der Zigeunerbaron,* 1885) (see ex. 2.3).

Popular styles were inclined almost from the start to mix promiscuously. In the later century, for instance, it is by no means unusual to find Viennese elements in music hall, or blackface minstrelsy (there is an *African Polka* in *Dobson's Universal Banjo Instructor* of 1882).[31]

Example 2.2 Adele's Lach-Couplets ("Mein Herr Marquis"), *Die Fledermaus,* act 2.

Examples 2.3 (a) "Champagne Charlie," words by George Leybourne, music by Alfred Lee (London: Charles Sheard, 1867); (b) "Wer uns getraut," duet: Saffi and Barinkay, *Der Zigeunerbaron* (1885), act 2.

A   noise all day,   and swim-ming in cham - pagne.

Und   mild   sang die Nach - ti - gall   ihr   Lied - chen in__ die   Nacht:__

Music Hall and Café-Concert

The diaries of Charles Rice, a comic singer who sang in London taverns during the 1840s, throw interesting light on the years leading up to music hall.[32] The tavern concert room, with its lower-middle-class patrons and professional or semiprofessional entertainment, has a more direct link to the music hall than do the song and supper rooms around Covent Garden and the Strand, which were frequented by the aristocracy and wealthy middle class. Evans's Late Joys, for example, had formerly been the residence of the earl of Orford, which had been converted into a high-class tavern by several peers of the realm in the eighteenth century.[33] West End halls, like the Oxford, were the only ones to attract higher-class patrons; suburban halls relied on patronage from the working class and lower middle class (tradesmen, shopkeepers, mechanics, clerks). Charles Morton had difficulty attracting middle-class patrons to his grand hall, the Canterbury, in Lambeth.[34] In the 1890s, middle-class attitudes became more favorable to music hall, swayed by the "new character of the entertainment,"[35] in a word, the respectability managers strove for (by encouraging the attendance of married women, for example). By that time, music hall had expanded to cover a wide range of performances, which included dancers, magicians, dramatic sketches, and some acts that would have been previously seen in a circus (such as acrobats and trapeze artists). That is the reason the French themselves started using the term *music-hall* for this type of entertainment, in order to distinguish it from the diet of romances, comic songs, and light-operatic arias usually associated with the café-concert.

The café-concert took off during the Second Empire (1852–70).[36] The first were established along the Champs-Elysées; the entertainment was given in the open air in summer on specially erected stages between the trees. Performing in this environment was exhausting for singers because of the noise, such as that of passing carriages. Cafés-concerts soon began to open in the city in winter, providing further employment for the same entertainers. The Eldorado was the first grand winter café-concert, built in 1858 on the boulevard de Strasbourg. It held 1,500, had a large orchestra and pit, and boxes, balconies, and galleries.[37] The musical accompaniment at other establishments could range from a single pianist to a small orchestra. Performers' names were shown on a board to the right of the stage; unlike British music hall, no chairman was used to announce performers and keep order. Other differences were that admission was generally free—patrons paid only for drinks—and singers were not permitted to wear stage costume until the late 1860s. In the 1880s, a café-concert was still allowed only one fixed scene, and the stage was to be without machinery, flies, or a cellar.[38] There was a certain amount of class mixing in the café-concerts, but separation was made possible by the designation of "best tables." The comic songs, smoke, and drink gave both music hall and café-concert a morally suspect air and kept many of the "respectable" at bay.

Of all the song novelties that came and went at the café-concert, perhaps none exasperated the high-minded critic more than the nonsense song. It was not an invention of the café-concert, but there was a sudden mania for this type of song in the 1860s, when it was known as a *scie* or saw.[39] The adjective *sciant* was used at that time to mean a mixture of tedious and tormenting. A typical device was to take a street cry, as Félix Baumaine did with "Hé! Lambert!"[40] and make up an irritating song that is halfway between sense and nonsense.

> Vous n'auriez pas vu Lambert,
> À la gar' du chemin de fer?
> Vous n'auriez pas vu . . .
> Lambert? (5 fois)
>
> S'est-il noyé dans la mer,
> S'est-il perdu dans l' désert?
> Qu'est-ce qui a vu Lambert?
> Lambert? (4 fois)
>
> Have you seen Lambert
> at the train station?
> Have you seen . . .
> Lambert? (5 times)
>
> Is he drowned in the sea,
> is he lost in the desert?
> Who has seen Lambert?
> Lambert? (4 times)

It drove some people to distraction. Jules de Goncourt wrote in 1864: "At this time in Paris, there is an epidemic of idiotic cries, of Ohé Lambert!, such that they need to be stopped by the police."[41] Sometimes these songs showed an interest in word play, as does "L'Amant d'Amanda," which was sung by Libert first at the Ambassadeurs then the Eldorado in 1876.[42] Here, "amant d'A" sounds identical to "Amanda" and initially suggests a crossdresser, an impression corrected only in the last line.

> Voyez-vous ce beau garçon-là,
> C'est l'amant d'A,
> C'est l'amant d'A,
> Voyez-vous ce beau garçon-là,
> C'est l'amant d'Amanda.
>
> Do you see that handsome guy there?
> It's A's lover [heard as "It's that Amanda"],
> It's A's lover.[43]
> Do you see that handsome guy there?
> It's Amanda's lover.

The humorous attraction of the *scie* may be best explained, perhaps, with recourse to the philosopher Henri Bergson's contention that repetition induces laughter because it suggests a "repeating-machine set going by a fixed idea" rather than something emanating from a thinking, living human being.[44]

The main clientele at cafés-concerts were the lower middle class, supplemented by some soldiers, students, and workers on a night out. Urchins and the Parisian poor would climb trees in the Champs-Elysées to catch glimpses of famous stars like Thérésa. The Eldorado remained open during the Commune, showing that the café-concert public was still in Paris, even if the theatergoers had left for Versailles. The *Réveil*, in 1886, described the patrons of the Alcazar d'été as "a wholly Parisian public of toffs, prostitutes, petits bourgeois with their families, and shop assistants."[45] Yvette Guilbert made her début, singing "Les Vierges," at the more upmarket Divan Japonais, which opened in 1888 at 75 rue des Martyrs. It held 200 at most, and singers were on a raised platform at the back of the room. Guilbert complained that the low ceiling meant she hit her hands if she made large gestures, and she was suffocated by the gas lighting.[46] Despite her artistic suffering, the *Figaro illustré* declared in 1896 that café-concert songs were the principal cause of the corruption of musical taste in France.[47] The songs had become associated with people letting their hair down and enjoying undisciplined leisure time. Saturday was payday for 85 percent of Parisian workers and their preferred evening for a café-concert or *bal*. It was also the day for leisure activities and a night out for workers in London, especially after Saturday half-day holidays became the norm in the 1870s. As with music halls, there were cafés-concerts in poorer areas. Between 1850 and 1860, many old cafés on the city's outskirts were falling into disrepair, and their owners "responded hastily to the new town planning of a metropolis recently industrialized and remodeled by Baron Haussmann, by transforming some of these buildings into cafés-concerts to meet the requirements of customers most often made up of workmen and unemployed farm laborers."[48] The working-class cafés-concerts were often known scornfully as *beuglants,* a reference to the audience singing along—*beugler* means to bellow. Cafés-concerts did, however, give an opportunity for people of working-class background, like Thérésa, to become famous.[49]

The attraction of the Champs-Elysées faded in the 1890s as interest increased in establishments around Montmartre, Pigalle, and place Blanche. The Moulin-Rouge had opened in 1889, and soon leaped to fame as the venue of the *quadrille réaliste* directed by the dancer la Goulue. The popular dance hall the Elysée-Montmartre was close to the first Chat Noir, an establishment that initiated a new and influential form of cabaret (discussed in chapter 8).[50] The working-class residents of Belleville and Ménilmontant did not go to the cabarets of Montmartre; they went to their own local establishments or to ad hoc venues for dances. The *cabarets artistiques* were not large: even the biggest venues, like the second Chat Noir (which had a shadow theater) or the Quat'z'Arts, catered for fewer than a hundred. On a much larger scale was the Oympia, which in 1893 brought the name *music-hall* to Paris, although the Folies-Bergère and the Casino de Paris already offered similar variety entertainment. It was *le music-hall* that began to attract the attention of modernist painters like Picasso in the early years of the twentieth century as the café-concert, cabaret, and theater came to be seen as too conventional and formula bound.[51]

Blackface Minstrelsy, Black Musicals, and Vaudeville

Shortly after the new style of dance music had developed in Vienna, and just before music hall and café-concert developed as new forms of entertainment in London and Paris, New York was developing its own distinctive popular form of entertainment in blackface minstrelsy. Charles Hamm remarks that the minstrel song "emerged as the first distinctly American genre."[52] It began when New Yorker Thomas Rice copied his "Jim Crow" dance routine from a disabled African-American street performer, and introduced it into his act at the Bowery Theatre in 1832.[53] The Virginia Minstrels, four in number, formed in New York in 1842. Rice visited London in 1836, and the Virginia Minstrels did so in 1843, and troupes soon formed in England (see chapter 6). Blackface minstrels reinforced racism, but subverted bourgeois values by celebrating laziness and irresponsibility, their blackface masks allowing an inversion of dominant values.[54] Their performances might be considered as presenting a special context: a social "frame" that Erving Goffman would analyze as one that allows people "to lose control of themselves in carefully controlled circumstances."[55] Minstrels rarely displayed any wild or eccentric behavior when off stage.

Minstrel troupes in the early period were seldom more than six strong. Following the example established by E. P. Christy in his minstrel hall at 472 Broadway, they sat in a semicircle, and the characters at each end were named Tambo and Bones after the instruments they played.[56] Known as the "corner men," they were the comedians, and were questioned to humorous effect by the "interlocutor," Mr. Johnson, who occupied the middle of the stage. Minstrel shows were in two halves, the first part featuring the black dandy character, who appeared in song almost on the heels of the ragged "Jim Crow" in the shape of "Zip Coon." Blackface minstrels had a broad appeal, and London soon had its own permanent troupe, the Moore and Crocker (later, Burgess) Minstrels, who took up residency at the smaller St. James's Hall as "Christy Minstrels."[57] The enormous cross-class popularity of the songs of Stephen Foster (1826–64) effectively created a "national music" for America.[58] His first big success, "Oh! Susanna," was first published under his own name in New York in 1848. "Massa's in de Cold Ground" and "My Old Kentucky Home, Good Night," published in New York in 1852 and 1853, respectively, were both labeled "plantation melodies," but one is in minstrel dialect, the other not. Dale Cockrell explains that Foster was beginning to condemn minstrel dialect as degrading.[59] His talent was not only for minstrel songs, as "Jeanie with the Light Brown Hair" (1854) confirms. Yet when Strauss Jr. visited New York and wanted to include something American in his *Manhattan Waltzes,* he chose Stephen Foster's "Old Folks at Home," perceiving that a characteristically American music had developed through minstrelsy.

The abolition of slavery after the American Civil War had little effect on theatrical representations of African Americans. Black minstrel troupes were formed that stressed the values of genuineness and authenticity, but since they adopted minstrel conventions, they continued to offer a distortion of black culture and plantation life. The first commercially successful black songwriter was James Bland (1854–1911), who worked for Callender and Haverly and whose songs included "Carry Me Back to Old Virginny"[60] and "Oh, Dem Golden Slippers!"[61] An alternative to minstrelsy was offered by the Jubilee Singers from Fisk University (founded for the education of African Americans) who toured, appearing in New York in 1871, and made such spirituals as "Go Down, Moses" widely known.[62] For the majority of black performers, however, minstrelsy was the only way of earning a living, and well over a thousand black entertainers had taken that route by the 1890s.[63] Some performers, for example Sam Lucas, and the Hyer sisters, tried to make a success of other forms of entertainment, but lacked audience support. Lucas was able to shake off minstrelsy in the 1890s, when black performers began to appear in vaudeville and the focus shifted from southern plantations to northern cities. In 1890, Sam Jack, a burlesque theater owner, produced *The Creole Show,* and paved the way for the future development of the all-black musical, although it still included minstrel routines. It was the first production, other than those given by the *Uncle Tom's Cabin* companies, to include black women performers.[64] A later all-black show, *Oriental America* (1896), made it to Broadway for a short run at Palmer's Theater. The first all-black musical comedy to triumph just off Broadway was Bob Cole's and Billy Johnson's *A Trip to Coontown*. It opened at the Third Avenue Theater in April 1898, a mere two months before the première of another successful black show, *Clorindy, or the Origin of the Cakewalk*, by Will Marion Cook (at the Casino Roof Garden, Broadway).[65] This indicates the beginnings of a shift in audience expectations regarding black performers, and also reveals how the presence of educated and entrepreneurial African Americans was having an effect on New York's musical life. Cole was a graduate of Atlanta University, and Cook had studied in Berlin and at the National Conservatory of Music in New York. Cook was to become associated with musicals that leaned heavily on the talents of the black entertainers Bert Williams and George Walker, such as *In Dahomey* of 1903—a success in New York, London, and then continental Europe. He was already cultivating African-American talent in *Clorindy*, which featured the ragtime star Ernest Hogan, whose infelicitously titled "All Coons Look Alike to Me" started the craze for syncopated "coon songs."[66] The title alone tells us unambiguously that the economics of cultural consumption at this time dictated that black artists needed to cater to a white subject position.

Ragtime was indebted both to the "jig piano" styles of African-American musicians and the European military march. This is not surprising, since black musicians could be found in nearly every regimental band in New York as early as the 1840s.[67] In 1896, Ben Harney was the first to make an impact playing ragtime piano in New York; his ragtime song "You've Been a Good Old Wagon" was published that year and, soon after that, his *Rag Time Instructor*. Ragtime developed as an original and idiomatic piano composition, especially in the hands of Scott Joplin at the turn of the century,[68] but in the 1890s its syncopated march rhythm was most often found in songs, or in band arrangements for dancing a two-step or a cakewalk. The American Dancing-Masters' Association launched the two-step in 1889, using John Philip Sousa's new march "The Washington Post."[69] That is not a ragtime piece, and contains a Viennese use of the sixth degree of the scale, but Sousa soon adopted the style and introduced ragtime numbers when he appeared with his band at the Paris Exhibition in 1900. Although the cakewalk had featured in minstrel shows of the 1870s, it was its performance by Charles Johnson and Dora Dean in *The Creole Show* that led to its becoming a rage. Johnson had developed some eccentric new features, and these helped to make international stars of him and his partner. It was performances by Johnson and Dean in Vienna that were responsible for the dance being taken up with such enthusiasm in that city.

Variety began as a free show in a concert saloon ("honky-tonk"), dime museum, or beer garden. After the Civil War, it was more usually found in theaters. It leaned on minstrelsy at first, but developed in its own way. Jokes directed at New York's Irish, Italian, and German immigrants were common, as many new immigrants were arriving in the city. Larger variety theatres had bands of around seven players, typically clarinet, cornet, trombone, violin, piano, double bass, and drums. If there were only three players, it would be cornet, piano, and drums. The drums were necessary for comic punctuations.[70] Vaudeville, which is usually traced back to the efforts of Tony Pastor at his Opera House on the Bowery in the late 1860s, came to mean variety entertainment suitable for the "double audience," that is, men and women. From 1881, Pastor was staging "high class" variety shows at his own theatre on Fourteenth Street. When Frederick Freeman Proctor opened his 23rd Street Theater in 1892, he decided to make it the home of continuous vaudeville (from 10:00 a.m. to 10:30 p.m.), suitable for "ladies and children"; his slogan was "After breakfast go to Proctor's, after Proctor's go to bed."[71] His shows included anything wholesome—from a baritone soloist to "comedy elephants." Proctor pioneered "popular prices" from 25 to 50 cents; yet the capacity of his theater meant he could afford the high salaries of the stars. Vaudeville soon replaced blackface minstrelsy as the major form of stage entertainment, so that, by 1896, only ten American minstrel companies remained.[72] The *comédie-vaudevilles* that were performed at Parisian theatres like the Odéon, the Gaîté, and the Vaudeville should not be confused with American vaudeville. These Parisian theaters featured traditional airs, songs from operetta, and a few original numbers; they were really the domain of actors who sang rather than singers who acted. A specific attempt to cater to a family audience in Paris was the founding of the Eden-Concert in 1881 at 17 boulevard de Sébastopol.

Operetta

The first *opéra-bouffe* (a term overtaken later by "operetta") was *Don Quichotte* (1847) by Hervé (real name Florimond Ronger), whose Folies Nouvelles theatre gave Jacques Offenbach (1819–80) the idea for his own Bouffes Parisiens, opened in 1855. *Orphée aux enfers,* an *opéra-bouffe* in two acts, was first performed there in 1858. A stage work like *Orphée* was not possible earlier because of the strict regulations of the prefecture of police, which in 1855 allowed Offenbach's company only three characters in musical scenes and no choruses without special permission, and restricted the entertainment to one act. *Orphée* pokes fun indirectly at aristocratic classical learning and the aristocracy's self-identification with classical figures. Significantly, the Marseillaise is quoted in the chorus of gods rebelling against Jupiter ("Aux armes! dieux et demi-dieux"). Orpheus and Eurydice are a bored husband and wife having affairs, though when Orpheus sings "On m'a ravi mon Eurydice," he quotes Gluck's famous melody. Part of Offenbach's popular appeal was his use of *couplets* (verse plus chorus) instead of arias and cavatinas. The *galop infernale,* however, was a sensation and often used for the cancan, though only in later years—Offenbach having distanced himself from this dance when it gained notoriety in Paris in the 1830s.[73]

The financial stability of the Théâtre des Variétés was assured when Hortense Schneider, for a fee of 2,000 francs a month, appeared in Offenbach's *La Belle Hélène* in 1864, and prompted this theater to engage in further fruitful collaboration with Offenbach.[74] Walter Benjamin remarks sourly: "The phantasmagoria of capitalist culture attained its most radiant unfurling in the World Exhibition of 1867. The Second Empire was at the height of its power. Paris was confirmed in its position as the capital of luxury and of fashion. Offenbach set the rhythm for Parisian life. The operetta was the ironical Utopia of the lasting domination of Capital."[75] However, as we shall see in chapter 4, the key word here for Offenbach and his collaborators Henri Meilhac and Ludovic Halévy is "ironical." The Theater an der Wien, next in importance to the Kärntnertortheater, was beset by financial problems in the 1850s, but its fortunes, too, were restored thanks to the success of Offenbach operettas. Vienna was the first foreign city to respond enthusiastically to Offenbach, and operetta took off at the Vorstadt theaters (those that had been outside the city walls). The quadrille *Hinter den Coulissen* (1859, no opus number) by Strauss Jr. and his brother Josef is based on themes in Offenbach's early stage works. He was invited to produce three of his works in person at the Carltheater in Leopoldstadt at the end of 1860, and he became a regular visitor thereafter.[76] Franz von Suppé was Offenbach's first imitator in Vienna: his *Die schöne Galathee* (1865) is indebted to *La Belle Hélène* (1864).[77]

The paper *Der Floh* hailed the premiere of Strauss Jr.'s *Indigo und die vierzig Räuber* at the Theater an der Wien (10 February 1871) as a defeat for the frivolous music of Offenbach.[78] A revised version, *La Reine Indigo,* was staged in Paris at the Théâtre de la Renaissance in 1875. It was also seen, though to no great success, as *King Indigo* in London at the Royal Alhambra Theatre in 1876. Strauss's most famous operetta, *Die Fledermaus* of 1874 (libretto by Carl Haffner and Richard Genée), was his third, appearing after he had already established the importance of the waltz in his stage work. Strauss's operettas, like those of Offenbach and Gilbert and Sullivan, are designed to appeal strongly to a bourgeois audience. There is an obvious middle-class subject position in Adele's "laughing song," which satirizes the idea that certain physiognomic features are the preserve of the aristocracy. Marie Geistinger, who played Rosalinde, had experience performing in parodies, having first established her reputation in *Die falsche Pepita* (1852) at the Theater in der Josefstadt.[79] In general, the satirical bite of Offenbach or Gilbert and Sullivan is absent in *Die Fledermaus,* but there were no London or New York operettas as sensual or hedonistic; he also added a Viennese quality that consisted of more than the waltz tunes: note, for instance,

Example 2.4 Refrain of the Champagne Song, *Die Fledermaus*, act 2, Finale.

Die Ma - je - stät wird an - er-kannt,   an - er-kannt   rings im Land,

the characteristic yodel-like rising sixths that appear in "Die Majestät wird anerkannt" (Finale, act 2; see ex. 2.4) and elsewhere.

Strauss had left political satire alone after *Indigo*, although his operettas continued to remain enmeshed in a social and political context.[80] Typical of operetta is the use of musical irony. The "wrong" musical mood for "O je, o je, wie rührt mich dies!" in the trio in act 1 betrays the characters' real feelings. Irony often works as an appropriation of a style: for example, the satirical text of "When Britain Really Ruled the Waves" (from *Iolanthe*) is strengthened by Sullivan's use of a style associated with patriotic music. Alternatively, a style may be chosen that contradicts the text, in which case the music becomes the primary vehicle for satire: for example, in the refrain of "Piff, Paff, Pouff" (from *La Grande-Duchesse de Gérolstein*) Offenbach eschews a grand operatic Meyerbeerian style and provides music that deflates the General's pomposity (see chapter 4 for a discussion of parody in operetta).

The success of Gilbert and Sullivan's *Trial by Jury*, first performed on the same bill as Offenbach's *La Périchole* at the Royal Theatre in 1875, opened the market for English operetta. Promoter D'Oyly Carte formed the Comic Opera Company the following year. Arthur Sullivan (1842–1900) is often indebted to Offenbach, an example being when a chorus repeats words of a soloist to humorous effect. The key to Gilbert's humor was his serious treatment of the absurd, showing the influence of burlesque. Musical burlesque in London, quite distinct from that in New York, occupied a middle ground between music hall and opera, including the music of both in its parodies.[81] Although it had a long history in England, the Victorian variety, characterized by punning, travesty, and satire, can be traced back to Planché's *Olympic Revels*, written for Lucy Vestris when she took over management of the Olympic Theatre in 1831.[82] The Gaiety Theatre, built in the late 1860s, became its home, but the success of Offenbach's *Grande-Duchesse* at Covent Garden in 1867 cast burlesque into the shade, creating an appetite for French operetta. In the 1880s, burlesque began to include much more original music, and gave rise to musical comedy in the 1890s. The new mixture of sentimental drama and light operatic music traveled well. The Theater an der Wien staged Ivan Caryll and Lionel Monckton's *The Circus Girl* (originally at the Gaiety, 1896); the Bouffes Parisiens put on Leslie Stuart's *Florodora* (originally at the Lyric, 1899); and Sidney Jones's *The Geisha* (1896) even outstripped the success of Gilbert and Sullivan's *The Mikado* (1885).[83]

Postbellum prosperity in America came to an end in 1873 with the collapse of Jay Cooke's financial empire. Industrial capacity was over-expanded, goods were in short supply, and inflation was rife. Musical organizations and performers were affected. Some minstrel troupes went bankrupt—New York had only one permanent troupe left in 1875.[84] Variety entertainment, being more adaptable, survived better.[85] The time was right to try new things. There had already been a sensational musical version of Charles Barras's play *The Black Crook* given at Niblo's Garden in 1866;[86] and it is significant that this occurred as opera was becoming more and more the restricted province of New York's "upper ten." With the closure of the Astor Place Opera House in the 1860s, the only place dedicated to opera was the Academy of Music—until wealthy New Yorkers who, for snobbish reasons, were being refused boxes at the Academy founded the Metropolitan Opera House in 1883. The import of operetta from London, Paris, and Vienna began to meet with success because of its cross-class appeal. During Offenbach's visit to New York in 1876, he had commented in his travel diary that there was no operetta theater that was "sure of two years of life;"[87] but in the next decade operetta was flourishing, and a native variety appeared with *The Pearl of Pekin* (1888), a Broadway operetta by Gustave Kerker, based on Charles Lecocq's Parisian success of 1868, *Fleur de thé*. Edward Harrigan and David Braham are often referred to as the American Gilbert and Sullivan for their musical plays of the 1880s in which Tony Hart performed as Harrigan's partner. Harrigan was the librettist and was first to make substantial use on stage of characters drawn from New York's ethnic minorities, commenting, "Polite society, wealth, and culture possess little or no color and picturesqueness."[88] However, Harrigan and Hart did not go in for political polemic, and their social comment never overrode their desire to create comedy and entertainment. Their shows were performed in London, Paris, and Vienna, and the title song from their *Mulligan Guards* of 1879 was a particular hit.[89] In fact, Karl Millöcker used it in the act 1 Finale of his most popular operetta, *Der Bettelstudent* (1882).

At the end of the nineteenth century, there were musicians in London, New York, Paris, and Vienna who had made sure that they were skilled in two or more of the various distinctive cultural goods that had originated in each of those cities. No longer did any impresario think it necessary to seek for performers in the places where the now internationally popular styles had first flowered. The reason for this is not surprising, and is put succinctly by Howard Becker: "Typically, no one small locality, however metropolitan, can furnish a sufficient amount and variety of work to serve a national or international market."[90]

3

Music, Morals, and
Social Order

The subject matter of this chapter raises large and thorny theoretical issues. Talcott Parsons says confidently as a fundamental principle that
"the stability of any social system" depends on the "integration of a set
of common value patterns," and that these values need to be internalized, to become part of people's personalities.[1] The internalization of
moral values was certainly recognized in the nineteenth century: John
Stuart Mill claims in his essay *Utilitarianism* (1863) that the ultimate
sanction of all morality is a "subjective feeling in our own minds."[2] But
just how these common values come to be internalized, and what role
that leaves for human agency, has been debated long and hard.[3] On
one side are those arguing that it is all a matter of consensus and shared
ideals.[4] On the other are those, among whom I number myself, insist-
ing that the seeming consensus actually conceals the working of a dominant ideology. This idea appears in its most direct form in Karl Marx's
statement "the ideas of the ruling class are in every age the ruling
ideas" (*Die deutsche Ideologie*, 1845–46).[5] It was reworked by Antonio
Gramsci as a theory of hegemony (*Quaderni del carcere*, 1929–35), by
Louis Althusser as a theory of ideological interpellation (*Lénine et la
philosophie*, 1969), and by Michel Foucault as a theory of power operating through legitimizing discourses (*Surveiller et punir*, 1975). And
these are by no means the only significant intellectual efforts that have
been made in the field of ideological critique. This book is primarily a
historical study of the rise of new forms of popular culture within
specific social structures and, as such, has limited space to elaborate on

theory; instead, I will draw on theoretical ideas only where they add more depth to the argument or a sharper focus to details under scrutiny.

Respectability and Improvement

Nineteenth-century bourgeois values were several, as were their ideological functions (thrift set against extravagance, self-help versus dependence, hard work versus idleness), but where art and entertainment were concerned, the key value in asserting moral leadership was respectability. It was something within the grasp of all, unlike the aristocratic values of lineage and "good breeding." Lineage was to become the butt of satire: Pooh-Bah in *The Mikado* is incurably haughty because he can trace back his ancestry to a pre-Adamite atomic globule. Respectability was not enforced from on high, however; it operated as part of a consensus won by ideological persuasion. Yet it never quite escaped its class character, as in the French working-class husband's mock-deferential term for his wife: *la bourgeoise*. In Offenbach's *Orphée aux enfers*, the outcry against Eurydice's lack of marital fidelity—and, thus, of respectability—is led by a character called, satirically, Public Opinion (a phrase that had become popular with the press). Thus, this stage work lends weight to the arguments of Jürgen Habermas that "public opinion" had become a problem for liberalism by the mid–nineteenth century and, whatever critical value it might previously have held, had now started to function as an institutionalized fiction that served to legitimize dominant values.[6]

To be a moral person and, indeed, to be respectable, Christianity was important—even if one's church attendance was less than regular. The Christian religion was used as a means of furthering the interests of the middle class in their dealings with the working class and, in so doing, functioned as bourgeois ideology. Marx argues in *Das Kapital* (1867) that for a society of goods producers, in which individual work is swallowed up in the standardized form of the commodity, Christianity with its cultivation of man in the abstract (especially in bourgeois developments, like Protestantism) is the most appropriate form of religion.[7] Max Weber makes a much lengthier case for linking the rise of capitalism to the "Protestant ethic," with its insistence that people were individually responsible for perfecting themselves and, therefore, should rationalize their conduct, work hard, and not waste time ("Zeitvergeudung is . . . die erste und prinzipiell schwerste aller Sünden").[8] It follows that even recreation should be rational, designed to be improving, and not merely idle amusement. Nonconformism was a major force behind English choral music in the nineteenth century.[9] Methodists, for example, had introduced congregational singing in the previous century, and a desire to encourage education and improvement made them strongly committed to sacred choral music. London's Sacred Harmonic Society, founded in 1832, began as a nonconformist organization. It met in the smaller of the two halls contained within the Exeter Hall, Strand, which had opened in 1831. Of its seventy-three members in 1834, thirty-six were artisans and twenty-seven shopkeepers—figures that reveal that it was dominated by the lower middle class.[10]

In Paris, it was the state that took an interest in similar developments. A commission chaired by the prefect of the Seine recommended the teaching of music in primary schools in 1835, having found that in schools where it was already being taught the pupils had "greater powers of application, courtesy, and good manners."[11] The Municipal Council put Guillaume Wilhem in charge. In 1836, the state awarded subsidy to his choir, which he called the Orphéon. As a consequence of that support, it had more prestige and a higher-class membership than the Sacred Harmonic Society.[12] (Offenbach's Orpheus, incidentally, is director of the Orphéon of Thebes.) Jane Fulcher may overestimate working-class participation in the Orphéon societies, but is right to stress that it was given official backing, because after the recent insurrection, it was seen as a move toward the creation of a harmonious art and a means of cultivating taste and the softening of manners.[13] The jury is still out regarding the musical standards achieved; France did not have the advantageous tradition of congregational singing found in Britain and Germany. It was many years later, in 1873, that Charles Lamoureux founded the Société de l'Harmonie Sacrée, modeled on London's Sacred Harmonic Society.

Oratorios dominated the choral scene in London, but took longer to find an enthusiastic response in New York. Walt Whitman remarked of the performance of Mendelssohn's *Elijah* by the Sacred Music Society in 1847: "it is too elaborately scientific for the popular ear," affording the audience "no great degree of pleasure."[14] There was no mass choral singing movement in Vienna because of the late decline of aristocratic power there and the aristocracy's suspicion (after the Napoleonic Wars) that choral societies were covert political organizations.[15] The Gesellschaft der Musikfreunde mounted oratorio performances on a scale similar to the Sacred Harmonic Society, but no regular choral society was relied on. The large choirs used for these events, however, drew much more of their membership from the middle class than did those in London.

The conviction behind Matthew Arnold's *Culture and Anarchy* (1869), to some extent fired by fear of the London crowd and growing concern about an ignorant mass, was that only culture could save society from anarchy. Edward Said has cited the Hyde Park riots of 1867 as important context for Arnold's idea of culture as a "deterrent to rampant disorder."[16] In America, similar ideas prevailed, as Nicholas Tawa has explained: "Prominent educators and social-minded leaders were confident that music could shore up humanity's ethical and emotional being, teach democratic principles, and encourage allegiance to an undivided national society."[17] Arnold's book was well received in America after its New York publication in 1875. Culture for Arnold is not a broad term: he spares no time on the music hall; people need to be led to cultural perfection through the pursuit of sweetness and light. His polarization of culture and anarchy indicates the importance of culture as a force of order. An audience may shout, stamp, applaud, or hiss at will at low entertainment, but a strict reception code operates for high art: you do not talk; you do not turn up late; you do not hum along; you do not eat, and so on.[18] John Kasson, in a study of manners in nineteenth-century America, speaks of "disciplined spectatorship" as the required code of behavior following the decline of communal working-class pursuits.[19] New York audiences were very vocal in their enthusiasm or derision, and the latter was likely to be underlined by missile throwing. In London, attempts were made to control rowdy behavior in music halls.[20] In Paris, there were attempts to impose a code of silence at high-status concerts by stressing bourgeois politeness;[21] but this did not apply at cafés-concerts, for even the grandest establishments were beset by public order problems. The Alcazar d'été, for example, became known by performers as the *loge infernale,* where groups of young men smoked and drank heavily, chatted loudly, and usually ended up being thrown out. The more elegant audience at the Ambassadeurs, however, was also prone to ragging and horseplay, which necessitated police action at times. In London, the police had the power to enter a music hall auditorium uninvited (unlike a theater), since they could always argue that they were ensuring that the licensing provisions were not being contravened (for instance, by serving those who were drunk). At the end of the century it was common for high-minded critics to relate rowdy behavior to there being one kind of culture that was elevating and another, a culture of the masses, that was degrading.

The working class was thought to need "rational amusement" such as choirs and not coarse entertainment.[22] The rational and the recreational were linked together in the sight-singing movement, even if the singing was not from conventional notation. Joseph Mainzer, the author of *Singing for the Million* (1842), John Hullah, and, last on the scene, John Curwen each offered competing methods to the singing classes; Curwen promoted the Tonic Sol-fa method, devised by Sarah Glover, a teacher in Norwich. It was not a cynical exercise in control: in their own lives the middle class were committed to self-improvement by going to concerts, buying sheet music, and performing it at home. Parisian *soirées,* Viennese *Hauskonzerten,* and "at home" functions in London and New York made demands on all those present. From the 1830s on, pianos were found in middle-class homes in all these cities, and girls were expected to learn to play them. While music was supposed to offer the poor "a *laborem dulce lenimen,* a relaxation from toil, more attractive than the haunts of intemperance," it was also believed to furnish the rich with "a refined and intellectual pursuit, which excludes the indulgence of frivolous and vicious amusements."[23]

For the middle class, culture was instructive but first required that people were instructed in it; hence the didactic character of attempts to encourage working-class "appreciation." The People's Concert Society, founded in 1878, was an amateur organization dedicated to making high-status music known among the London poor. The society began Sunday concerts of chamber music in South Place, Moorgate, in 1887. From the succeeding year, admission was free, or a voluntary contribution could be made, and attendance was good.[24] In 1882, the Popular Musical Union was founded "for the musical training and recreation of the 'industrial classes.'"[25] Concerts took place at the People's Palace in London's East End, and continued to do so until 1935. Persuasion was used, but no coercion was needed to interest the working class in music; the ideology of respectability and improvement meant that music, instrumental as well as vocal, could even be found on the timetables of instructive activities at Mechanics' Institutes, especially after 1830.[26]

The British brass band movement, in the second half of the century, was viewed, alongside choral singing, as another example of "rational and refined amusement," hence the willingness of factory owners to sponsor works bands.[27] They were to feel sour, however, when they discovered brass bands leading marches of striking workers.[28] These bands had their roots in the industrial North, but the steel, ironworks, and shipping companies of East London also had bands in the 1860s. Huge annual contests were held at the Crystal Palace during 1860–63. The first of these, a two-day event, attracted an audience of 29,000.[29] The test pieces for the contests at the Crystal Palace placed an emphasis on high-status music: selections from Meyerbeer's grand operas were the favorite choices, as at the Belle Vue contests in Manchester during the same decade. In the other cities of this study, regimental bands were a common sight. Paris's most famous military band was that of the Garde Republicaine (formed in 1854 as the band of what was then the Garde de Paris). It acquired a substantial reputation in America while on tour there in the early 1870s. Adolphe Sax was responsible for the instrumental organization of the band. It contained several families of instruments with six pistons (trumpets, trombones, saxhorns, and tubas) that were of his own invention, his desire being to enable a more consistent production of chromatic runs of notes than that possible on three-piston instruments.[30] In other respects, the band was not dissimilar in size or instrumentation from that of the Household Brigade in London. In the 1850s, the sale of refreshments was permitted on Sundays in certain London parks to coincide with military band performances. This met with strong opposition from those who wished to guard Sunday's importance as a religious day and who feared also that the excitement of listening to band music would trigger civil disturbance.[31] On the other hand, the right kind of music, in the right surroundings, was thought to act as "a civilising influence to which the lower classes were particularly responsive."[32] In Vienna, at midcentury, a license from the magistracy was required for permission to make "music for entertainment in public resorts," and the intention to include concert and operatic music alongside dance music was a great help in obtaining it.[33]

Physical Threats to Morality

A belief in the moral power of music was an all-pervasive ideology: "Let no one," the great champion of the improving powers of music the Reverend Haweis admonished, "say the moral effects of music are small or insignificant."[34] It was the activities that accompanied music making that raised suspicion of unwholesome conduct, not the music itself. Even in Vienna, for example, there were those who worried about the moral propriety of the waltz, its sensuality, and the close proximity of the couple dancing.[35] The waltz offers an example of how music could be perceived as being linked to a physical threat to public morality. When the waltz first began to be danced "in society," it provoked moral outrage in some quarters. Existing society dances were more decorous; the minuet and gavotte may have been dances for couples, but they emphasized graceful movement and involved delicate contact with the fingers only. In the waltz you could hold your partner, and not just with fingertips. Certainly, it was *de rigueur* for both men and women to wear gloves, but you could still hold your partner close. There were other subversive features, too, as Arthur Loesser explains with reference to the early waltz of the 1790s:

> it seemed utterly disorderly—it had no fixed number of steps, no prescribed direction of movement, no general pattern. It was for no settled number of couples: each pair danced without caring about any of the others—any couple could enter the dance or leave it at any second, as the whim might strike them. Truly, the waltz was an illustration of the two most intoxicating virtue-words of the age: the "people" and "liberty."[36]

The Empire line dominated women's fashions when the waltz was first introduced, and ball gowns allowed libidinous males considerable opportunity for groping, especially given the absence of corseting. Clothes were soon designed to place much more textile between partners, the outcome being the bell-shaped dress. Next, the development of the crinoline meant that heavy underwear was no longer necessary—though it is often forgotten that the cage collapsed as the man pushed forward.

Byron wrote a poem on the waltz in 1812 when it was little known in England. The following excerpts illustrate his (perhaps surprising) moral disgust:

> From where the garb just leaves the bosom free,
> That spot where hearts were once supposed to be;

Round all the confines of the yielded waist,
The strangest hand may wander undisplaced;
The lady's in return may grasp as much
As princely paunches offer to her touch.

Hot from the hands promiscuously applied,
Round the slight waist, or down the glowing side,
Where were the rapture then to clasp the form
From this lewd grasp and lawless contact warm?
At once love's most endearing thought resign,
To press the hand so press'd by none but thine;
To gaze upon that eye which never met
Another's ardent look without regret;
Approach the lip which all, without restraint,
Come near enough—if not to touch—to taint.[37]

The waltz combined closeness with a sensation of the room spinning around, and this could prove an erotic and giddy experience. Later in the century, this is what Madame Bovary discovers when she waltzes for the first time (the experience being heightened by her consumption of alcohol):

> They began slowly, and then went faster. They turned: everything around them turned—the lamps, the furniture, the wainscoting, and the floor, like a disc on a pivot. On passing near the doors, the hem of Emma's dress grazed[38] his trousers. Their legs entwined; he looked down at her, she looked up at him; a languor took hold of her; she stopped. They set off again; and, with a more rapid movement, the Viscount, dragging her, disappeared with her to the end of the gallery, where, panting, she nearly fell, and, for a moment, leant her head on his breast. And then, still turning, but more gently, he conducted her back to her seat; she leaned back against the wall and put her hand over her eyes.[39]

Queen Victoria's interest in waltzing helped to win it respectability in Britain, but moral concerns about dance music did not disappear, and were always ready to resurface.[40] They did so, for instance, in 1885, when Mr. Burnand of the Aberdeen Presbytery launched a widely reported attack on "balls, dancing parties, and promiscuous gatherings of people of both sexes for indulging in springs and flings and artistic circles and close-bosomed whirlings."[41] Ironically, it was not the waltz but the *galop* that ended up being banned in Vienna, after the authorities decided it was injurious to health in the 1840s. Strauss Jr.'s way around this was to develop the *Schnell-Polka*, which was more or less the *galop* under a new name. In 1854, when he produced his *Schnell-post-Polka* (Express Mail Polka, op. 159), a cholera epidemic was creating a more distracting health worry than that of purportedly dangerous dances.

Public and Private Morality

It was meaningless, of course, if the entertainment was respectable but the venue not. Concern about prostitution in theaters and music halls grew in the second half of the century.[42] In Vienna, prostitutes were found at some of the grandest dance halls, such as the Apollo in the 1820s.[43] The next decade the Apollo cleaned itself up entirely—by becoming a soap factory. In Paris, concern about prostitution in cafés developed in the 1860s, previous attention having been on other public spaces, such as boulevards and gardens. Alcohol consumption was another threat to morals and respectability, and fractional interests within the bourgeoisie used music as a medium of persuasion; for example, the temperance groups in London and New York promoted songs portraying the destructive effects of drunkenness on the home and family.[44] The music hall was especially disliked, not just because of the availability of alcohol there but also because it was celebrated in song (hence attempts to create "coffee music halls"). At one social level were Bessie Bellwood calling for her pint of stout and Gus Elen yearning constantly for half pints of ale, and at another were George Leybourne and Alfred Vance praising, respectively, champagne from Moët and from Cliquot.[45]

Music for the nineteenth-century middle-class home aligns itself with one of the fundamental "Victorian values"—that of improvement. It was the possession of an improving or edifying quality that allowed music to be described, in a favorite Victorian phrase, as "rational amusement." The quality that makes the nineteenth-century domestic ballad distinctive arises from its moral concerns and not from sentimental self-indulgence or a love of the maudlin, as some people mistakenly suppose. In short, American and British ballad writers and composers were often concerned to place sentimentality in the service of other aims, and these other aims were primarily social, moral, religious, and political rather than aesthetic.

The moral tone, whether we regard it now as healthy or not, is precisely what makes the Victorian ballad differ in character from the songs that came after. Early twentieth-century British and American ballads tend to shy away from the moral didacticism found in the previous century's ballads. The two closing decades of the nineteenth century were a transitional period, during which the variety of ballad types and ballad forms decreased. The structural diversity illustrated by songs like "Come into the Garden, Maud" (words by Alfred Tennyson, music by Michael Balfe, 1857) and "The Lost Chord" (words by Adelaide Procter, music by Arthur Sullivan, 1877) gives way to the more predictable shapes of post-1880 ballads, in which irregularities are accommodated to a more obvious overall verse and refrain form. This process was accelerated by the song sheet production of the group of firms in New York's Tin Pan Alley in the 1890s.

So let us begin by asking what themes were found suitable for the purpose of improvement. There are many songs that remind us of our own mortality, or place human life in a grander scheme of things, or contrast the secular and the divine. These, it should be stressed, do not always need to have an overtly sacred theme. There are other songs that take children as a theme, perhaps celebrating the love of parents for children, or touching on infant death, or presenting illustrations of the presumed innocence of children as a means of teaching adults a moral lesson. In addition to these, there are songs that deal with friendship, pride in one's country, and courage, whether that is exemplified in battle or in facing the grim realization that one has been jilted in love.[46]

The features that give the nineteenth-century domestic ballad its distinctiveness spring from a desire to teach a moral lesson, or educate people about appropriate social behavior, or edify and uplift them spiritually and drive them on to perform good deeds. Perhaps the first song that established firmly the kind of sentiment that was to be emulated by all songwriters who saw the middle-class home as their market was "Home, Sweet Home!" of 1823. Even at the end of the century, it was still felt to possess a remarkable moral and emotional power. In one story of an English colonial boy in the Australian outback, it is thanks to his pet bird being able to whistle "Home, Sweet Home" that he is saved from a gang of desperados: "strange and marvelous it was to see the tears trickling down the cheeks of these grizzled scoundrels at the thought of the homes into which they had probably brought nothing but shame and misery."[47] The song was, interestingly, a collaboration between an American, John Howard Payne, and an Englishman, Henry Bishop. In that, it foreshadowed the transatlantic traffic in this type of song that grew with every decade of the century. It featured in the English opera *Clari, or The Maid of Milan,* and it has an Italianate character suited to the opera's subject. However, the Italian connection is no more than that of a cantabile operatic style, rather than an Italian folksong, despite the fact that Bishop had tried earlier to pass it off as a Sicilian air in a book of national airs.[48]

The Italianate quality persisted in many of the songs composed by the Jewish English entertainer Henry Russell (fig. 3.1).[49] One such was "Woodman, Spare That Tree!" of 1837, another Anglo-American creation, with words by George Pope Morris.[50] A few sample measures will show that this is not a million miles from the famous aria "Casta diva" from Bellini's *Norma* of 1831 (see ex. 3.1).

This song brings us face to face more directly than does "Home, Sweet Home" with what some find the biggest obstacle to taking nineteenth-century ballads seriously: what is perceived as exaggerated sentimentality. Here is a narrative concerning someone whose emotional ties to a particular old oak are likely to seem excessive even to the most ardent tree-hugging hippie. However, Henry Russell is quite clear on this point: "sickening sentiment is born of a sickening mind," he pro-

Figure 3.1 One of New York and London's most popular socially committed and wholesome entertainers, Henry Russell, in later life.

claims, believing that his own songs, in contrast, exemplify a healthy moral tone.[51] Edgar Allan Poe was a champion of George Morris, claiming that "Woodman, Spare That Tree" was a composition "of which any poet, living or dead, might justly be proud." Poe was convinced it would make Morris's name immortal.[52]

The sternest moral fiber is to be found in temperance songs, although these frequently sounded too haranguing even for those who otherwise prided themselves on their respectability. All the same, 500 people were reputedly turned away from a concert in Niblo's Garden given by the teetotal Hutchinson Family.[53] Where alcohol was concerned, the middle-class watchword tended to be moderation, not prohibition. The most affecting type of temperance song overcame this resistance by putting its message in the mouth of a child—for example, "Come Home, Father!" (words and music by Henry Clay Work, 1864) and "Father's a Drunkard and Mother Is Dead" (words by Stella, music by Mrs. E. A. Parkhurst, 1866). The first of these bears the epigraph[54]

> 'Tis the SONG OF LITTLE MARY,
> Standing at the bar-room door
> While the shameful midnight revel
> Rages wildly as before.

The laboring poor may have been sung about and even felt to be understood in certain socially concerned drawing room ballads, but their lives often lay outside the experience of those who sang them (see fig. 3.2). Antoinette Sterling, who so movingly performed "Three Fishers Went Sailing," confessed that not only had she no experience of storms at sea but "had never even seen fishermen."[55] The subject posi-

Example 3.1 (a) Henry Russell's "Woodman, Spare That Tree!" (words by George Morris, music by Henry Russell); (b) "Casta diva" (Vincenzo Bellini, *Norma* (1831), act 1).

(a)

(b)

tion such ballads addressed was that of the middle class. So, too, did the Gilbert and Sullivan comic operas, parading middle-class prejudices, albeit in an ironic way, as in Ko-Ko's list of "society offenders" in *The Mikado*. The characters of this opera are, unmistakably, English in fancy dress. *The Gondoliers* (1889) satirizes antiegalitarianism, summed up in the lines "When every one is somebodee, / Then no one's anybody." It appeared at a time of antimonarchist sentiment and the growth of socialist and republican ideas. The issue of class distinction was especially to the fore, and the Duke of Plaza-Toro lampoons the buying of titles:

> Small titles and orders
> For Mayors and Recorders
> I get—and they're highly delighted.

The satire aimed at the House of Lords in *Iolanthe* (1882) is more plentiful than that targeting the Commons (Private Willis's song); reform of the Upper House was a contemporary issue. After the first night, a song was removed because a critic accused Gilbert of "bitterly aggressive politics" and pathos that "smacks of anger, a passion altogether out of place in a 'fairy opera.'"[56] The song offended middle-class values by sympathizing with a wretched pickpocket, suggesting that anyone "robbed of all chances" would turn to theft.

The respectability of the bourgeoisie was not beyond challenge, of course, in any of the cities that form the basis of this study. Samuel Smiles was aware of bourgeois hypocrisy: "We keep up appearances, too often at the expense of honesty."[57] In Paris, Yvette Guilbert represented bourgeois vices humorously in chansons like "Le Fiacre" (words and music by Léon Xanrof) and "Je suis pocharde!" (words by Léon Laroche, music by Louis Byrec). When she sang at the respectable Eden-Concert in 1890, she was allowed to sing the latter (concerning the effects of alcohol) but not the former (concerning marital infidelity). The context of "Je suis pocharde!" helped it to gain acceptability. Guilbert herself stressed that this is a girl from a "good family" who has been drinking champagne at her sister's wedding and is "gentiment grise" (slightly tipsy).[58] *Pochard* is both an adjective and a noun ("drunkard"), and it is easy to see how offensively vulgar it might have been in its feminine form.

The subject position of music halls and cafés-concerts was that of the upper-working-class or lower-middle-class male. Even the large Queen's Music Hall, situated in solidly working-class Poplar, assumed the audience would share the values of those social groups.[59] The performers themselves were of a mixed class background: of the *lions comiques* in London, for example, George Leybourne had been a mechanic and the Great MacDermott a bricklayer, but the Great Vance was formerly a solicitor's clerk. The toff or "swell" character of the 1860s appealed to socially aspiring lower-middle-class males. Leybourne, the most acclaimed of the swells, was given a contract in 1868, at the height

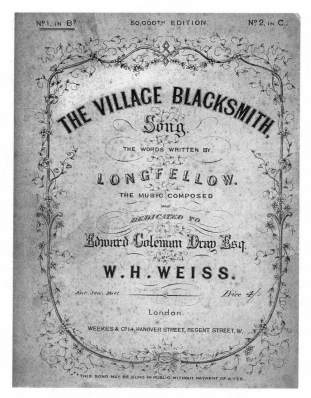

Figure 3.2 The title page of a morally uplifting drawing room ballad employing tasteful decoration and different type fonts.

of his success with the song "Champagne Charlie," requiring that he continued his swell persona off stage.[60] The swell, however, is double-coded: he might inscribe admiration for wealth and status, but he subverts bourgeois values in celebrating excess and idleness ("A noise all night, in bed all day and swimming in Champagne," Charlie boasts). Some of those attending cafés-concerts, also, were putting on appearances, like the *calicots* (Parisian slang for drapers' assistants, known in London slang as "counter-jumpers"). Hence the appeal of the Parisian swell, or *gommeux*, the most famous being Libert. Henriette Bépoix, a *gommeuse*, appeared fast on his heels. *Gommeuses* were common in the 1890s, wearing extravagant feathered hats, gaudy dresses, and lots of jewelry. They presented themselves as fun-loving and giddy, with rich, if unattractive, lovers. The renowned twentieth-century star of the *music-hall,* Mistinguett, began as an eccentric *gommeuse* at the Eldorado.

The efforts the bourgeoisie made in the interests of respectability were not always an unqualified success, and sometimes failure appeared unexpectedly. It would be easy to assume, given the association of French entertainment with the risqué, that London reacted more cautiously to the sauciness of Offenbach's operettas. On the contrary, in England they were sometimes lewder. *Punch* remarked of the productions of *La Grande-Duchesse de Gérolstein* and *La Belle Hélène* starring Hortense Schneider in 1868: "Schneider was far more vulgar in London than in Paris, though on her native heath her performance was witnessed chiefly by ladies of the faster set."[61] Once again, this opens up the issue of culture as an area of compromise where no complete dominance can be achieved. For the musical journalist Henry Chorley, *La Grande-Duchesse*, which many found so hilarious and tuneful, represented "opera in the mire"; he thought it the lowest point to which a stage work could sink "in offence to delicacy," and condemned its music as "trite and colourless."[62]

Much of the cultural change during the century can be seen as driven by the power and interests of fractions within the middle classes, but as Kathy Peiss points out, "the lines of cultural transmission travel in both directions," and the working class did not passively consume cultural messages.[63] For example, the African-American musical *A Trip to Coontown*, which ran for longer than any other nineteenth-century show in New York, was described by a Boston reviewer as having humor that "smacks far more of the street and barroom than of the drawing room."[64] And in 1899, the *Musical Courier*, with reference to the American ragtime craze, proclaimed: "A wave of vulgar, filthy and suggestive music has inundated the land."[65] The irony was that ragtime idiomatically suited the instrument most imbued with domestic respectability, the piano. However, the flipside was that pianos were also common in New York's brothels and honky-tonks.

The presence of different classes in the same venue did not mean that they mixed. Emile Blémont wrote about cafés-concerts in the *Evênement* of February 1891:

> There are two publics, different and totally distinct from one another in the Café Concerts. On the one hand you will find the masses, a trifle heavy, a trifle slow, but simple-minded, sympathetic and generous. . . faithful to the old traditional form of song. . . . . On the other hand . . . you will find another public which is, in some respects, more highly cultivated. They are the rakes, the *déclassés* of literature or trade, forming the bohemia of the more well-to-do middle class; free lances most of them in their particular professions of trade or art.[66]

Blémont commented that the two publics sat close together but did not intermingle, and that in some establishments the "popular element" dominated, while in others it was the "bohemian element." The double clientele was also found in the cabarets of Montmartre (see chapter 8). In London, the socially mixed music halls were in the center and attracted bohemian types from the beginning; the working-class halls were in the East End and south London. London's suburbs could be middle class in character (for example, South Kensington), whereas, historically, the working class of Paris have been located in the suburbs. There was no working-class "inner city" in Paris; this class would need to come into the center of Paris to see what was happening in the Champs-Elysées.

Threats to Social Order

Urban ballads rarely give voice to a particular community in the direct way that Tommy Armstrong's "Trimdon Grange Explosion" (1882)[67] does for his Durham coal-mining neighbors. "Let us think of Mrs. Burnett," Armstrong urges; but that means little to anyone outside of his community. The urban ballad generally appeared on the market as a commodity in the form of a broadside to be sold on the city streets, and so needed to have more general appeal. Publishers in Seven Dials were renowned for this material; a French visitor in midcentury provided readers of the *Revue at Gazette Musicale* with the much-exaggerated claim "It is in the smoky garrets of this neighborhood that the national *Lieder* of London are manufactured."[68] However, for much of the century, these ballads remained a repository of oppositional elements. "The New Poor Law," a song about the workhouse that followed that law's passing in 1834, chooses, satirically, the tune of "Home, Sweet, Home!"[69] Queen Victoria is represented as having very un-Victorian sexual interests in "Married at Last" (1840).[70] The striking women from Bryant and May's match factory sang a parody of "John Brown's Body" on their marches through the West End in 1888.[71] The next year, during the London dock strike, Jim Connell wrote "The Red Flag" (to the tune of "The White Cockade"), and during the same workers' struggle, Harry Clifton's "Work, Boys, Work" (the "*Marseillaise* of the Tariff Reform Party")[72] was parodied as "Strike, Boys, Strike." In America, the labor movement prompted the production of thousands of labor songs. A New York writer of such songs was Mary Agnes Sheridan, a carpet mill operative.[73] They were sung to traditional airs, hymn tunes, or minstrel melodies. The words typically accuse capitalists of betraying republican ideas of democracy and brotherhood. However, the increased use of repressive action by state and federal troops in disputes weakened the labor movement and, thus, the production of labor songs in the 1890s. In Austria, books of *Arbeiterlieder* were appearing in the 1860s;[74] and the newly formed Austrian socialist Arbeitergesangverein held its first Liedertafel on 4 May 1879.[75]

In France, the Saint-Simonians demanded a social art that would contribute to a better society. Rouget de Lisle's "Premier Chant des industriels" (1821) was written in praise of industrial workers, evidently at Henri de Saint-Simone's instigation.[76] Jules Vinçard, head of the Famille de Paris, a group of working-class and artisan Saint-Simonians in Paris, wrote songs showing the influence of the political chansons of

Pierre-Jean de Béranger, but for which, unlike Béranger, he also composed the music.[77] After 1848, chansonniers could be charged with incitement to hatred (*excitation à la haine*) as was Claude Durand for "Le Chant des vignerons" in 1850.[78] During the Second Empire, which followed Louis Napoléon's coup d'état of 2 December 1851, revolutionary and republican chansons were proscribed and only circulated secretly. Oppositional songs were still to be found at the *goguettes*, the working-class cafés in the *faubourgs*, although these songs, too, began to disappear during the Second Empire.[79]

After the defeat of Emperor Napoléon III in the Franco-Prussian War, the political and social aspirations that motivated insurrection in Paris and the formation of the Paris Commune (18 March–28 May 1871) soon found a vehicle in song.[80] A federation of authors and artists of theaters and concerts was organized under the Commune. Jean-Baptiste Clément's "Le Temps de cerises" (set to music by Antoine Renard in 1868) was sung by the Communards, who interpreted the return of spring as a metaphor for the return of liberty. Clément was one of the elected of the Commune.[81] The new Marseillaise of the Commune had as its refrain

> Chantons la liberté,
> Défendons la cité,
> Marchons, marchons,
> Sans souverain,
> Le people aura du pain.[82]

> Let us sing of liberty,
> Let us defend the city,
> Let us march, let us march,
> Without a sovereign,
> The people will have bread.

It was not just la Butte that echoed with such sentiment. Though rejected by the censor in May 1870, Augustine Kaiser sang "La Plébiéienne," an uncompromising republican chanson, at the Pavillon de l'Horloge.[83] Vialla sang a "Chant de l'Internationale (Hymne des travailleurs)" at the Eldorado, though this is not to be confused with Eugène Pottier's "L'Internationale." A woodworker from Lille, Pottier drafted the words of this most famous political chanson during the Commune but did not publish them until many years after its suppression (Pierre Degeyter provided music in 1888, the year after Pottier's death).[84] "La Semaine sanglante," sung to the tune of Pierre Dupont's "La Chant des paysans," takes as its theme the bloody end of the Commune, when the Versailles troops killed thousands. In the years after the Commune, few were eager to promulgate overt links between art and radical politics. The Festival of 1878, for instance, was to celebrate the new status quo and growing prosperity; a date without any political associations, 30 June, was chosen. Yet the Commune continued to be inspirational: the militant revolutionary Paul Brousse wrote "Le Drapeau Rouge" (The red flag) during his exile in Switzerland (he returned to Paris after the amnesty of 1880).[85]

Oppositional elements arose in Vienna in the 1840s, a time of growing dissatisfaction among the bourgeoisie and working class that culminated in the restless period known as the Vormärz. The outbreak of the Hungarian revolution in March 1848 triggered an uprising in Vienna a week later. It began when troops fired shots into a crowd and killed thirty. They were carrying a petition calling for freedom of the press and more civic power for the bourgeoisie. Unfortunately, the latter had called in support from Vienna's emergent proletariat, and this had created a sense of panic among the forces of law and order. The chancellor, Clemens Metternich, who had till then relied on repressive mechanisms and a huge network of spies, fled the country (eventually settling in London). The rebels held Vienna for around seven months, and Karl Marx seized an opportunity to address the Viennese Workers' Association in August. Strauss Jr. was sympathetic to the revolution, and he and his brother Josef were still at the barricades in October.[86] Some of his prorevolution works of the time, like the *Revolutions-Marsch*, op. 54, were published and have survived, though the counterrevolutionary authorities made attempts to confiscate as much as possible. The police confiscated his *Studenten-Marsch*, op. 56; [87] but it had already been published and so did not perish; nonetheless, over a half dozen unpublished works from 1848–49 have been lost.[88] He boldly played the Marseillaise at the barricades, and was probably saved only by his popularity when the revolution was crushed; however, he acquired a police record. [89] A warrant was also issued for the arrest of his brother Josef. A state of siege was declared in Vienna after the 1848 rebellion had been suppressed, and some of Strauss Jr.'s music was banned, including his *Burschen-Lieder* waltz, op. 55, based on students' songs and quoting in its introduction "Der Freiheit Schlachtruf" (Freedom's battle cry).

Their father, who had separated from the family, did not share his sons' republican sentiments and, after initial uncertainty, opposed the Revolution. This may have been welcome news for the authorities, given that it had been earlier written of him "he is a man who could do a great deal of harm if he were to play Rousseau's ideas on his violin."[90] His reactionary stance, however, prompted protests at some of his concerts during his postrevolution tour. His *Radetzky-Marsch*, op. 228 (1848), was for some an unappealing tribute to a Habsburg army general (though it celebrates a victory at Custozza, Italy, rather than any counterrevolutionary activity). Worse, he wrote a march for the bigoted and violent General Jellačić, who had helped to retake Vienna in October. Anyone who believed these were merely instances of political naïveté would have been shocked to learn that during his second trip to England he visited the exiled Metternich. Strauss discovered to his cost, however, that in London as in other major European cities, liberals who sympathized with the Austrian opposition to a nonconstitutional monarchy were shunning him. As a consequence, he was performing to half-empty houses; aristocratic support was no longer enough in his line of business. Strauss Jr.'s reputation suffered for different reasons: he spent well over a decade repairing the damage done by his sympathy for the revolution and trying to win over the new young emperor. The brothers Johann and Josef tried to put their rebellious past well behind them in their joint composition *Vaterländischer Marsch* of 1859. Austria was at war in northern Italy with the Piedmontese, whom the French Emperor Napoléon III was championing. This march quotes from the *Radetzky-Marsch* and the *Kaiserlied*. All the same, it would still take Strauss Jr. until 1863 to be appointed music director of the imperial balls at the Habsburg court (the position his father had held).

An often overlooked threat to public order in the city, though one not overtly political in character, is street music. Under a law of 1834, street singers in France were made to wear badges, the intention being to keep a record of their number and limit it.[91] Those who sang on the streets of New York, collecting money in a hat, were called buskers or guttersnipers. Vienna also had its itinerant street musicians and barrel organs. There is evidence throughout the century of street music creating social antagonisms. Michael T. Bass published *Street Music in the Metropolis* in 1864 in an attempt to amend the existing law to allow better regulation of street music in London.[92] The book contains much correspondence, and voices "the anxiety felt by so many persons for some effectual check to the daily increasing grievance of organ-grinders and street music." One correspondent sent Bass a list of the 165 interruptions (which included six brass bands) he had suffered in ninety days. Bass recalls how one person's decision to prosecute his "tormentors" caused the "poorer classes" who "took the offenders' part" to shout insults at him whenever they saw him. A householder at Hyde Park Gate admits that a majority of the population probably wished to retain street music, but his own views betray ingrained class arrogance:

> Among those who wish that this great nuisance should be done away with, we count the scientific man, the author, the artist, and others, who labour hard for the public benefit; while that other class, the members of which find pleasure in the performances of the organ-grinder and the ballad-singer, is composed mainly of household servants and others, whose wishes cannot surely be of any importance when weighed against those of such persons as I have mentioned above.[93]

Unfortunately, the problem of the street musician was a sensitive one for the bourgeois householder because, as the Reverend Haweis pointed out in the next decade, "your cook is his friend, your housemaid is his admirer."[94] As the century was drawing to a close, the problem was just as intractable: the *Musical Times* found in 1895 that practically nothing had improved, street music was present in "more aggravated forms," and "the organ fiend grins more diabolically than ever before our windows."[95]

Threats to Public Morality

Ensuring a consensus about public morality is an important part of hegemonic strategy, and when hegemony fails, Gramsci explained, it is replaced by coercion.[96] This is endorsed by C. Wright Mills, who observes: "at the very end, if the end is reached, moral problems become problems of power, and in the last resort, if the last resort is reached, the final form of power is coercion."[97] The music hall audience in London, however, defended its values and behavior when the law was used in a repressive manner, turning up in large numbers at the halls, at law courts and licensing sessions, and writing letters and petitions.[98] Indeed, when morality campaigner Laura Ormiston Chant initiated action in 1894 against the Empire Theatre of Varieties, Leicester Square, claiming that prostitutes frequented its promenade, there was even middle-class resentment. It is a case that challenges the usual assumption of Victorian prudery.

The clearest example of coercive control is censorship. Censorship of British music hall songs was left to managers. The contract offered to performers at Collins's Music Hall, Islington Green, required them to present any new song to the management for approval seven days before it was to be sung, and anyone "giving expression to any vulgarity" on stage was subject to instant dismissal.[99] Similar rules applied at the Middlesex. French censorship of songs was a matter for the police. It was relaxed during 1870, but returned after the end of the Commune, and songwriters vented their frustration by looking for ways of fooling the censors: for example, "Viens te rouler dans la mer, Dominique" changes its meaning dramatically when sung, since "mer" and the "d" of "Dominique" run together to form an obscenity.[100] A French official report of 1872 rails against the shamelessness of café-concert songwriters from all points of view, moral, political, and religious, and says that a large number of songs are refused absolutely, while "serious modifications" are required in others.[101] The physicality of some performers was a threat in itself. Thérésa had a loud, low-pitched voice and striking physical presence, an idea of which may be gained from Degas's studies of her performances, such as *Au Café-concert, le chanson du chien* (c. 1875–77). Some admirers deplored her later career, when they felt she had become absorbed by the bourgeoisie and no longer identified with ordinary people. It was what has now become the common complaint of the star "selling out." There is no doubt that in her early career, the censor scrutinized all her songs. However, it was the way she sang that had such an impact—her energy and defiance, and a use of argot that suggested sympathy with the Parisian working class. British journalist Charles MacKay was outraged by her vulgarity, and wrote in 1868: "In England we have not yet descended so low as to produce a 'Thérèse' [*sic*] to sing libidinous verses for the amusement of men (and women); but the songs which find most favor at our music-halls are by no means of a character to be commended either for their wit or their morality."[102] Her nearest equivalent in London was Jenny Hill, who was known for her presentation of aggressive lower-class female characters, servants and shopgirls who refuse to mind their place.[103]

Threats to sexual morality in the realm of vocal performance were considered in some ways more insidious than threats involving physical contact, as in dancing. Music hall and comic opera in London offer examples of these perceived threats. The music halls were diligently policed, and the law was sometimes used harshly. A hall could be closed if single women were seen entering without men, the assumption being that they were looking for business as prostitutes. It was more difficult to use the law to enforce moral rectitude where songs were concerned. The saucy song with a sexual theme was part of music hall from its beginnings.

The difficulty for those who morally disapproved was that suggestiveness was something awkward to pinpoint or prove. In "Jones's Sister" (1865),[104] the singer makes the mistake of courting his friend's wife under the impression that she is his friend's sister. Since she makes no attempt to correct the mistake, is this a song about licentious behavior? Or take a song the *lion comique* Arthur Lloyd wrote, composed, and sang whose title is still a well-known saying in the United Kingdom today, "It's Naughty but It's Nice" (1873).[105]

> I kiss'd her two times on the cheek,
> I would have kiss'd her thrice,
> But I whisper'd, ain't it naughty?
> She said, Yes, but it's so nice.

The words are innocent enough, but the implication that naughtiness is nice brings with it moral concerns. These were the types of comic song the respectable middle class found abhorrent, "destitute alike of wit and humour, even of the weakest description" and "set to music of the most contemptible character."[106] Another song, indeed, plays on fears of a moral hazard to women and girls of respectable families, presenting them with a picture of a seductive male who had easy access to the middle-class home: the piano tuner. We can only speculate about the anxious reaction of some parents to the chorus of "The Tuner's Oppor-tuner-ty."[107]

> At first he'd tune it gently, then he'd tune it strong,
> Then he'd touch a short note, then he'd run along,

Then he'd go with a vengeance, enough to break the key,
At last he tuned whene'er he got an opportunity.

Censorship was a blunt weapon when deployed against some performers. There is no doubt, for example, that it was the *way* Marie Lloyd performed that had such an impact on her audience—the lack of bodily discipline seen in the gestures, winks, and knowing smiles she employed to lend suggestiveness to apparently innocent music hall songs like "What's That For, Eh?" (1892; see fig. 3.3).[108] Marie Lloyd sang this song at the Oxford, and it was the subject of a complaint at a meeting of the London County Council in October 1896.[109]

Jacqueline Bratton draws a distinction between the innuendo of the broadside ballad and that of the music hall song:

> Where a broadside ballad making use of innuendo would most usually labour one point at length, wringing every last particle of fun out of a correspondence which had been set up or a train of puns which had been laid, music-hall songs of a very ordinary kind often had highly intricate and varied patterns of innuendo playing backwards and forwards across the text, even in printed versions, which would be supplemented a hundredfold by nuance and gesture in a good performance.[110]

One may imagine how Lloyd's famous wink may have been applied to her singing of "Oh, Mr. Porter" (1893), in which she finds her train is taking her on to Crewe when she only intended to go as far as Birmingham.[111] The device of innuendo is found in many of her best-known songs, such as "A Little of What You Fancy Does You Good"[112] and "When I Take My Morning Promenade."[113] In the latter, she acknowledges that her dress shows her shape just a little bit, but that's "the little bit the boys admire." Marie Lloyd used the device of feigned innocence as a form of double address: on the one hand it acted as a show of conforming to respectable bourgeois morality, but on the other it relied on a knowingness that others in her audience would not fail to pick up on. For instance, the music hall paper the *Era* claimed that she had keenly observed and imitated the soliciting techniques of Regent Street prostitutes.[114] Her winking could steer a thought in a different direction, but the meaning of a wink was difficult to define. As one of her songs, "The Twiddly Wink," puts it,

> What does it mean? Don't know. Do you?
> Still it's wonderful what a wonderful lot
> The twiddly wink can do![115]

Her song "Twiggy Voo?" is entirely about the role of innuendo in its diverse social contexts.[116] Vesta Victoria delighted in ingénue roles, and conveyed with an unknowing innocence the irony of "Our Lodger's Such a Nice Young Man," assuring the audience "Mummy told me so."[117] There is also considerable scope for queer readings of music hall, espe-

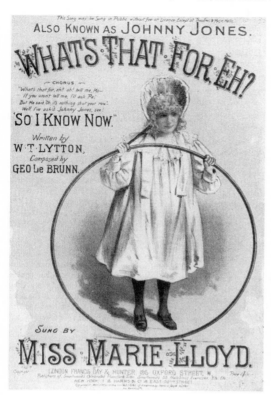

Figure 3.3 The title page of a music hall song using a lithographic image. Notice that it does not exploit the suggestiveness of the lyrics in any obvious way.

cially in travesty performances. Vesta Tilley made famous the song "Following in Father's Footsteps," in which she declares "He's just in front with a fine big gal, / So I thought I'd have one as well." [118] Vesta Tilley's contract prohibited her from wearing her male attire when off stage.

Married life tends to be portrayed via the stereotype of the nagged husband, and sometimes worse: Gus Elen's "It's a Great Big Shame"[119] and Dan Leno's "Young Men Taken in and Done For"[120] tell of husbands whom their wives beat violently, contrary to the Victorian norm in working-class domestic disputes. Such examples are a caution against viewing art as a reflection of reality. A song that stands as the exception to tales of marital strife is Albert Chevalier's "My Old Dutch."[121] Not surprisingly, it was one of the few music hall songs that such moral campaigners as Mrs. Ormiston Chant praised. Saucy songs, of varying degrees of vulgarity, continue unabated in the Edwardian music hall, an example being "Has Anybody Seen My Tiddler?"[122] Such songs clearly informed the repertoire of later variety artists like George Formby, whose father (of the same name) was a music hall entertainer.

Omitted in the foregoing account of music hall morality is the wholesome presence of entertainers like Harry Clifton and Felix McGlennon who prided themselves on their impeccable repertoire. Moreover, despite the variety of music hall audiences, and despite the presence at times of subversive elements in the entertainment provided, it must be stressed again that the values most commonly upheld were bourgeois in character. The songs offer strong evidence of this. Dave Russell, in his history of English popular music of this period, emphasizes the "profoundly conservative picture of life" that "emerges most forcibly from a detailed reading of music-hall song."[123] Even some of the songs that appear to have working-class subject positions can be seen as endorsing "Victorian values." Nelly Power sang "The Boy in the Gallery" (1885) affectionately to her imaginary lover, a young man making his living repairing shoes, who could afford only a cheap seat to watch her performance. [124] It can be read as a tribute to the loyalty and warmheartedness of working-class communities or as an example of how Victorian society encouraged people to accept their social station while at the same time holding out the promise that they might better themselves through hard work. In the final decade of the century, halls were being bought up, touring circuits and chains of halls were being established, and managers were seeking to enhance profits by promoting respectability and catering to the family audience. London County Council was playing its part by refusing drink licenses for the auditoriums of new music halls from 1894 onward (thus bringing them into line with theaters). Yet even at this time of increased moral propriety, there were still songs heavy with innuendo. Consider the refrain of "She's Going There Every Night" (1898):[125]

> She'd never been there before—never been there before!
> She felt so shy till Mister Brown
> Started to bounce her up and down,
> Then it was all serene—it filled her with delight;
> She'd never been there before, but now she's going there
>   every night.

There may be little that is found surprising in this account of the knowingness of music hall performers, which so often creates what Peter Bailey terms a "potent sense of collusion" between themselves and their audiences;[126] but is it something to be contrasted with a supposedly strait-laced and repressed bourgeoisie—or is that a stereotype asking to be challenged? Edward Pigott, examiner of stage plays for the Lord Chamberlain, informs the Select Committee on Theatres and Places of Entertainment in 1892: "generally, it is towards the West End of the town, and amongst richer, idler, and more fashionable audiences that a famished manager would prefer to seek in scandal and indecency the means of replenishing an exhausted treasury."[127] Perhaps operetta needs closer scrutiny in this regard. "Wer uns getraut" from Strauss Jr.'s *Der Zigeunerbaron* is certainly a most seductive duet about the pleasures of illicit sex: Saffi and Barinkay, having spent the night together, ponder the question "Who married us?" They declare it was the nightingale and a bullfinch. (*Dompfaff,* bullfinch, is a pun: *Dom* means cathe-dral, and *Pfaffe* is a pejorative word for priest.) French and Austrian op-erettas are known for their occasional disregard of bourgeois standards of moral decency. By contrast, it seems to be a widespread assumption that nothing could be more remote from the comic operas of Gilbert and Sullivan than reference to sexual matters. Gilbert was known to feel discomforted by the revealing costumes worn in French operetta, and made it his rule that "no lady of the company should be required to wear a dress that she could not wear with perfect propriety at a pri-vate fancy ball."[128] Yet certain members of the audience may have de-tected a lewd innuendo in his libretti at times. Did nobody ever smile during *Iolanthe* when the Fairy Queen wonders if Captain Shaw's hose is capable of quenching her great love, or when Strephon confesses he is a fairy down to the waist? Is it only a later, sophisticated, cynical, or decadent audience that could hear a double entendre in Grosvenor's cautionary rhyme "Teasing Tom was a very bad boy, / A great big squirt was his favourite toy" (*Patience,* act 2)? A sexual dimension seems to be confirmed by the poem's moral: "The consequence was he was lost to-*tally,* / And married a girl in the *corps de bally.*" It was received wisdom, however mistaken, that dancers in the corps de ballet were disrep-utable in their sexual behavior.[129] There is no doubt, either, that the popularity of St. James's Park with prostitutes would have added spice to Lord Tolloller's comment on Iolanthe's assignation with an unidenti-fied man:

> I heard the minx remark,
> She'd meet him after dark,
> Inside St. James's Park,
> And give him one!

Bracebridge Hemyng, writing on prostitution in London in 1862, had informed his readers: "Park women, properly so called, are those degraded creatures, utterly lost to all sense of shame, who wander about the paths most frequented after nightfall in the Parks, and consent to any species of humiliation for the sake of acquiring a few shillings."[130]

There are a number of occasions when one character shows a de-cidedly sexual interest in another. Pointing to the sentry, Private Willis, the Fairy Queen cries, "Do you suppose that I am insensible to the ef-fect of manly beauty? Look at that man!" However, she makes a great play of crushing these feelings; in other words, displaying her sexual self-control. The song "Oh, Foolish Fay" in which she invokes Captain Shaw (head of the Metropolitan Fire Brigade in real life), movingly de-scribes a "type of true love kept under." Ironically, Captain Shaw was keeping true love under in his private life, as was revealed in court two years after the première of *Iolanthe,* when Lord Colin Campbell accused him of having had an affair with his wife.

Characters are aware of social contexts in which the erotic can intrude. In *Ruddigore,* Mad Margaret and Sir Despard Murgatroyd take the precaution of informing the audience "This is one of our blameless dances." In *The Mikado,* Nanki-Poo and Yum-Yum are fully alert to the moral dangers of kissing and, in their duet, kiss each other merely to make absolutely clear, by concrete example, that this is what they will never do. Of course, this duet is a tease; it is inevitably sexually loaded, and is an example of how operetta marked out new possibilities—here, humorous flirtation—for the musical stage. The Japanese setting should fool nobody; wherever they are set, the Gilbert and Sullivan comic operas are always about the social and political condition of Britain.

Gilbert's young heroines are conscious of their allure, as Yum-Yum makes clear in her song "The Sun Whose Rays." On the other hand, many have deplored his use of spinsters as figures of fun. Jane Stedman has argued, however, that Gilbert's corpulent dames are used to satirize the value placed on youth and beauty in women as a conventional requisite for marriage, and they usually possess a strength of character denied his leading soprano characters.[131] They also have a part to play as sexual beings. When Lady Jane announces, in the context of the satire of artistic pretensions in *Patience* , "I am limp and I cling," suddenly the sexual dimension of the images of drooping women in pre-Raphaelite paintings is made blatant by the thought of a clinging, fleshly Lady Jane. In the same opera, the actions of the poet Reginald Bunthorne can be related directly to his sexual drive. He reveals to the audience that he has been playing the role of an aesthete solely to make himself attractive to the women of the neighborhood who have fallen under the spell of the aesthetic movement. In truth, Bunthorne despises the aesthetic realm as something opposed to worldly human appetites and desires, and he only occupies a place in this domain so as to acquire a means of attaining the fleshly satisfaction he yearns for. In such a manner, high-minded artifice and the realities of everyday life are bluntly juxtaposed.

In general, a nonromantic, even antiromantic ethos prevails in these comic operas. Marriage is often a solution to a problem: Private Willis, realizing that the Fairy Queen needs to marry to remain immortal, declares "I don't think much of the British soldier who wouldn't ill-convenience himself to save a female in distress." Bunthorne, accepting that Jane will never leave him, comments that after all, she's "a fine figure of a woman." This is not to say that more conventional love pairs do not exist. We have only to think of Strephon and Phyllis, who are also given a love duet complete with conventional melodic intertwining. However, such characters are rarely the focus point. And though Jack Point's death from love is moving in *Yeomen of the Guard,* so, in its own remarkable way, is that of the lovesick little bird in the deliberately ridiculous and absurdly sentimental "Tit Willow" from *Mikado.* The antiromantic qualities, and the masculine connotations of this attitude, may account for the numbers of men who are attracted to Gilbert and

Sullivan. Gilbert himself was a contentedly married if undemonstrative husband, and very much a man's man—although, running counter to his image as a misogynist, he died as a consequence of his courageous action in rescuing a woman from drowning. Sullivan was the philanderer. He was closest to Mrs. Mary Frances Ronalds, an American living in London separated from her husband. There is evidence in the form of love letters that, before this, he conducted affairs with two sisters simultaneously.[132] Nevertheless, Sullivan's high estimation of the moral value of music is beyond dispute: for corroboration, we can peruse his address to members of the Midland Institute, delivered in Birmingham, England, in 1888. Music, he claims, "is absolutely free from the power of suggesting anything immoral," and continues:

> Music can suggest no improper thought, and herein may be claimed its superiority over painting and sculpture, both of which may, and, indeed, do at times, depict and suggest impurity. This blemish, however, does not enter into music; sounds alone (apart from articulate words, spectacle, or descriptive programme) must, from their indefinite nature, be innocent. Let us thank God that we have one elevating and ennobling influence in the world which can never, never lose its purity and beauty.[133]

Here Sullivan offers a convincing reason why music was found to be such a powerful ally in the moral struggle. In actuality, erotic associations were not so easily forgotten in the context of certain musical devices.

The moral tone, as I remarked earlier, lends a character to Victorian ballads that makes them markedly different from the songs that followed. In the early twentieth century, there was something of a reaction to songs that preached messages, and in each successive decade the moral didacticism in the Victorian ballads appeared less and less congenial to new developments in the arts. The American composer Oley Speaks had a great success with his setting of "On the Road to Mandalay" in 1907, and though the Kipling poem "Mandalay" is earlier, the spirit of the song is that of a new age: the singer is given music that expresses vigorously his desire to escape to a place "where there ain't no ten commandments." That is not to say that sentiment was rejected simultaneously with moralizing. In the later ballad, emotion is frequently indulged in for its own sake—as, for example, in "Somewhere a Voice Is Calling," of 1911—whereas in the nineteenth century, that was rarely the case. [134] In the earlier ballads, children, for instance, were not just cute in their misery, as is the girl seeking her father in Denham Harrison's 1902 song "Give Me a Ticket to Heaven." The sick boy in "Put My Little Shoes Away" (1870) seizes the opportunity, as death approaches, to give his parents a lesson in unselfishness, as well as the value of recycling commodities, by asking them to hang on to his shoes because they will fit the baby when he is bigger. [135]

The importance of a moral tone to the American and European

bourgeoisie in the nineteenth century was a powerful incitement for many modernists' rejection of a moral dimension in the twentieth century, especially when the production of art for bourgeois consumption became strongly associated with notions of pandering to the marketplace and with personal insincerity, or a lack of artistic truthfulness. Thus, it became typical for twentieth-century high-status art to parade its complete lack of any kind of moral dimension—somewhat paradoxically—as a virtue. The license to shock without conscience became the prerogative of the modern artist, although, ironically, one aspect of bourgeois aesthetic ideology continued—the idea that art is *good for you.*

4

The Rift between Art and Entertainment

In my introduction to this study, I warned about mapping high or low culture directly onto high and low classes, but while the taste hierarchy does not neatly duplicate the class hierarchy, Herbert Gans usefully reminds us of similarities, "for in terms of prestige, high culture is at the top and low culture is at the bottom."[1] The status of high culture comes, of course, from its having been identified for many centuries with the rich and powerful. Pierre Bourdieu's *habitus* (the system of dispositions with which a person is invested by education and upbringing) is probably the richest, if not entirely unproblematic, concept to aid understanding of how cultural choices are made.[2] Taste is not a private matter but rather, as Hans Georg Gadamer puts it, "a social phenomenon of the first order."[3] Culture can be used as a marker of superiority, a taste for the "refined" over the "vulgar," which is why Bourdieu remarks that "art and cultural consumption are predisposed, consciously and deliberately or not, to fulfill a social function of legitimating social differences."[4] The increase in urban populations and rise of the bourgeoisie brought a need for public demonstrations of social standing, since it was no longer common knowledge who was important. Attending concerts was a means of displaying status.[5] By the second half of the century, a distinction had arisen between "art music" and "popular music," even if not expressed in exactly those terms. The next chapter shows how "light music" originated in Vienna, in the dance music of Joseph Lanner and Strauss Sr., which mixed traditional and classical styles in a new, exhilarating, rhythmic, and entertaining manner. As the end of the century approached, an individual's taste in music could have far-reaching consequences for his or her intellectual status. The terms "highbrow," first used in the 1880s, and "lowbrow," which emerged in 1900–1910, relate to the pseudoscience of phrenology: the high brow was considered a sign of intelligence, especially since it was believed to be a feature of the "civilized" European races.[6]

Carl Dahlhaus has argued that nineteenth-century popular music (that of the dance halls, promenade concerts, salons, and *variétés*) is lowbrow, and better described as "trivial music": "Eighteenth-century divertimentos were also designed to entertain, but no one would wish to place them alongside a nineteenth-century Viennese coffeehouse pièce."[7] Dahlhaus seeks to make a qualitative distinction, but explains it in terms of a betrayal of eighteenth-century philanthropy by nineteenth-century capitalists: the fault for the trivialization of those "philanthropic tendencies" lies with industrialization and the "compulsion to mass-produce and distribute commodities."[8] His example of *Trivialmusik* is Louis Lefébure-Wély's piano nocturne *Les Cloches du monastère*, op. 54, which he finds sadly deficient as a musical structure. He then rails against "trivialized listening," which ignores "the principle of self-absorption in the work as an aesthetic object," so that music "degenerates into a vehicle for associations and for edifying or melancholy self-indulgence."[9] The word "degenerates," in the context of what Dahlhaus describes as "a special form of lowbrow music," is not without its significance.[10] Finally, he spits it out: "Triviality offends against taste."[11] He suggests that "trivial" music is like a fashionable commodity that as soon as it ages is recognized as inconsequential and is rejected; yet the longevity of some nineteenth-century popular songs, for example "Home, Sweet Home," is unexplained.

For Percy Young, too, in *The Concert Tradition* (1965), the emergence of a new kind of popular taste in nineteenth-century London is part of a sad tale of falling musical standards. He writes, for example, of John Stevenson's arrangements of Irish songs "contorted by Tom Moore for suburban drawing-rooms" and, typical of criticism that follows the modernist line, he associates decline with loss of masculinity, speaking of "emasculated glees."[12] He lays out some of the causes of the "debasement of English musical taste" in the mid–nineteenth century: "The mixture of the run-down 'Gardens' song, the second-rate Italian opera aria, and the instrumental show-piece, the new vanities of singers able in the ballad age to command high fees and even royalties from composers, and the growing detachment of the English bourgeoisie, all contributed."[13] In presenting such opinions he reveals continuity with the views of musicians like John Ella and critics like Henry Lunn.[14] Strauss Sr. and Lanner have no part to play in Young's interpretation of the concert tradition. Yet, as early as 1894, one critic is beginning to think that the championing of *ernste Musik* has gone too far: "The tyranny of earnestness is to be deprecated as much as the unbridled dominion of frivolity."[15] He gives as an example of excessive high-mindedness the "great resentment and even hisses amongst a certain section of the audience" when Stanford introduced an item by Strauss Jr. into a concert at the Royal College of Music.

Light Music versus Serious Music

By the end of the 1820s a type of music had become established in Vienna that was widely enjoyed but at the same time was criticized for being fashionable and frivolous. The light-versus-serious opposition can be deconstructed readily: notice that this binarism is not formulated as light versus heavy or light versus difficult.[16] There are plenty of "serious" works that are easily assimilated by listeners, and the term "sublime simplicity" is not uncommonly applied to some "serious" compositions. Thus, "serious" is the dominant term, and "light" is defined negatively against it, as music *lacking* seriousness, as *Trivialmusik.* Johann N. Hofzinser, writing in the periodical *Sammler* in 1833, railed, "A just indignation must seize everyone who, when Strauss plays, hears the names 'art and artist' desecrated by such frivolous stuff."[17] Serious music might be simple in style, and it might be fun (scherzando), but it was regarded as music that ought always to be listened to attentively. Nonserious music was perceived as that which did not tax the mind and was consumed merely as an amusement, usually alongside the distractions of talking, laughing, or dancing. What defined music as nonserious was its supposed complicity with acts of effortless consumption. Distinctions were thus being made according to patterns of social behavior. Critics of light music may have been swayed by ideas about musical taste that were sometimes rooted in class hostility rather than aesthetics, but the argument was always sure to be formulated as an aesthetic one, and usually involved lofty comparisons with Haydn and Mozart, as if that illustrious pair were never complicit with the desires of the social world for which they composed.[18] Linke points to this period as that in which the concept of a "second-class music" grew, attributing its formulation to influential critics, among them Robert Schumann.[19] Yet when Schumann writes of the gold rattling in Strauss Sr.'s pocket as he conducts, he is not making any comment on the quality of the music; he is indicating his disgust at the intermingling of music and commerce.[20] The rupture between art and entertainment was caused primarily by an intense dislike of the market conditions that turned art into a commodity. Entertainment music was regarded as hand-in-glove with business entrepreneurs for whom popular music was a mere commodity and profits the main concern. Max Weber has stressed the frequency with which "every rational economic pursuit, and especially 'entrepreneurial activity,' is looked upon as a disqualification of status."[21]

This idea of a "second-class music" needs to be distinguished from ideas of "popular music" in the first half of the century. A correspondent to the *Musical Examiner* (London) in 1844, declares: "That popular music is totally without claims to excellence, we never assumed; but when it is vaunted to the depreciation of epic works of art, we consider it our duty to expose its poverty and assumption." But he does not mean by "popular music" what the term comes to mean in the second half of the century, as his following rhetorical question and statement make clear: "What would be our opinion of any ignoramus, who should attempt to place the glaring and popular works of Maclise above the harmonies of Rubens? Yet far worse would it be to class Donizetti with Mendelssohn, or Meyerbeer with Beethoven!" Then he advances an argument that becomes common later in the century: "Music, as an art, is the least understood; in its intellectuality, it is perfectly incomprehensible to any but refined and educated ears."[22]

In 1871, a lead article, "'Popular' Music," in the *Musical Standard* (London) acknowledges the impact education may have in forming musical taste:

> The term "popular music" is in very common use, but it would be difficult to define what description of music most deserves such a distinction. One class of music is popular with a certain standard of taste, and another class is considered popular by those with whose taste or degree of musical education it is most in accordance. Some consider cheap, that is low-priced music, "popular." Some write music under the idea that it will meet certain popular demands, either in consequence of its simplicity or its passages of a sensational nature.[23]

The writer recognizes that some composers now aim to satisfy what are perceived as popular demands but also suggests that a cheap edition of Beethoven's piano music would richly merit the designation "popular." Nevertheless, he proceeds to inform us that what "is widely understood as popular music" is the kind the New York preacher Henry Ward Beecher "would call clap-trap music." The article then praises Beecher's promotion of organ concerts, which offer the public music that is "grave and full of moral feeling."[24] So what is it that counts as "claptrap" music in 1871? Certainly not Donizetti or Meyerbeer. The only types of popular music mentioned are "dances and polkas."[25]

Significantly, the idea of a second-class music, or claptrap music, made it possible for a composition to be categorized as popular because of its style without its necessarily being popular in terms of sales. It was evident that some musical products aimed at popularity yet failed. Therefore, a shift occurred in the meaning of "popular," and this provided critics with a means of condemning any music that bore the *signs* of the popular—features they regarded as fashionable and facile (*leicht* meaning "easy" in German) rather than progressive and serious— whether or not such music enjoyed success in the marketplace. Albrecht Riethmüller has referred to Strauss's music as marked by the stain of popularity, noting that the perception of Strauss's light style (*leichte Musik*) led immediately to critical condemnation.[26] The Philharmonische Concert-Unternehmung mostly ignored the music of the Strauss family, thereby revealing fears of undermining their own artistic status and that of their concerts. This should be borne in mind before attributing inordinate significance to the admiration Brahms, Wagner, and from time to time Hanslick showed for Strauss waltzes. The growing acceptance of this music in the 1870s is indicated by Strauss's première of his waltz *Wiener Blut*, op. 354, in the Grosser Musikverein-saal, conducting (violin in hand) the Philharmonic Orchestra, and his performance of Viennese dance music with the same orchestra at the Vienna World Fair in 1873. Yet these were rare occasions that were received as good-humored opportunities for "letting one's hair down." A contemporary reviewer of the *Wiener Blut* première in 1873 remarked on the sensation caused by the combination of the Waltz King and serious (*ernsten*) Philharmonic players.[27] Collaborations remained few for the rest of the century. The seemingly age-old tradition of annual Strauss concerts by the Vienna Philharmonic was begun much later by Clemens Krauss, who gave annual Strauss concerts at the Salzburg Festival in 1929–33 and then initiated the Vienna New Year's Day concerts in 1941.

In England, the use of the term "royalty ballad" was a way of castigating drawing room ballads as commercial while also implying low artistic status: they are about money rather than art. For some critics the ballads were themselves fairly harmless, but it was exasperating to see them being accorded high artistic stature. Sydney Northcote wrote in 1942:

> when these products are raised to an undeserved status and importance it calls for very vigorous protest. We have only to reflect that less than eighty years ago Sullivan was appointed professor of pianoforte and *ballad singing* at the Crystal Palace School of Art to realize the extraordinary position attained by this form of song.[28]

In an article entitled "Popular Composers" that appeared in the *Strand* magazine in 1892, over a dozen composers are picked out, all of whom had enjoyed success with drawing room ballads, and there is no suggestion that the form is beneath them.[29] Of course, this also suggests that the *Strand* knows what its readers like and that these composers are popular with them. However, others thought that the sordid effect commerce was having on music needed to be cleansed by moral willpower: "It requires a great deal of moral courage to refuse money where it is offered . . . for popular compositions, but the conscience of having assisted in purifying music will in the end repay a trivial loss."[30] This argument is based on a fallacy that assumes any skilled musician could enjoy popular success by prostituting his or her talent, and it fails to recognize that popular forms were developing distinctive characteristics and conventions that were not found in classical forms or, if they were, had different meanings in the classical context (such as the "vulgarity" of the tonic triad with added sixth).

Popular music was unashamed to incorporate effects that "serious" composers would frown on. Often an attractive and unusual effect imprints a particular waltz on the memory. It does not have to be as gimmicky as the rifle shots in Strauss Jr.'s fast polka *Auf der Jagd,* op. 373 (1875); it can use entirely musical means: for example, the "donkey's bray" motive in the first waltz theme of his father's *Carnevals-Spende,* op. 60 (1833), or the grace notes that create a little *glissando* effect in the second half of the first waltz of *Sorgenbrecher,* op. 230 (1848). Strauss Jr.'s polka *Ligourianer Seufzer* (Liguorian sighs), op. 57, has a *Katzenmusik* (cat's music) Trio that calls for the players to sing a mocking song ("Ligouri ci gouri gouriani ani ani") and contains novel and raucous instrumentation that includes the sound of windows breaking. It was first performed at a Lerchenfeld tavern known as Zur blauen Flasche, during the revolution of 1848, and satirized an Order of Jesuits (founded by Alfonso Liguori [sic] in the previous century) who supported Metternich. They were expelled (temporarily) from Vienna after revolution broke out. The official censor found this *Scherz-Polka* too subversive, and he confiscated the piano version.

The Viennese are famous for being easygoing, and for seeking an escape from grim reality in gaiety. Austria and Germany share much in common, but have distinct personalities. As the Austrian satirist Karl Kraus put it, "In Berlin, things are serious but not hopeless; in Vienna, they are hopeless but not serious."[31] In the summer of 1866, the Prussians defeated the Austrians at the battle of Königgratz in a war about borders. It was during the carnival, in the winter of the following year, that Strauss presented the Viennese with *An der schönen blauen Donau* as part of a fund-raising event for the fallen. Hanslick considered this waltz a second Austrian national anthem: "one which celebrates the country and its people"[32]—an ironic comment, given that one of the things Metternich had clamped down on was nationalism. German bourgeois traits were being seen increasingly as national traits during the nineteenth century, as Norbert Elias has argued.[33] To be loyal to the Habsburg dynasty and to aristocratic values, however, one needed to be supranational in outlook.

Those attacking Viennese dance music on the grounds of its frivolity or lack of discipline could always point to the reveling in excess that is one of its distinctive features. An example is the percussion in Josef Strauss's *Feuerfest! Polka française,* op. 269 (1869), especially the relentless striking of the anvils in certain sections. Predictability, rather than something to be avoided, is used here and elsewhere as a humorous device—for instance, we wait to be amused by the bass drum's loud punctuation of musical phrases, the expectation of its arrival giving added pleasure. The sometimes extreme simplicity of melody found in Viennese dance music may have lent further persuasiveness to arguments about the facile: the main theme of Strauss Jr.'s *Auroraball-Polka,* op. 219 (1859), consists almost entirely of repetitions of one note. But how infectious it is![34]

In 1860, a writer in *Macmillan's* magazine identifies a "higher class of music," referring to music that, at that time, was beginning to be labeled "classical music." This is not of a kind to be associated with female accomplishments; it is a serious and quasi-religious "man's music"—in Lawrence Levine's terminology, a "sacralized" music.[35] The writer mentions an old friend who "would as soon have thought of sawing his beloved "Strad" up for firewood as of admitting his wife into the music-room during the celebration of the mysteries."[36] However, "young ladies" are implored to educate the ears of their fathers and brothers by playing a bit of Beethoven or Haydn occasionally. High-minded critics soon held composers to task for producing low (that is, entertaining) music. The London weekly *Figaro,* commenting on the first night of Gilbert and Sullivan's *Sorcerer* at the Opera Comique (15 November 1877), expressed its "disappointment at the downward art course that Sullivan appears to be drifting into."[37] Another review, in the *World,* remarked: "It was hoped that he would soar with Mendelssohn, whereas he is, it seems, content to sink with Offenbach."[38] This was a criticism he was to encounter often. The press greeted the première of *H.M.S. Pinafore* (Opera Comique, 25 May 1878) by damning it as undistinguished, disappointing, and feeble, despite its success with the audience.[39] This was a time when critical admiration began to grow for music that was challenging, difficult, or widening boundaries, and the composer-audience consensus was weakening.

Popular styles make a great deal of use of conventions, features Howard Becker aligns with sociological concepts such as "shared understanding" and "custom."[40] It is thus no surprise to discover that eliminating certain conventions is a practice associated with learned musical styles, since this means that special knowledge becomes a requirement. By the 1880s, "difficult" music brings high status to the composer and consumer. James D. Brown remarks in his *Biographical Dictionary of Musicians* of 1886: "Great composers, as a rule . . . uniformly confine themselves to the production of works calculated to please the learned."[41] An issue arises about the new in music, and the role of original and individual creativity. Gans comments: "Many popular culture creators want to express their personal values and tastes in much the same way as the high cultural creator."[42] Indeed, popular music cherishes novelty, but a question arises about when the new is to be deemed aesthetically worthy and when it is not. The qualities Samuel Smiles attributes to the inventors of the industrial age—"great force of character," "far seeing," "undaunted by failures"—could be transferred directly in most cases to the idealized romantic composer.[43] Yet in the arts as in industry, few innovations could fairly be claimed to be entirely the result of

unaided individual effort. In spite of that, once these thoughts are con-
nected to theories of race and evolution, and to imperialist discourse—
"widening boundaries," "pioneering," "ground breaking"—a comprehensive ideology of modernist creativity is in place. There is a recurring
image in Smiles of an ignorant mob that fails to understand the wonders of the industrial creators. It is not long before critics begin supple-
menting his "martyrology of inventors" by listing instances of suffering,
unappreciated composers. In other words, the "new" must be perceived not as novelty, but as synonymous with the "advanced." Despite
this clarification, it remains a conflicted ideological position, since a case
could easily be made for Strauss Jr. having advanced the genre of the
waltz. There was a conviction, inherited by twentieth-century modernism, that the accessible and the advanced could not go together. It is
found in Hanslick's dislike of Strauss's "advanced" waltzes (see chapter
5) and the emulation of grand opera in the act 2 Finale of *Der Zigeunerbaron*. At the same time, others thought that the popular could serve an
educational function, that dance music composers could "do valuable
service in educating the ear and sense of rhythm," if only they would
introduce "refreshing innovations," for example, "unusual harmonies."[44] Bernard Gendron suggests that the adoption of "high" features
in popular music leads to "the cultural empowerment of popular
music," but others may wish to argue that popular music loses political
or social power as it advances up the taste hierarchy.[45] The political
power of the popular was epitomized for the bourgeoisie by the fearful
image of those who were driven entirely by the profit motive feeding
an undisciplined urban crowd whatever music they were prepared to
pay to hear. It is a familiar trait of anti–urban music criticism. Henry
Davey, in his *History of English Music* (1895), believes the solution lies in
composers adopting a less dismissive attitude to "uncultivated taste," together with the instruction of the young in the "best old folk-tunes."[46]

Art, Taste, and Status

There have always been taste distinctions, of course, but until the nineteenth-century popular music revolution, they tended to be made in
the belief that preferences were based on an evaluation of quality in the
context of supposedly universal laws of music, rather than among competing musical styles that followed their own individual bylaws. William Weber points out that Charles Avison was criticizing some composers for producing a type of music "only fit for children" as early as
1752.[47] It is an accusation about "watering down" or "dumbing down"
an existing type of music, the values of which are widely accepted. In
another article, Weber confirms that in the eighteenth century the
"general public" remained the ultimate judge on matters of musical
quality.[48] This dovetails with Habermas's assessment of the influence
the public sphere wielded in Britain, France, and Germany at this time,

although Habermas is careful to stress that "a new stratum of 'bourgeois' people" had arisen "which occupied a central position within the 'public.'"[49] The notion of a "general taste" disguises such class distinctions (and the role taste plays in these) and tends to exclude the nonurban public, but it does help to clarify the way judgments about quality were perceived to be validated before the nineteenth century. Avison was writing before certain types of music took on commercial associations; following that development, *distrust* in the public begins, and reliable authority concerning musical value then occupies part of the province of specialized critics. Tia DeNora shows how Beethoven was assessed according to the norms of "general taste" in early reviews in the *Allgemeine Musikalische Zeitung,* but then became part of a critical discourse concerning connoisseurship and a "higher style" of music.[50] This may be taken as the first evidence of the erosion of "general taste" as a benchmark for musical quality, and it was to lead to a consequent erosion of trust in the judgment of the "general public." At the same time, the notion of a "general taste" remained widespread in the nineteenth century, and this term circumvents some of the problems associated with finding French and German equivalents for the Anglo-American description "popular."

One of the reasons aesthetic writing always has a moral tone is that, as Becker explains, it aims "to separate the deserving from the undeserving," rather than simply intending "to classify things into useful categories, as we might classify species of plants."[51] Along with the development of a new cooperative network, a new art world also needs a new aesthetic, the enunciation of "new modes of criticism and standards of judgment," or its activities will not be considered art.[52] In Vienna, for example, the quality of operetta began to be judged via the binarism natural (*echt*) versus artificial, the latter being associated with French operetta.[53] Becker sums up the institutional theory of aesthetics thus: "When an established aesthetic theory does not provide a logical and defensible legitimation of what artists are doing and, more important, what the other institutions of the art world—especially distribution organizations and audiences—accept as art, professional aestheticians will provide the required new rationale."[54] Hanslick helps to "aestheticize" the Viennese waltz. This begins to erode the sharp distinction between nonfunctional (i.e. not for dancing) "art" waltzes (like those of Berlioz, Chopin, and Brahms) and functional ones. Some of Strauss Jr.'s waltzes have indications for cuts to be made (in their codas) if used for dancing. Next comes the canon (or lineage) that goes Schubert–Lanner–Strauss Sr.–Strauss Jr., and from there to Wagner's Flower Maidens, Richard Strauss's *Rosenkavalier,* and Ravel's *La Valse.* Part of what Becker calls the "institutional paraphernalia" used to justify artistic claims are journals,[55] and it will be seen in chapter 8 that these were a feature of the *cabarets artistiques* in Paris. Peter Berger and Thomas Luckmann point to the conflict that may arise between experts and practitioners: "What is likely to be particularly galling is the experts' claim to know the ultimate significance of the practitioners' activity better than the practitioners themselves. Such rebellions on the part of 'laymen' may lead to the emergence of rival definitions of reality and, eventually, to the appearance of new experts in charge of the new definitions."[56] The choice of the word "rebellions" is not without significance to my claims that the new popular styles of the nineteenth century did, indeed, rebel against high-status styles, rather than diluting them. But what effect does artistic status have on the cultural products themselves? Further thoughts from Becker provide an answer: "Works in a medium or style defined as not art have a much shorter life expectancy than those defined as art. No organizational imperatives make it worth anyone's while to save them."[57] Nevertheless, this fails to explain why some popular music of the nineteenth century has lived on to the present, or why we can still respond with such pleasure to many of that century's popular songs—often the very songs that were most popular at the time.

Where the aesthetic status of Viennese dance music was concerned, the issue was whether it was art music or was functional music (*Gebrauchtmusik*) that ought to be regarded as part of a craft world rather than an art world.[58] It may be tempting to label the production of this music a craft in the 1820s, for it is not unusual to find that a craft world changes into an art world. This happens when values extraneous to the functional purpose become important. When Strauss Sr. began to be concerned with the aesthetics of waltz composition, he was moving from craft to art. One of the ways the status of art is ratified is by canonization. As soon as certain waltzes are picked out as "great"— such as Lanner's *Die Schönbrunner,* or Strauss's *Loreley-Rhein-Klänge*— acceptance of artistic status is certain to grow. When composers in an established art world took an interest in waltzes, as did Chopin, the perception of waltz composition as being merely a craft was, of course, further eroded—since, typically, a person from an art world will try to ensure that the final product is, in the practical meaning of the word, useless. When popular culture is absorbed into high culture, or even quoted, it is altered—although Gans reminds us that this also happens when popular culture takes up a high-culture product, style, or method.[59] Finally, art worlds depend on the reputations they help to create[60]—in the case of Viennese dance music, the waltz kings Johann Strauss father and son.

A movement against the miscellaneous concert and against musical *potpourris* becomes increasingly hostile in the 1860s, as illustrated by an article in *Dwight's Journal of Music:*

> No one objects to a felicitously *varied* programme. Indeed it is always desirable. But it is childish to suppose an incoherent medley, of Symphony and polka, Beethoven and sable minstrelsy, the sublime and the frivolous, the delicately ideal and the boisterously rowdy, essential to variety.[61]

It is clear from the examples given that the writer is objecting to concerts that do not recognize the schism between the "serious" and popular styles—those that lie outside what he later refers to as the "classical boundaries." He argues that variety is already more effectively available within the classical style:

> There is really more effective variety, more stimulating contrast, between the different movements of the same good Symphony, for instance, than there is between the different pieces of the most miscellaneous "popular" programme.[62]

The writer complains that the term "light" as applied to music means merely promiscuous or miscellaneous, and fails to acknowledge the existence of a high-quality alternative, a light *good* music:

> If you crave grotesque and fantastic recreation in your music, is not a Beethoven Scherzo, or a Mendelssohn Capriccio or Overture as daintily refreshing as a Jullien quadrille? Or do you like the glitter best without the gold? . . . Now we consider Mendelssohn's "Midsummer Night's Dream" light music;—light in the good sense;—its airy fairy fancies certainly are light. . . . The graceful Allegretto to Beethoven's eighth Symphony, so often played, is light.[63]

In this article, there is a tacit acknowledgment that popular music is now different stylistically from classical music, but the difference is perceived in terms of bad style versus good style. The problem, however, is that classical music itself is not a homogeneous style. In 1885, the *Musical Times* in London worried that Wagner's music might have an "upsetting and feverish effect" and, if served up to "the East Ender[s]," there should be no expectation "that his music will at once work miracles, and supply them with a soul-satisfying religion."[64] Even in *fin-de-siècle* Vienna, as Sandra McColl assures us, Wagner, Bruckner, and Wolf were yet to find favor "in the most influential circles of the conservative musical establishment."[65]

When Levine speaks of the "sacralization of culture," he means not only a quasi-religious reception of culture but also that culture is too sacred to be tampered with. This idea of culture is contrasted with the flexibility evident during one of the earliest New York performances of Rossini's *Il barbiere di Siviglia* in 1825, when Maria Garcia (later Mme. Malibran) happily sang "Home, Sweet Home!" as an encore in act 2.[66] It did not mean, of course, that the opera house was not segregated according to class. The possession of an expensive box at the opera in 1825 was, according to a former New York mayor, "a sort of aristocratic distinction."[67] In the first half of the nineteenth century, it was understood that, in New York, theater boxes were for fashionable society, the pit was for the middling class, and the gallery was for the lower class. However, as the decades passed, opera came to mean high-class culture: Italian opera was to be performed in Italian, not English; opera was refined and intellectual; and opera houses were for fashionable so-

ciety. The progress of a "sacralized" art becomes evident in comparing
Adelina Patti's two visits to New York, first in the 1850s, next in the
1880s, when some critics took offense at her giving a recital of "popular ballads," claiming that she had returned to "another America," an
"intelligent musically developed America," one "accustomed to hear
the greatest works of the greatest masters."[68] She had first visited when
there was strong support for a popular or "common man's" culture; it
was the time of popular urban stage characters such as Mose the
B'howery B'hoy (a brawling but fearless New York "fire-boy"). The
schism between the demands of the populists (which included most of
the "midding classes") and the elitists had resulted in a full-scale riot in
Astor Place in 1849 outside the Opera House, then New York's largest
theatre (capacity 1,500). It was triggered by rivalry between two actors,
a British tragedian admired by the "better families" and an American;
they represented competing claims on the future direction of American
culture. After the riot, which left 31 dead and 150 injured, the *Philadelphia Ledger* remarked: "There is now . . . in New York City, what every
good patriot has hitherto considered it his duty to deny—a high class
and a low class."[69] It is worth noting that culture has classified them.

Mindful of the Astor Place riot, when Barnum decided to promote
Jenny Lind, he emphasized her charity and simplicity and claimed she
wished to visit America to see its democracy in action. He also made
sure New York "b'hoys" as well as high society were at the dock to meet
her.[70] The broad-based appreciation of Jenny Lind's New York visit in
1850 suggested to some that the class divisiveness of the Astor Place
riot was beginning to heal. Lind's popularity was seen as evidence of
"the slightness of separation between the upper and middle class of our
country" in contrast to the situation in England.[71] Yet there was a new
assertiveness shown in the defense of popular taste in the 1860s. For example, a letter writer to the *Nation,* in September 1867, protests about
the scorn of the rich and educated for the "great mass of workers."[72]

The change in status of an artistic technique can be illustrated with
reference to yodeling. The Rainer Family, who left Switzerland for an
America tour during 1839–43, did not introduce the yodel to America,
but they popularized it through songs like "The Sweetheart."[73] The
American Hutchinson Family followed in their wake, and also included
some yodeling. Lest it be thought that Britain was untouched by yodeling, evidence to the contrary is found in Henry Bishop's "The Merry
Mountain Horn" (1828), written for Lucy Vestris (ex. 4.1), L. Devereaux's "The Swiss Herdsman" (c. 1835), and George Linley's "The Swiss
Girl" (c. 1845). Even a distinguished singer such as Lind had once been
happy to yodel her way through "The Herdsman's Song."[74] All the
same, it became an illegitimate technique in classical vocal production
after the middle of the nineteenth century. Tim Wise has suggested as
a reason that it contradicted the homogeneity of the classical sound, the
changes of vocal register being so striking and abrupt in the yodel.[75]

Example 4.1   "The Merry Mountain Horn" (words by J. Pocock, music by Henry Bishop (London: Goulding and D'Almaine, 1828).

However, this abruptness did not vanish altogether: there is a "yodel" between registers, for example, when Clara Butt moves from chest voice to head voice at the end of the first verse of her 1930 recording of "Land of Hope and Glory."[76] Moreover, yodel shapes did not disappear from some melodies (especially Viennese), as we have already seen in the refrain of Orlofsky's champagne aria in *Die Fledermaus* (ex. 2.4). They also persisted in instrumental music: in Josef Strauss's *Dorfschwalben aus Österreich*, there are passages where the falsetto of a yodel is suggested by a change of instrumentation midphrase, at moments when the human voice would break for the higher notes. I would suggest that yodeling became the "waste" byproduct of one of those drives to create order that Zygmunt Bauman has theorized as characteristic of modernity: "ambivalence is the main affliction of modernity and the most worrying of its concerns."[77] In classical technique, a falsetto note could be interpreted as cheating in one context but as acceptable if the context was a yodel. The impact of the popular music revolution was such that classical singers in the twentieth century felt obliged to avoid using falsetto when singing yodeling melodies: examples that can be heard on record are John Aler singing the *Tyrolienne* from act 2 of Offenbach's *La Belle Hélène* (1864),[78] and Guy Fouché in the duet "Le sort jadis" from Emmanuel Chabrier's *L'Ouvreuse de l'Opéra-Comique et l'employé du Bon Marché* (1888).[79]

Other aspects of popular performance become signs of tasteless vulgarity, such as stamping your foot to the beat. The banjo player was renowned for it, but so, too, was Strauss Sr., of whom it was said that "all the time he played, his right foot stamped the beat characteristically."[80] It is part of Georg Simmel's theory concerning the excess of mental stimuli in the metropolis that one of the side effects of attempting to reduce these stimuli is an increase in feelings of aversion.[81] Unsurprisingly, this involves matters of taste, since, as Gadamer explains: "Taste is defined precisely by the fact that it is offended by what is tasteless."[82] Henry Lunn remarks in 1878: "We have in the metropolis a large and rapidly increasing number of amateurs who cannot brook the degradation of art under any circumstances, and who instinctively, therefore, shrink from contact with those by whom they are surrounded even on the so-called 'classical nights' at the Promenade Concerts.'"[83] A solution for performers who wished to cross musical borders was to adopt a different identity: Emily Soldene sang at the Oxford music hall under the pseudonym Miss Fitzhenry.[84]

Lunn, despite his facetious tone about those who reacted strongly to the "degradation of art," had revealed himself in the 1860s to be a champion of the ideal of a higher art, of futurity not fashion, and of the need to resist the seduction of the popular, ignore the crowd mentality, and commit oneself to a quasi-sacred truth in art by worshiping true art and not popular idols.

> If the duty of the critic were simply to record the amount of ovation bestowed upon art and artists, to count the *encores*, register the number of bouquets thrown nightly from the boxes, and calculate the duration and violence of the rounds of applause, his task would be simple; but he who would judge with a higher aim, has to look boldly into futurity, and to shut his eyes and ears to the fascinations which would lure him from the worship of a true art, to bend with the multitude before a popular idol.[85]

This refusal to bend before an idol does not apply in the classical domain. The unveiling of the Beethoven monument in Vienna's Stadtpark in May 1880 was declared a "solemn occasion" by the presiding official, Nicolaus Dumba, and the English reporter predicted that the place in which it was erected would "be visited by thousands of devotees to the shrine of the great master."[86] *Kunstreligion* or the belief in a "higher world" of art grew in Vienna as elsewhere. This development may be regarded as antibourgeois, since the taste zone of the bourgeoisie was the most consistently despised by "serious" artists and art critics.[87] Ironically, the Viennese middle class did more than any class to support a "higher world" of art—the problem was that this class engaged simultaneously in selling art, and was thus associated with the "lower world" of pecuniary interest and commodification.

Eduard Hanslick's essay *Vom musikalisch-Schönen* (1854), which insists that music should be understood solely in its own terms, was an influential text where the growing status of instrumental music was concerned. [88] But other aesthetic criticism was soon being advanced that boosted the idea of "pure" music. Meirion Hughes and Robert Stradling hold up Walter Pater as the inspiration for a generation, his *The Renaissance* (1873) kindling a number of rebirths, including the English Musical Renaissance.[89] In explicating his maxim that all art constantly aspires to the condition of music, Pater argues that all art strives "to be independent of the mere intelligence, to become a matter of pure perception, to get rid of its responsibilities to its subject."[90] Notice Pater's crafty qualification of "intelligence" with the adjective "mere." He must have been aware that Hegel, in the third volume of his *Ästhetik* (1838), had given priority to music with text over "stand-alone music" (*selbständige Musik*) because of the latter's lack of a cognitive dimension.

Hegel points out that a gift for composition can reveal itself at an early age, and requires no profound cultivation of the mind (he adds some gratuitous and unkind remarks about the general intelligence of composers). Hegel believed that the composition of independent instrumental music would lead to thoughts of a subjective arbitrariness, deceptive tensions, surprising turns, whimsicalities, and the like.[91] The trajectory of musical modernism would appear to offer some validation of these comments. Despite the privilege Pater accorded to sensory perception, it remained important for the status of music and musicians to connect musical greatness to the intellect. Frederick Niecks, who was to occupy the Reid Chair of Music at the University of Edinburgh from 1891, wrote to the editor of the *Musical Times* in 1880 to refute the idea that the appreciation of music requires less education and intelligence than the other arts, and to posit that true musical greatness is commensurate with a musician's intellectual and moral power.[92] The uncritical were thought, at this time, to be able to cope only with music of inferior quality. In the mid-1880s, the music hall was charged by the composer Frederick Corder with appealing to a dimwitted, undiscriminating crowd: "I was only too clearly convinced that this was the musical food which our masses truly loved and enjoyed, not because they could get no better, but because it was most suited to their intelligence—to their minds, in fact, if I may venture to use such an expression."[93] His animosity was no doubt driven by concerns about the doubling of London's population over the previous twenty years and by fears of the power of the mob. Indeed, a major London riot, the first since the violent events in Hyde Park in 1866, was only a year away.

There were other commentators, however, who took a different viewpoint. In the 1880s, Friedrich Nietzsche, having been bowled over by Bizet's *Carmen,* was perhaps the most important writer on aesthetics to turn against "the great style" as represented by Wagner. In *Der Fall Wagner* (1888), he announced as the first proposition of his new aesthetic: "Das Gute ist leicht, alles Göttliche läuft auf zarten Füssen" (The good is light; everything divine runs on tender feet).[94] In London, the former chief music critic of the *Times,* James Davison, was recommending *Iolanthe* as a remedy for the "Parsifal sickness" in the *Musical World* (18 August 1883).[95] In the following decade the poet Arthur Symons wrote an article entitled "The Music Hall of the Future" in the *Pall Mall Gazette* (13 April 1892) in which he expressed his enthusiasm for music hall. Symons had high artistic expectations of the music hall of the future, and predicted: "Without losing the charm of its freedom, the flavour of its Bohemianism, it will cease to be vulgar by becoming consistently artistic."[96] Elizabeth Pennell soon provided music hall with a worthy cultural ancestry: "already in feudal days the idea of 'turns' had been developed: the minstrel gave place to the acrobat, the acrobat to the dancer, the dancer to the clever dog."[97] Among other bohemian music hall enthusiasts at this time was the painter Walter Sickert. In an article of 1894 with the same title as that by Symons, a writer in the *Musical Times* describes with irony a "wail" that has gone up among former music hall admirers who now complain "that its inspired artists are forsaking their high ideals, that individuality of treatment is giving way to 'anaemic vulgarity,' and that the attitude of the audience, with its craving for 'decency and domesticity,' is ruining the halls artistically."[98] These unhappy admirers are certainly the artistic bohemian element, since the writer notes how they place the blame squarely on the middle-class audience that has recently been attracted into the halls. The *Musical Times* critic regards this as "artistic cant" and, taking an opposite view, feels inspired by the bourgeois audience with hope for the future of the halls. Barry Faulk assesses the success of Symons's efforts to legitimate the aesthetic experience the halls offered, and suggests, teasingly, that the middle class made a subculture of late-Victorian music hall.[99] In fact, even allowing that this "subculture" might be attributed more cautiously to a fraction of the middle class, there is more evidence of a struggle between artistic status groups, and a willingness on the part of the bohemian literati to align themselves with entertainment of a lower-class character in pursuit of their own aesthetic agenda.[100] The same is true of the clash between the bohemian intellectuals of Montmartre and the Parisian arts establishment, such as the Salon des Beaux Arts (see chapter 8), with the important difference that the Montmartre chansonniers admired the gritty realism of the streets, and would not have wished their output to be mistaken for that of the café-concert. Michel Herbert sees the *cabarets artistiques* as fostering popular song of higher quality, in contrast to the "sous produits du café-concert."[101] Lionel Richard regards the Chat Noir as being in opposition to "l'industrialisation de la distraction, à l'art dégradé pour les foules qui culmine dans le café-concert."[102] Here is an example of the popular fighting the commercialization of the popular, or of the popular aspiring to something more than entertainment.

Opera versus Operetta

An illustration of the way the tensions between art and entertainment play themselves out within musical forms can be found by examining the relationship of opera and operetta. I use the term "operetta" for convenience, but it is worth noting that Sullivan's insistence on his stage works being called "comic operas" is also a comment on the friction between art and entertainment and its effect on aesthetic status. I am going to explore some general questions concerning the types of parody found in nineteenth-century operetta. The philosopher Henri Bergson has rebutted the argument that laughter of the kind parody produces is achieved solely by degrading or trivializing that which is dignified or solemn in the original. He comments that the process can be reversed to equally humorous effect, as when disreputable behavior is presented as respectable.[103] He finds that a peculiarly English device, and certainly Gilbert and Sullivan offer plenty of examples (most notably in *The Pirates of Penzance,* 1879). We can begin by asking what were the specifically musical features that lent themselves to parody. The answer, broadly, is any of those devices that draw attention to themselves as "arty" or, indeed, artificial. Take vocal flourishes, roulades, or lengthy melismas; the parodist has only to exaggerate in order to emphasize their artifice. The same goes for expressive devices; the parodist can reveal their mechanics by emphasizing the signs in which sentiment is encoded. This is found in scenes where characters boast of the varied roles they are able to play: examples are Adele's "Spiel' ich die Unschuld vom Lande" in *Die Fledermaus* (1874) and Nanki-Poo's "A wand'ring minstrel I" in *The Mikado* (1885). Ironically, the effect of all this is to make operetta a more contrived genre than opera itself.

I must add a few words about areas I am not focusing on but that are nevertheless relevant to my theme. These include parodies of subject matter, plot, and dramaturgical devices. An example is the tale of the abduction of Helen rewritten by Henri Meilhac and Ludovic Halévy in their libretto for Offenbach's *La Belle Hélène* (1864). The operatic *femme fatale,* such as Dido or Cleopatra, is also parodied—"Ah! Fatale beauté!" cries Helen at one point. Meilhac and Halévy also introduce a topsy-turvy version of the bedroom scene from Bellini's *La sonnambula* (1831). In that opera, Amina enters Rodolfo's bedroom innocently, because she is sleepwalking. In Offenbach's operetta, Paris walks into Helen's bedroom and tells her she is dreaming—an assurance she readily accepts and, in doing so, furnishes Sigmund Freud with a useful illustration of "secondary revision" in dreams (cases in which the dreamer is surprised or repelled in his or her dream).[104] Needless to say, the elevated artistic status and moral ethos of grand opera and classical literature is continually subverted. Another area I am passing over is direct quotation or parody of a specific aria or ensemble from an opera. An example of direct quotation is found in *Orphée aux enfers* (1858), when Orpheus complains to the gods of his anguish at losing Eurydice and borrows the melody of Gluck's poignant aria "Che faro senza Euridice." The effect is comic because Orpheus would much rather be rid of her, and has only been driven to try to bring her back as a result of demands made by the character Public Opinion. Examples of specific parody of other operatic music in Offenbach are the Patriotic Trio in *La Belle Hélène,* modeled on a number in Rossini's *William Tell,* and the chorus of courtiers in *La Périchole* (1868), based on a similar chorus in Donizetti's *La Favorite* (1840).

What I am more interested in, here, are generalities. *Why* did certain features lend themselves to parody, and for what reasons did composers like Offenbach and Sullivan seize on them? Operettas delight in parodying two things above all else: the stock situations or clichés of opera, and the artifices of the genre. The scene in which Reginald Bun-

Example 4.2   Recitative, "Pur, s'ella è spenta!" Amilcare Ponchielli, *La Gioconda* (1876), act 4.

thorne unmasks himself as an "aesthetic sham" in *Patience* (1881) also unmasks the artificiality of dramatic soliloquies delivered in recitative. In act 4 of Amilcare Ponchielli's *La gioconda* (1876), for example, the heroine is confessing her innermost thoughts, wondering if there is a possibility of finishing off her sleeping rival and getting her man back (see ex. 4.2). Compare that with Bunthorne, who is ready to confess his own inner thoughts—provided nobody is listening (ex. 4.3).

Bunthorne's recitative makes play with the ridiculousness of private confessions before an audience: he confirms he is alone and unobserved, yet we in the audience know we're watching him. This recitative also exaggerates the drama of such scenes: notice how the short rhyming scheme provided by Gilbert and the loud orchestral stabs provided by Sullivan undermine the dramatic tension by their deliberate triviality. ("This air severe . . . is but a mere . . . veneer!")

Another favored moment for parody is the inquisitive or commenting operatic chorus, a body of people who somehow manage to think up identical questions simultaneously and pose them in a perfectly syn-

Example 4.3   Recitative, "Am I alone and unobserved?" *Patience* (1881), act 1.

chronized manner. In act 1 of *La sonnambula*, Teresa announces that the hour has come when the phantom appears; the chorus declares, "That's true!" Rodolfo inquires, "What phantom?" The chorus replies, "It's a mystery." Rodolfo pronounces it foolish. "What are you saying? If you only knew!" cries the shocked chorus. Rodolfo wants to know, and this functions as a cue for a song in which the villagers narrate the entire history of the phantom in strict tempo. The artificiality of this kind of interaction between solo character and chorus can be heightened if it concerns more mundane matters, as when Captain Corcoran arrives on board *H.M.S. Pinafore* (ex. 4.4).

Fun can also be made of the conventional operatic use of the chorus by stressing the chorus's inability to perform furtive actions or achieve the appropriate level of discreet silence demanded by certain scenes. The initially hushed and circumspect Gallic warriors in act 2 of Bellini's *Norma* (1831) suddenly throw caution to the winds to declaim loudly: "Let us prepare to accomplish our great task in silence" (ex. 4.5). Offenbach parodied this sort of thing with his heavy-footed carabinieri in *Les Brigands* (1869), as did Sullivan with his pirates (ex. 4.6).

The parody of operatic choruses is certainly not exhausted by these examples. Consider the conspiratorial group revealing dastardly plans sotto voce in a sinister staccato, as does the gang of cutthroats in act 2, scene 2, of Verdi's *Macbeth* (1847), or the conspirators of *Un ballo in maschera* (1859), and compare them with those in Charles Lecoq's *La Fille de Madame Angot* (1872; exs. 4.7, 4.8).

I turn now to stock scenes and clichés. The operatic curse is a powerful weapon; witness its effect in Verdi's *Rigoletto* (1851) and *Simon Boc-*

Example 4.4   Entrance of Captain Corcoran, *H.M.S. Pinafore* (1878), act 1.

Example 4.5   Chorus, "E in silenzio," *Norma* (1831), act 2.

Example 4.6   Chorus, "With cat-like tread," *The Pirates of Penzance* (1879), act 2.

Example 4.7   Chorus, "E sta l'odio," *Un ballo in maschera* (1859), act 1.

Example 4.8   Chorus, "Quand on conspire, quand sans frayeur" *La Fille de Madame Angot* (1873), act 2.

canegra (1857). Indeed, its impact is undiminished in the latter, even though poor Paulo has been tricked into cursing *himself.* Thus we find, in *Patience,* it is enough for Bunthorne merely to threaten to curse Archibald Grosvenor in order to get his way. At the opposite extreme from the venomous curse is the scene of rapture as young lovers fall into each other's arms. The scene of operatic *ebbrezza,* or rapture, is so familiar that in *La Périchole* an overjoyed Périchole and Piquillo need only remind us with an economical "joie extrême, bonheur suprême, et cetera, et cetera." After having restricted Nanki-Poo to an expression of "modified rapture" in *The Mikado,* Gilbert and Sullivan rang a new change on this type of scene in *Yeomen of the Guard* (1888) when, in the act 2 duet "Rapture, rapture," what Dame Carruthers interprets as joyful Sergeant Meryll interprets as ghastly. Plenty of other stock scenes are ripe for parody. In *La Grande-Duchesse de Gérolstein* (1867), the grand operatic ceremonial scene is mocked, as the Duchess hands over with a ritualistic gesture that talismanic object, her father's sword. Offenbach works up a portentous and throbbing Meyerbeerian accompaniment for soloist and chorus in the "couplets du sabre." Family escutcheons and oaths also provide fodder for amusement in operetta.

Alongside satire of the high moral tone adopted by operatic heroes and heroines, there is a joy in sending up the heroic style of their music, especially their vocal pyrotechnics, extended melismas, and cadenzas. Also begging to be sent up are the vocal flourishes that principal sopranos so often add as decoration while a chorus sings—for example, Amina's "Sovra il sen la man mi posa" (*La sonnambula*). They reappear skittishly in songs like "Poor wand'ring one" from *Pirates.* Once more, the parody works by highlighting artifice. It often works though the effect of bathos, which is created by providing elaborate melismas for the least likely words. When Helen realizes that Paris stands before her, the man who, in his famous judgment, awarded the prize of an apple to Venus, she cries out "l'homme à la pomme!" and proceeds to lavishly embellish the phrase. Sometimes, an exaggerated flourish can poke fun at the sentiments being expressed. An example is the melisma Sullivan writes to underline the assertion "He remains an Englishman" in *Pinafore* (1878) (ex. 4.9), choosing to elongate the syllable "Eng-" rather than "remains," which would not have had such an absurd effect. In *La Belle Hélène,* the concern felt for Menelaus's honor is revealed as false by the absurdity of the vocal flourishes (ex. 4.10).

This brings me to a final question: how is musical irony used in operetta? Irony is employed, of course, in the serious as well as the comic domain. In serious opera, we usually find irony of situation rather than irony communicated through music. Think of Delilah singing to Samson of her love in Saint-Saëns's opera. She wants him to believe it, and it sounds like the truth to us, too, even though we know she hates him; therefore, we perceive the irony of the scene. In musical communication, no less than verbal communication, there is no convention that

Example 4.9 "He remains an Englishman," *H.M.S. Pinafore,* act 2.

acts as a guarantee of sincerity. Language philosopher Donald Davidson argues forcibly that the "ulterior purpose of an utterance and its literal meaning are independent."[105] There are examples of bitter irony in tragic operas but, again, usually created by situation—think of the party taking place at the very moment of Laura's supposed death from poison in *La gioconda.* The new departure for irony in operetta is that it operates through a radical appropriation of stylistic conventions and signs. The "wrong" musical sign is used to great ironic effect; in other words, a song or aria may be double coded. An example is the martial air sung by Général Boum in *La Grande-Duchesse.* The verse is single coded: the bellicose words are given the appropriate musical signs, a march rhythm and a melody containing fanfare-like intervals; but the

Example 4.10 Concern for Menelaus's honor, *La Belle Hélène* (1864), Finale, act 2.

refrain is double coded: while the words tell of battlefield explosions and assert the character's military rank, the tune has the mannerisms of a café-concert song, including an emphasis on the sixth degree of the scale. The result is a deflation of the pomposity and violence of the General's language (ex. 4.11).

The possibilities for musical irony are many. Besides using the wrong signs, there is the opportunity to use the right signs, but for words that can scarcely bear the weight of those signs. For instance, the music of "Tit Willow" from *The Mikado* never once suggests a knowing smile at the ridiculous narrative. Then there is the typical parodic device of exaggeration. An example is the overblown patriotic style Sullivan uses for "When Britain Really Ruled the Waves" from *Iolanthe* (1882). And that prompts me to end with a warning on the subject of irony: some people never get it. Among them can be numbered those who have interpreted this last song as an illustration of Sullivan's bombastic chauvinism. Thus, against all expectations, an audience may need more critical engagement to understand the workings of operetta than those of opera. This would accord, too, with Walter Benjamin's conviction that one of the most successful methods of stimulating critical

Example 4.11   "A cheval sur la discipline," *La Grande-Duchesse de Gérolstein* (1867), act 1.

thought is through humor: "There is no better start for thinking than laughter. And, in particular, convulsion of the diaphragm usually provides better opportunities for thought than convulsion of the soul."[106]

Operetta rejoiced in exposing the mechanics of its stage production (or, one might say, in breaking frame), while "serious" opera became more and more concerned with concealing them. The latter did so in an attempt to create the illusionistic theatrical reality that Bertholdt Brecht later wished to overturn, believing it encouraged passive wallowing in a "reality" that, in some respects, might be linked to the "false consciousness" the Frankfurt School condemned. Operetta is prepared to reveal how the real is constructed as an illusion: in *Utopia Limited,* Gilbert and Sullivan expose the stage illusion of "real" emotion by giving the tenor a song about the impossibility of singing when the emotion that he feels actually exists as an offstage reality.

> I could sing, if my fervour were mock,
> It's easy enough if you're acting—
> But when one's emotion
> Is born of devotion
> You mustn't be overexacting.
> One ought to be firm as a rock
> To venture a shake in *vibrato,*
> When fervour's expected
> Keep cool and collected
> Or never attempt *agitato.*
>
> But, of course, when his tongue is of leather,
> And his lips appear pasted together,
> And his sensitive palate as dry as a crust is,
> A tenor can't do himself justice.[107]

Folk Music: Edification for the Uncritical

One late nineteenth-century development, and its impact on aesthetic debate, is yet to be considered. After midcentury, the education of taste was seen as vital to the appreciation of music. For this reason, Manns had introduced program notes at his concerts, and annotated programs were also provided when the Philharmonic Society moved to St. James's Hall in 1858.[108] Theodore Thomas, who was based in New York, was praised for his tours with an orchestra (which appears to have been made up entirely of German players) and for setting a "standard of orchestral excellence" in order to "raise public taste as that it shall reach the level of classic art."[109] The trouble was, some began to think education might not be enough. In line with that part of evolutionary discourse known as "recapitulation theory"—that the embryo evolving to adulthood recapitulates the evolutionary stages through which a race has passed—a *Musical Times* editorial foresees problems in bringing highly cultivated music to people whose mental development has been "handicapped in the struggle for existence by the law of heredity," and who have been "stunted morally and physically by their surroundings."[110] Fortuitously, around the time this editor was expressing his melancholy thoughts, an unexpected type of "easy-but-good" music had sprung from English soil in the form of folk music.

Carl Engel, writing in the 1860s and 1870s on national song, had accused English scholars of falling behind the rest of Europe in folk song research; in return, later English researchers chose to "diminish and distort" the role he had played in the folk song revival.[111] The English were certainly slow off the mark. Empress Elisabeth had been presented with a handsome bound volume of national melodies of the Austro-Hungarian Empire on her marriage to Franz Joseph in 1854.[112] In France, in 1852, almost as soon as he came to power, Napoléon III called for a collection of *chansons populaires*. This supposedly communal art offered a vision of a more unified France, as well as "a pure, uncorrupted heritage."[113] Politically conservative groups as well as utopian socialists found qualities to admire in these chansons—at least, until left-wing ideas began to gain currency among country folk. This interest in national song signals, however, the beginnings of an ideological schism that separated popular music that was created to make money from another kind of "people's music" that was believed to represent the natural expression of a nation or race.

In England, William Chappell's *Collection of National English Airs* (1838) was a landmark publication in its historical concerns and its attention to tunes, although it was not without an antecedent, the publication of the work of eighteenth-century collector Joseph Ritson in 1829. Importantly, Chappell had laid the foundation for his celebrated later publication *Popular Music of the Olden Time* (1855–59), which was hardly a work of folk song research but, in its comprehensiveness and its inclusion of tunes, went far beyond anything achieved before.[114] However, its appeal was mainly to the middle class, evidenced by the fact that it formed the substance of an evening entertainment by Miss Poole at the Gallery of Illustration, Lower Regent Street—an establishment so very respectable that it trembled even to call itself a theater.[115] Chappell himself was inclined to think of popular music in terms of class rather than town and country, as when he informs us that "Early One Morning" is one of "the most popular songs among the servant-maids of the present generation."[116]

The term "folk music" served as a means of bracketing off a form of people's music that could be considered unsullied by commercial enterprise. At the first annual meeting of the English Folk Song Society, Hubert Parry (who, significantly, was regarded as the leader of the English Musical Renaissance) remarked on the superiority of folk song to music hall song: the latter puts him in mind of "sham jewellery and shoddy clothes" and is for people with "false ideals" who mistake "the commonest rowdyism" for the highest expression of human emotion. He throws in an apparently casual comment about its being made "with a commercial object," but it is evident that the commercial aspect contributes enormously to the disgust he feels. When Parry turns to folk song, he stresses that it "grew in the heart of the people before they devoted themselves so assiduously to the making of quick returns."[117] Cecil Sharp fervently hoped that folk song would oust coarse, commercial popular song entirely; and one of its great advantages was that it avoided the problem of having to educate people in its appreciation.

> Now, one of the most remarkable qualities of the folk-song is its power of appeal to the uncritical, to those who, unversed in the subtleties of musical science, yet "know what they like." Its value lies in its possession of this dual quality of excellence and attractiveness. Flood the streets, therefore, with folk-tunes, and those, who now vulgarize themselves and others by singing coarse music-hall songs, will soon drop them in favor of the equally attractive but far better tunes of the folk. This will make the streets a pleasanter place for those who have sensitive ears, and will do incalculable good in civilizing the masses.[118]

Sharp wished to make a distinction along German lines between the "merely popular" song (*volkstümliches Lied*) and what had previously been referred to as "national" song but was now, he considered, better designated by the term "folk-song." However, the German term *Volkslied* is not synonymous with Sharp's definition of folk song—a song "not made by the one but evolved by the many," an anonymous creation of the "common people" who have undergone no education or training.[119] In contrast, the cover of Spina's publication of Strauss Jr.'s *Erinnerung an Covent Garden*, op. 329 (1868), describes these waltzes as being based on English *Volksmelodien*, though they are a mixture of music hall songs and drawing room ballads ("Champagne Charlie" alongside "Home, Sweet Home"). Sharp is influenced by the pseudo-science of race, believing folk song to be a "communal and racial product" that "embodies those feelings and ideas which are shared in common by the race which has fashioned it."[120]

In putting together some concluding thoughts, the question arises: was the schism between the "popular" and the "classical" created solely by market conditions and the reaction to them, or were there other social and political factors at work? Tia DeNora suggests the possibility that some of the old aristocracy in early nineteenth-century Vienna embraced the new concept of greatness in music "as a proactive attempt to maintain status in the face of the loss of exclusive control over the traditional means of authority in musical affairs."[121] Later in the century, William Weber argues, the revolutions of 1848 "lent a powerful impetus to the hegemonic status of classical music," since this music was associated with morally uplifting and cosmopolitan cultural qualities.[122] He remarks on the number of European choral societies that were turning to the oratorios of Handel, Haydn, and Mendelssohn during 1848–49. Nicholas Tawa sees 1830–70 as a period of stylistic transition to an indigenous American style, but Judith Tick shows that women composers often bucked the trend, since female musical "accomplishment" meant something that resonated of the European salon, not blackface minstrelsy.[123]

A myth came to bedevil popular music: the idea that there is a formula for popular success.[124] The editor of the *Musical World* in 1855 puts down the success of the song "The Ratcatcher's Daughter" (see chapter 7) to the "vitiated taste of the public." His formula for a popular success is that you must simply bear in mind that "people will always be led by the ear, and the public ear must be pleased."[125] But he soon begins to contradict himself by recounting the different public tastes in evidence at the opera house, the concert room, and the promenade concert. Frederick Corder, writing in 1889, looks at the failure of an expected hit and the unpredicted success of another piece and declares: "the true reasons of popularity have ever been a secret and a mystery."[126] Around this time, however, the early Tin Pan Alley firms of New York thought that they had lighted on a formula for success, and today the big corporations have not given up belief in its existence. Much of the critical antagonism toward popular music in the twentieth century had in the background an image of conveyor belts carrying prefabricated sections to be bolted together before being delivered to a mass public of passive consumers. As I write (in 2006), Mike McCready, the chief executive of Platinum Blue Music Intelligence, claims that he is able to predict hits within twenty seconds using the firm's database of previous hits and a "spectral deconvolution" method of analysis that extracts forty pieces of information about "deep structure."[127] It is worth emphasizing that there has never been any scientifically substantiated evidence to suggest that the key to popular success can be found solely in a particular kind of musical structure. The belief that structure is the source of success neglects the importance of the social aspects of music, the influence of friends and family, and the lifestyles people wish to lead.

The rift between art and entertainment widened in Vienna toward the century's close. The Theater an der Wien thought it could span the gulf, and began to offer opera as well as its traditional fare of *Spieloper*. In 1896–97, when it faced artistic and financial difficulties, the music critic Richard Wallaschek warned it to make a choice between opera and operetta, "given the complete separation that exists between these genres today."[128] This was the period when Vienna witnessed an increase in learned articles on music, an emphasis on theory and analysis, and a preference for abstraction and structural listening among erudite musicians; it was, of course, home to Heinrich Schenker and Arnold Schoenberg. Yet Hanslick, while holding popular dance music responsible for a decline in intellectual effort on the part of listeners, hailed Strauss Jr. after his death in 1899 as Vienna's "most original musical talent," and praised the *Blue Danube* as "a symbol for everything that is beautiful and pleasant and gay in Vienna."[129] This parallels the admiration that still existed in London for the music of Arthur Sullivan at the time he died, a year after Strauss Jr. The *Times* obituary for Sullivan acknowledged this high regard, found everywhere except, it noted wryly, among those "musicians of earnest and highly cultivated taste."[130]

Notwithstanding the appeal of folk music to those who were "uncritical," efforts to cultivate taste were undiminished. Henry Wood, discussing the initial planning of promenade concerts at Queen's Hall, London, in 1895, quotes the musical entrepreneur Robert Newmand (the Hall's lessee): "I am going to run nightly concerts and train the public by easy stages . . . [p]opular at first, gradually raising the standard until I have *created* a public for classical and modern music."[131] Here we have the term "popular" being used clearly in the sense of inferior (music of a lower standard) and also as something to be contrasted with "classical" music. At the first prom, songs alternated with orchestral and instrumental items (which included a cornet solo). "This was," Wood explains, "a new venture, and as such *it had to be popular.*"[132]

"Serious music" in the later nineteenth century became more and more confused with autobiography—the belief that it was a portrayal of "inner feelings." Composers were presumed to be offering something of themselves, something personal, and certainly not something concerning the self of the listener, beyond the recognition of a common humanity. A paradoxical antidote to the idea of art as autobiography is Josef Strauss's waltz *Mein Lebenslauf ist Lieb' und Lust!* op. 263, which, far from conveying the conviction that the composer's life is all love and pleasure, is a composition designed to convince listeners or dancers that *their* lives are like that. As an emotional summation of Josef Strauss's own curriculum vitae (*Lebenslauf*), a brief journey filled with constant work and cigar smoke, it rings so hollow that it can as readily prompt sadness as joy.

Bourgeois female accomplishments and working-class rational recreations now seemed insufficiently dedicated to the shrine of art. A correspondent complained to the editor of the *Musical Times* in 1880 about an article on notation in Grove's *Dictionary of Music,* that said that Tonic Sol-fa "could never be used for any other purpose than that of very commonplace singing."[133] As if that were not insult enough, the preface by Lucy Broadwood and J. A. Fuller Maitland to *English Country Songs* (1893) reveals antagonism from another quarter, that of the new breed of folk song collectors, toward Tonic Sol-fa choirs and their "fatuous part-songs." Even the oratorio had now declined in status, although in 1861 it had received unstinting praise: "The oratorio is the highest form of musical composition, combining in itself the two great divisions, vocal and instrumental, in their most complete development."[134] In the summer of 1880, the *New York Times* ran three editorials opposed to the enthusiasm for brass instruments and brass bands. At this time, Sousa increased the number of reeds in his band, bringing it closer to the classical orchestra and making it more acceptable to the music critics, though not all approved of the way he mixed the "classics" and the "popular."[135] In the first half of the century, popular music was possible in the "best of homes," but from now on the message of "high art" was that there was a "better class of music" and another kind that appealed to "the masses." This laid the ground for mass culture critique, which proceeds from the following group of negative premises: there is a type of culture solely about profit; it debases high culture by borrowing from it; it harms people by offering spurious gratification and making them passive consumers; and it reduces a society's total cultural quality.[136] The friction between entertainment and art continued well into the twentieth century. A law passed in Austria in 1936, and not challenged until the 1970s, enabled 2 percent of royalties derived from "entertainment" music (*Unterhaltungsmusik*) to be reallocated to those making "serious" music.[137]

II

STUDIES OF REVOLUTIONARY POPULAR GENRES

5

A Revolution on the Dance Floor, a Revolution in Musical Style

The Viennese Waltz

This chapter investigates and evaluates evidence for the claim that the Viennese version of the revolving dance known as the waltz stimulated the development of a revolutionary kind of popular music that created a schism between entertainment music (*Unterhaltungsmusik*) and serious music (*ernste Musik*). As a consequence, the idea of the "popular" changed, and although the concept of a music liked by many people did not disappear, popular or light music soon began to be associated with business and commercial success. That is why calling pieces like Mozart's divertimenti "popular" leads to confusion. I gave some consideration in the previous chapter to Carl Dahlhaus's view (though it was a view I contested) that a distinction should be drawn between the desire for wide appeal that arises from eighteenth-century philanthropy and one that he regarded as springing from the manipulations of nineteenth-century capitalism. Adopting William Weber's term, we might say a "general taste" prevailed in eighteenth-century concert life; yet that taste consensus was dissipated as nineteenth-century capitalism brought an increasingly commodified structure to bear on musical production. The consequence was that some music came to be promoted as serious—demanding learning and attentive listening—and another kind was promoted as entertainment.

Most accounts of the popularity of the dance music of nineteenth-century Vienna have tended to concentrate on the social history of the period and autobiographical information about the Strauss family.[1] Yet the origins of the Viennese waltz, its revolving movement and its innovative musical style, are still matters of uncertainty. It has been common, for instance, to emphasize the importance of the *Ländler* to the waltz and neglect the influence of the *Dreher*. The whirling type of dance had been popular in the German countryside since at least the mid–sixteenth century, and various authorities attempted to prohibit dances with unseemly turns (*unziemblichen Verdrehen*).[2] The *Dreher*, in particular, was opposed by ministers of religion, and it was this dance that led most directly to the waltz.[3] Turning or rotating dances (*drehen* means to turn, *walzen* to rotate) were regarded as morally reprehensible in high society because they were likely to cause a woman's skirt to fly up. However, they were not banned in Vienna, where the aristocracy liked to believe they had not lost touch with ordinary people, an attitude they were able to sustain because Vienna at the end of the eighteenth century did not suffer the poverty found in London or Paris. There was already a mania for dancing at that time, and it was satisfied by a large number of suburban dance halls. One energetic dance was the *Langaus*, which had a slide instead of the *Ländler's* hop and could thus be danced at faster speed. The waltz, which also had a gliding movement, developed in bars and taverns along the Danube. The river was much used for transport, and musicians from the country sailed downriver playing to passengers and in establishments close to where the boats were moored. Strauss Sr.'s father was an innkeeper on an island in the Danube in the suburb of Leopoldstadt.[4]

J. H. Kattfuss's *Taschenbuch für Freunde und Freundinnen des Tanzes* (Leipzig, 1800) says that the only difference between the steps of the *Dreher*, *Ländler*, and waltz is that the pace of the *Ländler* is slower. Yet the waltz had already developed other differences. In the *Ländler*, the woman revolved beneath the man's raised arm while he stamped a foot, and each of them revolved in opposite directions and around each other back-to-back, as well as performing other figures that do not appear in the waltz. Moreover, the feet are dragged in the waltz, giving a gliding motion to the whirling that marks it out as an indoor dance; hopping movements in the *Ländler* were suited to rough terrain, and country shoes with nails lent emphasis to the stamping. A gliding motion could be faster on wooden floors, and outdoor boots were frowned on in dance halls.[5] The first parquet floor was laid at the Monschein Hall in 1806, although in 1797 the *Journal des Luxus und der Moden* was already claiming that the Viennese waltz was the fastest.[6] Naturally, the faster the waltz, the tighter the grip that was needed on the bodies of each partner; it meant that, allowing for due decorum, waltzes tended to be played more slowly for the aristocracy. The tempo of the waltz altered to suit fashions in women's dresses. It slowed down for the narrower styles of the early nineteenth century, but when fuller skirts began to develop in the 1820s it speeded up again.

The waltz entered France (via Alsace) in the late eighteenth century, and came to England at the same time, but possessed many *Ländler*-

like features. In Thomas Wilson's manual on waltzing issued in 1816, we are still far from the Viennese type of similar date. [7] Moral worries continued (see chapter 3), now being concerned with eroticism, the face-to-face position, and the contact between bodies unshielded by heavy corsetry. The biggest initial boost to the Viennese waltz was the holding of the Peace Congress in Vienna, 1814–15. Diplomats at the Congress of Vienna (at the Hofburg) visited the palace ballrooms so frequently that the well-known quip arose, "le Congrès ne marche pas, il danse."

Unterhaltungsmusik *and Popular Style*

A crucial development occurred in the 1820s, in the dance music of Joseph Lanner (1801–43) and Strauss Sr. (1804–49). As a writer looking back on this period in the *Musical Times* of May 1895 declared, "Haydn and Mozart . . . left the courtly dance of the last century pretty much where they found it, but the Strauss waltz is almost a distinct creation."[8] Lanner and Strauss, and especially the latter, saw the possibility of a popular revolution in music, and created a style that was often consciously at odds with the art music of its time. It was a style that gave new meaning to entertainment music: the thesis here being that the concept of the "popular" began to embrace, for the first time, not only the music's reception but also the presence of specific features of style.[9]

It is the accent on beat 1 that is crucial to the waltz, though there is often has an accent on beat 3 also. The *Ländler* has a characteristic accent on beat 2, as can be found in Franz Schubert's *8 Ländler, D378*, for piano (1816). It is especially noticeable in the seventh of these dances, since Schubert marks the accent (see ex. 5.1).

Schubert introduced unexpected modulations into his later piano waltzes of the 1820s, and began to make more use of "um-pah-pah" figures (the term is "Hum-Ta-Ta" in Vienna). The waltz he published in *Moderne Liebeswalzer* in 1826 (D979) reveals stylistically his familiarity with Lanner's music (see ex. 5.2).[10]

The accent on beat 1 in the waltz came about as it gained speed; it is not such a noticeable feature of early waltzes. The "um-pah-pah" accompaniment is rare, or scantily applied, before Lanner and Strauss.[11] Another distinction between the waltz and *Ländler* is that the violin had not traditionally accompanied the *Ländler*, yet Strauss and Lanner

Example 5.1   Schubert, no. 7 of *8 Ländler*, D378 (1816).

Example 5.2 Schubert waltz from *Moderne Liebeswalzer* (1826).

made the most of their skills as violinists and composed idiomatically for this instrument. Waltzes had commonly been published in groups of six, each waltz being in a binary form consisting of two repeated eight-measure sections. Strauss established a new waltz structure of an introduction, a sequence of five waltzes (each binary), and a coda reprising the best tunes. He first used this form in *Gute Meinung für die Tanzlust* (Good opinion for dance pleasure), op. 34, composed for the Carnival of September 1830. Before this, he generally preferred six waltzes and a coda with little or no introduction. The new form was, however, already there in embryo in his *Heitzinger-Reunion-Walzer,* op. 24 (1829).[12] Carl Maria von Weber's widely played "rondo brilliant" for piano, *Aufforderung zum Tanz* (Invitation to the dance) of 1819, was undoubtedly an influence, since its unique feature was that it framed a set of waltzes with an introduction building expectation, and a reflective epilogue. Strauss did more than set in place a structural convention; he also established a distinctive Viennese character and sound, partly drawn from traditional airs and partly invented.[13] *Gute Meinung für die Tanzlust* is again a crucial work in this regard, with its yodeling figures (waltz 1a and 2b), sighing appoggiaturas (1b, and the *wienerische Note* in 5a), and the ease with which it moves from modern syncopations (2a) and chromaticism (3b) to old *Ländler* patterns (4a and 5b). The new dance music of the 1830s consolidated the Viennese identification of themselves with this style. Composer Richard Heuberger, who experienced the music of this period as it first entered the ballroom, claimed that people recognized their own traits in it.[14]

Strauss began to extend the eight-measure sections of the waltz to sixteen measures, sometimes by having a varied repeat, so that instead of theme A (eight measures) × 2, we have A + A1 (making sixteen measures) × 2. Another technique was to return to the A section after the B section. Allowing ideas to reappear also gives coherence to the waltz sections. His willingness to introduce irregularities is evident even in his early *Täuberln-Walzer,* op. 1 (1827). The third waltz theme has a second half that is twelve measures long, and the final waltz theme, 7b (8b in the piano version) is also twelve measures.[15] All its other themes are eight measures, but some repeats are varied.[16] Waltz theme 6b (7b in the piano version) shows that Strauss's inventiveness regarding syncopation is with him from the beginning (see ex. 5.3).

Example 5.3   Strauss Sr., *Täuberln-Walzer,* op. 1 (1827), waltz 6b.

The short syncopated note as notated here might suggest an anticipation of the second beat of the measure that was to become one of the most recognizable features of Viennese waltz style, the Viennese lilt (the slight anticipation of the first "pah" of the "oom-pah-pah").

The *Täuberln-Walzer* is scored for a small orchestra consisting of flute, two clarinets, two horns (doubling trumpets), trumpet, three violins, double bass, and timpani (E and B, tonic and dominant). There has been speculation that Lanner had commandeered the viola and cello players for his own orchestra after his split with Strauss, but it may well be that Strauss liked this combination (in fact, when he began to increase the size of his orchestra, he added wind rather than strings). The sound of a double bass (often a smaller model than the norm) rather than cello has a history in Viennese dance music, and elsewhere in Austria, as some of Mozart's early divertimenti show.[17] Lanner composed his *Dornbacher Ländler,* op. 9 (c. 1824), for three violins and double bass. Early Viennese dance music often had two violins and a double bass, plus a guitar or clarinet and percussion.

The "pushed" note—the note played slightly ahead of the beat—became a characteristic feature of twentieth-century popular music. As just noted, it is already in evidence in the Viennese waltz, and evident from the notation (ex. 5.4).

Elsewhere, the "pushing" is not so mechanistic as to require or, indeed, gain clarity from being notated. It is often a question of "feel," as in the "swing feel" of jazz. It cannot be performed mechanically. In another pointer to the future of popular music (the importance of African-American music making), it is interesting to find that the person who might be thought of as the initiator of the popular music revolution (Strauss Sr.) was compared to an African by the writer Heinrich

Example 5.4   Strauss Sr., *Carnivals-Spende,* op. 60 (1833), waltz 5b.

Laube, later director of the Burgtheater, who heard him playing at the Sperl gardens in Vienna in 1833: "Typically African, too, is the way he conducts his dances; his own limbs no longer belong to him when the desert-storm of his waltz is let loose; his fiddle-bow dances with his arms; the tempo animates his feet."[18] As for the revolutionary angle, Laube remarks:

> The power wielded by the black-haired musician is potentially very dangerous; it is his especial good fortune that no censorship can be exercised over waltz music and the thoughts or emotions it arouses. . . . I do not know what other things besides music Strauss may understand, but I do know that he is a man who could do a great deal of harm if he were to play Rousseau's ideas on his violin. In one single evening the Viennese would subscribe to the entire *contrat social.*[19]

Richard Wagner, who first visited Vienna at age nineteen, endorses Laube's impression, describing in *Mein Leben* the frenzy he witnessed at Strauss's playing.[20] Strauss biographer Heinrich Jacob sums up the uniqueness of Strauss's achievement in the phrase "till then no music had had such demotic strength."[21]

His music was of a type that related little, however, to that which might previously have been considered "of the people." It was not music to accompany work, whether milking the cow or making the hay, nor did it function as part of traditional religious or secular rituals. It was music forming part of an entertainment provided not to everyone but rather to those prepared to purchase tickets. It was for the urban social dance, not the festive village dance. Unlike rural types of music, it was produced for urban leisure-hour consumption. That being so, it had the advantage of being more readily available for audiences elsewhere, since cities were beginning to share much in common in the nineteenth century. Even a locally marked artifact could be widely desirable if its origin was urban: a Parisian gown might be sought out by fashionable society in London or New York, although rural costume would be considered "fancy dress" outside its country of origin. The music of the Strauss family was, likewise, recognizably of a certain *place,* Vienna, but its primary purpose—at least, in the early days—was to satisfy expectations in a particular urban *space,* that of the dance hall. The music also had an urban subject position. When folk idioms were evoked, they were being served up for an urban audience. The drone effects and yodeling melodic phrases of *Dorfschwalben aus Österreich* (Village swallows), op. 164 (1864), a waltz by Josef Strauss (1827–70), are scarcely intended to be any more authentic than its imitation bird calls—there is a sense of an eyebrow being raised humorously over these devices. They are what an urban middle-class audience would recognize as rural and not what an Upper Austrian farmer would recognize as such. Even Jacob, who believed Josef had "a realistic feeling for nature," admits that this waltz was "the work of a man who spent his life in closed rooms."[22]

Stylistic Features

When examining Viennese waltz style, we should not neglect the importance of nonnotated performance practices such as the anticipated second beat, the use of accelerando, strongly marked ritardandi, and so forth. They all require musical "feel," just as do later features of popular music performance, such as "swing" and "groove." Strauss Sr. demonstrated his awareness of the importance of popular music performance conventions that are suggestive of spontaneity and intuition rather than inflexibility and subservience to a musical score when he asked Philippe Musard if he might play with his orchestra in order to acquire an idiomatic understanding of French quadrille playing. Other countries, in turn, needed to acquire the feel of the Viennese waltz. The anticipated second beat of the accompaniment is not something that happens relentlessly—it depends on context; but the context is judged as much by feel as by an assessment of the melodic rhythm. Similarly, you have to feel that a certain pushing and dragging of tempo is appropriate: for example, sensing the need to pull the tempo back slightly and to add gentle accents to each note as the melody strides downward after having reached its high point in the third phrase of the first waltz of Josef Strauss's *Sphären-Klänge,* op. 235 (1868). When New Yorkers finally got to hear a Viennese waltz played idiomatically (during Strauss Jr.'s tour), they were struck by the "life and color" in the performance: "It is really wonderful how a *pianissimo* or a *forte,* a *retardando* [*sic*] or a *crescendo,* an emphatic accent or other mark of expression animates, improves and heightens the effect."[23]

A crucial feature of the Viennese waltz style was its treatment of rhythm (as Berlioz recognized when he heard Strauss Sr. in Paris). Rhythm is more important to the music's functional purpose than is melody. Rhythm *makes* the dance, as well as signifying the dance type. Memorable rhythmic motives frequently take precedence over melodic development, nowhere more so than in the first waltz of *Carnivals-Spende,* which is something between a yodel and a donkey's bray (ex. 5.5).

Example 5.5   Strauss Sr., *Carnivals-Spende,* op. 60 (1833), waltz 1a.

Example 5.6   Strauss Sr., *Krapfen-Waldel-Walzer,* op. 12 (1828), waltz 6b.

Strauss Sr. also enjoys the kind of cross-rhythms that suggest two different meters are being played at the same time (ex. 5.6).

Even when longer melodic phrases appear, they tend to be characterized by unexpected rhythmic turns, accents (often emphasized by an *acciaccatura*), and syncopation. In the first waltz theme of Strauss Sr.'s *Erinnerung an Berlin,* op. 78 (1835), the imitations that punctuate phrases imitate the rhythm but not the pitches of notes. This prioritizing of the rhythmic level over the pitch level is rarely found in nineteenth-century "classical" music (with the exception of the dance-loving Austrian composer Anton Bruckner).

Strauss Sr. was fond of syncopation, especially in his polkas and *galops,* but the syncopated note is usually accented, unlike the novel kind of syncopation introduced in blackface minstrelsy (discussed in chapter 6). The syncopation in the Trio of the *Sperl Polka,* op. 133 (1842), for example (see ex. 5.7a), can be found already in Beethoven's Piano Sonata op. 31, no. 1, a sonata that also contains examples of "pushed" syncopation.

Example 5.7   (a) Strauss Sr., *Sperl Polka,* op. 133 (1842), Trio; (b) Beethoven, Piano Sonata No. 16 in G, op. 31, no. 1 (1802), first movement, bars 66–69.

Example 5.8   Strauss Sr., *Carnevals-Spende*, op. 60 (1833), waltz 4a.

The use of syncopation in Strauss Sr. acts as a foil to the predictability of the dance rhythm. The fourth waltz of *Carnevals-Spende* (Carnival donation), op. 60 (1833), contains timpani strokes that anticipate each new phrase by one beat (ex. 5.8).[24]

Max Schönherr has analyzed the different rhythmic waltz types, and arrived at sixteen rhythmic models.[25] Linke thinks he has missed some, and adds an interesting analysis of polyrhythmic patterns.[26] Schönherr relates the syncopated variety of waltz to the Bohemian *Furiant* (with its hemiola pattern). The hemiola rhythm is a characteristic of Lanner, and appears in the first waltz theme of one of his best-known waltzes, *Die Schönbrunner*, op. 200 (1842). Strauss Jr. makes use of this particular syncopated rhythm in the third waltz of *An der schönen blauen Donau* (On the beautiful blue Danube), op. 314 (1867).

Since the *Blue Danube* is so well known, I am going to use it to illustrate features of Viennese popular dance style. There is no great change in style between the music of Strauss father and son: Norbert Linke shows how Strauss Jr.'s style remained indebted to his father's.[27] Short motivic ideas continue to provide the material on which many waltzes are built, and antecedent–consequent structure is usually forgone in preference to call-and-response or dialogue between instruments (as in waltz 1a).[28] The orchestra Strauss Jr. employs in the *Blue Danube* is larger than that his father was accustomed to use, and the son uses his orchestral imagination (evident from the beginning of his career) to much effect in the introduction and coda. Nevertheless, many of the devices of orchestration that follow were already typical of his father's dance music: staccato and pizzicato (staccato violin and pizzicato cello in waltz 1b); short figures being highlighted with another instrument (the piccolo in waltz 2); shifting colors, as doubling instruments are changed during phrases of violin melody (the woodwind and brass in waltz 3a); cellos doubling the melody one or two octaves below (waltzes 1a, 2, and 4) or moving in parallel tenths below the melody (waltz 3a); trumpets being made to stand out by giving them a distinctive rhythm (waltz 4a); emphasizing the dance rhythm with percussion (the snare drum in waltz 3b); and saving additional percussion to bring excitement to a climactic section (waltz 5b). The use of a trumpet to double the melody (waltz 2b) is a feature of popular orchestration, creating an effect that would have been thought vulgar in *ernste Musik*. A change of texture, linked to contrasted dynamics, may be used for a responding phrase, as in waltz 1b (an example from Strauss Sr.'s output is the *Beliebte Annen-Polka,* op. 137, 1842). It is as if a hesitant, questioning "do you think we might . . ." receives a confident, affirmative "of course we can!"

A frequent melodic feature is the upward-leaping interval, often in Scotch snap rhythm or, as in waltz 1a of the *Blue Danube,* with the lower note written as an *acciaccatura.* The effect seems typically Viennese and may derive from the idiomatic violin technique of crossing strings with the bow, or it may be indebted to the yodels of the Tyrol. Another characteristic Viennese melodic device, this time surely of urban rather than rural provenance, is the use of chromatic appoggiaturas (waltz 4a). Three other melodic techniques are to hold a note at the end of a phrase while other melodic figures occur in the accompaniment (the cellos in 1a), to introduce melodic decoration by other instruments at a phrase ending so as to link to the next phrase (the cellos in 5a), and to write a countermelody (the flute in the closing section of the coda). Strauss Jr. did not invent these techniques; the last three can be heard in his father's *Fest-Lieder* waltz, op. 193 (1846). Moreover, that waltz shows that his father was extending some sections of the waltz beyond sixteen measures (though not to the thirty-two-measure sections found in the *Blue Danube*).

Waltz melodies are frequently characterized by grace notes, and the *Blue Danube* holds plenty of examples. Strauss Sr., in his early days, must have made an impact with the number of *acciaccaturas* he sometimes used (for instance, in the penultimate waltz of the *Täuberln-Walzer* or the first waltz of *Wiener-Carneval-Walzer,* op. 3, 1827). These grace notes had previously been most associated with the "Turkish style," rather than the typical "classical" style (though *acciaccaturas* developed as a way of giving an accent to certain notes in music for non-velocity-sensitive keyboard instruments of the seventeenth century). The arpeggio-based theme of the *Blue Danube* has an ancestor in Strauss Sr.'s *Loreley-Rhein-Klänge,* op. 154 (1843). Strauss Jr. had learnt about the dramatic use of chords from his father, and imitated the loud diminished seventh that begins the second half of the first waltz in *Loreley-Rhein-Klänge* in his *Sinngedichte,* op. 1 (1844). In the *Blue Danube,* abrupt changes of key have a similar effect: the second half of waltz 2, for instance, plunges suddenly into B-flat major, the first melody note D acting as a pivot point between the new key and the tonic D major.

What is most striking and revolutionary about the harmonic style is the use of free-floating major sixths and major sevenths. The *Blue Danube* has an example of the tonic with added sixth in the fourth phrase of waltz 1a (see ex. 5.9a). On a technicality, it may be argued that the sixth is resolved via octave transposition in the cello part, but the ear neither demands nor needs this reassurance of musical "correct grammar." A major sixth is added to the minor triad in waltz 2b of *Wein, Weib und*

Example 5.9   (a) Strauss Jr., *An der schönen blauen Donau,* op. 314 (1867), waltz 1a; (b) Strauss Jr., *Künstlerleben,* op. 316 (1867), waltz 4b; (c) Strauss Jr., *Geschichten aus dem Wienerwald,* op. 325 (1868), waltz 1a.

(a)

(b)

(c)

Gesang, op. 333 (1869). These dissonances—treated as if consonances—may be caused by parallel thirds or parallel sixths (see ex. 5.9b, c).

In the *Kaiser-Walzer* (Emperor waltz), op. 437 (1889), in addition to dissonant sixths and sevenths (waltz 1a), Strauss begins to use seconds and ninths: see the close of waltz 1a and measure 5 of waltz 3a. Josef had already pointed the way in the first waltz theme of *Dynamiden (Geheime Anziehungskräfte),* op. 173 (1865).

Peter Van der Merwe notes "the relation between melody and harmony had received a new twist" in the nineteenth century that perplexed theorists who were used to explaining the relationship of melody notes to accompanying chords.[29] The new popular style had begun to use notes that could not be explained with reference to the "rules" of classical harmony. Moreover, Van de Merwe points out that melody and harmony "seldom go in harness" as they do in the classical style: a sequential melody (like the opening waltz of *Künstlerleben,* op. 316, 1867) does not necessitate sequential harmonies, and vice versa.[30] Waltz 3b of Strauss Sr.'s *Sperls Fest-Walzer,* op. 30 (1829), is a very early example of his treatment of the sixth as an addition to the tonic chord in a way that scarcely demands resolution. (The melodic sequence suggests it is

Example 5.10   Strauss Sr., *Sperls Fest-Walzer,* op. 30 (1829), waltz 3b.

as much part of the tonic harmony as the leading note is part of the dominant in the first measure; see ex. 5.10.)

The added sixth permeates many of his waltzes, and it is part of the new Viennese sound that Linke sees as largely Strauss's achievement.[31] The free-floating sixth passed into popular music elsewhere and, as we shall see in chapter 7, was one of the things about London music hall songs that irritated high cultural critics like Hubert Parry. Another feature of the new Viennese sound is the *wienerische Note,* the leading note that falls rather than rises, producing a yearning effect over subdominant or supertonic harmony. It can be heard strikingly, approached uncompromisingly by a leap of a major seventh, in Strauss Sr.'s waltz *Heimath-Klänge* (Homeland sounds), op. 84 (1836) (see ex. 5.11).

Strauss Sr. moved toward more cohesiveness in his waltz structures as the 1830s wore on, using inner connections in his *Erinnerung an Berlin* of 1835. At the same time that he sought greater unity, he showed a concern with variety of phrasing—upbeat phrases, on-the-beat phrases, and phrases of different lengths, though usually obeying a regular hypermetric scheme of four-measure units.[32] In waltz 4 of *Erinnerung an-Berlin,* by delaying the entry of the bass and accompanying chords, Strauss Sr. deceives the listener into hearing the first measure as a three-beat anacrusis, thus creating an ambiguity between the phrasing structure and the regular measure groupings within the eight-measure sections (the hypermeter). This would not be possible in the old figure dances, but the waltz is not a figure dance—in a certain sense, as Mark Twain put it: "You have only to spin around with frightful velocity and steer clear of the furniture."[33]

The first waltz of the *Blue Danube,* the tune of which also forms the basis of the romantic introduction, has an anacrusis of a whole mea-

Example 5.11   Strauss Sr., *Heimath-Klänge,* op. 84 (1836), waltz 1b.

Example 5.12   (a) Strauss Sr., *Loreley-Rhein-Klänge,* op. 154 (1843), waltz 2a; (b) Strauss Jr., *An der schönen blauen Donau,* op. 314 (1867), waltz 1a.

sure's duration, extended further by an additional beat in succeeding phrases. There is almost a sense of bass and melody being one measure adrift, just as there is in waltz 2a of his father's *Loreley-Rhein-Klänge* (see ex. 5.12).

A five-measure melodic phrase synchronizes the parts (his father used a three-measure phrase to do likewise). Waltz 1b has a two-beat anacrusis, and begins without preparation in the dominant key. It shares melodic connections with 1a (see ex. 5.13).

Waltz 2a returns to the tonic, but begins with dominant seventh harmony. Against idiomatic string accompaniment, the new melody reveals rhythmic connections with the woodwind interjections in 1a, and varies a legato idea from the penultimate phrase of 1a. Waltz 2b is contrasted in key and dynamics and introduces a syncopated idea that anticipates the next waltz. Waltz 3 begins with a melody that introduces the cross-rhythm 3/2 against 3/4, while the second half introduces a cross-rhythm of 3/8 against 3/4 (see ex. 5.14).

Waltz 4, introduced by four measures of modulation, illustrates the necessity for knowledge about performance practice that is not to be

Example 5.13   Strauss Jr., *An der schönen blauen Donau,* op. 314 (1867),
waltz 1 (measures 30–32, 37–40).

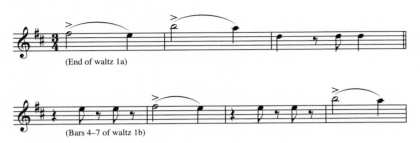

found written in the score. It begins with a tune that demands rubato
performance and proceeds to a second half that needs to be *più mosso*
but in strict tempo. Once more, thematic relationships are evident: the
rhythm of the first measure of 4a is that of the second measure of 3b,
and the rhythm of the sixth measure of 4b is akin to that of the third
measure of waltz 3b. There is an interesting harmonic sleight of hand
between the two halves of waltz 4. The end of the first half implies a
return to the tonic key, but it is thwarted by a sforzando chord. However, this is an example of Strauss's long-term planning, since this passage will be used to return the music to the tonic following the reap-
pearance of waltz 4a in the coda.

A modulating section of ten measures establishes the dominant
key, and the final waltz begins with an anacrusis of a whole measure's
duration, as did the first waltz. Its second half has no upbeat, and its

Example 5.14   (a) Strauss Jr., *An der schönen blauen Donau,* op. 314 (1867),
waltz 3a; (b) waltz 3b.

tune is related to the first half as well as to waltz 4b. It conveys clearly a sense of being a climactic section, with a feeling of exhilaration that is enhanced by the rhythmic figures on the bass instruments during the melody's sustained notes at phrase endings. The long coda then begins with its reminiscences of waltz themes 3a, 2a, 4a and, finally, 1a. After a general pause, there is a return to the romantic atmosphere of the introduction, but with echoing phrases on solo flute that convey a valedictory sentiment as the waltz concludes.

Music and Business

The categorization of a type of urban music as *Unterhaltungsmusik* was inextricably linked to the industrial production of sheet music and the growth of the music entertainment business. An international market for popular music had opened up in the West in which the popular managed to bear a local character at the same time as it transcended the local. At the end of his life, Strauss Sr. had succeeded in becoming the world's most popular musician.

> Strauss is the most popular musician on earth. His waltzes enrapture the Americans, they resound over the Wall of China, they triumph in the African bivouac, and a Viennese woman friend of mine wrote recently about how deeply it moved her, when she entered onto Australian soil and a beggar with a Strauss waltz asked for alms. In Europe, he spread personally the thrice-sweet teachings of the divine carelessness of the old Vienna.[34]

His early steps had been taken in partnership with Joseph Lanner, a glove maker's son born at Oberdöbling near Vienna in 1801. Lanner, an ex-member of Michael Pamer's dance band, had formed a trio consisting of two violins and guitar, and before long asked Johann Strauss— also of petit bourgeois origin—to join him.[35] The band next became a string orchestra, but Lanner and Strauss went their separate ways in 1825.[36] Rivalry began between the two, especially after the success of Strauss's *Kettenbrücke-Walzer*, op. 4 (1827), and each musician had passionate admirers—Strauss's music was found fiery, Lanner's sweeter, more sentimental.[37] Lanner was honored with the aristocratic engagement at the Redoutensäle; Strauss was hired at the bourgeois Sperl dance hall. It might have been thought that Lanner had achieved higher status, but Strauss was more aware of the new commercial age and its possibilities. He had been one of the first to realize that it was financially more advantageous to issue tickets for performances in parks and gardens than to take postperformance collections. He built up his own orchestra into a highly disciplined unit, gaining experience performing in inns and dance halls (several of which establishments appear in the titles of his early dances). He then set his sights on making money and fame by touring, something Lanner was not disposed to undertake.

Lanner was less inclined to embrace modernity; symptomatic of this was that he was fonder of the *Ländler* than Strauss (his early dance compositions were *Ländler*). However, his contribution to the new popular style was considerable, and he composed some hugely popular waltzes, such as *Pesther-Walzer,* op. 93 (1834), *Hofball-Tänze,* op. 161 (1840), and *Die Romantiker,* op. 167 (1840).

Strauss was a skilled businessman who understood well how commerce and music might mix effectively. An exhibition held in Vienna in 2004 that focused on the "show business world" of Strauss Sr. revealed how he became a model of "how to plan and achieve success in the entertainment industry."[38] He knew the publicity value of the topical or fashionable when seeking ideas and choosing titles for his compositions, and how to gain celebrity by developing a charismatic stage persona and involving himself in open-air spectacles with sensational effects of scenery, lighting, and fireworks, designed and arranged by his friend Carl Hirsch. The tours, however, were what, more than anything, helped to promote sales of his publications and to make him an international star.

New forms of organization are necessary for the growth of a new art world: the Strauss Orchestra was crucial to building Strauss's reputation and disseminating the new music via its many tours. Having triumphed in Berlin in 1834, and within the next two years toured throughout Germany, Belgium, and the Netherlands, he set his sights on France and England. During his stay in Paris in 1837, he gave a series of thirty concerts in association with Musard. He was initially concerned that his orchestra was a third the size of Musard's (Berlioz counted twenty-six players), but these concerts sealed his fame.[39] He toured much of Britain the next year (making plentiful use of the railways) and also gave concerts in Ireland. The *Times* described his first English concert in Hanover Square, 17 April 1838, as "most extraordinary and altogether novel," the reviewer being much taken with the precision of the playing.[40] On 28 June that year he played with his orchestra in the open air, in front of London's Reform Club, for Queen Victoria's coronation. He was very busy in London, playing for dances as well as for garden parties and concerts, and creating an appetite for Viennese dance music that lasted long after his departure. The editor of the *Musical World,* writing of the Lyceum Promenade Concerts in 1839, says: "As for Strauss and Lanner, they turn our heads."[41] This editor then explains to readers the functional nature of the structure of a Viennese waltz, that it has an introduction for partners to greet each other, a four- or five-movement waltz, and a coda that recapitulates ideas. Even the overall duration of the waltz is perceived to have a social significance: "Each piece lasts about ten minutes; being the time during which a sober person is thought capable of spinning without nausea or prostration."[42]

Strauss toured with his dance orchestra primarily to give concerts, which was very much a new departure. Dance orchestras played at dance halls not concert halls. The desire to exhibit the skill of his musicians lies behind a witty piece like *Erinnerung an Ernst,* op. 126 (1840), which acts as an early "guide to the instruments of the orchestra," featuring among other things a piccolo solo and a double bass solo.[43] Linke calls the *Strauss-Kapelle* the world's first touring orchestra.[44] Strauss did, indeed, wish to tour the world: his desire to visit America after Britain was thwarted only when his homesick orchestra refused to go. Because Strauss directed as the lead violinist, and not with a baton, there was more sense of immediacy in his concerts than in those of Jullien. As tribute to the newness of Strauss's music and his vigorous style of playing, the adjective "electric" was common.[45] It was necessary to see him to feel the whole effect (one suspects he may have inspired "air violin" playing among some of his admirers). The energy of the performance seemed to be drawn from the composition like a charge from a battery: the *Wanderer* in January 1846 said of his new waltz *Moldau-Klänge,* op. 186, that it was full of electric energy.[46] In the late 1830s and early 1840s, electricity was associated with sparks and magnetism (the battery had already been invented). It was a fresh and exciting field of scientific research: the first volume of Michael Faraday's *Experimental Researches in Electricity,* important to the development of the electric motor and dynamo, appeared in 1839.

Strauss was the international Waltz King by 1840. He had gradually expanded the orchestral forces used in dance music, and had also collaborated with military bands and male choirs (*Liedertafel* groups). He had made lots of money in his lifetime, but much of it had been spent on travel and accommodation, and paying his orchestra a good salary. It is difficult to get an idea of the value of money at this time except by comparing costs. A statement of expenditure for a summer concert in the Brühl, near Vienna, runs as follows (sums are in gulden):

Illumination	700
Installation (platform, etc.)	c. 700
Police (to keep order)	90
Advertising (newspapers, posters, etc.)	180
Travel expenses	30
Other costs	600

The box office takings were 2,800, so Strauss on this occasion earned 300 gulden.[47]

Capitalist enterprise grew swiftly during the years of Strauss's rise to fame: sheet music publishers and instrument makers began to build thriving businesses in the 1820s. The capitalist market demanded that music should not only serve a purpose, but should do so with the greatest possible economic success.[48] Music making in the home was on the increase among the bourgeoisie—a side effect of Metternich's repressive control of the public sphere.[49] Tobias Haslinger published Strauss's music in many different arrangements to cater to the variety of instruments used in domestic performances. Title pages of these arrangements were given eye-catching illustrations to ensure they were as attractive to customers as possible. Strauss was the first to see the value of the youth market for sheet music; in 1839, he and Tobias Haslinger introduced a waltz series for girls, containing piano arrangements "in leichtem Style und in leichten Tonarten" (in easy style and easy keys).[50] Other collections followed, such as easy quadrilles in 1841. Strauss also published in other countries: Robert Cocks was publishing his music in London, including his set of waltzes *Huldigung der Königin Victoria von Grossbritannien* (Homage to Queen Victoria), op. 103 (1838), which had an introduction based on "Rule, Britannia!" and a coda quoting "God Save the Queen!"

A characteristic of the consumption of commercial popular music, then as now, is the appetite for novelty. Viennese publishers made much more money out of Strauss than Schubert and Chopin, because the novel was exactly what Strauss supplied. His sons continued to do so: Strauss Jr. sometimes included attention-grabbing effects that might be considered gimmicks—or might be accepted simply as good fun— such as the rifle shot near the end of his *Jäger-Polka*, op. 229 (1859) and the cracking of the whip in his quick polka *Im Sturmschritt!* op. 348 (1871). In the years when an interest in old music was developing alongside the formation of a canon of classical works, Viennese dance music was a business thriving on the desire for the new and fashionable, and on expectations of dancing excitedly to the hits of the Carnival season.

Strauss Jr.'s publisher in Vienna until late 1851 was Pietro Mechetti, though H. F. Müller had also issued some of his music. Then he moved to Carl Haslinger (son of Tobias), till arguments arose in 1863 over missing fees from Haslinger's partner Büttner, who had been publishing his music in Russia. Strauss was then thinking of starting his own firm, but C. A. Spina, who had already signed Josef (since Haslinger had secured Johann), contracted to publish his music from *Morgenblätter*, op. 279 (1864), onward. Haslinger cut his losses and set his sights on the emerging waltz star Carl Ziehrer. Spina soon reaped the reward of his investment in Strauss, and no more so than when he had to make one hundred plates (sufficient for a million copies) to cope with demand for the *Blue Danube*. His business success ensured that other publishing businesses saw his firm as prey for horizontal integration; it changed hands twice in the 1870s. *An der schönen blauen Donau* had been commissioned for the Wiener Männergesang-Verein (Men's Choral Association) by their director, Johann Herbeck; the association's poet, Josef Weyl, was to add his much-criticized words when Strauss supplied the waltz.[51] Its reception had been muted when the choral version had its premiere on 15 February 1867 at a masked ball in the Dianabad-Saal in Vienna, but in instrumental form it had triumphed in Paris at the World Exhibition of that same year.[52] The coda, much extended for the instrumental version, was praised particularly. Yet *Aus den Bergen*, op. 292 (1864), had a 184-measure coda, so it was not a sudden innovation. Strauss Sr. may well have been music's first world star, but his son's *Blue Danube* was the first worldwide hit.[53] Spina sold it all over the globe (including Africa, Australia, and South America).[54]

Biedermeyer Vienna has a reputation as a time of comfort and docility, despite the repressive censorship and control imposed by the chancellor, Clemens Metternich, but public quiescence was encouraged in the 1830s by there being plenty of food, and it was further ensured by the absence of an organized working class.[55] This state of affairs did not continue: factories were being built in the 1840s, and soon poverty, alienated labor, and unemployment were on the rise. After several years of economic depression, revolution broke out in 1848 (see chapter 3); yet by the mid-1850s, the bourgeoisie had regrouped and were sufficiently strong in number, influence, and affluence to hold their own society dances. Strauss Jr.'s *Handels-Elite-Quadrille*, op. 166, was composed for the merchants' ball at the Sperl that took place during the Carnival of 1855. The Sperl began to go downmarket as it widened its appeal in this decade, and high-status patrons became discomforted by encountering there too many of Leopoldstadt's petite bourgeoisie. Fasching was a big time for dancing: the playing order from a ball given by the Strauss orchestra during the Carnival of 1864 shows that waltzes alternated with either polkas or quadrilles, with pauses of four to seven minutes between dances. This was probably done to make sure people were not made too giddy by the whirling motion of waltzes. There was an interval of forty-five minutes, and the program lasted three hours in total.[56]

Johann Strauss Jr. was born in 1825, and his quarrels as a young man with his father, especially over his father's determination that he should not become a musician, have been well covered by biographers. When Strauss Sr. separated from his wife and family, however, he lost much of his control over his son's behavior. The young Johann set out on his own in 1844, age nineteen, at the relatively new establishment Dommayer's Casino, Hietzing (near Schönbrunn), because his father, aided by Hirsch, had managed to prevent his performing elsewhere in Vienna. He had managed to put together an orchestra from the many unemployed musicians he found at various inns, and had rehearsed them well before making his impressive debut. It was supposed to be a *soirée dansante*, but the place became too full. As a gesture of filial loyalty, he included a performance of his father's recently acclaimed waltz *Loreley-Rhein-Klänge*. Competition with his father was, nevertheless, thrust uncompromisingly before the public when a now famous review of the occasion concluded with the words "Gute Nacht, Lanner! Guten Abend, Strauss Vater! Guten Morgen, Strauss Sohn!"[57] His father's efforts to put a boycott in place had failed because the entertainment industry, like other capitalist industries, did not operate through a system of personal loyalties; its only concern was profit. Someone would always be ready to seek that profit: if the father could use his personal influence to prevent his son being engaged at the Sperl, he was unable to do so at Dommayer's; and if Haslinger feared annoying the father by publishing music of the son, then Mechetti had no hesitation in doing so—especially after the waltz Strauss Jr. labeled his Opus 1 (*Sinngedichte*) had allegedly received nineteen encores at Dommayer's.

In his first year, Strauss Jr. was engaged at the Casino Zögernitz as well as Dommayer's, and he also became bandmaster of the Second Regiment of Citizens' Guards (his father was bandmaster of the First). He began to tour in the early 1850s, although when he was at home in this decade, his program of events was full: he might be in a restaurant one evening, the Volksgarten another, and a dance hall the next. He was, in fact, in demand every day of the week.[58] He composed nothing but dance music up to the age of forty-four; Jacob snarls: "The dance industry had him in its tyrannical clutches."[59] But it was certainly his choice and doing: when his withdrawal from conducting in the 1860s in favor of his brothers allowed him more time, he chose to spend it developing the "symphonic waltz," not the symphony.

The Strauss family business, as built up by Strauss Jr.'s mother, Anna (whose input should not be underrated), and his two brothers Josef and Eduard, had over 200 employees at one stage. It was precisely the complex network you would expect to find in an efficiently operating art world: there were musicians and music copyists, ushers and coach drivers, and administrators, such as bookkeepers.[60] Strauss Jr.'s music, like his father's, circulated in a variety of forms, tailored for concert hall, dance hall, *Hausmusik,* and military bands (of which there were several in Vienna).

Since there was economic depression in Vienna in 1846–55, Strauss Jr. made a great deal of his money through his visits to Russia, especially his concerts during the Pavlovsk season from mid-May to mid-September. Once again the importance of bourgeois engagements is revealed: it was not an aristocrat who invited him there to perform, but the director of a rail company whose purpose was to attract people onto the trains from St. Petersburg to Pavlovsk, where the company had developed a summer resort. Of course, Strauss did give concerts to the Russian aristocracy, but was soon made bitterly aware of the significance of class divisions when he was unable to marry Olga Smirnitzki because of her family's objections.

Russia was not the only country that welcomed him. He and his brother Josef appeared at the Paris World Exhibition in 1867. He visited Britain later that same year, and directed a series of promenade concerts at the Royal Italian Opera House, Covent Garden (see chapter 2). He had a 100-strong orchestra of London players and conducted, like his father, with violin in hand. A few years later, Strauss was lured to Boston and the World's Peace Jubilee by the offer of an advance fee of $100,000.[61] His *Autograph Waltzes* date from this 1872 visit; they were published by White and Goullaud of Boston, and in Britain by A. Hammond of London. Unlike a lot of Strauss's music for America, they were original compositions. Another original piece was *Greeting to America*, which quotes "The Star-Spangled Banner." Strauss went on to New York afterward, where he gave three concerts. It is not surprising that New York proved more to his taste: he told a reporter that he found Boston too puritanical, with no life in the street; with New York he was perfectly charmed—except for the poor beer—and he found the city gayer than London.[62]

Class and the Metropolis

For popular music to circulate widely as a commodity in the nineteenth century, it was necessary for it to be popular with the haute bourgeoisie and petite bourgeoisie. Since these were classes that shared similarities in their urban experiences wherever they resided, the music of the city was never too circumscribed by local meanings, and metropolitan life became more and more distinct from village life as the century wore on. Among the experiences that typify life in the metropolis, Georg Simmel cites the "intensification of nervous stimulation," leading to social reserve, a head-over-heart attitude, and the necessity for precise timetabling of activities.[63] In discussing the anonymity of the metropolis, Simmel conjures up a compelling and influential image, that of the individual being reduced to "a mere cog in an enormous organization of things and powers."[64]

The early 1830s were looked back on as a "golden age," that of *Alt Wien*, when Vienna was prosperous and the waltz craze was a distraction that communicated no dissident ideas—*Heiter auch in ernster Zeit* (Cheerful also in serious times), as one of Strauss Sr.'s waltzes puts it—although social problems were to come to the fore in the following decade. After the revolution of 1848, the new emperor, Franz Josef, was keen to promote railway developments, trade, and commerce. He decreed the city walls should go in December 1857, and the Ringstrasse, which opened in 1865, was created, encircling the city in their place. As a grand and spacious boulevard, it completed the city's modernization and showed the influence of Baron Hausmann's redevelopment of Paris. Austria was industrializing rapidly in the 1860s, and a new class friction was developing between the aristocracy and the industrial rather than mercantile bourgeoisie—especially those industrialists who could afford to build luxurious homes on the Ringstrasse. These people were, in fact, those with whom Strauss Jr. was most comfortable, as someone who had not inherited his own substantial wealth. Vienna, like London, New York, and Paris, grew rapidly—it doubled in population between midcentury and 1890. In 1830, there were some 318,000 residents, while at the end of the nineteenth century there were over a million. Austria remained absolutist, but with a growing socialist movement.

Urban popular styles of music were not as marked by their place of production as rural styles. Cities were more like each other than were rustic areas, and merchants had long accustomed themselves to trading commodities between cities. Composers could see a similar opportunity opening up with the development of the commercial music industry (sheet music sales, international tours). Certainly, the most popular waltz music was in origin and character Viennese, but its meanings and attractions were broader. Robert Stolz explained the success of the waltz by describing its three-quarter time in generalized romantic terms as "a quarter spring, a quarter love, a quarter wine."[65]

An emphasis on the local is found in some titles and the descriptive effects that follow from them: for example, Strauss Jr.'s *Geschichten aus dem Wienerwald* (Tales from Vienna Woods), op. 325 (1868), which features a zither to evoke an atmosphere of Viennese folk tradition. Nonetheless, the appeal to local cultural experience is never asserted to such a degree that it would create difficulties of understanding elsewhere. Strauss Sr. was aware of this back in 1833 when he wrote the first of his several souvenir pieces of European cities: his waltz *Emlék Pestre* (Souvenir of Pest), op. 66, begins with a quotation of a Hungarian dance tune and is dedicated to "the noble Hungarian nation," but one does not need to be Hungarian to enjoy it fully.

The local is in this context embedded in capitalist rather than agrarian social relations, so that evocations of the *Volk* or of rusticity are prepackaged for urban consumption. The local is thus inevitably available for a much wider market. To dance a *Ländler* in the 1840s was to dance an Austrian dance, but to dance a waltz in the same decade was to enjoy a fashionable European dance *from* Austria that had circulated from city to city in the same way as might any other capitalist commodity. The *Ländler* was still being danced in the country long after the waltz had replaced it in the city. The waltz was part of an urban entertainment industry rather than a rustic tradition, and it readily linked itself to other industrial ventures: for instance, Strauss Sr.'s *Eisenbahn-Lust,* op. 19, celebrated the opening of Vienna's first railway in 1837, and his son's *Jux-Polka,* op. 17, was composed specially for a ball Vienna's industrialists held in 1846. The Austrian waltz seemed available for all, of any nationality or ethnic background, just as the American foxtrot did in the 1920s. When Strauss Jr. gave the title "The Austrians" to one of his waltzes (*Die Österreicher,* op. 22) of 1845, it is significant that it was an old-fashioned *Ländler*-influenced waltz, since ideas about the roots of a national character are always closely tied to countryside traditions. A strong folk influence is also felt in his *Berglieder* waltz, op. 18, of the same year, which was composed for a festival of friendship for Vienna's Tyrolean residents. When Strauss Jr. strives to depict the East, he adopts the same Orientalist framework as other nineteenth-

A *Revolution on the Dance Floor, a Revolution in Musical Style* **139**

century composers. The *Egyptischer Marsch,* op. 335 (1869), makes use of Liszt's Hungarian "Gypsy scale," a favorite device for signifying an indistinctly known cultural Other.[66] When Strauss needs to represent the much more familiar Hungary, he is much subtler, and this is evident in his earliest efforts, such as the *Pesther Csárdás,* op. 23 (1846).

Strauss Jr.'s music is a record of the social, cultural, and even technological history of his times; so much is evident from titles alone, for instance, the *Elektro-magnetische Polka,* op. 110, of 1852. He also documented the expansion of Vienna, composing the *Demolirer-Polka,* op. 269 (1862) as the walls were coming down, and the *Neu-Wien-Walzer,* op. 342 (1870) when the borders of the city spread even further, to its old outer defense (the Linienwall). His *Accelerationen-Walzer,* op. 234 (1860), one of the first pieces of music to be inspired by a machine—here, a motor accelerating—was composed for the Valentine's Day Ball of Vienna University's student engineers. This waltz launches a decade in which Vienna's industrial bourgeoisie became a significant social and cultural force, holding *soirées* in their grand new houses. A reversal of fortune set in with the collapse of the Vienna Stock Exchange on 9 May 1873 ("Black Friday")—with most unfortunate timing, too, because it was Vienna's turn to hold a World Exhibition,[67] which had opened at the beginning of that very month on the Prater. The reverberations were felt throughout Europe, since capitalism was already international in scope.

Josef Strauss also enjoyed commissions from Vienna's industrial bourgeoisie. He composed his Polka française, *Feuerfest!* op. 269 (1869), to celebrate the production of the twenty-thousandth fireproof iron safe made by Franz Wertheim's factory. *Feuerfest!* was the company's advertising slogan, so those championing the art side of the art/entertainment schism must have thought this composition represented a new low point in the abjection of the artist. It is not just a matter of its title, since it is clear that the subject matter has influenced unmistakably the character and sound of the composition—anvils are called for in the orchestra and are struck vigorously. In the twentieth century, this would become known as "selling out." In the nineteenth century it would be regarded as art put to meretricious purposes. Yet this promotional piece is one of the wittiest and most vivacious polkas ever written.

To map *Unterhaltungsmusik* onto the middle class, assuming that it comprehensively defined their taste, is revealed as patently erroneous when the aristocratic patronage of music declines in the second half of the nineteenth century. Indeed, the Gesellschaft der Musikfreunde would have been unable to promote *ernste Musik* without middle-class support. The industrialist Nicolaus Dumba became that society's president at the same time he was lending his support to Strauss Jr. It would be another error to align popular dance music too closely with working-class interests. We should remember how much the aristocracy loved waltzing. Strauss Sr. was promoted after Lanner's death in 1843 to the position of director of court balls (*Hofball-Musikdirektor*) and, when on tour, also played for aristocracy (such as the duke of Sutherland and Queen Victoria in England). Nevertheless, Jacob maintains that he was "not at home in the salons of the great, much as they loved him; he played there, but he never ceased to be the petit bourgeois."[68]

Artiness and Seriousness

In his introduction to the collected edition of his father's music, Strauss Jr. remarks that dance composition in his father's day was "eine leichtere Kunst," adding that nobody can now bring out a polka unless the entire music literature has been studied and perhaps a philosophical system, too. Formerly, he tells us, you just needed to come up with an idea, and you always managed to do so.[69] Strauss Jr. and Josef Strauss extended the sixteen-measure sections to even longer spans (a move anticipated in some sections of their father's later waltzes), and made use of extended introductions and codas. Greater efforts were also made to ensure the formal cohesion of a waltz (e.g. anticipating themes, recalling themes, interrelating themes) that served no functional purpose as far as the dance was concerned. Waltzes in the 1860s developed a dual character, becoming both functional pieces for dancing and objects for aesthetic contemplation—although it is fair to say that the waltzes of Strauss Sr. and Lanner were never designed solely to regulate foot movement and, as noted concerning his father's tours, were not always played for dancing.[70] In the music of Strauss Jr., there is often an indication of a cut to be made (usually in the coda) if the waltz is to be performed in a dance hall. Symphonic waltzes now have a market value; that was not the case in the 1830s. Then, there was a strict division between the ballroom waltz and concert waltzes, like the waltz in Berlioz's *Symphonie fantastique* (1829), or the waltzes Chopin composed for his piano recitals in the 1830s.

Chopin, of course, was working within the category of *ernste Musik*, but the idea that entertainment music must be "easy" was challenged as early as the second half of the 1850s by Josef Strauss, who provocatively called *Perlen der Liebe*, op. 39 (1857), a "concert waltz." It might lay claim to be the first example of an aspiration to the status of art from within a commercial popular style. Strauss Jr. also became interested in crossover works at this time, composing music for dance that was at the same time redolent of the concert hall, and especially of those features that were associated with high-status music: adventurous harmonies, dissonances, strong evocation of atmosphere, intricate orchestral effects, and imaginative timbres. The result is what is frequently termed the "symphonic waltz." In the years to come, it would not be uncommon to find popular forms that from time to time emulated, with varying degrees of success, higher-status forms. The tendency to incorporate high cultural features within the popular has remained a characteristic of what happens to popular styles once they have established themselves. It manifests itself either in a desire to take from an existing tradition or to be associated with contemporary high art practices. This can occur whatever style of popular music is involved, and in the twentieth century it manifested itself in "symphonic" jazz, "third stream" jazz, and "progressive" rock.[71] Those in the business of selling musical commodities may be worried by such developments, as, indeed, was Strauss Jr.'s publisher, Carl Haslinger, who showed no enthusiasm for a waltz like *Gedankenflug,* op. 215 (1858), with its unusual themes and orchestration and a dedication to mood creation that almost overrides its dance elements.

Programmatic elements, common in concert hall Romanticism, were present in much early dance music. In Strauss Sr.'s *Tivoli Freuden-fest-Tänze,* op. 45 (1831), the repeated quavers in waltz 1 could have been suggested by the rolling carriages of the Tivola slide on the Green Hill, Obermeidling. In his ambitious piece *Der Raub der Sabinerinnen,* op. 43 (1831), described as a "charakterisches Tongemälde" (characteristic tone-painting), he seems to be seeking an art music crossover; even so, it was composed for a ball at the Sperl. It consists of a march (the arrival of Roman soldiers), a *galop* (the abduction), and a set of waltzes (the reconciliation).

Josef's *Sphären-Klänge* bears features resembling a symphonic poem, beginning with its sensitive, poetic introduction (by no means an unusual feature of his waltzes). It is very much a post-*Lohengrin* piece—yet, again, it was composed for a ball and not a concert. Josef and his brother Johann showed an interest in Wagner that calls for explication. It was Josef who performed publicly excerpts of *Tristan und Isolde* and other later works of Wagner before their formal premieres elsewhere. He appeared to find no conflict between this activity and his normal role as a dance music conductor. Was it because of an apparent kinship between the novel and the innovative? If so, it must be admitted that the novelty in dance music was intended to be immediately attractive, whereas there was no commercial imperative for Wagner's innovations to be so. Nevertheless, there has often been a comradely alliance between the popular and the "advanced"—one has only to think of the image of Karlheinz Stockhausen on the cover of the Beatles' album *Sgt. Pepper's Lonely Hearts Club Band.*

In his waltz *Die Extravaganten,* op. 205 (1858), Strauss Jr. appropriates the harmonies of *Zukunftsmusik,* much to the annoyance of Eduard Hanslick, who was otherwise an admirer of the melodic invention and animated rhythms of both Strauss father and son.[72] However, he believed that *Die Extravaganten* demonstrated that Strauss had misguided "serious" ambitions for the waltz, and he failed to see how Strauss might adopt "advanced" harmonies while retaining a popular appeal. The waltz, in fact, proved a success.[73] The *Fremden-Blatt* commented on its "sehr hübsche Motive" (very pretty themes) and had no doubt that it would be reckoned one of the season's best dance compositions.[74] In confirmation of its enduring melodic appeal, a tune from this waltz (added to one from *Vermählungs-Toaste*, op. 136) was used for the duet "Warm" in the film musical *The Great Waltz* (MGM, 1972).

Strauss Jr. enriched the waltz in terms of harmony and timbre (his orchestra swelled in size to around fifty, because he absorbed his father's players after his father's death), and he composed melodies that outlasted his father's in memorability. Strauss Jr. was responsible for the *Verzückungswalzer*, which exercised a seductive charm with its rhythm and harmony (*Verzückung* is a state of ecstasy). In an instance of popular art influencing "high" art, it had an influence on Wagner's music for the Flower Maidens in *Parsifal*. Perhaps Strauss Jr. in the mid-1860s stands in the same relationship to his father's music as, a century later, the Beatles and "Strawberry Fields" did with respect to Elvis Presley and "Jailhouse Rock." There is more obvious artistry and refinement, but there is also something earthy and spontaneous (or could the word be "electric") that has been lost. Early rock 'n' roll was very definitely intended to be danced to, just as were the waltzes of Lanner and Strauss Sr., but the "art rock" that developed in the 1960s had the same dual character as the "symphonic waltzes" of the 1860s. Public esteem may be carried along with such developments, though it often turns against them (especially if pretentiousness is suspected).

Excursions into the domain of high art notwithstanding, the serious music art world continued to cold-shoulder Strauss. When his music was heard in the grand surroundings of the recently opened Goldener Saal of the Musikverein, 13 March 1870, some critics thought it inappropriate for this high cultural venue. The concert's success, however, led to thirty more years of Sunday afternoon concerts. In the fiftieth anniversary year of his debut concert at Dommayer's Casino, Strauss was made an honorary member of the Gesellschaft der Musikfreunde, and was thereby accorded recognition as a composer of status, albeit a mere five years before his death. As for Johann's youngest brother, Eduard, who survived into the twentieth century, he remains a neglected figure, though he produced over 300 compositions and enjoyed a big success in London in 1885. He became conductor of the Strauss Orchestra after Josef's death in 1870 (having already been its conductor during Johann's and Josef's absences in Russia), and after Strauss Jr. was relieved of his duties as Hoffball-Musikdirektor because of ill health in 1871, Eduard took over the following year. He disbanded the Strauss Orchestra in 1901.

Today, millions watch the New Year's Day concert from Vienna on television, imagining that the link between the Vienna Philharmonic Orchestra and the music of the Strauss family is lost in the mists of time. In fact, the Wiener Philharmoniker was reluctant to play this type of music in the nineteenth century, and when the orchestra did so on

14 October 1894, it was intended as a special honor to Johann Strauss as part of the fiftieth-anniversary celebrations of his debut. Many more years were to elapse before the New Year concerts at the Musikverein were established; the very first of these was conducted by Clemens Krauss during wartime in 1941.

6

Blackface Minstrels, Black Minstrels, and Their European Reception

African Americans and their cultural practices were first seen through the distorting medium of blackface performance, which began when New Yorker Thomas Rice copied his "Jim Crow" dance routine from an African-American street performer, and introduced it into his act at the Bowery Theatre, 12 November 1832.[1] Charles Hamm remarks that the minstrel song "emerged as the first distinctly American genre."[2] Rice visited London in 1836. The first troupe, the Virginia Minstrels (fiddle, banjo, tambourine, and bone castanets) formed in New York in 1842, calling themselves minstrels after the recent success enjoyed by the Tyrolese Minstrel Family. Stephen Foster (1826–64), who composed for E. P. Christy, another pioneering troupe, had helped to win approval for the genre. He boasted, "I find that by my efforts I have done a great deal to build up a taste for the Ethiopian songs among refined people."[3] His first big success, "Oh! Susanna," was published in New York in 1848. "Massa's in de Cold Ground" and "My Old Kentucky Home, Good Night," published in New York in 1852 and 1853, respectively, were both labeled "plantation melodies," though the words of the former are in minstrel dialect and those of the other are not. Visitors to America sometimes mistook Foster's songs and other blackface minstrel songs for African-American songs. Moritz Busch collected and published some of them as Negro songs in *Wanderungen zwischen Hudson und Mississippi, 1851 und 1852*,[4] they included "O Sussianna" ("Oh! Susanna") and "The Yellow Rose of Texas," which became "Gelbe Röslein von Indiana."[5] Minstrelsy overshadowed the achievements of black composers in the 1840s, such as the dance-band leader Frank Johnson.[6]

The conditions for the British reception of blackface minstrelsy, an entertainment purporting to depict the recreational activities of black plantation slaves, differed in various respects from those in America, and for historic reasons. Slavery had been illegal in Britain since 1772, and after the campaigning efforts of William Wilberforce and others, the slave trade had been abolished in 1807. Those opposed to abolition had failed in their arguments that black slaves led happy and contented lives on American plantations and that their Christian masters were striving to save the souls of heathens. Another issue that forced the reconsideration of slaving interests was that Britain, at that time, was having to define its understanding of freedom in the wake of the revolutionary interpretation of *la liberté* in France and the circulation of French political ideas in Britain. This was fueled by the founding of radical groups like the London Corresponding Society and the appearance of publications such as Thomas Paine's *Rights of Man* (1791–2) and Mary Wollstonecroft's *Vindication of the Rights of Men* (1790), in which she condemned the slave trade—"a traffic that outrages every suggestion of reason and religion."[7] Slavery was eventually abolished throughout the whole British Empire in 1833. Later in that decade, radicalism was reawakened by the Chartist movement, which associated freedom with the right to vote. In 1843, the year the Virginia Minstrels, the first established blackface troupe, visited Britain, the leader of the London Chartists was William Cuffey, the grandson of an African slave.

The reaction to the early minstrel troupes in the 1840s, then, was not one of uniform praise throughout England, and often entailed some unease, especially in the industrial Northwest. To win approval, blackface performers stressed the wholesomeness of their entertainment and their personal respectability. This had been true of the pioneering solo blackface performer Thomas Rice, whose visit in 1836, according to the *London Satirist,* spread a "Jim Crow" mania though "all classes."[8] Ten years later, the Ethiopian Serenaders made their first London appearance at the prestigious Hanover Square Rooms, charging hefty prices of 2 and 3 shillings for tickets. Their status was assured when they were invited to perform before Queen Victoria. From then on, although it was true that blackface minstrels did appeal to British working-class audiences, in Britain they always had a bourgeois audience more firmly in their sights, and thus left available a cultural space that was to be filled by the music hall. In contrast, minstrelsy remained the most popular form of urban working-class entertainment in America until the rise of vaudeville in the 1880s—though, ironically, vaudeville came about as a deliberate attempt to attract the "middling class" into theatres.

I do not wish to give the impression that minstrelsy automatically endorsed slavery. There are, indeed, antislavery minstrel songs, for example, by Henry Russell and, later, Henry Clay Work. In New York, the Hutchinson Family sang their abolitionist song "Get off the Track" to the tune of "Old Dan Tucker," one of the Virginia Minstrels' biggest hits.[9] Many minstrel troupes were also quick to incorporate scenes from Harriet Beecher Stowe's highly successful novel *Uncle Tom's Cabin* (1852). The primary purpose of the blackface mask was to signify a particular theatrical experience, and to allow performers to behave on stage in a way that would not normally be condoned.[10] Blackface minstrels were double coded, inscribing racism, but at the same time subverting bourgeois values by celebrating idleness and mischief rather than work and responsible behavior. An example of how the blackface mask produces a character transformation on the Virginia Serenaders can be seen on the front cover of a collection of their songs (see fig. 6.1).

Such humor works on its own terms and requires no knowledge of African-American behavior—and just as well, because most Europeans

Figure 6.1   The Virginia Serenaders.

had none. The unruly humor may explain why minstrelsy appealed to British audiences, providing them with a release of tension in an age of social restraint and inhibition. The influence on British society of those campaigning on behalf of black emancipation had declined by the middle of the century, though slavery remained an issue of public interest until the 1870s.[11] British minstrels retained their cross-class appeal in these succeeding years, borrowing from music hall on occasion, but always selling themselves to the middle class as wholesome entertainment and displaying a more eloquent wit in their burlesques and comic songs than that found in the music hall. Even British banjos began to differ from those in America, with the development of five- and six-string models as well as the zither banjo. That said, it is highly likely that minstrelsy in Britain encouraged the acceptance of imperialist ideology by depicting emotional and hyperactive blackface characters who needed to be kept in check by a firm but fair Mr. Interlocutor. It easy to see how this could extend to the idea that a colonial presence was required to ensure a paternalistic regulation of conduct in countries overseas.

The Virginia Minstrels commenced their English tour at the Concert Rooms, Concert Street, Liverpool, on 21 May 1843. They sang in solo or unison, and accompanied themselves on fiddle, banjo, tambourine and bone castanets (made of cow ribs). [12] They were not particularly successful in Liverpool, but earned enough to travel to Manchester, where they appeared in the upmarket Athenaeum Rooms. There was hardly an enthusiastic response from the Manchester critics; one wrote, "As a specimen of Negro holiday enjoyment, the entertainment is worth seeing once."[13] The Virginia Minstrels were finally given a warm critical reception when they appeared at the Adelphi Theatre, London, in June 1843, for a fee, the manager claimed, of £100 a week. Manchester remained unconvinced about minstrelsy; when the Ethiopian Delineators arrived in 1846, the *Manchester Guardian* advised its readers, "The Ethiopian Delineators are amusing enough to hear and see once."[14] Remarkably, when the Ethiopian Serenaders performed to a rather empty Free Trade Hall later that year, the press handed out accolades. Fresh from their London success, they sang in harmony, wore concert dress, and did not dance. They were six strong, favored songs of a sentimental hue, and accompanied them with two banjos, accordion, guitar, tambourine, and bones. A song they sang that became a great favorite in England (see fig. 6.2) was "Lucy Neal," which reinforced antislavery feelings with its tale of enforced separation and heartbreak on the plantation.[15]

(*Final verse*)
Dey bore her from my bosom, but de wound dey cannot heal;
And my heart, my heart is breaking, for I lub'd sweet Lucy Neal.
O! yes and when I'm dying, and dark visions round me steal,
De last low murmur ob dis life shall be, sweet Lucy Neal.

(*Refrain*)
O! poor Lucy Neal, O! poor Lucy Neal!
If I had you by my side, how happy I should feel!

The year after the visit of the Ethiopian Serenaders, the *Manchester Guardian* returned to berating minstrelsy, calling the songs "musical abortions."[16] They were not alone; the *Manchester Courier,* having witnessed the New Orleans Serenaders at the Free Trade Hall, declared, "one exhibition of the kind is quite sufficient in one generation."[17] The general tenor of these quotations does make evident, however, that the citizens of Manchester had no objection to trying out anything once. Interestingly, Manchester, renowned for its freethinking and radicalism, received a visit from a seven-strong troupe, the Female American Serenaders, in 1847, a time when female minstrels do not seem to have performed publicly in America. The *Manchester Guardian,* with characteristic distaste, described their performance as a "questionable entertainment."[18] The attitude of the Manchester press could easily be interpreted as defensiveness in the face of a new kind of popular music. One

TOO POPULAR BY HALF.

Boy (singing). "LOVER-LY LUCY NEAL, OH LOVER-LY LUCY NEAL, HIF I 'AD YOU BY MY SI-I-HIDE, 'OW 'APPY I SHOULD FEEL!"

Figure 6.2 "Too Popular by Half" (1847), cartoon by John Leech, in *John Leech's Pictures of Life and Character from the Collection of "Mr. Punch"* (London: Bradbury, Agnew, 1886), 250.

remembers that it was in Manchester's Free Trade Hall that Bob Dylan was booed for picking up an electric guitar.

Seeking the Black beneath the Blackface

Hans Nathan and other scholars have shown that early minstrel songs often bear a kinship to English theatre music and Irish and Scottish dance music, but it is a more difficult matter—particularly in the absence of contemporary documentation—to demonstrate African influence. However, it seems highly likely that minstrelsy in the 1840s was a fusion of black and white cultural elements. After all, would the early minstrels be so keen to copy the instruments of plantation music making[19] but not the actual music those instruments played? Among what strike me as black elements are the following ten features.

The Constant Pulse

This was usually emphasized by the banjoist tapping his heel. If playing solo in, say, a circus, a banjoist would stand on a small wooden platform to help the taps resonate, thus showing it was considered an important percussive feature and not merely a crude means of keeping time. This steady background pulse, with which the rhythmic foreground interacts, is important to syncopation and polyrhythmic devices. It also encourages the omission of notes on strong beats and prompts, instead, the playing of accented offbeat notes. Heel tapping is absent from the sheet music, of course—with the exception of the operatic parody song "Stop Dat Knocking," which at one point refers jokingly to a "Solo wid de heel." [20]

The Drone

The banjo has an inverted drone (on the dominant in the nineteenth century); it is the highest string, but positioned to be played by the thumb. It affects harmonies and creates clashes that were unfamiliar in European music of that time. Joel Sweeney, who is often given credit for adding the fifth string to the banjo, added an extra low string, not this short drone string (as is sometimes assumed).

The Use of Slides

These are not common in European playing practices, especially when accented, and their effect would be more pronounced on older nonfretted banjos. (Henry Dobson is credited with being the first to add frets, around 1878.)

Motivic Structure

Many of the early songs are dominated by repeated motives. An example is "Old Dan Tucker" (which Emmett claimed as his own composition, though evidence suggests otherwise). One of the most popular

songs in the Virginia Minstrels' repertoire, it contributes a musical newness to complement the newness of dance and words that had already
been established with "Jim Crow" (ex. 6.1).

Example 6.1 "Old Dan Tucker," attributed to Dan Emmett (New York:
Atwill, 1843). A and B indicate repetitions of melodic-rhythmic motives.

A manuscript of Emmett contains a dance entitled *Genuine Negro Jig*
that has the kind of two-measure cell structure that would later, in the
language of twentieth-century jazz, be unhesitatingly called a riff.[21] It
also contains minor third versus major third ambiguity, another feature
of blues and jazz (ex. 6.2).

Example 6.2 *Genuine Negro Jig,* collected by Emmett, MSS 355 Daniel D.
Emmett Papers, c. 1840–1880, Archives/Library of the Ohio Historical
Society. Columbus, OH.

Syncopation

This is not the usual European syncopation of this period, in which the
syncopated note is accented. The syncopated note tends to have no accent; instead the accent falls on the preceding note.[22] The difference be-

tween the two types can be heard by comparing a syncopated passage in Suppé's *Poet and Peasant* Overture with "Buffalo Gals" (ex. 6.3). Note that the accent is on "come," not on "out" (the syncopated note). Similarly, toward the end of the refrain of Stephen Foster's song "Angelina Baker" the accent is on the note before the syncopated note.

Example 6.3 (a) *Dichter und Bauer* (1846), Franz von Suppé; (b) refrain of "Buffalo Gals," as published in Davidson's *Universal Melodist* (London, 1853); (c) "Angelina Baker" (1850).

It took awhile for this kind of unaccented syncopation to embed itself as a popular feature. For example, there are no syncopations on the "out" of the "get out" refrain of some versions of "Old Dan Tucker" (ex. 6.4).

Example 6.4 (a) "Old Dan Tucker," attributed to Dan Emmit (*sic*) (Boston: Keith, 1843); (b) "Old Dan Tucker," attributed to Henry Russell (London: Davidson, *Universal Melodist*, 1853).

Syncopation was being defined even in 1877 as an "abnormal *emphasis*," but Emmett is aware of this different type of syncopation from early on.[23] In his dance *My First Jig*, he cuts short the duration of the syncopated note (a practice often found later in ragtime piano). Syncopation becomes rare in minstrelsy of the 1860s, but returns vigorously in the 1890s with ragtime and the renewed input of African Americans into popular music.

Call-and-Response Patterns

Call and response, which has become almost a defining feature of black music making, is found in songs like Foster's "De Camptown Races" and Emmett's "Dixie's Land" (exs. 6.5 and 6.8d).[24]

Example 6.5. "De Camptown Races," words and music Stephen Foster (Baltimore: Benteen, 1850).

Pentatonic Shapes

Although these shapes are insufficient in themselves to enable us to verify anything, they become significant as an African-American feature once they are recognized as forming part of a chain of other signifiers of black music making (ex. 6.6a). Example 6.6b provides, for purposes of comparison, alternative pitches typical of a nineteenth-century European popular style for the words "I hear de noise den saw de fight" in "Old Dan Tucker."

Example 6.6 (a) "Old Dan Tucker," original pentatonic form; (b) a more typical nineteenth-century European popular tune shape.

(a)

(b)

Ambiguous Thirds and Flattened Sevenths

These are sometimes present in a way that prompts parallels to be made with the "blue notes" of jazz. Hans Nathan finds that "My Old Aunt Sally" resembles in parts Charles Dibdin's "Peggy Perkins";[25] but surely the most striking feature in the former is the use of flattened sevenths in the refrain (see ex. 6.7). Henry Russell retains these when he varies the tune for his song "De Merry Shoe Black."[26]

Example 6.7 "My Old Aunt Sally," as published in Davidson's *Cheap Edition of the Songs of the Ethiopian Serenaders* (London, c. 1848).

The Important Role of Dance

Some songs were danced and sung simultaneously, and almost all songs incorporated bodily movement, if not what might be described strictly as dance.

The Texts

Song lyrics can sometimes be linked to African cultural interests, for example, animal fables or trickster humor. Rice's "Jim Crow," which was taken, as mentioned earlier, from a black street performer, seems European in musical style; yet the lyrics appear indebted to the Yoruba trickster, who was a crow. The character of Jim Crow established the ragged, raucous joker stereotype of the minstrel show.

> (*Second verse*)
> I us'd to take him fiddle
> Ebry morn and arternoon,
> And charm de old buzzard,
> And dance to the racoon.
>
> (*Refrain*)
> Wheel about, and turn about, and do jis so,
> Ebry time I wheel about, I jump Jim Crow.

According to William Mahar, even the dialect used in minstrelsy approaches, at times, "period attestations of spoken dialect."[27] The dialect was, however, always going to be compromised, since it had to be recognizable and understood by a white audience while at the same time signifying difference and a black Other.

The fusion of styles in minstrel songs was effected from a variety of directions (America, Africa, Europe) and by people of varying social and cultural backgrounds. Henry Russell, for example, was Jewish, and George Dixon, whose song "Zip Coon" established the black dandy stereotype, was of black and white parentage.[28] Thus, the songs are too fluid to be dissected analytically so as to reveal conclusively the provenance of their constituent parts. Black musicians on southern plantations were accommodating European music to their own aesthetic demands, just as white musicians were reworking plantation songs and dances to suit themselves. For instance, there were claims that Dan Emmett's "Dixie's Land" was based on a southern African-American air "If I Had a Donkey," but if so, then that song must itself have been based on Henry Bishop's "Dashing White Sergeant," to which "Dixie's Land" bears clear resemblances (see ex. 6.8).[29]

This cultural "to-ing and fro-ing" does not mean that the question of cultural appropriation may be ignored but, rather, that it should be seen as a matter of unequal power relations in the social domain rather than as an abstracted question of musical aesthetics. The white musician was able to define the nature of black music and dominate its reception, leaving the black musician with an identity at odds with his or her subjectivity. Thus, one consequence of whites' power to define black culture was that African Americans were left dispossessed of a means of representing themselves on stage, and this was to last a long time—even Louis Armstrong was never able to shake himself entirely free of minstrel gestures.

In England, minstrels quickly lost the raucousness and challenging of dominant moral values found in their early American context. As the 1850s wore on, instead of wanting to bet money on the horses at

Example 6.8   (a) "The Dashing White Sergeant," from the opera *The Lord of the Manor,* by Henry Bishop (London: Goulding and D'Almaine, 1812); (b) "Dixie's Land," by Dan Emmett (New York: Firth, Pond, 1860); (c) "The Dashing White Sergeant"; (d) "Dixie's Land."

the Camptown racetrack, they were content to dream about what it might be like to be a daisy.[30] They were also tending to sit with their legs together, and the banjo was not displayed in such an obviously phallic manner as it had been (see fig. 6.3).

However, even in America, the catastrophe of the Civil War was to dampen the minstrels' high spirits. As the songs were increasingly taken over by sentiment after 1860, mothers became popular figures. Here are half a dozen sample titles:

"Mother I'll Come Home Tonight"
"Mother Kissed Me in My Dream"
"I'm Lonely since My Mother Died"
"Who Will Care for Mother Now"
"Let Me Kiss Him for His Mother"
"Dear Mother, I've Come Home to Die"

The mother fixation was to linger on into the twentieth century in Al Jolson's impassioned appeals to his mammy.

London became a center of minstrel sheet music production to equal New York. Hopwood and Crew advertised themselves as "Publishers of the Whole of the Songs and Ballads, sung by the ORIGINAL CHRISTY MINSTRELS"—by which they referred not to the original troupe organized by E. P. Christy, but to the troupe under the proprietorship of Moore and Burgess at St. James's Hall, Piccadilly. Many of

Figure 6.3 The Virginia Serenaders'
banjoist, J. P. Carter, in blackface.

the songs were also being published in Charles Sheard's *Musical Bouquet* series. Most of Stephen Foster's songs, too, were published in the *Musical Bouquet*. A cheaper publisher, Davidson, was selling "Negro Songs" at threepence each in his series the *Musical Treasury*, which he styled "the original and only genuine music for the million." It is not surprising that minstrel songs, being often of vague provenance, led to battles over rights between publishers.

Hopwood and Crew knew that the middle-class market for their music hall songs was limited, but not that for their minstrel songs, which they proclaimed "have taken such a permanent hold in the esteem of the musical public, ever welcomed and highly appreciated in the drawing room, and the greatest favourites with teachers in Class Instruction."[31] One attraction was the ease with which many minstrel songs (especially of the early variety) could be sight-read at soirées, should an unfamiliar one be placed in front of the accompanist. As a character remarks in Bernard Shaw's novel *The Irrational Knot,* "you need only play these three chords. When one sounds wrong, play another."[32] Thus were the pleasures of a three-chord aesthetic indulged in well before the days of punk rock. The songs were also taken up by the Tonic Sol-fa Agency and published in Sol-fa notation for singing classes and choirs. With the passing of time, the harmonies of some songs became more sophisticated and employed passing modulations, as found in "Annie Lisle" (see ex. 6.9), a song Hopwood and Crew advertised as

Example 6.9   "Annie Lisle," words and music by H. S. Thompson
(Boston: Oliver Ditson, 1857), beginning of the refrain.

one of the songs "sung with the greatest success by the Christy Minstrels' eminent Tenor, Mr J. Rawlinson at St. James's Hall."[33] There is
unmistakable evidence in such advertisements of the British *embour-
geoisement* of American minstrelsy.

England's Preeminent Minstrel Troupes

The Reverend Hugh Haweis called the Moore and Burgess Minstrels
the "princes of the art," but continued, "From St. James's Hall, and not
from 'Old Virginny,' come constant supplies of new melodies. The original melodies, such as 'Lucy Neal,' 'Uncle Ned,' some of which were no
doubt genuine American Negro productions, are almost forgotten."[34]
His comment reveals that the production of minstrel songs was in full
swing in England in the 1860s and 1870s.

The smaller of the two halls inside what was referred to in singular
fashion as St. James's Hall (Piccadilly) was a home of minstrelsy from
1859 to 1904. The Moore and Burgess (originally Moore and Crocker)
Minstrels began their long residency there on 16 September 1865. It
lasted the rest of the century, by which time the troupe was sixty
strong. They advertised their shows as suitable for families.[35] Even the
clergy frequented the smaller St. James's Hall with enthusiasm. Harry
Reynolds reports it being said that "this was the only entertainment
Catholic priests were allowed to attend."[36] Charles Dodd, a respectable
head teacher from Wrexham who would stay only in temperance ho-
tels, remarks of his visit with friends in 1878: "With the entertainment
we are delighted. We hear some grand music, both vocal and instrumental, conundrums, speeches, etc."[37] An anonymous reviewer toward
the end of the century, looking back at the troupe's many years of success, comments: "It has always been the aim of the conductors of the
Moore & Burgess Minstrels to give an entertainment at which no sen-
sible person can take offence."[38] When George Washington Moore (a
principal performer and one of the resident troupe's proprietors) per-

Figure 6.4   George Moore.

formed in blackface, it was without the grotesqueness found in many of the American burnt cork caricatures (fig. 6.4). The makeup had originally been of a crude variety: corks were simply soaked in alcohol, set on fire, and then mixed with water into a paste.

The Moore and Crocker (soon to be Moore and Burgess) Christy Minstrels program for an unspecified afternoon in 1867 shows the two contrasting halves of a typical entertainment (fig. 6.5).[39] Ballads and comic songs fill most of the first half, which concludes with a narrative, "The Old Jaw Bone," which probably included "stump speech" conventions. The second half is dominated by parody and burlesque. The Japanese fiddle may refer to a one-string instrument—such was the "Japanese fiddle" on which the Cockney blackface performer G. H. Chirgwin played with much skill later in the century.[40] The show concludes with an opera burlesque. Arthur Sullivan hit back at their fondness for burlesquing opera when he included a parody of their music making in the ensemble piece "Society has quite forsaken" in act 2 of *Utopia Limited* (1893). The troupe was large by 1867 standards, having thirty-one members.

As an example of their satirical humor, let us examine "The Grecian Bend," written, composed, and sung by George Moore. In the 1860s, it became fashionable to bunch skirts at the back into panniers

ST. JAMES'S HALL,

PICCADILLY (1867).

The Only Original and Veritably Legitimate

CHRISTY MINSTRELS

Messrs. G. W. Moore & J. P. Crocker, *Proprietors.*   *Manager,* Mr. Frederick Burgess.

PROGRAMME FOR THIS AFTERNOON.

PART I.

INTRODUCTORY OVERTURE, - - -	Christy Minstrels
NEW BALLAD, "Softly o'er the rippling waters," -	Mr. Winter Haigh
NEW BALLAD, "Bright-Eyed Jenny Lee," -	Mr. Vernon Reed
NEW COMIC, "Ada with the golden hair," Written, Composed, and Sung by	Mr. G. W. Moore
NEW AMERICAN BALLAD, "Far away," -	Mr. H. Norman
BALLAD, "Mill May," - - -	Mr. John Adams
COMIC REFRAIN, "Off to Brighton," - -	Mr. Harry Templeton
NEW BALLAD, "Mother kissed me in my dream," -	Mr. L. Rainford
CHORUS, "Hark again," - - - -	Christy Minstrels
NEW BALLAD, "The Birds will come again" -	Mr. A. Brenner
PATHETIC BALLAD, "Poor old Joe," - - -	Mr. J. Romer
COMIC SONG, "Picayune Butler," - -	Mr. G. W. Moore
BALLAD, "I'll meet thee in the lane," -	Mr. John Rawlinson
DESCRIPTIVE NEGRO LEGEND, "The old jaw bone,"	Mr. J. B. Ellis & Company

PART II.

In which the entire Company of Thirty-one Performers appear.

ETHIOPIAN PAS SEUL, - - - -	Mr. Pedro Stirling
BURLESQUE SCENA, - - -	Mr. Frank Pieri
SOLO ON THE JAPANESE FIDDLE, - -	Mr. W. P. Collins

To be followed by the Christy's Burlesque on a

CHINESE DANCE

SOLO CORNET, - - - - -	Mr. W. Ryder
BALLAD, - - - - -	Mr. John Rawlinson

DOUBLE AMERICAN JIG,
Messrs. Anderson and Norton.

BALLAD, - - - - -	Mr. C. Ernest

To conclude with a novel and wildly extravagant Burlesque upon the

GRAND ITALIAN OPERA

Figure 6.5   Program for the Christy Minstrels.

worn below the waist; the bustle was then developed to fill the gap between panniers and lower back. Understandably, women needed to bend forward to keep their balance, and the posture was dubbed the "Grecian bend."[41] This furnished ample excuse for a topical satire that would appeal across classes. Middle-class families must have bought the song because the sheet music was expensively produced, having a lithograph on the title page in which the green color of a slim umbrella was skillfully registered without blotches at a time when lithographic stones were still being used. It retailed at 3 shillings (fig. 6.6).

I am sure affluent, fashion-conscious women laughed at the song, as no doubt in more recent times lovers of designer clothes have laughed at the fashion excesses of Patsy and Edwina on the television comedy series *Absolutely Fabulous*. The dance interlude is a Schottische, which might seem bizarre but for the knowledge that style mixing was never something that unduly bothered blackface minstrels.

The Grecian bend now go it ladies,
Shake yourselves and set us crazy,
Double up, and show the men,
The style is now the Grecian bend.

The Mohawk Minstrels were England's other celebrated troupe.
They were formed by James and William Francis (who worked for the
music publisher Chappell) to rival the Moore and Crocker Minstrels.
After first working semiprofessionally, they moved into Berners Hall in
1873, next to the Agricultural Hall in Islington. They soon had rivals
themselves in the Manhattan Minstrels, but they determinedly approached the leader of that troupe, Harry Hunter (1840–1906), and
made him an offer he couldn't refuse. He was already an accomplished
actor, singer, and sketch writer. The Mohawks now became so successful they moved to the nearby St. Mary's Hall, which held 3,000. Since
so much of the troupe's material was original, the Francis brothers got

Figure 6.6   "The Grecian Bend," title page lithograph.

together with David Day of Hopwood and Crew to form a new publishing company. Later they were joined by Hunter himself to become the huge and successful music business Francis, Day and Hunter. The firm also sold minstrel requisites, such as plain wigs at 2 shillings and sixpence and "eccentric" wigs for a shilling more.

The Mohawks included some fine singers, and an unusual feature of their accompanying instrumental ensemble was that it included a harp. For a while, they employed a black artist, Billy Banks, who had come to England with Callender's Colored Minstrels. Unfortunately, he died after having been with them one year only. In the 1890s, George D'Albert won plaudits as their female impersonator; he was a fine dancer with an excellent falsetto voice. To add to the many contradictions of minstrelsy, a great many of his most fervent admirers were women. In 1900, Francis and Hunter took over the St. James's Hall lease and created the Mohawk, Moore and Burgess Minstrels. Admirers of both troupes were dissatisfied, however, and business was unhealthy. In 1904, minstrelsy at St. James's Hall came to an end, and Harry Hunter died two years later.[42]

The Mohawk Minstrels' "Grand New Programme," (reproduced in fig. 6.7) follows the norm of two contrasting halves. Minstrel troupes sat in a semicircle with Tambo at one end and Bones at the other. These corner men, or end men, were the comedians. The emcee came to be known as the Interlocutor, since he was frequently asking the corner men questions. Perhaps the most famous of minstrel jokes runs as follows:

Corner man: "My dog's got no nose."
Interlocutor: "How does he smell?"
Corner man: "Awful!"

Harry Hunter played Tambo when he joined the Mohawks, but became the Interlocutor, a role he plays here, punctuating a succession of ballads and comic songs until the cast comes together for a "Japaneasy Absurdity" before the interval. The second half looks a little like a variety show, minus the performing dogs and acrobats, but note that it contains a selection from Balfe's *Bohemian Girl*.

The Mohawks' satirical songs could have at times an acerbic quality, even a political character, as illustrated by Hunter's "Because He Was a Nob":

> There was a man, a nobleman,
> A nob of high degree,
> But he knew how to work it, though
> No working man was he;
> For though there might be thousands out,
> And looking for a job,
> He had a job brought thousands in,
> Because he was a nob.[43]

MOHAWK MINSTRELS

Proprietors & Managers   -   Messrs. JAMES FRANCIS, WILLIAM FRANCIS
& HARRY HUNTER.

GRAND NEW PROGRAMME

PART I.

Interlocutor   -   -   Mr. HARRY HUNTER.

NEW OPENING CHORUS	-	-	-	-	-	MOHAWK MINSTRELS
BALLAD	-	-	"' Sunny golden rays "		-	Mr. ERNEST GORDON
COMIC SONG		-" The Concert in the old Green Lane "			-	LITTLE THOMAS
BALLAD	-	-	" Left by Angel's hands ajar "		-	Mr. F. RUSSON

(HARP OBLIGATO   -   -   Master JOHN FRANCIS).

COMIC SONG	-	" I hope she'll never come back "		-Mr. WILL PARKER
BALLAD	-	" Don't go like that darling "	-	-Mr. JOHN FULLER
SONG	-	-	" On to the front " -	-	Mr. R. OLIVER
COMIC SONG		-" She ought to have a muzzle on "-		Mr. JAMES FRANCIS
BALLAD	-	-" Ah, never deem my love can change "		-Mr. CHAS. OSWELL
COMIC SONG		" There's always something happening "		Mr. WALTER HOWARD
BALLAD	-	-	" Love's after-glow "		Mr. W. C. HAWKINS
COMIC SONG		" I'll send you down a letter from the sky "		Mr. J. H. DANVERS

(His First Appearance with the Mohawk Minstrels)

SONG   -   -" When the ship comes back again "   Mr. THOS. CAMPBELL

Concluding with a New Original and Japaneasy Absurdity, by HARRY HUNTER
and EDMUND FORMAN, entitled

"COME LET US BE JAPPY TOGETHER."

PART II.

OPERATIC SELECTION from Balfe's "BOHEMIAN GIRL,"
MOHAWK MINSTRELS' CHOIR AND ORCHESTRA.

FIRST APPEARANCE OF

MR. JOHN M. DANVERS
IN A NEW SPECIALITY.

THE GREAT MINSTREL COMEDIAN,

MR. WALTER HOWARD
IN HIS DROLLERIES WITH THE BANJO.

THE

MARVELLOUS BOISSETS
IN THEIR ECCENTRIC ENTERTAINMENT,
"MELOMANIA"

Figure 6.7   Program for the Mohawk Minstrels.

It continues in similar vein, but any suggestion of an inflammatory call to engage in class struggle is defused by the chorus, which begins "I wish I was a nob," thereby suggesting that personal envy overrides a sense of social injustice. Thus it was that British minstrels were able to do a balancing act and appeal across classes even on the touchiest of subjects. In the same year that the Mohawks gave their last performance, St. James's Hall was destroyed by fire; its place is now taken by the Piccadilly Hotel.

Frederick Corder gives a sour view of the later nineteenth-century British minstrel show in an article in the *Musical Times* in 1885. He relates that after a considerable period of absence abroad, he decided to visit a London minstrel show to see if any of its former "quaint charm" still survived. He describes seeing a thirty-strong "Christy" minstrel troupe that was almost certainly the Moore and Burgess Minstrels. Although one must make allowances for Corder's scorn, his review is interesting and unusual in providing information about the musical side of the show.

Well, the instrumental portion of the troupe was as follows:—two fiddles and a cello, a flute, a cornet, a harp, and a big drum and cymbals, to which were added ten pairs of bones and six tambourines. Imagine, if you can, the effect of any orchestral piece whatever played by such a collection of instruments. But no one could who had not heard it. A few odd periods from one of Auber's best known overtures were strung together, and this prelude, though it lasted but a minute and a half, so completely deafened me that I could hardly catch a word of the first two songs. One was a tenor ballad, which seemed very touching, every fourth line ended with the word "mother," which was brought out with a jerk thus—"moth-a-ar," and affected the bystanders profoundly; indeed, I saw one poor woman in tears, and was sorry to think that she should have perhaps her most sacred feelings stirred by so coarse a touch. After each verse the chorus sang the air harmonized (not over correctly), without accompaniment, the last time in a whisper, which was a pretty effect, till I found it was done to nearly every song, after which it became silly. I soon discovered that there were only two kinds of songs; the sentimental, with whispered chorus, and the grotesque comic, with the full force of the percussion instruments.[44]

Black Troupes

Before the American Civil War, the most famous African-American performer was Master Juba. His real name was William Henry Lane, and he has a claim to be acknowledged as the father of American tap-dancing.[45] His performances as "Juba" were greatly admired. Dance historian Marian Hannah Winters has claimed that he was the "most influential single performer of nineteenth century American dance."[46] He made his reputation in the early 1840s, and was hailed by Charles Dickens on the latter's visit to America as "the greatest dancer known."[47] Juba had been promoted by Barnum, who found him too pale, so he was blacked up and given a woolly wig and bright red lips (the earlier convention, before white was used for lips). This was also a practice not uncommon for some later performers in supposedly authentic black troupes. Juba performed as a dancer and tambourine player with Pell's Serenaders at Vauxhall Gardens in 1848. He danced the "Virginny Breakdown," "Alabama Kick-up," "Tennessee Double-shuffle," and "Louisiana Toe-and-Heel," all of which the *Illustrated London News* took to be "Negro national dances."[48] Juba broke many social taboos of the day. He toured—as top of the bill—with white blackface performers in 1845, and settled in England after marrying a white woman.[49] He was only twenty-seven years old when he died in 1852.

The aftermath of the American Civil War and the abolition of slavery had little effect on theatrical representations of African Americans. Black troupes were formed, the first being the Georgia Minstrels in 1865. They stressed the values of genuineness and authenticity, but since they adopted the minstrel code, they continued to reproduce a simulacrum of black culture and plantation life, all the more insidious for seeming natural. Sam Hague brought his Slave Troupe of Georgia Minstrels to England in June 1866. They were twenty-six emancipated slaves, and performed for the first time on 9 July 1866, at the Theatre Royal, Liverpool. They were not a great success. Hague thought the strength of his company was their genuineness: they were the real thing. Audiences, however, saw only what appeared to be a crude version of a stage entertainment they thought was accomplished in a more polished and professional manner by blackface minstrels. A dejected Hague paid for half of his troupe to return home and employed white performers to make up the missing number. One successful black member of the troupe was Aaron Banks, especially so when performing the song "Emancipation Day." Reynolds remarks, "No white man could have put the same amount of enthusiasm and realism into this song."[50] The comment reveals that the success of black minstrels was, indeed, linked to recognition of their authenticity. Nevertheless, only in certain moments, such as this, were black minstrels able to erase the stage from the audience's mind. Hague eventually took the lease of Liverpool's St. James's Hall, but his company grew whiter with each passing year. In the 1870s he had a separate touring company, and as evidence of the popularity of minstrelsy, it has been estimated that he played to around 10,000 people a day during the first weeks of his Christmas season at Birmingham's Bingley Hall.[51]

Barney Hicks's Georgia Minstrels were another early all-black troupe, and included Billy Kersands, inventor of the soft-shoe shuffle.[52] They became Callender's Georgia Minstrels in 1872 and engaged many exceptional performers, such as the comedian Sam Lucas.[53] They were taken over by J. H. Haverly in 1878, expanded to huge size, and featured the celebrated banjoists the Bohee Brothers—one of whom, James, gave banjo lessons to the Prince of Wales. Haverly employed the first commercially successful black songwriter, James Bland (mentioned in chapter 2). Haverly toured Europe with what were now the Colored Minstrels in 1881. One difference between black and blackface troupes was that the latter avoided improvisation whereas the former made use of it, especially in dancing. Haverly dominated the minstrel scene in the 1870s. The mood of the time was for a grand scale: his United Mastodon Minstrels were advertised as "Forty—40—Count 'em—40—Forty."[54] He had theatres in New York and Chicago, went in for spectacle, and was not much concerned about historical accuracy or cultural consistency. One of his shows was set in a Turkish palace, but managed to include a scene of "basket ball."[55] In 1894, Primrose and West, who also favored extravagance, staged a "big minstrel festival" with forty white and thirty black minstrels. Of course, black and white were given separate slots in the show; an integrated performance, unlike the mixed shows that had taken place in Britain, was not tolerated in the United States. The final stage of minstrelsy was reached when the Primrose and West troupes stressed artistry and refinement, and sometimes chose to appear in the attire of the court of Louis XI. The older style of minstrelsy was kept alive by Lew Dockstader, who was to coach Al Jolson.

People went to the blackface minstrel show to see a certain kind of theatrical entertainment; they did not go to learn about African-American culture. This inevitably meant that black troupes found themselves having to conform to blackface conventions in order to achieve success. That does not mean that white audiences could not accept black performers as anything other than minstrels. Minstrelsy was still in its prime when the Jubilee Singers from Fisk University decided to tour Europe. They arrived in England in 1873, and enjoyed an entirely different reception from that given to black minstrels.[56] Here was a group of black Americans introducing a novel genre, the Negro spiritual, which raised no existing expectations on the part of their white audiences. Religious music rarely featured in minstrel shows, so there were no conventions to adhere to. The Jubilee Singers commented on the lack of color prejudice they found in Britain, though Paul Gilroy has cited evidence to the contrary.[57] Certainly, their reception could not have been entirely free of the racial ideology that was growing in Europe and North America with every decade of the century.

The first collection of spirituals had been published as *Slave Songs of the United States* (New York, 1867). Black spirituals invited metaphorical interpretation: in "Go Down Moses," old Pharaoh could seen as representing the slaveowner, and frequent references to Canaan or to "crossing over Jordan" might, in addition to being interpreted in a religious way, also mean the North and freedom from slavery. "Roll, Jordan, Roll" appeared in the *Slave Songs* collection and also featured in slightly different form in the Jubilee Singers' repertoire. Its use of a flattened seventh, and even a flattened third in its very first printed version, as collected by Lucy McKim in 1862, would have confirmed those features as characteristic of African-American music making (see ex. 6.10).[58] Black gospel took another leap into prominence after the Golden Gate Quartet performed at Billy McClain's huge show in Ambrose Park, Brooklyn, in 1895.

Toward the end of the century, minstrelsy was being squeezed out

Example 6.10   "Roll, Jordan, Roll," in G. D. Pike, *The Jubilee Singers* (London: Hodder and Stoughton, 1874), 171.

by vaudeville and ragtime musicals in America. Theatre owners were putting together their own variety shows rather than renting out their premises to visiting troupes. In Britain, minstrelsy faced the challenges of Pierrot troupes (especially at seaside resorts) and variety entertainment. It was a time when minstrel troupes had swollen in size and were sometimes dressed bizarrely in court wigs and breeches. In the 1890s, black American entertainers were abandoning minstrelsy in favor of the Broadway musical. Ragtime songs became popular and were taken up by both black and blackface performers. In England, Salford-born composer Leslie Stuart developed a peculiarly British form of not-quite-ragtime song, such as "Little Dolly Daydream" (1897) and "Lily of Laguna" (1898). "Lily" is remarkable for its extended verse section, and its distant modulations—at one point a modulation from C minor to G minor is succeeded by an abrupt switch to B-flat minor (see ex. 6.11). There is little in the way of syncopation, but "blue" inflections (flattened thirds) are found frequently. Ragtime songs were sung in England by blackface performers like Eugene Stratton, as well as black performers like Pete Hampton.[59]

African-American music had little impact in nineteenth-century Austria (despite tours by the Jubilee Singers and minstrel troupes).[60] The same was true of France (the Ethiopian Serenaders flopped in Paris) until 1892, when the song "Tha-ma-ra-Boum-di-hé" arrived. It has an infectious refrain that songwriter Henry Sayers took from the singing of Mama Lou in a notorious St. Louis cabaret.[61] Originally entitled "Ta-Ra-Ra Boom-Der-É," it had been published in New York the previous year, and had already been made famous in England by Lottie Collins, who performed it as a song and dance at the Grand Theatre, Islington. Marguerite Duclerc then introduced it at the Ambassadeurs, the large café-concert on the Champs-Elysées, and it took Paris by storm. However, it was not the crest of a wave. Not only was Paris host to a new style of cabaret at this time (see chapter 8) but France, like Austria and Germany, already enjoyed a style of popular music that fulfilled similar functions to that of minstrelsy in America and Britain: Gypsy music. Tzigane music in France and Zigeunermusik in Austria

Example 6.11 "Lily of Laguna," words and music by Leslie Stuart (London: Francis, Day and Hunter, 1898), part of the verse.

and Germany started to become popular around the same time as the rise of minstrel troupes. The Romanian Cabaret that opened on the Boulevard Montmartre during the *Exposition Universelle* of 1889 gave a boost to the music in Paris. It led to Gypsy ensembles being engaged at other establishments, such as the Restaurant du Rat Mort and, at the turn of the century, Maxim's. The same issues relating to authenticity and cultural otherness apply.

The Viennese were certainly familiar with minstrelsy and the songs of Stephen Foster. However, the style was never taken up with any effort. Philipp Fahrbach Jr.'s quadrille *Les Minstrels*, op. 206, does not identify any of the tunes, and they may be of his own invention, since they make few gestures in the manner of minstrel style, and are for the most part merely simple melodies with simple harmonic accompaniment (tonic, dominant, and subdominant). Symptomatic of the lack of interest in minstrelsy in Vienna is that there is only a handful of minstrel songs in the music collection of the Österreichische National Bibliothek. Strauss Jr.'s *Der Zigeunerbaron* (1885) ensured that pseudo-Hungarian Gypsy music would dominate the stage for many years, and the popularity of this style delayed the conquest of Austria by jazz. When the cakewalk was introduced in Vienna in 1903, it was soon fashionable across the different classes and became associated with the cultural and social values of modernity.[62] It was not until the 1920s, however, that the battle for supremacy between African-American and Gypsy styles was finally fought out in Austria, and the struggle continues to rage onstage in Emmerich Kálmán's operetta *Die Herzogin von Chicago* (1928).

Minstrel Contradictions

To accuse the blackface minstrel show of being simply racist would invite the question why slavery was not found a fit subject for jokes. Many minstrels were opposed to slavery, and some minstrel song composers, like the Englishman Henry Russell and the American Henry Clay Work, strongly so. Ironically, even the nineteenth century's most famous antislavery text, Harriet Beecher Stowe's *Uncle Tom's Cabin* (1852), seems at times closer to the minstrel show than the plantation; indeed, when it circulated as a stage play it invariably included blacking up and minstrel songs. It is unfair to chastise Stowe for that, when even Herman Melville dishes up a minstrel-style stump speech for a black character in chapter 64 of *Moby-Dick*, a work widely acclaimed as one of the greatest American novels.[63]

To add to the racial contradictions of minstrelsy, it had from the beginning a strong Irish dimension.[64] In the American North, the African-American and Irish working classes shared similar social conditions, which sometimes led to fighting and at other times to friendships and intermarriage. In addition, many important figures in minstrelsy were

Irish American, such as Stephen Foster, Dan Emmett, and George Christy. This Irish side to minstrelsy was not ignored in England. Issue number 14, volume 5, of the *Mohawks Minstrels' Magazine* is described as a "Special Irish Number."

Among the questions the reduction of minstrelsy to racial issues raises is "Would anybody practice the banjo for hours simply to make fun of black banjoists?" John Boucher's *Glossary*, published in London in 1832, describes the banjo as a lower-class instrument.[65] In the 1850s, a clergyman declared the banjo the best adapted of all instruments to the "lowest class of slaves," and "the very symbol of their savage degradation."[66] So why, a few decades later, do we find the future King Edward VII taking banjo lessons from black banjoist James Bohee? Young "society ladies" in New York began to take up the banjo after Lotta (Carlotta Crabtree), who could play the instrument well, became a theatrical star in the late 1860s.[67] By the 1890s, the high-class banjoist was no rarity in Europe or the United States. The banjo, in addition to being the subject of tuition books, was one of the first instruments to be the subject of periodicals aimed at players. *Banjo World* was published in London from 1893 to 1917, running to 271 issues.

Eric Lott has suggested that the early blackface performers were genuinely attracted to black music making, but employed ridicule as a result of white fears and anxieties. That contradictory behavior can be accounted for by the mixture of fear and attraction found frequently in encounters with cultural otherness. Lott maintains that, rather than being its raison d'être, derision in blackface was a means of controlling the "power and interest of black cultural practices."[68] He stresses, as does Eileen Southern, that minstrels did explore these practices, though they were more likely to have pursued their research in urban bars and theatres rather than on plantations.[69]

In disgust at the racism of minstrelsy, it is tempting to relegate it to the periphery of cultural history. There is no mention of blackface minstrelsy in Ronald Pearsall's *Victorian Popular Music* (1973).[70] Yet, in avoiding minstrelsy, we neglect its role in the battle of ideas concerning how people should live and what values they should espouse. Minstrelsy certainly marginalized black concert musicians;[71] but we do not remedy that by marginalizing those black popular musicians that were involved with minstrelsy, such as composer James Bland and dancer Billy Kersands. Moreover, studying minstrelsy forces us to consider such questions as "What is black culture?" and "Who has the power to define black culture?"

Theories of the carnivalesque adapted from Mikhail Bakhtin's work on Rabelais cannot furnish sufficient justification for admiring minstrelsy, since the values being derided and inverted do not always, or even most of the time, have as their satirical target the powerful in society. [72] Issues of class are often well served, but not those relating to ethnicity or gender, which are sometimes linked satirically together, as in the stump speeches on women's rights delivered by the blackface female impersonator. Jokes about big feet (to which, I should inform the reader, I am personally sensitive) are hardly likely to start a revolution against social injustice. How, then, should one listen to blackface minstrelsy now? With one ear in the critical present, I would suggest, and the other listening historically. Locating a pair of hermeneutic ears may appear to be an awkward task, but media scholars have already found the hermeneutic eyes that enable them to watch the old *Carry On* films without wincing.

Minstrelsy allowed things to be said that could not be said in another form, because the mask provided, metaphorically as well as literally, a cover. The social critique was perceived to emanate from a cultural outsider who could not be taken as a genuine threat and, in any case, was assumed to be just acting silly. In the same way, these all-male troupes used female impersonators to say things that no respectable woman could say. This still required careful assessment of the audience's perceived sensitivities. In England, given minstrelsy's predominantly bourgeois subject position, there were limits to the vulgarity of the female impersonator. By contrast, in America they might complain more knowingly on the subject of female rights, for example, proclaiming suggestively that it wasn't fair for women to be "always under men." No minstrel, once the burnt cork was removed, expected to have to account for what he had said or done on stage.[73]

The Minstrel Legacy

Minstrelsy was the catalyst for the unbridgeable rift between popular and art song in the nineteenth century. Before blackface minstrelsy, popular song had often been seen as diluted art song, but now there appeared a kind of song, especially in the 1840s, that seemed to some the antithesis of art song—which is not to say it was not enjoyed, even by some of those who concurred with that estimation. In the early twentieth century, blackface was absorbed into British variety entertainment in the shape of performers like G. H. Chirgwin, Eugene Stratton, and G. H. Elliott. There were some British women, too, who had shown themselves not averse to blacking up, such as May Henderson. Later, blackface emerged in film—in the first talkie, indeed, starring Al Jolson.

A favorite form of minstrel show humor was the "parade skit," in which one person after another enters the scene and confronts the person on stage, who may be a bureaucrat in an office. Frank Sweet points out the longevity of this humorous device, noting that it even featured heavily in the *Monty Python* television series.[74] We also have to remind ourselves that the minstrel trickster reappears in Disney's animated cartoons, not Jim Crow, perhaps, but Bugs Bunny.

It might be argued that the Virginia Minstrels set the pattern for the pop band containing four young men, which reemerged in the late

1950s. Once again, the young men were white and leaned heavily on the practices of black musicians. Rock-and-roll is not a million miles from minstrelsy, as a quick comparison of "Old Dan Tucker" and Elvis Presley's early hit "Jailhouse Rock" (Jerry Leiber and Mike Stoller, 1957) makes clear. Even the lyrics have parallels: both involve characters on the wrong side of the law. I noted earlier that twentieth-century tap-dancing owes a debt to Master Juba, but in addition, dance historian W. T. Lhamon has shown that many of the dance moves made by black dancers of the 1980s and 1990s, including those of Michael Jackson, can be directly related to minstrel show dance steps.[75] We could broaden this out even more, perhaps, and argue that the whole idea of incorporating gesture and bodily movement or dance into the performance of popular song has its roots in minstrelsy. It is something easily overlooked, when this manner of performing popular song has become the norm. Lhamon argues elsewhere that minstrel transgression continues in the performances of white rappers like the Beastie Boys. The significant difference is that blacking up is no longer on the agenda, since self-definition is now in the control of black artists.[76] Looking back on how all this has come about, you may be embarrassed by the role played by minstrelsy, or be offended by minstrels, or despise minstrelsy, but you cannot ignore its impact on popular music.

7

The Music Hall Cockney

*Flesh and Blood,
or Replicant?*

Despite its significance as the major form of working-class stage entertainment over a sixty-year period, the music hall remains a neglected
area in musicology. Much of the scholarly work available tends to focus
on social and economic issues, which are usually linked to the troubled
relationship between popular culture and public morality.[1] Treatment
of music hall performance has been confined mainly to biographical
discussions of the stars of the halls, especially the *lions comiques*. In the
late 1980s, however, questions of performance and style, and the representation of character types, such as the "swell," formed the subject
of a few critical studies.[2] This chapter moves on from there to consider
not just parodic representation or character acting but the "imagined
real" of certain music hall characters. Leading the confusion of the real
and the imaginary in the 1890s was the portrayal on stage and in song
of the Cockney, often a costermonger (or, more familiarly, coster). These
were itinerant street traders who usually sold fruit or vegetables from
a donkey-drawn barrow (the name was derived from costard, a type of
apple). My argument is that from the 1840s to the 1890s the representation of the Cockney in musical entertainments goes through three
successive phases: it begins with parody, moves to the character-type,
and ends with the imagined real. In this final phase, the stage representation is no longer derived from the flesh-and-blood Cockney; instead,
it consists of a replication of an already-existing representation.[3]

Phase 1: Parody

When Charles Dickens introduced the Cockney character Sam Weller into his serialized *Pickwick Papers* in 1836, the impact was enormous; for a start, sales increased a thousandfold over those for the previous issue. The binders had prepared 400 copies of the first number, but "were called on for forty thousand of the fifteenth."[4] In consequence, the character was to have a lasting effect on the representation of Cockneys elsewhere.

Many of the features of what became familiar as "literary" Cockney language are already in place in the anecdote Sam Weller delivers on his first appearance in *Pickwick Papers:*

> "My father, sir, wos a coachman. A widower he wos, and fat enough for anything—uncommon fat, to be sure. His missus dies, and leaves him four hundred pound. Down he goes to the Commons, to see the lawyer and draw the blunt—wery smart—top boots on—nosegay in his button-hole—broad-brimmed tile—green shawl—quite the gen'lm'n. Goes through the archvay, thinking how he should inwest the money—up comes the touter, touches his hat—'Licence, sir, licence?'—'What's that?' says my father.—'Licence, sir,' says he.—'What licence?' says my father.—'Marriage licence,' says the touter.—'Dash my veskit,' says my father, 'I never thought o' that.'—I think you wants one, sir,' says the touter. My father pulls up, and thinks abit—'No,' says he, 'damme, I'm too old, b'sides I'm a many sizes too large,' says he.—'Not a bit on it, sir,' says the touter.—'Think not?' says my father.—'I'm sure not,' says he; 'we married a gen'lm'n twice your size, last Monday.'—'Did you, though,' said my father.—To be sure we did,' says the touter, 'you're a babby to him—this way, sir—this way!'—and sure enough my father walks arter him, like a tame monkey behind a horgan, into a little back office, vere a feller sat among dirty papers and tin boxes, making believe he was busy. 'Pray take a seat, vile I makes out the affidavit, sir,' says the lawyer.—'Thankee, sir,' says my father, and down he sat, and stared with all his eyes, and his mouth vide open, at the names on the boxes. 'What's your name, sir,' says the lawyer.—'Tony Weller,' says my father.—'Parish?' says the lawyer.—'Belle Savage,' says my father; for he stopped there wen he drove up, and he know'd nothing about parishes, *he* didn't.—'And what's the lady's name?' says the lawyer. My father was struck all of a heap. 'Blessed if I know,' says he.—'Not know!' says the lawyer.—'No more nor you do,' says my father, 'can't I put that in arterwards?'—'Impossible!' says the lawyer.—'Wery well,' says my father, after he'd thought a moment, 'put down Mrs. Clarke.'—'What Clarke?' says the lawyer, dipping his pen in the ink.—'Susan Clarke, Markis o' Granby, Dorking,' says my father; 'she'll have me, if I ask, I des-say—I never said nothing to her, but she'll have me, I know.' The licence was made out, and she *did* have him, and what's more she's got him now; and *I* never had any of the four hundred pound, worse luck. Beg your pardon, sir," said Sam, when he had concluded, "but wen I gets on this here grievance, I runs on like a new barrow with the wheel greased."[5]

The characterizing features of Sam Weller's language can be grouped together as follows.

1. Addition, subtraction, and substitution of letters: for example, "horgan" (organ), "babby" (baby), "gen'lm'n" (gentleman), "dessay" (dare say), "arter" (after), "archvay" (archway), "inwest" (invest).
2. Use of catch phrases or sayings: for example, "Dash my veskit" (waistcoat); "struck all of a heap"; "I runs on like a new barrow vith the wheel greased."
3. Use of the present tense for the past: for example, "His missus dies and leaves him four hundred pound"; "up comes the touter."
4. Use of nonstandard vocabulary (neologisms, metaphors, malapropisms, and dialect words): for example, "broad-brimmed *tile*"; "draw the *blunt*."

Backslang does not appear, nor the rhyming-slang so associated with Cockney speech. Cockney humor is there in the association made between roofs and heads—the reference to wearing a "broad-brimmed tile." Compare the examples of slang that Henry Mayhew cites in his *London Labour and the London Poor* (1861) as being used by the coster-mongers.[6] These show the common use of back-slang, which sometimes, though not always, changes a meaning to its opposite: for example, a "trosseno" means not an honest sort ("onessort") but a bad sort of person (as "yob" now means a bad boy). They also offer insight into Cockney humor—"do the tightener" means to go to dinner, that is, cause one's clothes to become tight at the waist. Dickens is restricted in the use he can make of actual Cockney slang, because his middle-class readers would not understand it; therefore, some phrases Mayhew cites are ruled out. In *A Few Odd Characters out of the London Streets* (1857), Mayhew quotes a London costermonger speaking about his use of language:

A penny ve calls a "yennep,"—a shilling is a "ginillhis,"—and a half-crown a "flatch-enorc." For "I've got not money," ve says "I tog on yenom;" and for "look at the policeman," "kool the esilopnam." A pot of beer, is "a top o' reeb" in our lingo; a glass of gin or rum ve dubs "a slag o' nig or mur": and if you vos to ax me vot fammerley I'd got, vy, instead of telling on ye as I'd "three boys and two gals besides the old 'ooman at home," I should say in reg'lar coster there vos "erth yobs and ote elrigs besides the delo namow at emotch."[7]

It is to be wondered, even here, how much of this passage is Mayhew's interpretation. He writes "girls" phonetically as "gals," for instance, yet the backslang version "ote elrigs" would appear to establish that the costermonger is guided by received pronunciation when using backslang.

Dickens, who had less reason than Mayhew to strive for accuracy, may have invented some features of Cockney language and character, while he no doubt exaggerated other features: for example, the extent to which an initial *w* is replaced by *v*, and vice versa.[8] We also have to bear in mind that Dickens was not writing for a Cockney readership. A literate Cockney would not, after all, require special Cockney spellings. Moreover, there is often a moral prejudice at work when Dickens writes nonstandard English. The description for this used to be "substandard English," a phrase that could easily suggest that it might be accompanied by substandard morals: this helps to explain why some of Dickens's characters, like the good Oliver Twist, unaccountably resist what may be interpreted as the "corruption" of the street vernacular. Even a middle-class character who uses slang, like James Harthouse in *Hard Times*, demonstrates a tendency to moral weakness (Harthouse's "idle" use of language is symptomatic of his indolent life; he is continually "going in" for things but lacks application).

Now let us examine an example of parodic representation in song: "The Ratcatcher's Daughter," a "serio-comic ballad" that enjoyed immense success in the 1850s. A correspondent to the *Musical World* in 1855 declares: "Everywhere I go in London . . . I cannot escape the infliction of having my ears stunned with some hideous words relating to the daughter of a ratcatcher and a seller of sand, set to a most vile tune."[9] The song was also being advertised in the *New York Musical World* with not a little exaggeration as the "greatest comic song of the age . . . sung throughout England and Scotland by everybody from Queen to Peasant."[10] It purports to be a tale of costermonger romance and tragedy sung by a Cockney. The words, in fact, issued from the pen of the Reverend Edward Bradley;[11] the music (headed with the expression mark *comicoso con jokerando*) is attributed to the comedian Sam Cowell (1820–64).[12] Cowell was born in London but, from the year after, grew up in America, where he gained his acting experience.[13] He returned only in 1840 and, later that decade, made this song popular at Evans's Song and Supper Rooms. These formed part of a hotel located in Covent Garden, an area where costermongers were a common sight, thus enabling patrons of Evans's to make an on-the-spot comparison between the real and the parody. Costermongers may have set up their barrows or gone to collect food in London's West End, but this was not, of course, a Cockney area of the city. Those were the East End and across the Thames in Lambeth; both places were inclined to assert that they were home to the genuine Cockney. The Song and Supper Rooms of the 1830s and 1840s, whether in Covent Garden or in and around the Strand, cannot be considered remotely working-class in character or clientele, although some of the performers there were later to make the transition to the stages of the more socially varied and geographically dispersed music halls. The tune and first two verses of "The Ratcatcher's Daughter" are given in ex. 7.1.

Repeating the previous taxonomy of Cockney features, a lyric analysis of the complete song reveals the following.[14]

Example 7.1 "The Ratcatcher's Daughter," words by the Reverend E. Bradley, music attributed to Sam Cowell (London: Charles Sheard, 1855).

1. Addition, subtraction, and substitution of letters: for example, "haccident," "'at," "nuffink," "arter," "Vestminstier," "woice."
2. Use of catch phrases or sayings: for example, "bunch of carrots"; "cock'd his ears"; "dead as any herrein'" (herring).
3. Use of the present tense for the past: for example, "so 'ere is an end of Lily-Vite Sand."

4. Use of neologisms, malapropisms, and dialect words: for example, "putty" (pretty); and in the spoken passage after the last verse, "resusticated," "seminary" (cemetery).

No reality effect is achieved by the lyrics of this song, for a variety of reasons: first, because of its satirical character (for example, the reference to her "sweet loud woice"); second, because of the random way it drops an initial *h* (for example, "hat" is in the first verse, "'at" in the second); third, because of the mechanical way it exchanges an initial *v* for *w* (which highlights a glaring inconsistency in verses 8 and 9, where "what" appears in the former and "vot" in the latter); and fourth, because of its mocking or patronizing use of malapropisms, like "seminary" for "cemetery." One expression, "t'other" (for "the other"), stands out oddly, since it is normally associated with the speech of West Yorkshire. Sam Cowell, as the singer, would have been constructing a working-class persona for the audience not to laugh with but, rather, to laugh at. Another Cowell song, "Bacon and Greens," reveals the social class of the audience he expects to be performing to in the unidentified musical quotations used for its interludes. There would be no point choosing quotations that would go unrecognized (they are Bishop's "Home, Sweet Home," Haynes Bayly's "Long, Long Ago," and Balfe's "The Light of Other Days"). It need hardly be added that the musical style of "The Ratcatcher's Daughter" is itself more redolent of the drawing room than the street; this "polite" musical character, indeed, enhances the humorous effect by contrasting incongruously with the "vulgarity" of the Cockney words.

Another example of the Cockney parody song is "Villikins and His Dinah," which was sung by Frederick Robson as the character Jem Bags in a "comedietta" at the Olympic Theatre entitled *The Wandering Minstrel* (1853).[15] It was again made famous by Sam Cowell.[16] The Villikins of the title is offered as a Cockneyfied version of the name William, but that there is nothing particularly Cockney about the tune in terms of topography or style is evident from its being known in the United States as the melody of "Sweet Betsy from Pike." A selection of words and phrases will give its flavor: "wery," "siliver," "parient," "consikvence," "inconsiderable" (malapropism for "inconsiderate"), "diskivery," "unkimmon nice," "mind who you claps eyes on." A *Punch* cartoon of 1854 depicts a middle-class couple trying to capture the spirit of this "low" language (fig. 7.1).

It is instructive to compare these parodic songs with "Sam Hall," a ballad the Scottish entertainer W. G. Ross adapted from the earlier "Jack Hall."[17] He made it famous at the Cyder Cellars, one of the West End's less salubrious venues, located at No. 20 Maiden Lane (which runs parallel to the north side of the Strand).[18] Melodramatic in its cursing and brutality, it has little in common with the songs so far discussed. However, we need to find out what was taking place in venues

TASTE IN THE DRAWING-ROOM.—VILLIKINS AND HIS DINAH.

Young Lady (who ought to know better). "NOW, WILLIAM, YOU ARE NOT LOW ENOUGH YET. BEGIN AGAIN AT 'HE TOOK THE COLD PIZEN.'"

Figure 7.1 Cartoon (1854) by John Leech, in *John Leech's Pictures of Life and Character from the Collection of "Mr. Punch"* (London: Bradbury, Agnew, 1886), 250.

that were even further downmarket to obtain an idea of what coster-mongers were watching and listening to at this time. Evidence, admittedly in prejudiced form, can be gleaned from the journalist James Ritchie's description of a costermongers' "Free and Easy," a singsong in the concert room of a public house:

> I once penetrated into one of these dens. It was situated in a very low neighbourhood, not far from a gigantic brewery, where you could not walk a yard scarcely without coming to a public house. . . . Anybody sings who likes; sometimes a man, sometimes a female, volunteers a performance, and I am sorry to say it is not the girls who sing the most delicate songs. . . . One song, with a chorus, was devoted to the deeds of "those handsome men, the French Grenadiers." Another recommended beer as a remedy for low spirits; and thus the harmony of the evening is continued till twelve, when the landlord closes his establishment.[19]

Further insight is provided by Henry Mayhew's account of a "penny gaff," in this instance, a public entertainment taking place on a small stage in a converted room above a warehouse:

> The "comic singer," in a battered hat and . . . huge bow to his cravat, was received with deafening shouts. Several songs were named by the costers, but the "funny gentleman" merely requested them "to hold their jaws," and putting on a "knowing" look, sang a song, the whole point of which consisted in the mere utterance of some filthy word at the end of each

stanza. Nothing, however, could have been more successful. . . . The lads stamped their feet with delight; the girls screamed with enjoyment. When the song was ended the house was in a delirium of applause. The canvass front to the gallery was beaten with sticks, drum-like, and sent down showers of white powder on the heads in the pit. Another song followed, and the actor knowing on what his success depended, lost no opportunity of increasing his laurels. The most obscene thoughts, the most disgusting scenes were coolly described, making a poor child near me wipe away the tears that rolled down her eyes with the enjoyment of the poison.[20]

To summarize phase 1, the subject position of the parodic Cockney song was middle class. It was influenced in its language by Dickensian Cockney, and in its music by bourgeois domestic song. It represented Cockneys as figures of fun for those who had little cultural understanding of working-class Londoners. Consequently, these songs that supposedly issued from the mouths of Cockneys bore no relation to what was happening in pubs and penny gaffs of the East End.

Phase 2: The Character-Type

In the 1860s, the Cockney becomes one among several character-types available to the music hall performer; others can be, for example, Irish, blackface, rustic, or a city "swell." The character-type differs from the parodic Cockney in that he or she is no longer viewed through a satirical lens. This is not to deny that character-types can slip easily into stereotypes. An important feature to note during this phase, however, is that the identity of the performer is not confused with that of the character. The performer is unmistakably *acting* a role on stage, as Harry Clifton played the part of a brokenhearted Cockney milkman in one of the enduring songs of this decade, "Polly Perkins of Paddington Green."[21]

Alfred Vance (real name Alfred Peck Stevens, 1839–88), one of the *lions comiques,* was the first to represent the coster on the music hall stage.[22] His "The Ticket of Leave Man" (1864) is very different from "The Ratcatcher's Daughter" in both its lyrics and its Jewish melodic and rhythmic character (see ex. 7.2).[23] The presence of Jewish elements should come as no surprise, given that Mayhew, basing his figures on calculations by the chief rabbi, had estimated the number of Jews living in London at midcentury as 18,000.[24] A later survey suggests that the figure may have been around 25,000.[25] The majority of the Jewish working class lived in the East End, especially in or near Whitechapel. There had been in existence there, at least since the 1880s, a Jewish Working Men's Club with a license for music and a seating capacity of 640.[26] The overall population of Whitechapel was 73,518 when Charles Booth was writing in 1891;[27] but by then many more Jews had arrived (London's Jewish population, native and foreign born, increased to 140,000 by 1900). One might speculate as to

Example 7.2 "The Ticket of Leave Man," excerpt, words by A. G. Vance, music by M. Hobson (London: Hopwood and Crew, c. 1864).

(continued)

Example 7.2   *Continued*

whether or not Cockney backslang owes anything to the fact that Hebrew is read from right to left, in other words, backward compared to English.[28] Certainly, in a Cockney backslang expression like "esilop" for "police," it is a reversal of how the word is read rather than how the word sounds (which would have produced "seelop"). Interestingly, the Cockney music hall performer Charles Coborn sings the chorus of his well-known "Two Lovely Black Eyes" in several languages, including Hebrew, on a record he made in 1904.[29]

Until they began to be undersold by poor Irish immigrants, Jewish street traders had almost a monopoly on the sale of oranges and lemons, the former fruit being as popular in music halls then as popcorn is in cinemas today. More than anything, perhaps, Jews were associated with clothes and tailoring, providing the "slap-up toggery" for a Cockney night out or Sunday jaunt. Because of the strength of the Jewish community in the East End, the Jewish Cockney was a well-known character. The father of a popular songwriter of the 1930s, Michael Carr (born Maurice Cohen), for example, was a boxer known, significantly, as "*Cockney* Cohen." Whether being a Jew or being a Cockney came first was probably no more an issue than whether, say, on Merseyside being a Catholic came before being a Scouser (Liverpudlian).

It is difficult to find contemporary Jewish secular music to compare with Vance's "Ticket of Leave." One of the melodies for Hallel, however, has several points of resemblance and was published in a collection of music of the Sephardic liturgy seven years before Vance's song appeared (see ex. 7.3).[30] Sephardim were originally the dominant Jewish community in Whitechapel but, as they became affluent, began to leave the area. Their place was taken, in the main, by Ashkenazim from Poland and Russia. I also offer, perhaps less reliably, an example of a traditional Jewish folk song, "Ale Brider" (We are all brothers), because of the interesting comparison it provides with Vance's song (see ex. 7.4).

It will be noted that most of the melodic material of all three occurs between the tonic and fifth above, that minor gives way to relative major, and that they all feature a melodic stepwise descent from fifth to tonic. The latter is most striking at the final cadences of examples 7.2 and 7.4 (see bracketed passages), which also share in common a 2/4 rhythm and vigorous accompaniment.[31] Vance's song's kinship to a Jewish musical style is not flattering, however: the singer is a Cockney member of the criminal fraternity: to be given a "ticket of leave" was to be released on probation.

Vance's coster representations met with resounding success from the moment he introduced his coster songs, like "The Chickaleary Cove," on the music hall stage in the 1860s. However, it should be borne in mind that he was not just a Cockney character actor or coster

Example 7.3   Hallel Festival Hymn, excerpt, Sephardic liturgy, published London 1857, transposed up a tone to aid comparison.

comedian; he was "The Great Vance" and played other character-types, such as the "swell"—the exhibitionist toff or swaggering "man about town." Example 7.5 gives a taste of the very different character of music and lyrics found in his celebrated swell song "The School of Jolly Dogs."

To summarize phase 2, the identity of the performer remains separate from that of the character portrayed. The cultural experience of Cockneys is mediated by performers who are character-acting on the music hall stage, and hence the appeal of the Cockney character-type is broader in class terms than that of the parodic type.

Example 7.4 "Ale Brider," music traditional, the Yiddish text is based on the poem "Akhdes" by Morris Winchevsky (1856–1932).

Phase 3: The Imagined Real

When we reach phase 3 in the 1880s, the performer is no longer thought of as playing a role, but as *being* the character. In putting forward this argument, I must warn against too close a link being made to Jean Baudrillard's theory of simulacra. I am, certainly, claiming that just as in Baudrillard's third-order simulation, this third phase substitutes "signs of the real for the real itself";[32] but Baudrillard sees third-order simulation as a feature of twentieth-century postmodernity: it is a "generation by models of a real without origin or reality."[33] As far as the music hall Cockney ceases to relate to the real world and is, instead, generated by stage models, this phenomenon might be considered to adumbrate the type of postmodern hyperreality Baudrillard has in mind. He did, after

Example 7.5 "Slap Bang, Here We Are Again, or The School of
Jolly Dogs," excerpt, words and music by Harry Copeland
(London: D'Alcorn, c. 1865).

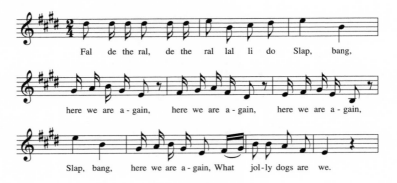

all, make the following pertinent comments on the role of art: "For a
long time now art has prefigured this transformation of everyday life.
Very quickly, the work of art redoubled itself as a manipulation of the
signs of art. . . . Thus art entered the phase of its own indefinite *reproduction*."[34]

The music hall Cockney song becomes increasingly reflexive. Bessie
Bellwood's "What Cheer 'Ria" (Herbert/Bellwood, 1885) has a title that
is a catch phrase in the making: in the lyrics to later songs (discussed
later) it moves, over time, to "Wot Cher" and "Wot'cher," gradually
transforming itself into the "wotcha" still heard around the East End
today.[35] Bessie Bellwood (1857–96) was regarded as a real Cockney,
and she took a hand in the writing of this her best-known song. Actually, she was born Kathleen Mahoney, and as one might expect from
such a name, she started out as a singer of Irish songs.[36] So now we see
the influence of the Irish Cockney as well as the Jewish Cockney.[37]

The song concerns someone attempting to rise above her station,
speculating a "bob" (1 shilling) for a posh seat in the stalls rather than
sitting with her friends in the cheap gallery seats (see ex. 7.6). It might
be thought that Jewish elements can still be detected in this song, in the
melodic style of the minor key verse and in the key change to the relative major for the refrain, but perhaps these features came now as a
influence from already-assimilated elements in other music hall songs.
From now on, it becomes difficult to say exactly *where* Jewish elements
come from, even in twentieth-century musical theatre such as Lionel
Bart's *Oliver!* (1960).[38]

A clear example of how inward-looking music hall song has become in the 1880s appears in the chorus of "What Cheer 'Ria," in the
line "she looks immensikoff [*sic*]," which refers back to a Cockney swell
song hit, "Immenseikoff," written and sung by another star of the halls,
Arthur Lloyd (who, we might note, was actually Scottish) in 1873 (see

Example 7.6 "What Cheer 'Ria," chorus, words by Will Herbert, music by Bessie Bellwood, arranged by George Ison (London: Hopwood and Crew, 1885).

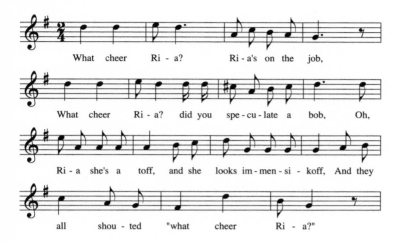

ex. 7.7). It is evident that this particular Cockney dandy has learned from the Viennese popular style, since his song is a polka. Dance rhythms from Vienna were making their mark on British music hall songs. Another swell song, "The Marquis of Camberwell Green,"[39] contains a waltz refrain complete with a characteristic Viennese hemiola rhythm.

It should be mentioned, perhaps, that the swell was not a character-type restricted to male performers: Jenny Hill (1850–96) performed in drag, singing about another Cockney would-be swell, in "'Arry," in the 1880s.[40] The character remained male, however; there was no London music hall equivalent of the female swell or *gommeuse* seen in Parisian cafés-concerts. The female counterpart of 'Arry and his pearly buttons

Example 7.7 "Immenseikoff, or The Shoreditch Toff," chorus, words and music by Arthur Lloyd (London, 1873).

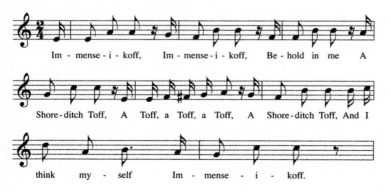

was his "donah" 'Arriet and her feathered bonnet. It was she Bernard Shaw had in mind for Eliza Doolittle when he set about writing *Pygmalion* in 1913: "Caesar and Cleopatra have been driven clean out of my head," he remarked, "by a play I want to write for them in which he shall be a west-end gentleman and she an east-end dona with an apron and three orange and red ostrich feathers."[41]

The reflexivity of music hall song is evident in both the title of "Wot Cher!" (Chevalier/Ingle) of 1891 and, musically, in its use of minor key verse and relative major key chorus. However, some details of pronunciation have changed: we are given "very," not the "werry" that was used in the first verse of Bellwood's song. "Wot Cher!" enjoyed enormous popularity and helped to establish a jerky dotted rhythm and leaping melody as standard features of coster songs. The overall effect can be enhanced with lurching stage movements and cracks in vocal delivery (see ex. 7.8).

The song was made famous by Albert Chevalier (1861–1923), who was important to the growing respectability of the halls. The music hall management were, at this time, concerned to emphasize that men took their wives to the music hall rather than going there to consort with "loose women." The police had become very persistent in looking out for prostitutes: they even opposed a license to London's lavish Oxford Music Hall in 1874 on the grounds that women had been admitted without men, which they assumed could mean only one thing.[42] Mayhew's research had shown that costers usually cohabited in an unmarried state, so Chevalier's coster song "My Old Dutch" (1892) strikes a blow for respectability.[43] It is a eulogy to forty idyllic years with his wife ("Dutch" is short for "Duchess of Fife," Cockney rhyming slang for "wife"). With his theatrical flair, however, Chevalier raised the emotional temperature of the song, as well as introducing social comment, by singing it in front of a stage set consisting of the doors to a workhouse, a place that was often a last refuge for many poor elderly couples and that segregated them by sex. Notice how respectability pervades the music itself, in the guise of features that would have been associated with the middle-class drawing room ballad (see ex. 7.9). Similar repeated quaver chords appear, for example, in the final repeat of the refrain of Balfe's "Come into the Garden, Maud" (1857). The song has untypical harmonic richness, and more attention has been given to the bass line than is the norm for music hall songs. It has an unusually active harmonic rhythm, too, lending it hymn-like associations.

Mrs. Ormiston Chant, the moral crusader outraged by the likes of Marie Lloyd, recorded visiting a music hall in the "poorest part" of London and being moved by the audience's singing of the chorus to this song. She thought the emotion it generated "might be a means of introducing into lives a tenderness and a sentiment not hitherto displayed."[44] Unlike the style of "Wot Cher!" however, the refined style of "My Old Dutch" had no lasting impact on music hall songs. In 1911,

Example 7.8 "Wot Cher!" words by Albert Chevalier, music by
Charles Ingle (his brother) (London, 1891).

Last week   down   our   al - ley   come   a toff,
"Ma'am,"   says   he,   "I   have   some   news   to   tell,

Nice   old   geez - er   with   a   nas - ty   cough,
Your   rich   un - cle   Tom   of   Cam - ber - well,

Sees   my   Mis - sus,   takes   'is   top - per   off,
Popped   off   re - cent,   which   it   ain't   a   sell,

In   a   ve - ry   gen - tle - man - ly   way!
Leav - ing   you   'is   lit - tle   don - key   shay."

"Wot   cheer!" [sic]   all   the   neigh - bours   cried,

"Who're   yer   goin'   to   meet,   Bill?

Have   yer   bought   the   street,   Bill?"   Laugh!   I

thought   I   should   'ave   died,   Knock'd   'em   in   the   Old   Kent   Road!

Hubert Parry felt able to draw a general comparison between music hall
songs and Cockney speech; they were both, he considered, "the result
of sheer perverse delight in ugly and offensive sound."[45]

Ernest Augustus Elen (1862–1940) was, and still is, often put forward as the "real" to Chevalier's "sentimental" coster, as the "tough"
and "true to life" character found out on the streets of London. Gus
Elen's working-class background is often cited approvingly; Chevalier's
background was lower middle class. Elen had worked as a draper's assistant, an egg-packer, and a barman, though how much such experi-

Example 7.9   "My Old Dutch," excerpt, words by Albert Chevalier, music by Charles Ingle (his brother) (London, 1892).

ences informed his stage persona is impossible to say. He spoke of the influence of Chevalier when interviewed in the *Era* (a music hall paper) in 1905, yet on being asked if he had studied actual costers he replied, "unconsciously, perhaps." To point the contrast between Chevalier and Elen, my next example turns from the lovely wife to the horrid wife.

There is a short film of Elen, late in life, performing "It's a Great Big Shame," a song about a large, burly man who has fallen victim to a tiny, bullying wife.[46] Elen's detailed notebook has survived, showing how carefully he worked out gestures and routines ("Business Make-ups," as he called them).[47] Stage movements can, of course, be timed with precision when accompanied by music. In the Pathé short of 1932, he reproduces the directions in the notebook. Such a meticulous approach is not one associated with "being yourself" or "getting into character" using the Stanislavski method. His movements (the shamble and the jerk) and his demeanor (the grim and "deadpan" face to suit a tragi-comic role) point to the kinesic and mimic codes of music hall. His characteristic vocal delivery (little falsetto breaks in the voice before plunging down onto a melody note) also indicates a stylized performance. In fact, not even these cracks in the voice are left to be improvised; their precise locations are set down in his notes:

> When singing lines—at scrappin' 'e 'ad won some great
>   renown.
> It took two coppers for to make 'im move along.
> And annover six to 'old the feller dow-own.
> On word 'renown' Jerk this out—latter part of word like
>   double note
> (Re-now-own)—an extra Jerk out word (down)[48]

The music to these words is reproduced in ex. 7.10.

The melodic style developed for Elen by composer George Le Brunn is designed to enhance such a vocal delivery. The style permeates one of Elen's best-known songs, "If It Wasn't for the 'Ouses in Between" of 1894 (see ex. 7.11).[49] Notice, also, that there is not a plain "vamp till ready" between verses, but something suggesting an opportunity for comic stage business.

The musical style would have driven Parry to fury. "Ugly and offensive sounds" begin almost at once: for example, the first measures of the introduction have the leading note falling to the sixth he hated so much, a product, as we have seen, of the Viennese popular revolution. There are also what he would have regarded as crude dissonances in the second half of measure 3. These two songs show the lyricist Edgar Bateman introducing features of the "new Cockney" accent that is found in the work of Andrew W. Tuer (notably, *The Kaukneigh Awlminek* of 1883) and, later, in the work of Bernard Shaw.[50] Both writers listened to actual Cockneys speaking and, concluding that the Dickensian Cockney had passed away, introduced phonetically a new range of

Example 7.10 "It's a Great Big Shame," verse 2, excerpt, words by Edgar Bateman, music by George Le Brunn (London: Francis, Day and Hunter, 1895).

sounds—not that this stopped other writers, like George R. Sims and Somerset Maugham, from continuing in the older vein. Bateman uses the new *f* for *th* in words like "think," and the new *ah* for *ow*. In the song sheet of "If It Wasn't for the 'Ouses in Between," he finds it necessary to add a footnote explaining that "kah" means "cow." Other features of the "new" pronunciation, for example, "down't" for "don't," "loike" for "like," "grite" for "great" or Cockney glottal stops in words like "little" ("li'le"), were not indicated in the song as published, but then Elen was not restricted to reproducing only the phonetic spellings provided by Bateman, as his extant recordings demonstrate. For example, in "It's a Great Big Shame," although Bateman writes "I've lost my pal," Elen sings "I've *lorst* my pal." However, he retains the long *a* in "great big shame," in preference to Shavian Cockney, which would be "gryte big shyme."[51]

An idea of the critical reception of Elen in the 1890s can be ascertained from the typical praising of his performances as "authentic Cockney," "true pictures," and an "ungarnished portrayal of the coster as he really is."[52] Sixty years later, the abiding memory of Elen was that he was "the real thing . . . not an actor impersonating a coster, but a real coster, or, at any rate, a real Cockney of the poor streets."[53] For those who chose to interpret Elen's stage persona as the real Cockney, the sign had, to borrow words from Umberto Eco, abolished "the dis-

Example 7.11 "If It Wasn't for the 'Ouses in Between," excerpt, words by Edgar Bateman, music by George Le Brunn (London: Francis, Day and Hunter, 1894).

tinction of the reference."[54] As a result, it now became difficult for performers like Elen to get out of character, either to play other characters
on stage or to be themselves offstage. It is interesting to note that the
requirement to continue an onstage character when *off*stage (as in the
case of Leybourne's swell, discussed in chapter 3) is now overturned by
the desire for a performer to retain an offstage character when *on*stage.

There are serious problems with the picture of Elen as the real
Cockney, however, and they can be illustrated easily with reference to
"It's a Great Big Shame" and his performance of that song. The song is
a *joke;* it is not a slice of real life. How often do men 6 feet 3 inches tall
marry women who are 4 feet 2 inches tall? Of those who do, how many
become victims of marital bullying? The reality does not square with
the song, especially since the reverse, the beating of wives or female
partners, was not uncommon in coster communities. In fact, the social
reality forms the substance of a joke in the last verse and following patter in another Cockney song, Charles Coborn's "He's All Right When
You Know Him" (1886). W. S. Gilbert wickedly intimated in "The Policeman's Song" (from *The Pirates of Penzance*) that far from being intimidated by women, the coster is not averse to "jumping on his mother"
followed by "basking in the sun." A poker-faced Henry Raynor cites this
as an example of Gilbert finding the working class "unamiably funny."[55]

If, nevertheless, Gus Elen's character comes across in "It's a Great
Big Shame" as being built of typical coster determination and a blunt
Cockney "I won't stand for any nonsense" attitude, how do we react
when we find him adopting a passive role as the victim of a bullying
wife himself? In the ironically titled "I'm Very Unkind to My Wife" (Nat
Clifford), he is married to a woman who is even prepared to stab him
with a kitchen knife. If Elen's voice is the voice of the true coster, why
does his language change (if not always his pronunciation), depending
on who has written the lyrics to his songs? There is little Cockney vernacular, for example, in "Down the Road" (Fred Gilbert, 1893). Of
course it may be objected that Elen simply has to sing whatever lyrics
others have written; but that is partly my point: his Cockney character
is textually rather than genetically constructed. Moreover, he bears the
sign of "the star entertainer" in what was in the 1890s a well-established
star system; thus, his own star persona makes a significant contribution
to the way his presence on stage is received. Finally, for a "real" coster,
his language is remarkably free of swearing; not even the extremely
common Cockney expletive "Gawblimey!" is to be found.

Turning to the reception of Elen and Chevalier, one is inclined to ask
why toughness is perceived as real and sentimentality as phony. Are we
to assume that the latter mood was unknown among costers—there is
evidence to suggest otherwise[56]—or is it that sentimentality is a mark of
untruth for those who espouse the values of high art? And what if the
reception of Elen as "real" arises, ironically, from a sentimental disposi-
tion toward the working class, a desire to see a coster as a "rough dia-

mond," on the part of middle-class theatre critics? It was not uncommon for middle-class perceptions of the working class to be colored by what was seen in the music hall. Richard Hoggart has even accused the "stringent and seemingly unromantic" George Orwell of doing just that.[57]

Marie Lloyd (real name Matilde Wood, 1870–1922), like Elen, had a reputation for being the real thing on stage. George Le Brunn, who had composed hits for Elen, also went on to provide songs for Marie Lloyd, and in her coster girl songs, she was to adopt voice breaks similar to those worked out by Elen. Yet despite those who thought she "expressed herself, the quintessential Cockney," [58] her recordings reveal that she could put on and take off the Cockney accent at will. Her recorded performance of "Every Little Movement Has a Meaning of Its Own" (Cliffe/Moore, 1910), for example, is not Cockney.[59] Moreover, she characterizes her material: the Cockney persona she adopts on her recording of "A Little of What You Fancy Does You Good" (Leigh/Arthurs, 1912)[60] is not the same as that on "The Coster Girl in Paris" (Leigh/Powell, 1912);[61] even though the song has the same lyricist and was recorded in the same year. Dare one suggest that rather than being herself, Marie Lloyd was *acting?* This is not to deny Lloyd's pride in being an East End Cockney, nor is it to argue that Cockneys did not recognize themselves in or identify with the music hall Cockney;[62] rather, it is to recognize that such behavior can be persuasively explained with reference to Louis Althusser's theory of interpellation, and the propensity for human beings to identify with desired images of themselves or others.[63] The case I have been making here is that the coster character becomes an example of a desired image created by the music hall and perpetuated by the music hall's feeding on itself rather than by drawing ideas from, or representing, the world outside. That is why the issue of reflexivity is so important. My contention is that a representational code is learned and reproduced and, bingo, you have a Cockney. Isn't that how Dick Van Dyke did it in *Mary Poppins* (Walt Disney, 1964)? In other words, *a real figure is not represented anymore; an already-existing representation is replicated.* Here is an example in a nutshell: a much-admired impressionist represents, say, a politician on television; then another impressionist comes along intending to represent that same politician but, instead, offers a replication of the previous impressionist's representation. If this continues, the politician can sometimes seem to be empty and lifeless compared to the replicant.

It may help to clarify the argument by giving an example of a late-twentieth- and early-twenty-first century simulacrum that replaces something that was formerly part of the lives of a specific community. This is the ubiquitous "Irish Pub." Originally representing a friendly, welcoming, down-to-earth alternative to the soulless urban pub owned by one of the profit-hungry big brewers, these establishments can now be found in every major European city. The result is not a proliferation of imitations of pubs that exist in Ireland, but rather a generation from an imaginary model of an Irish pub, a model encoded with every desirable sign of Irishness. Yet because these pubs replace rather than *symbolize*, and replace rather than *displace*, the phase may already have been reached when some people feel persuaded that an "Irish Pub" in Berlin or Rome is more convincingly Irish, more real for them, than a pub in Ireland. What is more, just as Cockneys were able to identify with the Cockney replicant, Irish people are able to identify with the Irish Pub simulacrum. Cultural insiders and outsiders alike can be willingly sucked into the experience of hyperreality.

The influence of African-American styles of music, particularly as mediated through dance bands, began to erode the dominance of music hall and variety theatre in British popular culture after World War I. But when the Cockney did reappear in song, it was as the replicant—

Example 7.12 "Wot'cher Me Old Cock Sparrer," excerpt, words by Billy O'Brien, music by Billy O'Brien and Jack Martin (1940).

think of "Wot'cher Me Old Cock Sparrer" (1940)[64] and "My Old Man's a Dustman" (1960).[65] A glance at the lyrics of the first of these will satisfy anyone that this is a Cockney picture produced with the most economical of imaginative means (see ex. 7.12). The Old Kent Road and Lambeth are dropped in as talismanic words, and the merely impressionistic function of "Wot'Cher" is evident in its redundant midpoint apostrophe—there is now no sense of that expression's historical origins in "What Cheer!"

The tune adopts the jerky rhythm found in many Chevalier and Elen songs. It is surely not without significance that this rhythm reappears in the song "Wouldn't It Be Luverly" from Lerner and Loewe's *My Fair Lady* (1956). At one stage in the 1990s, the Cockney replicant seemed about to make a comeback in the shape of Damon Albarn on the pop group Blur's album *Parklife* (1994), but this direction was not pursued further. He was stung, perhaps, by accusations of being a "Mockney." Yet this was a misconception on the part of his critics: like others before him, Albarn was faithfully reproducing a copy of a copy; he was not imitating or mocking an original.

Replication and reflexivity in Cockney stage and screen images in the twentieth century have been most obvious in television series like *On the Buses* and in the long-running series of *Carry On* films. However, the new realism of British television soaps like *Eastenders* may have put an end to the replicant. Or is such a judgment premature? Here is a quotation from a review in the *Times* (London) of a television drama broadcast in March 1998 on BBC 1 and entitled, of all things, *Real Women*.

> the worst disaster to befall the characters was that most of them were possessed by unquiet spirits from an old episode of *On the Buses* and started rabbiting on like gor-blimey Cockneys. At first they just said things such as, "Me bunion's playin' me up." . . . Then the poltergeists got angry and started commenting on the script, "A flamin' farce where the 'usband from 'ell's been knockin' off me best mate!" raged one. "I must 'ave been so stupid!" wailed another. "I don't think I could take much more," moaned the spirit occupying the character of the bride, and you could see the point.[66]

Indeed, I hope this chapter has been a further contribution to elucidating the same point. As a final example of Cockney generated purely by code, I must mention the "dialectizer" at www.rinkworks.com, which will instantly translate any internet website into Cockney. For example, the phrase "the creative process and aesthetic response to music" is immediately translated as "the bloomin' creative Queen Bess and aesffetic response ter music." It is apparent that while the code is indebted to Shavian Cockney, it nevertheless allows for the production of some innovative rhyming-slang. Moreover, the rhymes it finds are not rigidly controlled—it generates a variety of rhymes, apparently at random, for words ending "–ess." The effect, of course, is that they seem to emanate from a real person.

8

No Smoke without Water

The Incoherent Message of Montmartre Cabaret

Montmartre was still a hilltop village in the 1880s, though Paris had annexed it in 1860. The Montmartre *cabarets artistiques* were originally designed to attract not the general public but instead an informal gathering of musicians, theatrical performers, poets, and artists. The Chat Noir, founded in 1881, appealed to the Hydropathes and the Incohérents, groups of Left Bank writers, performers, and bohemian intellectuals committed to *l'esprit fumiste* (hoaxing and joking) and to socializing during the hours of darkness when artistic work proved difficult. Erik Satie also frequented this cabaret, and accompanied the chansonnier Vincent Hypsa. This strange mixture of artistic activity, and the contradictions it throws up, accounts for the title I have given this chapter.

Art historians have long considered that the Chat Noir was important to the rise of modernism, and cultural historian Bernard Gendron has made a case for its impact on music, but musicologists, with the notable exception of Steven Whiting, have largely ignored it.[1] Yet these artistic cabarets raise important questions about the relationship between avant-gardism, modernism, and popular culture that have particular relevance for understanding musical developments in the second half of the twentieth century. As well as assessing the musical significance of the cabaret's performers, this chapter examines the contradictions of Montmartre cabaret, asking to what extent the *chansons réalistes* were a mouthpiece for the Parisian underclass and to what extent they were entertainment for the more affluent who enjoyed the idea of "slumming" in Montmartre. Aristide Bruant, who became a Chat Noir regular in 1884, sang of the dispossessed and disaffected, though he was of provincial middle-class origin himself. Moreover, these once subversive cabarets were relying on wealthy middle-class patronage before the century was out and, in the opinion of some critics, had nothing more to offer than silly songs.

The cabarets and artistic cafés fostered a unique atmosphere of elitism mixed with rebellion, in which social satire was nurtured and bourgeois values were ridiculed. The first to open, and the first to adopt the gothic style, which in this context brought Rabelais to mind for the French, was the Grande Pinte (28, avenue Trudaine) in 1878.[2] At around six in the evening you would enter and "choke a parrot" (*étouffer un perroquet*)—that is, drink a glass of (bright green) absinthe[3]—then later recite your verse or sing your songs while keeping your throat lubricated with beer (a drink made popular by the Paris World Expositions in 1867 and 1878). Cabaret reinvigorated the chanson, bringing back its concern with social issues, such as injustice, corruption, poverty, and crime. Jules Jouy's "Le Réveillon des Gueu," for example, warns of imminent conflict between the hungry poor and the wealthy. Though songs at cafés-concerts were subject to censorship, less attention was given to cabaret.[4]

Chanson is not synonymous with song or, for that matter, sung poem in France. Chanson usually demands a theatrical style of performance involving collaborative effort (words, music, staging), is a mixture of low and high features, and has a tradition of social comment.[5] A chanteur simply sang songs; a chansonnier was a singer-poet, though this did not necessarily entail composing the music. The precursors of nineteenth-century chanson were the songs sung to existing tunes and disseminated by words alone. A famous chansonnier from the first half of the nineteenth century was Pierre-Jean de Béranger (1780–1857), who became known for his politically charged performances in the Caveau moderne from 1813. However, the term *chansons populaires* was used to describe songs of a rustic character that we would now label folk songs, and so reminds us that there are different nuances in the French use of the word "popular." These songs took on political resonances during the Second Empire;[6] and there is no doubt that, being perceived as simple and realistic "songs of the people," they influenced the ideological character of Montmartre chansons.

The Chat Noir and Aristide Bruant

Rodolphe Salis opened the Chat Noir in 1881 at the premises of a former post office, 84 boulevard De Rochechouart. Most of the Hydropathes (1878–81), led by journalist and poet (but not chansonnier) Emile Goudeau, moved there, and were to be highly influential on the cabaret's beginnings, as well as what happened more generally in Montmartre.[7] Goudeau took the name Hydropathes from Joseph Gung'l's *Hydropathen Waltz,* but for him and his friends it had nothing to do with water cures; it was the rejection of water for alcohol. [8] Such reversals— here turning temperance to its opposite—were typical of fumist wit. The cabaret moved to larger premises at 12, rue de Laval (now rue Victor Massé) in 1885 and survived until 1897. It became, according to a regular, Maurice Donnay, "en effet une école chansonnière."[9] It was originally advertised as a Louis XIII cabaret (a reference to its bizarre but by no means authentic décor) founded by a *fumiste.*[10] A *fumiste,* as described by the composer Georges Fragerolle in 1880, was a lion in an ass's skin.[11] *Fumisme* was dedicated to the deflation of smugness and pomposity. Salis dressed his waiters in the formal robes of the Académie des Beaux Arts, provoking the latter to bring a lawsuit against him in 1892, though it was unsuccessful.[12] The Incohérents (1882–96), founded by Jules Lévy, were another group of writers, artists, and performers equally committed to fumist wit. An example was the composition produced by Alphonse Allais for the 1884 exhibition of "incoherent paintings" at the Café des Incohérents, rue Fontaine. It is a completely silent funeral march for a "great deaf man" (ex. 8.1).[13]

The Incohérents also became a prominent force at the Chat Noir, and were the cause of the added political edge found in pages of the house journal, though the tone remained humorous and satirical rather than polemical. Allais became editor of this journal in 1891, with his belief that jokes were the only defense against solemnity.[14] The paper

Example 8.1   Alphonse Allais, *Marche Funèbre* (1884) (my facsimile).

MARCHE FUNÈBRE

COMPOSÉE POUR LES

FUNÉRAILLES D'UN GRAND HOMME SOURD

Lento rigolando

attracted a wide circulation, stimulated no doubt by the new law on press freedom passed in 1881.[15] Allais's biggest *blague* (teasing pretense) was pretending to be the conservative critic Francisque Sarcey, attributing Sarcey's name to ironic articles he'd written. He sometimes invited people to dinner, giving Sarcey's address instead of his own, and warning them that he had a mad servant who might try to stop them from entering.[16]

Erik Satie, called by Allais "Esoterik Satie," was hired by Salis as second pianist in the Chat Noir, and accompanied the chansonnier Vincent Hypsa, who specialized in parodies—including one of the Toreador's Song from *Carmen* putting forward the bull's point of view. Satie also wrote a fumist essay on the musicians of Montmartre in 1900, which offers a mock social-historical survey.[17] Satie's humor was much affected by his association with the Chat Noir.[18] The café-concert was the subject of scorn there, and unresponsive audiences would be told to get off to one. Rodolphe Salis adopted an entertaining way of being rude to his audience; he was particularly fond of exaggerated politeness ("Take a seat, your grace").

Aristide Bruant (1851–1925), who had started off as a performer with a dandy persona in the Scala and the Horloge cafés-concerts, was taken to the Chat Noir by Jules Jouy. Bruant represented the *chanson populaire* and wrote the cabaret's theme song, the "Ballad of the Chat Noir," which appeared in issue 135 of the house journal (9 August 1884). He then decided to reject his former lively, bantering types of song and become a bard of the street.[19] He remodeled his image and repertoire so that words, music, and persona all became part of the aesthetic experience he offered. His high boots, wide-brimmed black hat, cloak, and red scarf caught the attention of Henri Toulouse-Lautrec and are, therefore, still well known from Toulouse-Lautrec's posters.[20] His impact on popular music, especially his development of the genre of the *chanson réaliste* (influenced by reading Zola), has received much less attention.[21] Bruant's method of distancing himself from emotional involvement had a lasting effect in cabaret and the cabaret-influenced music theatre that was to develop elsewhere in Europe. It is perhaps most immediately apparent in the blunt delivery found at times in the chansons of Georges Brassens, Barbara, and Léo Ferré, but a song like "Die Moritat von Mackie Messer" (Brecht/Weill, 1928), for example, also demands Bruant's treatment.

When the Chat Noir moved to bigger premises in 1885, Bruant stayed on and created Le Mirliton (The reed pipe), which remained a *cabaret artistique*. Bruant was, in fact, honored with membership of the Société des Gens de Lettres in 1891, despite *vers mirliton* being the French for doggerel. Salis was keen to move in order to expand, but was also desirous of avoiding the brawls that had afflicted his previous establishment, often as a result of friction between locals and some of his well-to-do clientele.[22] Bruant found he could keep the *Alphonses*

Figure 8.1
Aristide Bruant.

(pimps) out and handle rowdiness better with his blunt remarks like "Shut your row, blast you all, I'm going to sing."[23] This he did, accompanied by a pianist and with two men he paid to join in refrains.[24] He could also deliver certain songs in an apparent rage. Lisa Appignanesi calls Bruant's Mirliton "the initial theatre of provocation";[25] patrons were picked on if they happened to wander in or out while he was performing.

Bruant sang of the dispossessed and disaffected, building a celebrated repertoire of songs of the *barrières*—"A la Villette," "A Grenelle," "A la Chapelle," "A la Bastille," and so forth. The original barriers were taxation points for those entering the city with goods; the *faubourgs* (suburbs) themselves were home to the Parisian working class. Bruant, himself, was of provincial middle-class origin and knew nothing of the Parisian *faubourgs* before the age of seventeen. In fact, he confesses that he was at first shocked by the slang he heard there, but was soon attracted to its originality, liveliness, brutality, cynicism, and rich use of metaphors and neologisms.[26] Bruant does not proclaim a direct political message, but as Peter Hawkins remarks in his book on chanson, "without being politically explicit, the spirit is anarchist and populist, even if it is not elevated to the level of a doctrine."[27] This was certainly the impression a seller of the anarchist newspaper *La Libertaire* had of him, until he realized Bruant had no intention of buying the paper he was selling.[28] Having been a soldier, Bruant also wrote some patriotic songs: "Serrez les rangs" (Close ranks) may have come back to haunt him when his son died doing just that when leading an attack during World War I.

To choose a typical example of Bruant's output, "A la Villette" (1885) has a trite tune and banal rhythm that, along with his unflinching, deadpan delivery, act as a perfect match for the monotonous and impoverished existence of its antihero, Toto Laripette, and increase the sense of brutality as the song ends with his neck held ready for the guillotine (ex. 8.2). [29] There is no overt indignation, though it is implied, and there is no judgmental attitude.

Verse 1
Il avait pas encor' vingt ans.
I'connaissait pas ses parents.
On l'app'lait Toto Laripette
A la Villette. . . .

Verse 6
De son métier i'faisait rien.
Dans l'jour i'baladait son chien:
La nuit i'comptait ma galette,
A la Villette. . . .

Verse 9
La dernièr' fois que je l'ai vu,
Il avait l'torse à moitié nu,
Et le cou pris dans la lunette
A la Roquette.

Verse 1
He wasn't yet twenty.
He didn't know his parents.
They called him Toto Laripette
at la Villette. . . .

Verse 6
He made nothing of his job.
He walked his dog during the day:
at night he shared my money
at la Villette. . . .

Verse 9
The last time I saw him,
his chest was half bare,
and his neck was held ready for the guillotine
at Roquette prison. [30]

Example 8.2 "A la Villette" (1885), words and music by Aristide
Bruant.

Bruant's coldness prevented his song from being seen as sentimental. His concern with social injustice was heightened by singing in the
first person, suggesting personal involvement, though the "I" of the
songs is usually another narrative voice rather than Bruant himself.
Surprisingly, perhaps, given Bruant's strongly masculine persona (see
fig. 8.1), the narrative voice in "A la Villette" is feminine (though if his
recordings are anything to go by, he omitted the stanza with the line "I'
m'app'lait sa p'tit' gigolette"). Having lived near Mazas prison and visited
it regularly, he acquired knowledge of criminal language and behavior.
The overall effect was one of authenticity, his listeners feeling that his
songs "take the real life of poor and miserable and vicious people, their
real sentiments . . . and they say straight out, in the fewest words, just
what such people would really say, with a wonderful art in the reproduction of the actual vulgar accent."[31] Yet we may wonder how that reception squared with the theatricality of the red scarf, big hat, and cape.

Bruant's costume indicated a theatrical frame for his performance,
reassuring his listeners that it was, after all, an act. Francis Carco suggests that Bruant's audience was seeking sensation: "the fine ladies
shuddered with horror, without doubting that Bruant, after having
troubled them, would laugh about it."[32] Hawkins, following a line similar to Carco, proposes that Bruant's songs appealed to the bourgeoisie
because they were "tales from the other side of the tracks," inspiring "a
sentiment of gratitude for the security of the bourgeois lifestyle" while
allowing them to enjoy "the thrill of imagining themselves in touch
with the dangerous life of the streets."[33] The rudeness with which he
often addressed directly individual patrons, and which he had inherited
from Salis, added to the engrossment of his audience. As Erving Goffman explains of audience-insulting routines: "the recipient of the
frame-breaking remark is forced into the role of performer, forced
sometimes to project a character. He, in consequence, floods out, and
this provides a source of involvement for the remaining members of
the audience."[34]

Bruant's theatrical frame was, in fact, loosely applied. He walked
up and down while singing, thus avoiding a set space, such as a stage
or platform that would delineate a represented world separated from a

real world. Yet one could argue that the Mirliton itself was his stage set. In this regard, it is significant that when he was asked to perform at the Ambassadeurs and the Eldorado, he agreed to do so only if the Mirliton were recreated on stage. Bruant also adopted practices typical of real-life social communication that enhanced the perception of the authenticity of his characterizations. It was not just his frequent use of the first person, or the sense that he knew personally the characters he sang about; it was his use of slang and casual references to working-class mores delivered with the implication that he need not explain himself. At the same time, he needed to ensure, as did the Cockney singers discussed in chapter 7, that his audience could follow him. Like the music hall costers, he avoids backslang, for example, *le verlan*, a form of French prison slang that typically reverses the order of syllables (*verlan* is derived from *envers*). He made sure he gave listeners enough intelligible vocabulary to help them follow the narrative, as can be seen in the excerpted verses from "A la Bastoche" (ex. 8.3).

Verse 1
Il était né près du canal,
Par là . . . dans l'quartier d'l'Arsenal,
Sa maman qu'avait pas d'mari,
L'appelait son petit Henri . . .
Mais on l'appelait la Filoche
A la Bastoche. . . .

Verse 5
Un soir qu'il avait pas mangé,
Qu'i'rôdait comme un enragé;
Il a, pour barbotter l'quibus,
D'un conducteur des Omnibus,
Crevé la panse et la sacoche
A la Bastoche.

Verse 1
He was born by the canal,
over there . . . in the Arsenal district.
His mother, who hadn't a husband,
called him her little Henry. . .
But they called him the shirker
at la Bastoche. . . .

Verse 5
One evening when he hadn't eaten
and was prowling around like a madman,
he punctured both the belly and the bag
of a conductor of the local trains
in order to steal money
at la Bastoche.[35]

Example 8.3   "A la Bastoche" (1897), words and music by Aristide Bruant.

Bruant's chanson "A la Bastoche" has a structure of four two-measure phrases followed by one three-measure phrase (with an ac-celerando), which makes for a satisfying sense of completeness. How-ever, the fast interludes in a different meter are a puzzle. These appear to quote the melody of one of his wryly humorous chansons, "Belleville-Ménilmontant," but the purpose is unclear—it may be there merely in order for its jollity to make an ironic and dramatic contrast with the mood of the verses. Beyond the thought given to phrasing, the piano accompaniment is, as usual, very basic, and the song melody itself has no carefully shaped structure (for example, it lacks internal symmetries) and suggests something originally improvised as a vehicle for the words. These seem to demand a three-quaver anacrusis rather than the existing one quaver with the other two pushed into the following measure; however, French does not require the same kind of stress as English, and thus the issue of verbal stress coinciding with musical accent is not the same. The skeletal melody resembles the kind often found in the work of amateur songwriters and invites an improvisatory flexibility when sung.[36] Yet whatever corners have been cut musically, the words have been given considerable thought, and have been carefully structured to provide the desired narrative pace, as well as to lead back to the first stanza at the end, with its suggestion of the youth having been doomed from the beginning and of a fresh cycle of misery beginning for those born by the canal.[37] "The Bastoche" is a vernacular term for the Bastille district. Little Henri is not the sort to excite sentimental sympathy; yet Bruant does elicit our empathy for the brutality and poverty of the lives of the unfortunates he sings about. This is partly achieved by the contextualized portraits he paints of his characters, often incorporating details of childhood and parents (or their absence) into the character's past history.

Other Cabaret Artists

Jules Jouy (1855–97) was in many ways closest to Bruant in his repertoire. He wrote topical and political songs that he sang to his own piano accompaniment at the Chat Noir and, later, at its rival the Chien Noir (created by Victor Meusy with other Chat Noir performers in 1895) and at his own Cabaret des Décadents (opened 1893). His "La Veuve" (1887) became a well-known antiguillotine song. In 1886, Jouy reworked Jean-Baptiste Clément's song "Le Temps de cerises" ("Cherry Time") as "Le Temps des crises" (Crisis time).[38] In doing so, he made a more overtly political statement out of a song that had earlier been a favorite of the Communards of 1871, who interpreted the return of spring as a metaphor for the return of liberty.

It should not be assumed, however, that all cabaret performers chose the same themes. The postal employee Maurice Mac-Nab (1856–89) sang ironic songs of working-class life at the Club des Hydropathes, then with the breakaway group the Hirsutes. He enjoyed his first success as an *auteur-interprète* (author-performer) in the basement of the Café de l'Avenir. He specialized in macabre and grotesque songs, such as "Suicide en partie double," in praise of double suicides;[39] and "Les Fœtus," in which he concludes that aborted fetuses enjoy the singular good luck of being dead before they are born. The subject matter of this chanson certainly points to the sometimes striking difference in repertoire between the cabaret and the café-concert, and the effect of the text being set as a waltz melody is bizarre (ex. 8.4). One of his milder

Example 8.4   "Les Fœtus" (1892), words by Maurice Mac-Nab, music by
Camille Baron.

satires that reached a wider audience was "Le Pendu," in which a hang-
ing man dies while one person after another calls for someone to help
in the emergency. Mac-Nab also sang chansons with anarchist sympa-
thies, like "L'Expulsion." Michel Herbert describes him as the leader of
the topical chansonniers.[40] Ill health forced him to give up performing,
and he died of tuberculosis at the early age of thirty-three.

He sang with a piano accompaniment, and his voice was of a memorable, if not very musical, character:

> Mac-Nab possessed the most hoarse and out of tune voice that it is possible
> to imagine; it was like listening to a seal with a cold. But that bothered him
> little. He sang all the same, without worrying about the desperate gestures
> of Albert Tinchant, his usual accompanist.[41]

A favorite Mac-Nab political-satirical chanson at the Chat Noir was "Le
Grand Métingue du Métropolitain," which celebrates the strike by metal
workers at Vierzon (Mac-Nab's birthplace, near Bourges) in 1886. It
pokes fun at the municipal police, and makes ironic use of phrases associated with appeals to patriotism.

Verse 1

C'était hier, samedi, jour de paye,
Et le soleil se levait sur nos fronts.
J'avais déjà vidé plus d'une bouteille,
Si bien qu'j'm'avais jamais trouvé si rond!
V'là la bourgeoise qui radine devant l'zinc:
"Feignant!"—qu'elle dit—"t'as donc lâché l'turbin?"
— "Oui," que j'réponds, "car je vais au métingue,
Au grand métingue du Métropolitain!"

Verse 2

Les citoyens, dans un élan sublime,
Etaient venus, guidés par la raison;
A la porte, on donnait vingt-cinq centimes
Pour soutenir les grèves de Vierzon.
Bref, à part quatre municipaux qui chlinguent
Et trois sergots déguisés en pékins,
J'ai jamais vu de plus chouette métingue
Que le métingue du Métropolitain!

Verse 1

It was yesterday, Saturday, payday,
and the sun rose on our faces.
I'd already emptied more than one bottle,
so well that I'd never, indeed, found myself so drunk!
Suddenly, the missus turns up in front of the counter:
"Idler!" She says. "So, you've left work?"
"Yes," I reply, "because I'm going to the meeting,
to the big meeting of the Métropolitain!"

Verse 2

The citizens, in a sublime enthusiasm,
had come, guided by reason;
at the door, you gave 25 centimes
to support the strikers of Vierzon.
Briefly, to the side were four stinking municipal guards
And three policemen disguised as civilians.
I've never seen a finer meeting
than the meeting of the Métropolitain![42]

The well-crafted melody, the modulations in the harmony, and the detail in the piano accompaniment reveal the skill of composer Camille Baron, and place this chanson at the opposite pole musically from those of Bruant; here, rather than a spontaneous quality suggesting the street, the influences of the bourgeois salon are much in evidence—though they feature in the context of parody (see ex. 8.5). The abruptly juxtaposed loud and soft dynamics give the song an excitable, fidgety character. The quiet beginning of the refrain suggests a conspiratorial

Example 8.5   "Le Grand Métingue du Métropolitain" (1890), words by Maurice Mac-Nab, music by Camille Baron.

hush. The knowing artifices of the song prevent it from having the kind of authenticity effect that those of Bruant create. The ironic reception called for in the text is also demanded by the music. In particular, the overloud fanfares that punctuate phrases convey a satirical mood, mocking the military use of such figures (reminding us that the *blague* was a favorite fumist device). The unexpectedly delicate and graceful codetta adds to the humor.

The satirical effect of *fumisme* can be gleaned from the following incident. One evening, it is related, Mac-Nab was singing (with his *voix de fausset*) a touching chanson about how a warm stove in a cold room raises the spirits and encourages fond thoughts. He suddenly broke off singing to recommend the purchase of a particular movable stove-on-wheels (*poêle mobile*) costing 100 francs. His sales pitch was delivered with the same intensity as his poetically expressed verse.[43] Thus the poetic appreciation of the stove was contrasted starkly with an apprecia-

tion of the stove as commodity. The crude juxtaposition of use value
and exchange value was something he returned to in his two volumes
of *Poèmes mobiles.*

The interests of the composer Paul Delmet (1862–1904) contrast
markedly with those of Mac-Nab. Pierre d'Anjou praises Delmet for his
charm, sentimentality, and tenderness.[44] He was not without his eccen-
tricities, however, such as taking out his glass eye and clinking it on his
glass to attract the attention of a waiter.[45] Moreover, his sentiment
could be ironic, as in his musical setting of "Les Petits Pavés," written
by Maurice Vaucaire. Herbert suggests that Delmet's music took such a
hold on the public that they forgot to pay attention to the words in a
song like this.[46] It becomes clear that the singer is a violent stalker.

Verse 1

Las de t'attendre dans la rue,
J'ai lancé deux petits pavés
Sur tes carreaux que j'ai crevés,
Mais tu ne m'es pas apparue.
Tu te moques de tout, je crois,
Tu te moques de tout, je crois;
Demain, je t'en lancerai trois!

Verse 3

Si tu ne changes pas d'allure,
J'écraserai tes yeux, ton front,
Entre deux pavés qui feront
A ton crâne quelques fêlures!
Je t'aime, t'aime bien, pourtant,
Je t'aime, t'aime bien, pourtant;
Mais tu m'en as fait tant et tant!

Verse 1

Tired of waiting for you in the street,
I threw two small paving stones
at your windows, which I smashed,
 but you didn't appear to me.
You make fun of everything, I believe,
You make fun of everything, I believe;
Tomorrow, I'll throw three at you!

Verse 3

If you don't change your style,
I'll crush your eyes, your face,
between two paving stones,
which will make some cracks in your skull!
I love you, love you much, however,
I love you, love you much, however;
but you made me like this![47]

Delmet provided the music for poems by others. According to Emile Goudeau, he was already composing a sentimental type of chanson in the Latin Quarter. Goudeau calls him the "musician of young love," and remarks that a distinctive feature of the Latin Quarter (not shared by Montmartre) was its focus on youth. Goudeau specifies twenty years old as the perfect age for enjoying that locality.[48]

Yvette Guilbert (1867–1944) did not perform at the Chat Noir,[49] but she was recognized as having been influenced by it. An article in the *Echo de Paris* claimed, "Montmartre . . . has made her what she is, cadaverous and intensely modern, with a sort of bitter and deadly modernity which she must have acquired at the Chat Noir."[50] She adopted a pale, unfashionably thin look for that time. She had endured poverty when young, helping her seamstress mother, and was responsive to the *chansons réalistes* of Bruant; "A la Villette" was in her repertoire. "La Soûlarde" (music by Eugène Poncin, 1884) was perhaps the most famous of her Jouy songs. Like all her *chansons modernes,* she sang it with her red hair worn up, wearing a simple green satin evening dress and long black gloves (well known from Toulouse-Lautrec's posters), and she was felt to convey more of a sense of realism than more elaborately costumed performers. As a *diseuse,* she gave primary attention to enunciating words expressively.[51] An admirer wrote of her "grace anémiée et maléfique" in this song.[52] She made a big impact

Figure 8.2
Yvette Guilbert.

with it in London: Harold Simpson comments that it revealed "something new and hitherto undreamt of in the power of song as a medium of dramatic expression."[53] It concerns a drunken, wretched old woman dragging herself down a street, enduring jeers and abuse. It avoids sentimentality, though it includes a plea for pity, and was probably found morally acceptable as a warning of the degrading effects of alcohol.

Her repertoire was far from being unremittingly grim, and she replaced Thérésa as Paris's star singer-comedian (and, like Thérésa, returned with different and more "refined" repertoire in later life). When performing at the café-concert, the scene of Thérésa's greatest triumphs, Guilbert had to find a middle course for her *chansons modernes*. Henry Bauer, in the *Echo de Paris*, December 1891, writes:

> Between the songs of inane depravity, which reigns supreme in the Café Concert, and the artistic picturesque and powerful verses of Jules Jouy and Bruant, there is now a middle kind . . . songs of delicate fancy, pointed without being ill-natured, and not broad enough to be unpleasant. This class of song has its own particular bard, whose name is Fourneau, or in Latin Fornax, whence by anagram, Xanrof . . . On the scenario of these songs, and others like them, Mdlle. Guilbert has built up by her own individual genius the fabric of her art.[54]

She represented bourgeois vices humorously in chansons like "Le Fiacre" (Xanrof, 1888) and "Je suis pocharde!" (Laroche/Byrec, 1890). When she sang at the respectable Eden-Concert in 1890, she was allowed to sing the latter (concerning the effects of alcohol) but not the former (concerning marital infidelity). As mentioned in chapter 3, it was Guilbert's introduction to "Je suis pocharde!" that helped to win it acceptability, since she took care to provide a narrative frame concerning a respectable girl who had become slightly tipsy (*gentiment grise*) drinking champagne at her sister's wedding.[55] "Pocharde," especially in this its feminine form, would have registered disapproval and pity, whereas "gentiment grise" is a benevolent expression. Besides, it has a forerunner in "Griserie," the eponymous character's tipsy song in Offenbach's *La Périchole* (1868). Having taken all that into account, however, Guilbert was particularly skilled at innuendo.[56] What she did not possess was the political awareness of Eugénie Buffet (1866–1934), who was also singing the *chansons réalistes* of Bruant and others in the 1890s, one such being Jouy's "La Terre" (a chanson dedicated to Emile Zola). Buffet had been sentenced to fifteen days in prison for shouting "Vive Boulanger!" (the discredited general) in 1889, and this experience had given her the idea for her stage persona of the *pierreuse* or low-class prostitute. She sang politically engaged songs, perhaps her best known being "Pauvre Pierreuse!" (1893) (ex. 8.6). Her success enabled her to run her own cabaret, La Purée, at 75, boulevard de Clichy.

Although a new market had developed for these cultural goods,

Example 8.6 "Pauvre Pierreuse!" (1893), words by Paul Rosario, music by G. Marrietti.

A - vez vous, le soir, par ha - sard, Ren - con - tré
sur le bou - le - vard U - ne ro - deu - se

certain classes and class fractions could only acquire the new goods if they were made available in a socially suitable market. In Paris, the Mirliton was not a suitable venue for some. Though Bruant obtained permission to open till 2:00 a.m. (establishments with music normally had to close at midnight) and held a *jour chic* with higher prices on Fridays (as Salis had done), he attracted only a higher-class bohemian crowd who went there after the theatre. Yvette Guilbert says it was a revelation for the audience at the Divan Japonais, 75, rue des Martyrs, when she began singing chansons by Bruant there in 1891; for the first time these songs had left their home ground and, through her, were to become popularized.[57] Perhaps she was persuaded she might use Bruant's material by the way Bruant himself was prepared to sing from a female perspective in chansons like "A la Villette," "A la Grenelle," and "A Saint-Lazare." Bruant actually encouraged Guilbert to sing his chansons, saying, "tu as ton talent et ton coeur qui saigne."[58] She made her reputation and developed her characteristic repertoire at the Divan Japonais. Like the Chat Noir, it had a *jour chic* on Fridays, when a more upmarket audience would attend.

Next, it was the haute bourgeoisie who wished to hear her, but who felt uncomfortable frequenting the café-concert. Therefore, arrangements were made for her to appear at the Théâtre d'Application, rue Saint-Lazare. The proprietor begged the many women in the audience not to be shocked[59]—although that is probably the reason they had turned up. She successfully "crossed over" and, by the mid-1890s, had admirers in all classes. After her appearance at London's Empire in 1894, a press reception was held at the luxurious Savoy Hotel, and she was soon being welcomed in fashionable society. On her second visit to London, in 1896, she was invited to dine with the Prince of Wales. She was at that time performing at the Duke of York's Theatre with the respectable British music hall entertainer Albert Chevalier, whom she later joined for a combined tour of the United States. Her repertoire had now mellowed even further, and she and Chevalier made an appropriate coupling.

The Proliferation of Artistic Cabarets

It would be pointless to produce a telephone directory–style list of all
the important artistic cafés and cabarets around Montmartre.[60] Some of
the most important, not so far mentioned, were the gothic Abbaye de
Thélème (1, place Pigalle) and the rustic Auberge du Clou (30, avenue
Trudaine, next to the Grande Pinte). The Rat Mort (Dead rat), place Pigalle, catered to a double clientele, as did many others: Goudeau mentions anarchists and authoritarians, writers and businessmen existing
side by side.[61] Alphonse Allais thought the beer there terrible, and was
not averse to smuggling in a bock purchased from the Nouvelles Ath-
ènes across the street.[62] On the boulevard de Clichy were the twin cabarets Le Ciel et L'Enfer (Heaven and Hell), with the waiters dressed as
angels in the one and as skeletons in the other. Also on the same boulevard, at number 62, was the long-lived Quat'z'Arts cabaret (1893–
1924), which featured poets and chansonniers of Montmartre and became the preeminent *cabaret artistique* after the Chat Noir closed in
1897.[63] It contained a gothic café room, a restaurant, and a theatre at
the rear with around 150 seats. It was the first cabaret to put on a revue
(in 1894) and had a journal edited by Goudeau from 1897. Jarry's *Ubu
Roi*, though first performed in 1896, was given for the first time with
puppets, as he preferred, at the Quat'z'Arts in 1901 (running for sixty-
four performances). However, this should not be taken as an indication
that the Quat'z'Arts was committed to provoking the bourgeoisie: the
popular Anglo-French entertainer Harry Fragson also had his début
there. The artistic cabarets of Montmartre were relying on wealthy
middle-class patronage before the century was out and, as Goudeau
commented, "saw at their formerly modest doors the throng of embla-
zoned carriages and the wealthiest bankers contributing their subsidy
to this former Golgotha transformed into Gotha of the silly songs."[64] By
then, Bruant had himself retired to a country estate.[65]

Maurice Boukay, looking back on the final years of the Chat Noir
just after it had closed, wondered what had really been achieved. He
describes the legacy of artistic cabarets as the tail of the Chat, but notes
that the cat's tail is very long, and suspects it has been pulled too far. He
expresses his irritation at the number of imitators of Bruant and Guilbert, and declares his weariness of scatology, the macabre, and ugli-
ness. He recounts his attempt, with Delmet, to renew the love song
without all the "sickening banalities" heard in low-class entertainment
venues (*bastringues*). He remarks despondently that he and his friends
did not succeed in chasing away the inanity or pornography of the café-
concert.[66] Yet some things of enduring value had undoubtedly been
achieved: Carco, for example, praises Bruant for creating the folklore of
the outlying quarters of Paris.[67]

Lest the artistic freedom of the cabarets be exaggerated, it is important to remember that they were always under the necessity of being

alert to the perils of censorship and closure. The Chat Noir was an exception, since it was the first cabaret of its kind, and thus its official authorization was retrospective. Moreover, because it was made up of "poètes et de chansonniers dont les œuvres avaient une valeur artistique," it avoided the normal censorship process (that is, having to submit its programs in advance to the censor).[68] Bruant's Mirliton inherited the same concession, since it occupied the same premises as the original Chat Noir. All other cabarets, however, were opened only after official authorization and were, therefore, subject to normal censorship. In 1895, the year Bruant retired, the chansonnier Joanot waved a red flag at the Cabaret du Coup de Gueule (108, boulevard Rochechouart), claiming that he was demonstrating how railway workers controlled carriages. The Préfecture de Police closed the establishment down for having permitted the exhibition of a seditious emblem.[69]

Steven Whiting sourly sums up the *cabarets artistiques* as designed to package bohemian Montmartre for Parisian consumption, suggesting that, instead of being artistic haunts that the bourgeoisie gatecrashed, they from the beginning "made wry obeisance to art, to youth, to social concern, and to a romanticized past, all the while exploiting their profit-making potential."[70] I think he overplays the manipulative character of the cabarets; the Hydropathes, for example, met to pursue their artistic interests, not to make money, and they did not change overnight when they decamped to the Chat Noir. Boukay points to the rejection of the "muse of Montmartre" by legitimating institutions: "L'Académie nous fait la moue" (the Academy pulls its face at us).[71] Moreover, Salis did not pay chansonniers to perform until forced to by competition from elsewhere; therefore, they had no incentive, at first, to appeal to the bourgeoisie. Certainly, things had changed at the end of the century. Théodore Botrel, for example, whose début was at the Chien Noir and whose social conscience is evident in his earlier chansons like "Le Couteau," moved politically to the right and even produced *chansons royalistes*. Yet this should not cloud our judgment about the original motivations of Montmartre cabaret, nor should the fact that many of the newer cabarets opened with only commercial aims.[72] Lisa Appignanesi has argued that the Chat Noir artists "identified with the people in their immediate Montmartre environment";[73] and Armond Fields supports this "artist in the community" view: "The artists and writers who frequented the cabaret and contributed to its operation were themselves mostly residents of Montmartre. They represented the locals."[74] Bruant himself lived in Montmartre, in the rue des Saules at the corner of rue Cortot.[75] Nevertheless, the cabarets participated in a professional art world rather than a folk tradition. In her preface to Emile Bessière's *Autour de la Butte: Chansons de Montmartre et d'ailleurs* (1899), Yvette Guilbert speaks of the international success of Bessière's "Au Clair de la lune" in Paris, London, and America, and explains that this is because the words are tender, human, and may be understood by all.[76] What makes these chansons different from those of the café-concert, however, is their ability to turn at any moment from broad and inoffensive lyrics to the harshest social realism, as Bessière exemplifies in "Les Morphinomanes," perhaps the first song about drug addiction:

> A la morphine chaque jour,
> Elles se piqu'nt avec amour
> Chacqu' parti' du corps tour à tour,
> En vicieuses courtisanes.[77]

> Every day they prick
> lovingly with morphine
> each part of the body in turn,
> like lecherous courtesans.

Cabaret and the Avant-Garde

The artistic cabarets of Montmartre—of which only the Lapin Agile of 1903 survives (2, rue des Saules)[78]—raise important questions about the relationship between avant-gardism, modernism, and popular culture that have particular relevance today. Fields has claimed the Chat Noir characterized the "heart and spirit" of the Parisian avant-garde of that time.[79] It is obvious that something unique was happening in the arts in Montmartre in the 1880s, and equally obvious that it involved a mixing of high and popular culture. A typical reading of the events in Montmartre sees them as paving the way for modernism; but it can also be argued that a new kind of popular culture was created there with the birth of poster art and a new type of cabaret that soon spread throughout Europe (among the first successors being the Quatre Gats, Barcelona; the Elf Scharfrichter, Munich; Schall und Rauch, Berlin; and Die Fledermaus, Vienna).[80] The influence of Montmartre lived on longer than that, and not just in France; in Britain and United States, Tom Robinson, Jake Thackray, Scott Walker, and Leon Rosselson are all names that spring to mind.

Henri de Saint-Simon, the first to apply the military term "avant-garde" to art,[81] believed that art could and should play an active role in the struggle for a freer and fairer society. The morale of the Saint-Simonians and Fourierists (who also adopted this term) was sapped by the failure of 1848, the coup d'état of 1851, and the establishment of the Second Empire. The avant-garde artists of the 1860s maintained a concern with contemporary Parisian life, but put most of their energy into challenging the official art of the Académie. When a Prussian victory ended the Second Empire in 1871, huge war reparations followed and caused an economic depression. The meaning of "avant-garde" grew vaguer from then on and, in the 1880s, began to refer to art that had no explicit connection to politics, such as impressionism—an early example of turning a "revolt into a style."[82] An avant-gardist was now someone interested primarily in aesthetic progress (attacking "official" art) rather than social progress, and that is how the avant-garde became linked to modernism in the arts. Aesthetic rebels, like those of the Salon des Indépendants, replaced political rebels. In the twentieth century, however, avant-garde formations in western Europe seemed to be competing against each other in the absence of an official art to attack. Whereas nineteenth-century avant-gardism had a social impetus, the twentieth century variety had an aesthetic impetus: art as a vehicle for experimentation in style and structure; art as artistic problem solving; art as radical departure from existing art; art as challenge to artistic convention; art that moves away from subjects to abstract ideas; and art that makes its own materials explicit. The Montmartre artists often championed the popular against the high, but for a mid-twentieth-century critic like Clement Greenberg, avant-gardism was at the opposite pole to *Kitsch* and was driven by a search for the autonomous artwork.[83] The move to detach art from society and dissolve content into form is what other theorists have regarded as the hallmark of modernism. Adorno, in his *Aesthetic Theory,* follows a line not dissimilar to Greenberg: the avant-garde is either conflated with modernism or rejected for merely fetishizing the new. [84] Another writer who conflates avant-gardism and modernism is Bernard Gendron.[85] It is to be wondered if there is not room for a separate theory of the avant-garde. Dada does not seem to fit Greenberg's theory. Tristan Tzara's *Dada Manifesto* (1918) condemned "laboratories of formal ideas" and proposed that there was "a great negative work of destruction to be accomplished."[86]

Peter Bürger, in his *Theory of the Avant-Garde,* sees the avant-garde arising as a response to aestheticism in bourgeois society, where art is "no longer tied to the praxis of life" and has become socially functionless. [87] For Bürger, avant-gardists, though they do not restore the social function of art, do negate the autonomy of art, as, for example, when Duchamp exhibited a mass-produced urinal, entitled it *Fountain,* and signed it R. Mutt (a sanitary engineer). The artists of the Chat Noir and the Quat'z'Arts liked to confuse fake and real, and often concealed identities with nicknames or pseudonyms. An important feature of avant-gardism, for Bürger, is its rejection of an artistic tradition; thus, Dada fits well into his conception, while cubism (which was no problem for Greenberg) is more awkward for him to accommodate. Nevertheless, the Montmartre artists did not so much break with tradition as create new fusions of high and low art. Well-known musical examples would be Satie's *Gymnopédies* and *Gnossiennes.* The chansons of Bruant, Jouy, and Mac-Nab were at home neither in concert hall nor café-concert (though, as mentioned earlier, Bruant was persuaded to appear at the Ambassadeurs in 1992, on condition that the stage set reproduced the interior of his own cabaret).

The Montmartre avant-gardists fit better into the postmodern theorizing of Andreas Huyssen, who suggests that avant-gardists are those that have challenged the "great divide" between modernism and "commercial mass culture." The Montmartre chansonniers, of course, frequently drew on popular forms, or raised the status of the "trivial" as a means of critiquing the artistic values of their society. Carco calls Bruant "un grand poète populaire";[88] and Bruant's work certainly asserts the category of the demotic in both vocabulary and technique (he avoids, for example, high-art Alexandrines in his verse). Huyssen holds that "the historical avant-garde aimed at developing an alternative relationship between high art and mass culture and thus should be distinguished from modernism, which for the most part insisted on the inherent hostility between high and low."[89] At the same time, he accepts that the boundaries between avant-gardism and modernism were fluid. I have to say I do not like the term "mass culture," which immediately suggests a now discredited theoretical paradigm in which there are manipulative producers and passive consumers; however, reworked as "popular culture," I can accept much of Huyssen's argument. Yet I want to go further. Huyssen, like Bürger, sees avant-gardism springing out of "high culture"; I would like to broaden the perspective and consider the implications of viewing certain developments in the popular arena as avant-garde. For example, what would it mean to regard Pink Floyd, the Doors, and Frank Zappa as avant-garde, or the Beatles in their albums *Revolver* and *Sgt. Pepper?*[90] The mood of the boulevard de Rochechouart in the 1880s may have been not unlike that of Carnaby Street, London, in the 1960s. Perhaps Bob Dylan might be seen as the Aristide Bruant of the 1960s: think of his creation of a provocative new rock and folk hybrid style coupled to lyrics of social concern, as heard, for example, in "Desolation Row." Perhaps, when we give the label "counterculture" to events in the 1960s, we are really referring to an avant-garde culture in the older sense of that term.

Notes

Introduction

1. *Music and Society since 1815* (London: Barrie and Jenkins, 1976), 147. Adorno mentions the "scars of capitalism" that afflict all forms of twentieth-century art in a letter to Walter Benjamin, 18 Mar. 1936, in *Theodor W. Adorno: Über Walter Benjamin,* ed. Rolf Tiedemann (Frankfurt: Suhrkamp Verlag, 1970), 126–34.

2. See Howard Becker, *Art Worlds* (Berkeley: University of California Press, 1982), 35, 78. Becker accepts that a number of specific art worlds may share certain activities and features that allow them to be considered as part of a more general art world (161).

3. *Art Worlds,* 305, 307. Becker's arguments then begin to depart from my own, because he concentrates on revolutions in an art world that lead to new accepted practices, whereas I am interested in revolutions that leave a state of continuing struggle. For example, the added sixth continues throughout the nineteenth century to be rejected in the musical high-art world as a vulgarism. I conceive of the practices I'm discussing as revolutions that lead to new art worlds. Becker sees a revolution as something that causes changes in an existing art world, while he understands new art worlds as those that bring together "people who never cooperated before" and "conventions previously unknown" (310); he regards rock music, for example, as a new art world (313).

4. Theodor W. Adorno, *Introduction to the Sociology of Music,* trans. E. B. Ashton (New York: Continuum, 1989; originally published as *Einleitung in die Musiksoziologie* [Frankfurt: Suhrkamp Verlag, 1962]).

5. "Nicht bloss werden die Ohren der Bevölkerung so mit leichter Musik

überflutet, dass die andere sie nur noch als der geronnene Gegensatz zu jener, als 'klassisch' erreicht." *Philosophie der neuen Musik* (Frankfurt: Europäische Verlaganstalt, 1958), 17.

6. "Die Unterschiede in der Rezeption der offiziellen 'klassischen' und der leichten Musik haben keine reale Bedeutung mehr." *Dissonanzen. Musik in der verwalteten Welt* (1956), in *Gesammelte Schriften* (Frankfurt: Suhrkamp Verlag, 1973), 14:21.

7. *Philosophy of Modern Music*, trans. Anne G. Mitchell and Wesley V. Blomster (New York: Seabury Press, 1973), 8. Adorno actually wrote "von Gebrauch ganz sich losgesagt" (quite renounced use), 15.

8. Michel Foucault and Pierre Boulez, "Contemporary Music and the Public," trans. John Rahn, *Perspectives of New Music* (fall–winter 1985), 6–12; see 8 and 11, excerpted as "On Music and Its Reception," in Derek B. Scott, ed., *Music, Culture, and Society: A Reader* (Oxford: Oxford University Press, 2000), 164–67; see 165 and 167.

9. Carl Dahlhaus, *Esthetics of Music*, trans. William Austin (Cambridge: Cambridge University Press, 1982; originally published as *Musikästhetik* [Cologne, 1967]), 96.

10. Henry Lunn, in 1866, refers to the worship of the "popular idol" in "The London Musical Season," *Musical Times and Singing Class Circular* 12, no. 283, 1 Sep. 1866, 363–65, 363. Even those twentieth-century pop idols who rose to fame on their "street credibility" but then developed aristocratic aspirations merely replicate the behavior of nineteenth-century stars like cabaret performer Aristide Bruant, who bought himself an estate and ended his life as a respectable *châtelain*.

11. A seminal study of class and music in three of the cities I am dealing with—London, Paris, and Vienna—is William Weber, *Music and the Middle Class: The Social Structure of Concert Life in London, Paris and Vienna between 1830 and 1848*, 2nd ed. (Aldershot, England: Ashgate, 2003; originally published London: Croom Helm, 1975), but it focuses on the earlier part of the nineteenth century (1830–48). Weber is currently working on a book with further parallels to my own work, entitled *The Great Transformation*. An important study of antecedents of twentieth-century popular music is Peter Van der Merwe, *Origins of the Popular Style* (Oxford: Clarendon Press, 1989), but it lacks the kind of historical and cultural contextualization that characterizes my work and instead spends much time tracing stylistic features from one piece to another in a fairly traditional "genealogical" manner. Moreover, it does not identify or explain the significance of the four particular cities I have singled out to changes in Western popular musical style. (The index has eight page references for Vienna, four for New York, and none for London and Paris.)

12. See M. Maretzek, *Revelations of an Opera Manager in Nineteenth-Century America*, pt. 1 (New York: Dover, 1968; originally published as *Crotchets and Quavers*, [n.p.: 1855]), 25; see also Charles Hamm, *Yesterdays: Popular Song in America* (New York: Norton, 1979), 69. While accepting that many features of American society, such as fluidity of status, can be related to the absence of a feudal era, C. Wright Mills complains that this has been confused with lack of class structure and class consciousness; *The Sociological Imagination* (New York: Oxford University Press, 1959), 157.

13. For instance, you will find no Offenbach, no Lanner or Strauss, and definitely no London music hall or New York black musicals in Richard L.

Crocker's compendious *A History of Musical Style* (New York: McGraw-Hill, 1966). The few French popular elements that are mentioned are only seen as relevant in the context of the canonized work of Les Six and Stravinsky.

14. Oscar A. H. Schmitz, *Das Land ohne Musik: Englische Gesellschaftsprobleme*, 8th ed. (Munich: Georg Müller, 1920), 30.

15. David Ewen, *American Popular Song* (New York: Random House, 1966), 74.

16. *From Max Weber: Essays in Sociology*, trans. and ed. by H. H. Gerth and C. Wright Mills (New York: Oxford University Press, 1946), 185. Weber designates a "status situation" as "every typical component of the life fate of men that is determined by a specific, positive or negative, social estimation of *honor*" (187). This expresses itself in a specific lifestyle (for example, one that rejects the pretensions brought about by riches). Nevertheless, "[t]he differences between classes and status groups frequently overlap" (193). Weber's arguments were put forward in *Wirtschaft und Gesellschaft [Economy and Society]* (1922), pt. 3, chap. 4.

17. See Pierre Bourdieu, *Distinction: A Social Critique of the Judgement of Taste*, trans. R. Nice (London: Routledge, 1984; originally published as *La Distinction. Critique sociale du jugement* [Paris: Editions de Minuit, 1979]), 14–18.

18. *Music and the Middle Class*, viii–xv, 8–10, and 140; and in "The Muddle of the Middle Classes," *19th Century Music* 3 (1979), 175–85.

19. A class fraction is an identifiable grouping within a particular class whose behavior or opinions may not be characteristic of the class as a whole and who may even play an oppositional role at times; for example, middle-class temperance campaigners who cut across the dominant middle-class view of a free market. A class fraction should not be confused with a social stratum—for example, bachelors under the age of forty.

20. "Popular Music," in Stanley Sadie, ed., *The New Grove Dictionary of Music and Musicians*, 2nd ed., 29 vols. (London: Macmillan, 2001), 20:128–30.

21. See Derek B. Scott, *From the Erotic to the Demonic: On Critical Musicology* (New York: Oxford University Press, 2003), 38. Weber discusses his idea that there existed a "general" taste for popular music in the first half of the nineteenth century in *Music and the Middle Class*, xxiii. However, the term "general" suggests a taste consensus achieved without struggle, without contest over meanings.

22. Van Akin Burd, ed., *The Winnington Letters* (London: Allen and Unwin, 1969), 528–29, cited in Sara M. Dodd, "Ruskin and Women's Education," paper presented at the Association of Art Historians conference, Sheffield, Apr. 1988.

23. See Carl Dahlhaus, *Nineteenth-Century Music*, trans. J. B. Robinson (Berkeley: University of California Press, 1989), 110–11.

24. See Dave Harker, *Fakesong: The Manufacture of British "Folksong" 1700 to the Present Day* (Milton Keynes, England: Open University Press, 1985), 155–56.

25. Raynor, *Music and Society since 1815*, 132.

26. Discussion of both, as well as of productive forces (mentioned in the next sentence), is in Karl Marx and Friedrich Engels, *Die deutsche Ideologie* (1846), full text based on the original manuscript in Marx-Engels-Lenin Institute, Moscow, www.mlwerke.de/me/me03/me03_009.htm. Class and class struggle is featured in Marx's English journalism, for example, "The Chartists," *New York Daily Tribune*, 25 Aug. 1852, in T. B. Bottomore and M. Rubel, eds., *Karl Marx: Selected Writings in Sociology and Social Philosophy*, 2nd ed. (Harmondsworth, England: Penguin, 1961), 204–7.

27. *Principles of Political Economy,* 3rd ed. (London: John W. Parker, 1852), 2:327. Letters from Mill to Taylor indicate collaboration on this work, though it was published under Mill's name only.

28. See Raymond Williams, *Keywords* (London: Fontana, 1976), 61. The "Industrial Revolution" may have begun in Britain, but the term was first used in France in the 1820s; see Raymond Williams, *Culture and Society 1780–1950* (Harmondsworth, England: Penguin, 1961; originally published London: Chatto and Windus, 1958), 14.

29. Williams, *Culture and Society,* 15.

30. Ibid.

31. There is also a reference to the lower middle class in Henry James, *Portrait of a Lady* (London: Macmillan, 1881), chap. 15.

32. Heinrich Eduard Jacob, *Johann Strauss: A Century of Light Music,* trans. Marguerite Wolff (London: Hutchinson, 1940; originally published as *Johann Strauss und das neunzehnte Jahrhundert. Die Geschichte einer musikalischen Weltherrschaft, 1819–1917* [Amsterdam: Querido-Verlag, 1937]), 74.

33. *Music in the New World* (New York: Norton, 1983), 183.

Chapter 1

1. William *Weber, Music and the Middle Class: The Social Structure of Concert Life in London, Paris and Vienna between 1830 and 1848,* 2nd ed. (Aldershot, England: Ashgate, 2004; originally published London: Croom Helm, 1975), 7.

2. Richard Leppert, *The Sight of Sound: Music, Representation, and the History of the Body* (Berkeley: University of California Press, 1993), 207.

3. Leonard B. Meyer, *Style and Music: Theory, History, and Ideology* (Chicago: University of Chicago Press, 1996), 183.

4. Café-concert entrepreneurs are discussed in Concetta Condemi, *Les Cafés-concerts: Histoire d'un divertissement* (Paris: Quai Voltaire, 1992), 101–32, and music hall entrepreneurs in Peter Bailey, ed., *Music Hall: The Business of Pleasure* (Milton Keynes, England: Open University Press, 1986).

5. "The Black Opera," *New York Tribune,* 30 Jun. 1855, reprinted in *Musical World* 36, no. 32, 7 Aug. 1858, 502–3, 503.

6. Quoted in Lois Rutherford, "'Managers in a Small Way': The Professionalization of Variety Artistes, 1860–1914," in Bailey, *Music Hall,* 93–117, 95.

7. Figures given by James Graydon, manager of the Middlesex Music Hall, Drury Lane, in answer to question 2895, *Minutes of Evidence taken before the Select Committee on Theatres and Places of Entertainment* (London: Eyre and Spottiswoode for HMS0, 1892), 4 May 1892, 197.

8. Cyril Ehrlich, *The Music Profession in Britain since the Eighteenth Century: A Social History* (Oxford: Clarendon Press, 1985), 54.

9. "The multiplication of specific tasks brought about by the division of labor requires standardized solutions that can be readily learned and transmitted." Peter L. Berger and Thomas Luckmann, *The Social Construction of Reality: A Treatise in the Sociology of Knowledge* (New York: Anchor Books, 1967), 77.

10. Peter Maurice, "What Shall We Do with Music?" letter to earl of Derby, chancellor of Oxford University (1856), quoted in Ehrlich, *The Music Profession in Britain,* 42.

11. See Simon McVeigh, "The Society of British Musicians (1834–1865)

and the Campaign for Native Talent," in Christina Bashford and Leanne Langley, eds., *Music and British Culture, 1785–1914: Essays in Honour of Cyril Ehrlich* (Oxford: Oxford University Press, 2000), 145–68.

12. Cyril Ehrlich, *The Music Profession in Britain*, 51. He gleans this information from occupations given on census returns, as well as in directories, reports, and surveys.

13. "The Musical 'Cheap Jack,'" editorial, *Musical Standard* [1], 17 Mar. 1871, 117–18, 117. Lessons were being advertised at around twopence instead of the professionally accepted fourpence halfpenny.

14. Robert Elkin, *Royal Philharmonic: The Annals of the Royal Philharmonic Society* (London: Rider, 1946), 9. Another informative history of the Philharmonic Society is in Reginald Nettel, *The Orchestra in England: A Social History* (London: Jonathan Cape, 1946), 103–99.

15. Elkin, *Royal Philharmonic*, 67.

16. For a general history of concert life in Vienna, see Eduard Hanslick, *Geschichte des Concertwesens in Wien*, 2 vols. (Vienna: Braumüller, 1869–70; reprint, Hildesheim: Georg Olms, 1979).

17. See Tia DeNora, *Beethoven and the Construction of Genius: Musical Politics in Vienna, 1792–1803* (Berkeley: University of California Press, 1995), 37–39, 53.

18. See Erwin Mittag, *The Vienna Philharmonic*, trans. J. R. L. Orange and G. Morice (Vienna: Gerlach and Wiedling, 1950; issued simultaneously as *Aus der Geschichte der Wiener Philharmoniker*).

19. Weber, *Music and the Middle Class*, 87.

20. See John Erskine, *The Philharmonic Society of New York: Its First Hundred Years* (New York: Macmillan, 1943).

21. Census figures quoted in Arthur Loesser, *Men, Women and Pianos: A Social History* (New York: Simon and Schuster, 1954), 456.

22. Weber, *Music and the Middle Class*, 30.

23. Nettel, *The Orchestra in England*, 215.

24. For contemporary histories of these concerts, see Henry Saxe Wyndham, *August Manns and the Saturday Concerts: A Memoir and a Retrospect* (London: Walter Scott, 1909), and Joseph Bennett, *A Story of Ten Hundred Concerts, 1859–87* (London: Chappell, 1887). The latter is a history of both the Monday and Saturday Popular Concerts.

25. For an informative study of the concertina in social context, see Allan W. Atlas, *The Wheatstone English Concertina in Victorian England* (Oxford: Clarendon Press, 1996).

26. On the fire, see reports in *Times* (London), 21 Oct. 1856, 6, col. c, and 12 Jun. 1861, 5, col. f.

27. *Musical Standard* 3, no. 50, 30 Jul. 1864, 40.

28. See Ehrlich, *The Music Profession in Britain*, 57.

29. Philip Rutland, solicitor to the Proprietors of Entertainments Association, questioned, minute 1372, in *Minutes of Evidence taken before the Select Committee on Theatres and Places of Entertainment*, 6 Apr. 1892, 101.

30. For a survey tracing the changes of provision from "convivial meeting" to "grand music hall" and beyond, see John Earl, "Building the Halls," in Bailey, *Music Hall*, 1–32.

31. See Peter Bailey, "A Community of Friends: Business and Good Fellowship in London Music Hall Management c. 1860–1885," in Bailey, *Music Hall*, 33–52, 34.

32. Music by Bessie Bellwood, words by Will Herbert (London: Hopwood and Crew, 1885). The song is reproduced in John M. Garrett, *Sixty Years of British Music Hall* (London: Chappell, 1976), n.p.

33. "Champagne Charlie," words by George Leybourne, music by Alfred Lee (London: Charles Sheard, 1867); "Cliquot," words by Frank W. Green, music by J. Riviere (London: Hopwood and Crew, 1870).

34. For an overview of the various societies, see Rutherford, "'Managers in a Small Way,'" app. 5.1, 115.

35. Harold Scott, *The Early Doors: Origins of the Music Hall* (London: Nicholson and Watson, 1946), 221.

36. Annie Glen, "Careers for Singers," *Woman's World* 2 (1889), 82–85, cited in Paula Gillett, *Musical Women in England, 1870–1914* (London: Macmillan, 2000), 201. Paula Gillett offers an overview of music as a profession for women, 189–227.

37. For example, Helen, countess of Radnor, was inspired to found and conduct one of her own. See Paula Gillett, "Entrepreneurial Women in Britain," in Weber, *The Musician as Entrepreneur, 1700–1914: Managers, Charlatans, and Idealists* (Bloomington: Indiana University Press, 2004), 198–220, 210.

38. George Bernard Shaw, *Shaw's Music,* ed. Dan H. Laurence, vol. 1, *1876–1890* (London: Bodley Head, 1981), 335–40, 337–38. Eduard Strauss and the Strauss Orchestra appeared at the Inventions Exhibition in 1885; see James D. Brown, *Biographical Dictionary of Musicians* (Hildesheim: Georg Olms, 1970; originally published Paisley, England: Alexander Gardner, 1886), 581.

39. Ibid., 339–40. The conductor was distinguished by a black silk skirt. It is not clear, incidentally, why Shaw thought a baton was essential for "an original interpretation of a classical work."

40. See Margaret Myers, "Searching for Data about Ladies' Orchestras," in Pirkko Moisala and Beverley Diamond, eds., *Music and Gender* (Urbana: University of Illinois Press, 2000), 189–213.

41. "Mrs. Hunt's Orchestra," *Strand Musical Magazine* 5, May 1897, 268–69, 268.

42. Gillett, *Musical Women in England,* 199.

43. There is a photograph of the Salvation Army's first woman cornet player in *War Cry,* 31 Jul. 1880, and she was soon joined by others. See Brindley Boon, *Play the Music, Play! The Story of Salvation Army Bands* (London: Salvationist, 1966), 13–15.

44. Ibid., 269.

45. See ibid., 192.

46. Henry J. Wood, *My Life of Music* (London: Victor Gollancz, 1938), 372.

47. At the time of writing in January 2007, the *Wiener Philharmoniker* still has only two women players.

48. Wood, *My Life of Music,* 96.

49. Victoria L. Cooper, *The House of Novello: Practice and Policy of a Victorian Music Publisher, 1829–1866* (Aldershot, England: Ashgate, 2003), 13, based on figures from William Weber, *Music and the Middle Class,* 160, and Peter H. Lindert and Jeffrey G. Williamson, "English Workers' Living Standards During the Industrial Revolution: A New Look," *Economic History Review* 36 (1983), 1–25, 4. Weber also discusses disposable income for leisure products in *Music and the Middle Class,* 28–29.

50. *Mid-Victorian Britain, 1851–1875* (London: Fontana, 1971), 102.

51. A. Hyatt King, *Four Hundred Years of Music Printing* (London: British Museum, 1964), 28.

52. Russell Sanjek, *American Popular Music and Its Business: The First Four Hundred Years*, vol. 2, From 1790 to 1909 (New York: Oxford University Press, 1988), 95.

53. Heinrich E. Jacob, *Johann Strauss: A Century of Light Music*, trans. Marguerite Wolff (London: Hutchinson, 1940; originally published as *Johann Strauss und das neunzehnte Jahrhundert. Die Geschichte einer musikalischen Weltherrschaft, 1819–1917* [Amsterdam: Querido-Verlag, 1937]), 193.

54. Michael Twyman, *Early Lithographed Music* (London: Farrand Press, 1996), 47.

55. Figures from the *New York Musical Review* (1855), cited in Sanjek, *American Popular Music and Its Business*, 71–72.

56. See Sanjek, *American Popular Music and Its Business*, 76–77.

57. Ibid., 370.

58. See Nicholas Tawa, *The Way to Tin Pan Alley: American Popular Song, 1866–1910* (New York: Schirmer Books, 1990), 44–53.

59. Sanjek, *American Popular Music and Its Business*, 403.

60. See ibid., 165.

61. Ehrlich, *The Music Profession in Britain*, 103.

62. *Musical Opinion*, Mar. and Aug. 1898, cited in Cyril Ehrlich, *Harmonious Alliance: A History of the Performing Right Society* (Oxford: Oxford University Press, 1989), 5.

63. Letter of 26 Oct. 1837, in Hans Leneberg, ed. and trans., *Breitkopf and Härtel in Paris: The Letters of Their Agent Heinrich Probst between 1833 and 1840* (Stuyvesant, N.Y.: Pendragon Press, 1990), 26.

64. Ibid., 28.

65. *A Short History of Cheap Music* (London: Novello, Ewer, 1887), and *A Century and a Half in Soho: A Short History of the Firm of Novello* (London: Novello, 1961), 8.

66. *A Century and a Half in Soho*, 18–19.

67. David Gramit, "Selling the Serious," in Weber, *The Musician as Entrepreneur*, 81–100, 91–92.

68. On periodicals in Paris, see Katharine Ellis, *Music Criticism in Nineteenth-Century France: "La Revue et Gazette musicale de Paris," 1836–1880* (Cambridge: University of Cambridge Press, 1995). *La Revue et Gazette musicale de Paris* has been reprinted in 13 vols. by Répertoire International de la Presse Musicale (Bethesda, Md.: National Information Services, 1998–99).

69. See Irving Kolodin, Francis D. Perkins, and Susan Thielmann Sommer, "New York," in Stanley Sadie, ed., *The New Grove Dictionary of Music and Musicians*, 2nd ed. (London: Macmillan, 2001), 17:171–89, 187.

70. See Leanne Langley, "The Musical Press in Nineteenth-Century England," *Notes*, 2nd ser., 46, no. 3 (Mar. 1990), 583–92, 588.

71. Harvey Grace, article in *Grove's Dictionary of Music and Musicians*, 5th ed., vol. 6 (London: Macmillan, 1954), quoted in *A Century and a Half in Soho*, 25.

72. Death notice, *Dwight's Journal of Music* 24, no. 13, 17 Sep. 1864, 311.

73. Loesser, *Men, Women and Pianos*, 162.

74. Cyril Ehrlich, *The Piano: A History* (London: Dent, 1976), 15.

75. See Loesser, *Men, Women and Pianos*, 234–36.

76. See ibid., 345.

77. List of prices in Rosamond E. M. Harding, *The Piano-Forte: Its History Traced to the Great Exhibition of 1851* (Cambridge: Cambridge University Press, 1933), 379–80.

78. Ibid., 381.

79. See Dennis G. Waring, *Manufacturing the Muse: Estey Organs and Consumer Culture in Victorian America* (Middletown, Conn.: Wesleyan University Press, 2002).

80. "The Pianoforte Virtuoso," Paris, 25 Mar. 1843, excerpt (via a translation in *Dwight's Journal of Music*), *Musical World* 36, no. 32, 7 Aug. 1858, 500–501, 500.

81. Loesser, *Men, Women and Pianos*, 386.

82. Ibid., 387.

83. Ehrlich, *The Piano*, table 1, 28.

84. Cited in Harding, *The Piano-Forte*, 376.

85. Peter Maurice, "What Shall We Do with Music," 43.

86. Sanjek, *American Popular Music and Its Business*, 347.

87. See Ruth A. Solie, *Music in Other Words: Victorian Conversations* (Berkeley: University of California Press, 2004), 89–90. For the piano as preeminent bourgeois instrument, see Derek B. Scott, *The Singing Bourgeois: Songs of the Victorian Drawing Room and Parlour*, 2nd ed. (Aldershot, England: Ashgate, 2001; originally published Milton Keynes, England: Open University Press, 1989), 46–49.

88. See Loesser, *Men, Women and Pianos*, 560–62.

89. Ehrlich, *The Piano*, 92–93.

90. Percy A. Scholes, *The Mirror of Music 1844–1944: A Century of Musical Life in Britain as Reflected in the Pages of the "Musical Times"* (London: Novello, 1947), 1:305.

91. The various "taxes on knowledge" are discussed in Cooper, *The House of Novello*, 114–20.

92. Ehrlich, *The Piano*, 75.

93. Ibid., 54.

94. See Ehrlich, *The Piano*, 63, for their tactics at the Vienna International Exhibition of 1873, when they had no pianos on exhibit.

95. See ibid., 128–42.

96. Raymond Williams, *Culture* (London: Faber, 1981), 47.

97. *Noise: The Political Economy of Music*, trans. Brian Massumi (Manchester: Manchester University Press, 1985; originally published as *Bruits: Essai sur l'économie politique de la musique* [Paris: Presses Univeritaires de France, 1977]), 77.

98. *La France Musicale*, 10, 10 Mar. 1850, quoted in Attali, *Noise*, 78.

99. Ehrlich, *Harmonious Alliance*, 2–3. See also Scott, *The Singing Bourgeois*, 125–26, and James Coover, comp., *Music Publishing, Copyright and Piracy in Victorian England* (London: Mansell, 1985), 6.

100. See Ehrlich, *Harmonious Alliance*, 3, and Gavin McFarlane, *Copyright: The Development and Exercise of the Performing Right* (Eastbourne, England: Offord, 1980), 86.

101. John Tasker Howard, *Stephen Foster: America's Troubadour*, 2nd ed. (New York: Crowell, 1953; originally published New York: Crowell, 1934), 305. Howard provides a detailed study of Foster's finances, 265–305.

102. Sanjek, *American Popular Music and Its Business*, 32–33.

103. Ibid., 139–40.

104. William Boosey, *Fifty Years of Music* (London: Ernest Benn, 1931), 23–24.

105. Sullivan's reminiscences, recorded in Arthur Lawrence, *Sir Arthur Sullivan: Life Story, Letters, and Reminiscences* (London: James Bowden, 1899), 136.

106. Leslie Baily, *The Gilbert and Sullivan Book*, rev. ed. (London: Spring Books, 1966), 184–85.

107. *Musical Opinion and Music Trade Review*, Dec. 1882, 115, excerpted in Coover, *Music Publishing, Copyright and Piracy*, 13.

108. See Coover, *Music Publishing, Copyright and Piracy*, 59–65.

109. See William Weber, "From the Self-Managing Musician to the Independent Concert Agent," in Weber, *The Musician as Entrepreneur*, 105–29.

110. Thérésa [Emma Valadon], [with Victorien Monnier], *Mémoires de Thérésa écrits par elle-même*, [with Victorien Monnier] (Paris: E. Dentu, 1865), 221. She developed her comic repertoire at the Alcazar.

111. Attali, *Noise*, 77.

112. Paulus, *Trente Ans de café-concert*, Souvenirs recueillis par Octave Pradels (Paris: Société d'édition, 1927).

113. See Sterling Mackinlay, *Origin and Development of Light Opera* (London: Hutchinson, 1927), 116.

114. Soldene became an opera manager, specializing in productions of comic opera and operetta. Her troupe toured the United States in the 1870s. See Paula Gillett, "Entrepreneurial Women in Britain," in Weber, *The Musician as Entrepreneur*, 198–220, 209.

115. See Sanjek, *American Popular Music and Its Business*, 316–18.

116. Richard Wagner, "Farewell Performances," in *Wagner Writes from Paris: Stories, Essays, and Articles by the Young Composer*, ed. and trans. Robert L. Jacobs and Geoffrey Skelton (London: Allen and Unwin, 1973), 124, cited in Henry Raynor, *Music and Society Since 1815* (London: Barrie and Jenkins, 1976), 63.

117. Henry C. Lunn, "The London Musical Season," *Musical Times and Singing Class Circular* 12, no. 283, 1 Sep. 1866, 363–65, 365.

118. Scott, *The Singing Bourgeois*, 72–77; see reproduction of Boosey's *List of Popular Songs*, 70.

119. Harold Simpson discusses a number of singers at the Ballad Concerts in *A Century of Ballads 1810–1910: Their Composers and Singers* (London: Mills and Boon, 1910), 212–36.

120. Boosey, *Fifty Years of Music*, 26.

121. Ibid., 22.

122. See Scott, *The Singing Bourgeois*, 134–68.

123. For a discussion of the romance and its popularity in salon music making, see David Tunley, *Salons, Singers and Songs: A Background to Romantic French Song 1830–1870* (Aldershot, England: Ashgate, 2002), 58–71.

124. *Hymns Ancient and Modern* sold sixty million copies by 1904 (Scholes, *The Mirror of Music*, 2:542).

Chapter 2

1. Henry C. Lunn, "The London Musical Season," *Musical Times and Singing Class Circular* 12, no. 283, 1 Sep. 1866, 363–65, 363.

2. Ibid., 364.

3. Georg Simmel, "The Metropolis and Mental Life," in Kurt H. Wolff,

trans. and ed., *The Sociology of Georg Simmel* (New York: Free Press , 1950), 409–24, 411, 420. Simmel's essay was originally published as "Die Grossstädte und das Geistesleben," *Die Grossstädte: Vorträge und Aufsätze* 9 (1902–3), 185–206.

4. J. E. Ritchie, *The Night Side of London* (London: William Tweedie, 1857), 200.

5. William Weber, ed., *The Musician as Entrepreneur, 1700–1914: Managers, Charlatans, and Idealists* (Bloomington: Indiana University Press, 2004), 8, 15.

6. Leonard B. Meyer, *Style and Music: Theory, History, and Ideology* (Chicago: University of Chicago Press, 1996; originally published Philadelphia: University of Pennsylvania Press, 1989), 171. Samuel Smiles argues against hereditary genius, although he holds that talent is transmissible, in *Life and Labour* (London: John Murray, 1887), 186–239.

7. "Und ob ihr der Natur noch seid auf rechter Spur, das sagt euch nur, wer nichts weiss, von der Tabulatur." Richard Wagner, *Die Meistersinger von Nürnberg* (1868), act 1, Hans Sachs.

8. Samuel Smiles, *Self-Help* (London: John Murray, 1859), 35–67. Smiles links national economic growth to the "free energy of individuals."

9. The Society left its library to the Royal College of Music.

10. Reginald Nettel, *The Orchestra in England: A Social History* (London: Jonathan Cape, 1946), 159 (no source given).

11. Ruth A. Solie, *Music in Other Words: Victorian Conversations* (Berkeley: University of California Press, 2004), 123.

12. *Beethoven and the Construction of Genius: Musical Politics in Vienna, 1792–1803* (Berkeley: University of California Press, 1995), 11–36. An important study of nineteenth-century salon music is Andreas Ballstaedt and Tobias Widmaier, *Salonmusik: Zur Geschichte und Funktion einer bürgerlichen Musikpraxis* (Stuttgart: Steiner Verlag, 1989).

13. Nettel, *The Orchestra in England*, 162.

14. Editorial, *Musical World* 13, no. 192, new ser., 5, no. 109, 21 Nov. 1839, 461–62, 461.

15. "Jullien's Concerts," *Musical Examiner* 110 [wrongly published as 109], 7 Dec. 1844, 70–71.

16. Frances Trollope, letter 24, 27 Sep. 1836, in *Vienna and the Austrians* (Paris: Galignani, 1838), 229. Two examples of reviews of Strauss Sr.'s Volksgarten concerts in the next decade are in *Allgemeine Wiener Musik-Zeitung*, 9 Sep. 1843, 456, and 20 Jul. 1844, 347.

17. See programs reproduced in William Weber, *The Great Transformation of Musical Taste: Concert Programming from Haydn to Brahms* (Cambridge: Cambridge University Press, forthcoming).

18. Weber, *The Great Transformation*, chap. 6.

19. Vladimir Ivanoff, "From the Danube to the Bosporus: The Ecstasy of the Waltz and the Mysticism of the Dervishes," notes to *The Waltz—Ecstasy and Mysticism*, compact disc, Archiv Produktion, 00289 477 5420 (2005), 9–11, 10.

20. Waltzes 4 and 5 of *Die Osmanen* can be heard on *The Waltz: Ecstasy and Mysticism*, compact disc, Concerto Köln and Sarband, Archiv Produktion, 00289 477 5420 (2005), track 15. Abdülaziz's waltz can be heard on *Invitation to the Seraglio*, compact disc, London Academy of Ottoman Court Music: Period Dances, Marches and Occasional Pieces, Warner Classics 2564 61472–2 (2004), track 7.

21. *Das Fremden-Blatt*, 16 Aug. 1867, quoted in Peter Kemp, notes to *Jo-*

hann Strauss, Jr. Edition, compact disc set, 51 vols., vol. 45, Marco Polo 8.223245 (1995), 17.

22. Quoted in Peter Kemp, *The Strauss Family: A Portrait of a Musical Dynasty* (London: Omnibus, 1989; originally published Tunbridge Wells, England: Baton, 1985), 75.

23. Heinrich Eduard Jacob, *Johann Strauss: A Century of Light Music,* trans. Marguerite Wolff (London: Hutchinson, 1940; originally published as *Johann Strauss und das neunzehnte Jahrhundert. Die Geschichte einer musikalischen Weltherrschaft, 1819–1917* [Amsterdam: Querido-Verlag, 1937]), 213.

24. See William M. Johnston, *The Austrian Mind: An Intellectual and Social History 1848–1938* (Berkeley: University of California Press, 1972), 130.

25. *Musical Opinion and Music Trade Review,* Sep. 1888, 562, excerpted in James Coover, comp., *Music Publishing, Copyright and Piracy in Victorian England* (London: Mansell, 1985), 38.

26. Raymond Williams, *The Long Revolution* (Harmondsworth, England: Penguin, 1965; originally published London: Chatto and Windus, 1961), 291.

27. Henry Raynor, *Music and Society since 1815* (London: Barrie and Jenkins, 1976), 149.

28. Charles Hubert Parry, *Style in Musical Art* (London: Macmillan, 1911), quoted in Peter van der Merwe, *Origins of the Popular Style: The Antecedents of Twentieth-Century Popular Music* (Oxford: Clarendon Press, 1989), 223.

29. See the Eulenburg miniature score (no. 910) of *Götterdämmerung* (Zurich), 998.

30. Van der Merwe, *Origins of the Popular Style,* 242.

31. Henry C. Dobson and G. Clifton Dobson, *Dobson's Universal Banjo Instructor* (Boston: Oliver Ditson, 1882); for the polka, see 36.

32. Laurence Senelick, ed., *Tavern Singing in Early Victorian London: The Diaries of Charles Rice for 1840 and 1850* (London: Society for Theatre Research, 1997).

33. Harold Scott, *The Early Doors: Origins of the Music Hall* (London: Nicholson and Watson, 1946), 117. The name of the establishment contains a pun: Evans took it over from a Mr. Joy.

34. Dagmar Höher, "The Composition of Music Hall Audiences 1850–1900," in Peter Bailey, ed., *Music Hall: The Business of Pleasure* (Milton Keynes, England: Open University Press, 1986), 73–92, 76.

35. Höher, "The Composition of Music Hall Audiences," 86.

36. A useful survey is provided by Concetta Condemi in *Les Cafés-Concerts: Histoire d'un divertissement (1849–1914)* (Paris: Quai Voltaire, 1992).

37. Martin Pénet, comp., *Mémoire de la chanson: 1100 chansons du Moyen-Age à 1919* (Paris: Omnibus, 1998), 441.

38. Article 101 of the bylaws of 16 May 1881. Parisian regulations are in *Minutes of Evidence Taken before the Select Committee on Theatres and Places of Entertainment,* 1892 (London: Eyre and Spottiswoode for HMSO, 1892), app. 2, 407–12.

39. See H. Gourdon de Genouillac, comp., *Les Refrains de la rue de 1830 à 1870,* (Paris: E. Dentu, 1879), for information on the *scie.*

40. Baumaine fit his words to the tune of "La Belle Polonaise" (words by Paul Avenel, music by Marc Chautagne, 1863).

41. 20 Aug. 1864. Edmond and Jules de Goncourt, *Journal: Mémoires de la vie littéraire,* vol. 6, 1863–64 (Monaco: Fasquelle and Flammarion, 1956), 233.

This entry of 20 Aug. 1864 did not appear in the first publication of vol. 2 of the *Journal* (1862–65) edited by Edmond de Goncourt; see <http://freresgoncourt.free.fr/scies/pageune.htm>.

42. Words by Emile Carré, music by Victor Robillard (Paris: Feuchot). The full texts (without music) of this, and "Hé! Lambert," are in Pénet, *Mémoire de la chanson*, 506 and 572.

43. The definite article is used with names to indicate someone known, hence my translation "It's that Amanda."

44. *Laughter: An Essay on the Meaning of the Comic*, trans. Cloudesley Brereton and Fred Rothwell (London: Macmillan, 1911; reprint, New York: Dover, 2005; originally published as *Le Rire: Essai sur la signification du comique* [Paris: Félix Alcan, 1900], reprinted from three articles in the *Revue de Paris*), 37.

45. "Chronique—Le Café-concert," *Le Réveil*, 29 Sep. 1886, quoted in Timothy J. Clark, *The Painting of Modern Life: Paris in the Art of Manet and His Followers* (London: Thames and Hudson, 1985), 214.

46. Yvette Guilbert, *La Chanson de ma Vie (Mes Memoires)* (Paris: Bernard Grasset, 1927), 86, quoted in Marie Oberthür, *Cafés and Cabarets of Montmartre* (Layton, Utah: Gibbs M. Smith, 1984), 85.

47. Victorin Joncières, quoted in François Caradec and Alain Weill, *Le Café-concert* (Paris: Hachette, 1980), 30.

48. "Aménagés à la hâte pour répondre au nouvel urbanisme d'une métropole récemment industrialisée et rémodelée par le baron Haussmann, certains de ces locaux se transforment en café-concert pour répondre aux exigences d'une clientèle le plus souvent composée d'ouvriers et de paysans au chômage." Condemi, *Les Cafés-concerts*, 58.

49. See Thérésa [Emma Valadon; with Victorien Monnier], *Mémoires de Thérésa écrits par elle-même* (Paris: E. Dentu, 1865), 9–10.

50. "Il n'existe nulle part ailleurs de cabaret à la manière du *Chat Noir*, pas plus dans un autre endroit de Paris que dans le reste du monde." Lionel Richard, *Cabaret, Cabarets: Origines et décadence* (Paris: Plon, 1991), 87.

51. See Jeffrey S. Weiss, "Picasso, Collage, and the Music Hall," in Kirk Varnedoe and Adam Gopnik, eds., *Modern Art and Popular Culture: Readings in High* and *Low* (New York: Museum of Modern Art, 1990), 83–115.

52. Charles Hamm, *Music in the New World* (New York: Norton, 1983), 183.

53. Don B. Wilmeth, *Variety Entertainment and Outdoor Amusements: A Reference Guide* (Westport, Conn.: Greenwood Press, 1982), 119.

54. See Michael Pickering, "White Skin, Black Masks," in Jacqueline S. Bratton, ed., *Music Hall: Performance and Style* (Milton Keynes, England: Open University Press, 1986), 70–91. Some important scholarship on blackface minstrelsy appeared in the 1990s, revealing the complexities of issues of ethnicity and class raised by this entertainment. See, for example, Eric Lott, *Love and Theft: Blackface Minstrelsy and the American Working Class* (New York: Oxford University Press, 1993); Dale Cockrell, *Demons of Disorder: Early Blackface Minstrels and Their World* (Cambridge: Cambridge University Press, 1997); and William J. Mahar, *Behind the Burnt Cork Mask: Early Blackface Minstrelsy and Antebellum American Popular Culture* (Urbana: University of Illinois Press, 1999).

55. Erving Goffman, *Frame Analysis: An Essay on the Organization of Experience* (Boston: Northeastern University Press, 1986; originally published New York: Harper and Row, 1974), 33.

56. Carl Wittke, *Tambo and Bones: A History of the American Minstrel Stage*

(New York: Greenwood Press, 1968; originally published Durham, N.C.: Duke University Press, 1930), 136.

57. The success of Edwin Pearce Christy's troupe (formed in 1843 in Buffalo, New York) caused "Christy Minstrels" (or "Christy's Minstrels") to become a generic name for blackface minstrels.

58. See Hamm, *Music in the New World,* 230–31.

59. "Nineteenth-Century Popular Music," in David Nicholls, ed., *The Cambridge History of American Music* (Cambridge: Cambridge University Press, 1998), 158–85, 172, no source given. Ken Emerson makes no mention of Foster's opinion of minstrel dialect, and suggests that the use of standard English allowed Foster to overcome "the blackface/parlor ballad, possum fat/flowrets dichotomy that had long bedeviled him." *Doo-dah! Stephen Foster and the Rise of American Popular Culture* (New York: Simon and Schuster, 1997), 195. William W. Austin makes no comment when referring to Foster's removal of dialect from an earlier sketchbook version of the song, in *"Susanna," "Jeanie," and "The Old Folks at Home": The Songs of Stephen C. Foster from His Time to Ours* (London: Macmillan, 1975), 233–34.

60. Boston: Oliver Ditson, 1878.

61. Boston: John F. Perry, 1879.

62. The first collection of spirituals was compiled by Francis William Allen, Charles Pickard Ware, and Lucy McKim Garrison, and published as *Slave Songs of the United States* (New York: A. Simpson, 1867). A selection of their Jubilee Singers' songs was first published in G. D. Pike, *The Jubilee Singers and Their Campaign for Twenty Thousand Dollars* (London: Hodder and Stoughton, 1874; originally published Boston: Lee and Shepard, 1874), which appeared in an expanded edition the next year as J. B. T. Marsh, *The Story of the Jubilee Singers with Their Songs,* with a supplement by F. J. Loudin (1875; reprint, Mineola, NY: Dover, 2003).

63. Allen Woll cites census figures in *Black Musical Theatre—From Coontown to Dreamgirls* (New York: Da Capo Press, 1991; originally published Baton Rouge: Louisiana State University Press, 1989), 2. See also Henry T. Sampson, *Blacks in Blackface: A Source Book on Early Black Musical Shows,* 2nd ed. (Lanham, Md.: Scarecrow Press, 1995; originally published Metuchen, N.J.: Scarecrow Press, 1980).

64. Tom Fletcher, *100 Years of the Negro in Show Business* (New York: Da Capo Press, 1984; originally published New York: Burdge, 1954), 103.

65. For information on *Clorindy,* see Will Marion Cook, "Clorindy, the Origin of the Cakewalk" (1947), in Rosamond Gilder, Hermine Rich Isaacs, Robert M. MacGregor, and Edward Reed, eds., *Theater Arts Anthology* (New York: Theater Arts Books, 1950). Information on Robert Cole can be fond in Thomas L. Riis, "'Bob' Cole: His Life and His Legacy to Black Musical Theater," *Black Perspective in Music,* 13/2 (Autumn, 1985), 135–50. A general survey of black musical theater of the 1890s is given in Thomas L. Riis, *Just before Jazz: Black Musical Theater in New York, 1890 to 1915* (Washington, D.C.: Smithsonian Institution Press, 1989).

66. The words and music are in Eileen Southern, *The Music of Black Americans: A History,* 2nd ed. (1971; reprint, New York: Norton, 1983), 312–13.

67. See Dena J. Epstein, *Sinful Tunes and Spirituals: Black Folk Music to the Civil War* (Urbana: University of Illinois Press, 1977), 119–20.

68. See Edward A. Berlin, *King of Ragtime: Scott Joplin and His Era* (New York: Oxford University Press, 1994).

69. Nicholas E. Tawa, *The Way to Tin Pan Alley: American Popular Song, 1866–1910* (New York: Schirmer Books, 1990), 183.

70. See Douglas Gilbert, *American Vaudeville: Its Life and Times* (New York: McGraw-Hill, 1940), 32.

71. William M. Marston and John H. Fuller, *F. F. Proctor Vaudeville Pioneer* (New York: Richard R. Smith, 1943), 50.

72. See Wilmeth, *Variety Entertainment and Outdoor Amusements*, 121.

73. Siegfried Kracauer, *Offenbach and the Paris of His Time*, trans. Gwenda David and Eric Mosbacher (London: Constable, 1937; originally published as *Jacques Offenbach und das Paris seiner Zeit* [Amsterdam: Allert de Lange, 1937]), 33–5.

74. See David Hillery, *The Théâtre des Variétés in 1852*, Modern Languages Series (Durham: University of Durham, 1996), 45.

75. Walter Benjamin, "Paris: Capital of the Nineteenth Century," *Perspecta*, 12 (1969), 163–72; extracted from the incomplete *Arcades Project* [*Passagen-Werk*], 1927–40), 169.

76. Kracauer, *Offenbach*, 219. For Offenbach in Vienna, see also Camille Crittenden, *Johann Strauss and Vienna: Operetta and the Politics of Popular Culture* (Cambridge: Cambridge University Press, 2000), 11–15.

77. See Richard Traubner, *Operetta: A Theatrical History* (New York: Oxford University Press, 1989; originally published New York: Doubleday, 1983), 106.

78. *Der Floh*, no. 7 (1871), quoted in Peter Kemp, notes to *Johann Strauss, Jr. Edition*, compact disc set, 51 vols., Marco Polo 8.223249 (1995), 48:5.

79. See Crittenden, *Johann Strauss and Vienna*, 79–80. Geistinger took over as director of the Theater an der Wien in 1869.

80. See Moritz Csáky, "Der soziale und kulturelle Kontext der Wiener Operette," in Ludwig Finscher and Albrecht Riethmüller, eds., *Johann Strauss: Zwischen Kunstanspruch und Volksvergnügen* (Darmstadt: Wissenschaftliche Buchgesellschaft, 1995), 28–65. Camille Crittenden discusses the political context of *Der Zigeunerbaron* in *Johann Strauss and Vienna*, 170–209.

81. In New York it was rough humored, and fond of presenting young women dancers in scanty costumes or body stockings.

82. A short survey of Victorian burlesque can be found in Sterling Mackinlay, *Origin and Development of Light Opera* (London: Hutchinson, 1927), 202–14.

83. See Andrew Lamb, "Music of the Popular Theatre," in Nicholas Temperley, ed., *The Romantic Age 1800–1914*, vol. 5 of *The Blackwell History of Music in Britain* (Oxford: Blackwell, 1988; originally published London: Athlone, 1981), 92–108, 99.

84. The San Francisco Minstrels. George C. D. Odell, *Annals of the New York Stage* (reprint, New York: AMS Press, 1970, originally published in 15 vols., 1927–49), 10:98.

85. Tawa, *The Way to Tin Pan Alley*, 122.

86. See David Ewen, *All the Years of American Popular Music* (Englewood Cliffs, N.J.: Prentice Hall, 1977), 83–85, and Russell Sanjek, *American Popular Music and Its Business: The First Four Hundred Years*, vol. 2, *From 1790 to 1909* (New York: Oxford University Press, 1988), 303–5.

87. Jacques Offenbach, *Orpheus in America*, trans. Lander MacClintock (Bloomington: Indiana University Press, 1957; originally published as *Offenbach en Amérique: Notes d'un musicien en voyage* [Paris: Calmann Lévy, 1877]), 70.

88. Quoted in Robert C. Toll, *On with the Show: The First Century of Show Business in America* (New York: Oxford University Press, 1976), 185.

89. E. J. Kahn Jr., *The Merry Partners: The Age of Harrigan and Hart* (New York: Random House, 1955), 3–5.

90. Howard S. Becker, *Art Worlds* (Berkeley: University of California Press, 1982), 329.

Chapter 3

1. Talcott Parsons, *The Social System* (London: Routledge and Kegan Paul, 1951), 41–42.

2. *On Liberty and Other Essays* (Oxford: Oxford University Press, 1991), 161.

3. Anthony Giddens defines agency thus: "the stream of actual or contemplated causal interventions of corporeal beings in the ongoing process of events-in-the-world." *New Rules of Sociological Method: A Positive Critique of Interpretative Sociologies,* 2nd ed. (Cambridge: Polity Press, 1993; originally published London: Hutchinson, 1976), 81.

4. Geoffrey Best, for instance, makes a case for the common acceptance of the "practice of deference, the 'removable inequalities' theory of society, and the concept of the gentleman" in mid-Victorian Britain, and cites the success of friendly societies or benefit clubs as evidence of shared ideals between the different classes. *Mid-Victorian Britain 1851–75* (London: Fontana, 1979; originally published Weidenfeld and Nicholson, 1971), 279–92.

5. "Die Gedanken der herrschenden Klasse sind in jeder Epoche die herrschenden Gedanken." Karl Marx and Friedrich Engels, *Die deutsche Ideologie* (1845–46), introduction. Full text based on the original manuscript in Marx-Engels-Lenin Institute, Moscow, www.mlwerke.de/me/me03/me03_009.htm.

6. Jürgen Habermas, *The Structural Transformation of the Public Sphere: An Inquiry into a Category of Bourgeois Society,* trans. Thomas Burgeri with the assistance of Frederick Lawrence (Cambridge: Polity Press, 1989; originally published as *Strukturwandel der Öffentlichkeit* [Darmstadt: Luchterhand, 1962]), 237, 240. It is significant that Phil Park decides to turn the moral bully Public Opinion into Orpheus's mother in his English version, *Orpheus in the Underworld* (London: Weinberger, 1966).

7. "Für eine Gesellschaft von Warenproduzenten, deren allgemein gesellschaftliches Produktionsverhältnis darin besteht, sich zu ihren Produkten als Waren, also als Werten, zu verhalten und in dieser sachlichen Form ihre Privatarbeiten aufeinander zu beziehn als gleiche menschliche Arbeit, ist das Christentum mit seinem Kultus des abstrakten Menschen, namentlich in seiner bürgerlichen Entwicklung, dem Protestantismus, Deismus usw., die entsprechendste Religionsform." *Das Kapital. Kritik der politischen Oekonomie* (Hamburg: Otto Meissner, 1867), chap. 1, sec. 4.

8. *The Protestant Ethic and the Spirit of Capitalism,* trans. Talcott Parsons (New York: Routledge, 1992; originally published as *Die protestantische Ethik und das Geist des Kapitalismus,* in Archiv für Sozialwissenschaft und Sozialpolitik, vols. 20 and 21 [1904–5]), 100, 104–5; full text, <http://de.wikisource.org/wiki/Die_protestantische_Ethik_und_der_Geist_des_Kapitalismus>.

9. See Henry Raynor, *Music and Society since 1815* (London: Barrie and Jenkins, 1976), 93.

10. See William Weber, *Music and the Middle Class: The Social Structure of Concert Life in London, Paris and Vienna Between 1830 and 1848,* 2nd ed. (Aldershot, England: Ashgate, 2004; originally published London: Croom Helm, 1975), 167, table 21.

11. Quoted in Bernarr Rainbow, *The Land without Music: Musical Education in England 1800–1860 and Its Continental Antecedents* (London: Novello, 1967), 102.

12. See ibid., 105–6.

13. Jane Fulcher, "The Orphéon Societies: Music for the Workers in Second-Empire France," *International Review of the Aesthetics and Sociology of Music* 10 (1979), 47–56. Howard Becker characterizes the interest of the state in art thus: "Some art makes people discontented, destroys their moral fiber, and makes them unfit to play the roles and do the work the state wants done. Other art works implant and support habits and attitudes the state finds congenial or thinks necessary to its own goals." *Art Worlds* (Berkeley: University of California Press, 1982), 166. However, relations between the state, cultural institutions, and the cultural market place are anything but simple; see Raymond Williams, *Culture* (London: Faber, 1981), 102–8.

14. C. Rodgers and J. Black, eds., *The Gathering of the Forces, by Walt Whitman* (New York: Knickerbocker Press, 1920), 2:353–54, quoted in Charles Hamm, *Music in the New World* (New York: Norton, 1983), 206–7.

15. See Heinrich Eduard Jacob, *Johann Strauss: A Century of Light Music,* trans. Marguerite Wolff (London: Hutchinson, 1940; originally published as *Johann Strauss und das neunzehnte Jahrhundert. Die Geschichte einer musikalischen Weltherrschaft, 1819–1917* [Amsterdam: Querido-Verlag, 1937]), 188.

16. Edward W. Said, *Culture and Imperialism* (New York: Vintage, 1994; originally published London: Chatto and Windus, 1993), 157–58.

17. Nicholas E. Tawa, *A Music for the Millions: Antebellum Democratic Attitudes and the Birth of American Popular Music* (New York: Pendragon Press, 1984), 21–22.

18. For a general discussion of audiences and order in nineteenth-century America, see Lawrence M. Levine, *Highbrow/Lowbrow* (Cambridge, Mass.: Harvard University Press, 1988), 178–95.

19. See John F. Kasson, *Rudeness and Civility: Manners in Nineteenth-Century Urban America* (New York: Hill and Wang, 1990), 252–56, cited in Simon Frith, *Performing Rites: On the Value of Popular Music* (New York: Oxford University Press, 1996), 34.

20. Peter Bailey remarks that magistrates were generally tolerant toward the halls, however, "when not under immediate pressure from reform lobbies." *Leisure and Class in Victorian England: Rational Recreation and the Contest for Control, 1830–1885* (London: Methuen, 1987; originally published London: Routledge and Kegan Paul, 1978), 157.

21. James H. Johnson, *Listening in Paris: A Cultural History* (Berkeley: University of California Press, 1995), 228–36.

22. For the idea of culture as "instructive" and "harmonizing," a force for moral order in America, see Levine, *Highbrow/Lowbrow,* 200–207; for culture as rational recreation in England, see Bailey, *Leisure and Class in Victorian England.*

23. From the end of George Hogarth, *Musical History, Biography, and Criticism* (London: John W. Parker, 1838; reprint, New York: Da Capo, 1969 [repro-

duction of the American edition (New York: Redfield, 1848(]), quoted in Reginald Nettel, *The Orchestra in England: A Social History* (London: Jonathan Cape, 1946), 160. The phrase "laborem dulce lenimen" ("sweet solace of labor") is from Horace, *Odes* 1.32.14–15. Horace is, indeed, using it to describe the effect of music.

24. See Cyril Ehrlich, Simon McVeigh, and Michael Musgrave, "London," sec. 6.2.2, "Concert Life: 1850–1900," in Stanley Sadie, ed., *The New Grove Dictionary of Music and Musicians* (London: Macmillan, 2001), 14:141–44, 144, and E. D. Mackerness, *A Social History of English Music* (London: Routledge and Kegan Paul, 1964), 201–2, who says incorrectly, however, that the South Place Concerts began in 1878.

25. Quoted without source in Percy M. Young, *The Concert Tradition: From the Middle Ages to the Twentieth Century* (London: Routledge and Kegan Paul, 1965), 230.

26. Mackerness, *A Social History of English Music*, 148. The London Mechanics' Institute was founded in 1823; others followed throughout the country.

27. The quotation is from Charles Dickens's description in the first issue of *Household Words* (1850), quoted in Cyril Ehrlich, *The Music Profession in Britain since the Eighteenth Century* (Oxford: Clarendon Press, 1985), 67.

28. Reginald Nettel, *The Orchestra in England: A Social History* (London: Jonathan Cape, 1946), 168.

29. See Roy Newsome, *Brass Roots: A Hundred Years of Brass Bands and Their Music, 1836–1936* (Aldershot, England: Ashgate, 1998), 38–42.

30. "The Garde Republicaine Band," *Dwight's Journal of Music* 32, no. 9, Jul. 1872, 277.

31. See Mackerness, *A Social History of English Music*, 185–86.

32. Lord Mount Temple speaking in 1884, quoted in Denis Richards, *Offspring of the Vic: A History of Morley College* (London: Routledge and Kegan Paul, 1958), 67, and in Mackerness, *A Social History of English Music*, 202.

33. See Jacob, *Johann Strauss*, 119.

34. Hugh Reginald Haweis, *Music and Morals* (1871; reprint, London: Longmans, Green, 1912), 112.

35. See Alice M. Hanson, *Musical Life in Biedermeier Vienna* (Cambridge: Cambridge University Press, 1985), 163.

36. Arthur Loesser, *Men, Women and Pianos: A Social History* (New York: Simon and Schuster, 1954), 159.

37. George Gordon, Lord Byron [Horace Hornem, pseud.], *The Waltz: An Apostrophic Hymn* (London: John Murray, 1813). The poem was written the previous year.

38. The use of the reflexive verb *s'enrafler* conveys an erotic tone here by suggesting something akin to human action. I am grateful to Mireille Ribière for alerting me to this point.

39. "Ils commencèrent lentement, puis allèrent plus vite. Ils tournaient: tout tournait autour d'eux, les lampes, les meubles, les lambris, et le parquet, comme un disque sur un pivot. En passant auprès des portes, la robe d'Emma, par le bas, s'éraflait au pantalon; leurs jambes entraient l'une dans l'autre; il baissait ses regards vers elle, elle levait les siens vers lui; une torpeur la prenait, elle s'arrêta. Ils repartirent; et, d'un mouvement plus rapide, le vicomte, l'entraînant, disparut avec elle jusqu'au bout de la galerie, où, haletante, elle fail-

lit tomber, et, un instant, s'appuya la tête sur sa poitrine. Et puis, tournant tou-
jours, mais plus doucement, il la reconduisit à sa place; elle se renversa contre
la muraille et mit la main devant ses yeux." From Gustave Flaubert, *Madame
Bovary* (1856), chapter 8, my translation.

40. See Curt Sachs, *World History of the Dance*, trans. Bessie Schönberg (New
York: Norton, 1937; originally published as *Eine Weltgeschichte des Tanzes* [Berlin:
D. Reimer/E. Vohsen, 1933]), 427–34, and Sevin H. Yaraman, *Revolving Em-
brace: The Waltz as Sex, Steps, and Sound* (New York: Pendragon Press, 2002).

41. "The Educational Value of Dance Music," *Musical Times* 26, no. 507,
1 May 1885, 253–55, 253.

42. See Dagmar Kift, *The Victorian Music Hall: Culture, Class and Conflict*,
trans. Roy Kift (Cambridge: Cambridge University Press, 1996; originally published as *Arbeiterkultur im gesellschaftlichen Konflikt: Die englische Music Hall im 19.
Jahrhundert* [Essen: Klartext Verlag, 1991]), 136–39, and Dagmar Höher, "The
Composition of Music Hall Audiences," in Peter Bailey, ed., *Music Hall: The Business of Pleasure* (Milton Keynes, England: Open University Press, 1986), 73–92,
74–75.

43. See Joseph Wechsberg, *The Waltz Emperors: The Life and Times and Music
of the Strauss Family* (London: Weidenfeld and Nicolson, 1973), 44.

44. See Derek B. Scott, *The Singing Bourgeois: Songs of the Victorian Drawing
Room and Parlour*, 2nd ed. (Aldershot, England: Ashgate, 2001; originally published Milton Keynes, England: Open University Press, 1989), 189.

45. "What Cheer, 'Ria" (words by Bessie Bellwood, music by Will Herbert,
1885); "'Arf a Pint of Ale" (words and music by Charles Tempest, 1905); "Champagne Charlie" (words by George Leybourne, music by Alfred Lee, 1867);
"Cliquot" (words by Frank W. Green, music by J. Riviere, 1870).

46. For a representative selection of drawing room ballads, see Michael R.
Turner and Antony Miall, eds., *The Parlour Song Book: A Casquet of Vocal Gems*
(London: Pan, 1974; originally published London: Michael Joseph, 1972), and
Michael R. Turner and Antony Miall, eds., *Just a Song at Twilight: The Second Par-
lour Song Book* (London: Michael Joseph, 1975).

47. James Workman, "Home, Sweet Home," *Strand Musical Magazine* 2
(1895), 252–56, 255.

48. In its original incarnation it had words by Thomas Haynes Baily, "To
the Home of My Childhood in Sorrow I Came," in Bishop's *Melodies of Various
Nations* (London: Goulding and D'Almaine, 1821).

49. Henry Russell is one of the first internationally famous Jewish composers of popular song. Jewish songwriters became very important to the history of popular music. The success of Irving Berlin, Jerome Kern, George
Gershwin, and Richard Rodgers is not a twentieth-century novelty but can, like
so many other popular music developments, be traced back to the nineteenth
century.

50. Morris's poem was first published in the *New York Mirror* in 1830, and
was republished (after the song had appeared) in *The Deserted Bride and Other
Poems* (New York, 1838).

51. Henry Russell, *Cheer, Boys, Cheer!* (London: John Macqueen, 1895), 253.

52. See Edgar Allan Poe, "George P. Morris," in Rufus Wilmot Griswold,
ed., *The Works of the Late Edgar Allan Poe*, vol. 3, *The Literati: Some Honest Opinions
about Autorial Merits and Demerits* (New York: Redfield, 1850), 255–56, 256.

53. Charles Hamm, *Yesterdays: Popular Song in America* (New York: Norton, 1979), 152.

54. Printed on the original song sheet published by S. Brainard's Sons, Cleveland.

55. Harold Simpson, *A Century of Ballads 1810–1910* (London: Mills and Boon, 1910), 121. This song is a setting of Charles Kingsley's verse by John Hullah (1857).

56. W. Beatty-Kingston, critic of the *Theatre*, quoted in Leslie Baily, *The Gilbert and Sullivan Book* (London: Spring Books, 1966; originally published London: Cassell, 1952, rev. 1956), 238.

57. *Self-Help* (1859; reprint, London: John Murray, 1936), 255. Gilbert was similarly aware of bourgeois hypocrisy: his Pirate King declares, "I don't think much of our profession, but, contrasted with respectability, it is comparatively honest" (*Pirates of Penzance*, act 1).

58. Yvette Guilbert and H. Simpson, *Yvette Guilbert: Struggles and Victories* (London: Mills and Boon, 1910), 116–17.

59. Matthew Hanly, a representative of the London United Workmen's Committee (established in 1878), says that the music halls in the East End and in southeast London (home to a population of two million) are "considered the great entertainment of the working man and his family." He gives the example of the Queen's music hall at Poplar. He then adds, "at the present time music halls have reached a very high state of morality, and can compare very favourably with the theatres." Minute 5171, in *Minutes of Evidence taken before the Select Committee on Theatres and Places of Entertainment* (London: Eyre and Spottiswoode for HMS0, 1892), 23 May 1892, 327.

60. See Peter Bailey, "Champagne Charlie: Performance and Ideology in the Music Hall Swell Song," in Jacqueline S. Bratton, ed., *Music Hall: Performance and Style* (Milton Keynes, England: Open University Press, 1986), 49–69, 50–51, and Peter Bailey, *Popular Culture and Performance in the Victorian City* (Cambridge: Cambridge University Press, 1998), 102–4.

61. Quoted without date in Baily, *The Gilbert and Sullivan Book*, 90.

62. Henry Fothergill Chorley, "Depths and Heights of Modern Opera," *All the Year Round*, 9 Oct. 1869, 450–54, 451, quoted in Robert Terrell Bledsoe, *Henry Fothergill Chorley: Victorian Journalist* (Aldershot, England: Ashgate, 1998), 274.

63. Kathy Peiss, *Cheap Amusements: Working Women and Leisure in Turn-of-the-Century New York* (Philadelphia: Temple University Press, 1986), 8.

64. "A Bostonian reviewer" in 1896, quoted in Robert C. Toll, *On with the Show: The First Century of Show Business in America* (New York: Oxford University Press, 1976), 190.

65. Quoted in Ian Whitcomb, *After the Ball: Pop Music from Rag to Rock* (1972; reprint, New York: Limelight, 1986), 16.

66. Quoted in Guilbert and Simpson, *Yvette Guilbert: Struggles and Victories*, 204–5.

67. See Albert L. Lloyd, *Come All Ye Bold Miners: Ballads and Songs of the Coalfields*, rev. ed. (London: Lawrence and Wishart, 1978; originally published 1952), 183.

68. M. de Rodenburg, *Journal d'un voyage à Londres*, translation from *La Revue et Gazette Musicale*, *Musical World* 36, no. 30, 24 Jul. 1858, 467.

69. See Roy Palmer, *A Ballad History of England* (London: Batsford, 1979), 110–11.

70. Ibid., 120–21.

71. Roy Palmer, *The Sound of History: Songs and Social Comment* (Oxford: Oxford University Press, 1988), 108.

72. Robert Tressell, *The Ragged Trousered Philanthropists* (London: Grafton Books, 1965; originally published London: Lawrence and Wishart, 1955), 446. Tressell's work remained unpublished at the time of his death in 1911. Clifton's song was sung to the tune of George Root's "Tramp! Tramp! Tramp!"

73. See Clark D. Halker, *For Democracy, Workers, and God: Labor Song-Poems and Labor Protest, 1865–95* (Urbana: University of Illinois Press, 1991), 55, 70 and 206. For a general survey, see Philip S. Foner, *American Labor Songs of the Nineteenth Century* (Urbana: University of Illinois Press, 1975).

74. Johann W. Seidl, *Musik und Austromarxismus: Zur Musikrezeption der österreichischen Arbeiterbewegung im späten Kaiserreich und in der Ersten Republik* (Vienna: Böhlau, 1989), 96–97.

75. Ibid., 85.

76. See Ralph P. Locke, *Music, Musicians and the Saint-Simonians* (Chicago: University of Chicago Press, 1986), 33, 235–37; complete song reproduced 238–39.

77. Five of Vinçard's songs are reproduced with music in Locke, *Music, Musicians and the Saint-Simonians,* app. C, 247–50. On Béranger, see Ralph P. Locke, "The Music of the French Chanson, 1810–1850," in Peter Bloom, ed., *Music in Paris in the 1830s* (Stuyvesant, N.Y.: Pendragon Press, 1987), 431–56.

78. Robert Brécy, *La Chanson de la Commune: Chansons et poèmes inspirés par la Commune de 1871* (Paris: Éditions Ouvrières, 1991), 23.

79. See Bernard Gendron, *Between Montmartre and the Mudd Club: Popular Music and the Avant-Garde* (Chicago: University of Chicago Press, 2002), 49–51.

80. "Les chansons et poèmes créés dans les premiers jours du pouvoir populaire illustrent bien, par-delà leur forme souvent maladroite, les aspirations des diverses couches de la population parisienne, en particulier le double aspect, patriotic et social, les mobiles qui ont animé les communards." Brécy, *La Chanson de la Commune,* 67. See also Georges Coulonges, *La Commune en chantant* (Paris: Messidor, 1970).

81. In 1886, Jules Jouy reworked the song as "Le temps des crises," making a more explicit political statement.

82. Brécy, *La Chanson de la Commune,* 68.

83. Ibid., 43. The words of "La Plébiéienne" are by A. Philibert and H. Chatelin, the music by F. Chaissaigne.

84. The vexed question of the date of Pottier's first draft of "L'Internationale"—whether it was September 1870 or June 1871—is discussed by Brécy, *La Chanson de la Commune,* 106–8. Pottier did not publish it until 1887, although he had opportunity to do so while in exile.

85. Ibid., 186.

86. Biographers usually play down his involvement with the revolution, but Norbert Linke shows that it was considerable; see *Johann Strauss* (Reinbek bei Hamburg: Rowohlt, 1996), 45–47.

87. Wechsberg, *The Waltz Emperors,* 101.

88. Peter Kemp lists seven lost unpublished works from 1848–49. "Strauss," in Sadie, *New Grove II,* 24:474–96, 486.

89. Two decades later, Jakob Audorf's version of the Marseillaise became one of the most popular songs of the German workers' movement (*Arbeiterbewegung*). Seidl, *Musik und Austromarxismus*, 96–97.

90. Heinrich Laube, *Reise durch das Biedermeyer* (Hamburg: Hoffmann und Campe, 1965; originally published as *Reisenovellen* [3 vols, Mannheim: H. Hoff, 1834–37]), 250.

91. Jacques Attali, *Noise: The Political Economy of Music,* trans. Brian Massumi (Manchester: Manchester University Press, 1985; originally published as *Bruits: essai sur l'économie politique de la musique* [Paris: Presses Univeritaires de France, 1977]), 74.

92. London: John Murray.

93. Lengthy quotation is made from Bass's book in "From My Study," *Musical Times* 36, no. 627, 1 May 1895, 297–301.

94. Haweis, *Music and Morals*, 535.

95. "From My Study," 301.

96. Antonio Gramsci, *Selections from the Prison Notebooks,* ed. and trans. Quintin Hoare and Geoffrey N. Smith (London: Lawrence and Wishart, 1971), 12.

97. *The Sociological Imagination* (New York: Oxford University Press, 1959), 77.

98. Kift, *The Victorian Music Hall*, 183.

99. Contract reproduced in *Minutes of Evidence Taken before the Select Committee on Theatres and Places of Entertainment* (London: Eyre and Spottiswoode for HMS0, 1892), app. 4, 441.

100. See François Caradec and Alan Weill, *Le café-concert* (Paris: Hachette, 1980), 66.

101. "Le nombre des chansons que l'on soumet au visa est incalculable; on ne peut imaginer à quel degré de dévergondage en arrivent les auteurs de ces chansons, à tous les points de vue: morale, politique, religion, question sociale. Un très-grand nombre est refusé absolument; la plus grande partie de celles qui sont autorisées, ne le sont qu'après les plus sérieuses modifications." Report of Nov. 1872, Archives nationales, series F21, no. 1338, p. 2, quoted in Timothy J. Clark, *The Painting of Modern Life: Paris in the Art of Manet and His Followers* (London: Thames and Hudson, 1985), 304 n. 10. On the censorship of café-concert songs, see Concetta Condemi, *Les Cafés-concerts: Histoire d'un divertissment* (Paris: Quai Voltaire, 1992), 31–38.

102. [Charles MacKay], "Modern Cynicism," *Blackwood's Edinburgh Magazine* 103, no. 627 (Jan. 1868), 62–70, 67. The publisher William Blackwood had a London branch; this is not to be taken as a comment restricted to Scottish music halls.

103. Jacqueline S. Bratton, "Jenny Hill: Sex and Sexism in the Victorian Music Hall," in J. S. Bratton, ed., *Music Hall: Performance and Style* (Milton Keynes, England: Open University Press, 1986), 92–110, 107.

104. Harry Sydney (London: H. D'Alcorn).

105. London: D'Alcorn.

106. "Popular Music," *St. James's Magazine,* June 1868, excerpted in *Musical Standard* 8, no. 203, 20 Jun. 1868, 246–47. The magazine was edited by Mrs. J. H. Riddell, and was aimed primarily at respectable and elderly female readers.

107. Words by Harry Adams, music by Fred Coyne (London: Hopwood and Crew, 1879); reprinted in John M. Garrett, *Sixty Years of British Music Hall* (London: Chappell, 1976), n.p.

108. Words by John P. Harrington, music by George Le Brunn (London: Francis, Day and Hunter).

109. Susan Pennybacker, "'It Was Not What She Said, but the Way in Which She Said It': The London County Council and the Music Hall," in Bailey, *Music Hall*, 118–40, 131. The London County Council had become responsible for regulating and licensing music halls after the passing of the Local Government Act in 1888.

110. Jacqueline S. Bratton, *The Victorian Popular Ballad* (London: Macmillan, 1975), 195.

111. Words by Thomas Le Brunn, music by George Le Brunn (London: Francis, Day and Hunter). Reprinted in Garrett, *Sixty Years of British Music Hall.*

112. Words and music by Fred W. Leigh and George Arthurs (London: Francis, Day and Hunter).

113. Words by A. J. Mills, music by Bennett Scott (London: Star Music, 1910); reprinted in Peter Davison, comp. and ed., *Songs of the British Music Hall,* Jerry Silverman, music ed. (New York: Oak, 1971).

114. *Era*, 30 Apr. 1892, cited in Peter Bailey, "Conspiracies of Meaning: Music-Hall and the Knowingness of Popular Culture," *Past and Present,* no. 144, Aug. 1994, 138–70, 164.

115. Words by Fred W. Leigh, music by Orlando Powell (London: Francis, Day and Hunter, 1912).

116. Words by Richard Morton, music by George Le Brunn (London: Francis, Day and Hunter, 1892); reprinted in *Sixty Old-Time Variety Songs* (London: EMI, 1977), 126–28.

117. Words by Fred Murray, music by Laurence Barclay (London: Francis, Day and Hunter, 1897); reprinted in Peter Gammond, ed., *The Good Old Days Songbook* (London: EMI, 1983), 76–78.

118. Words and music by E. W. Rogers (London: Francis, Day and Hunter, 1902); reprinted in Davison, *Songs of the British Music Hall.*

119. Words by Edgar Bateman, music by George Le Brunn (London: Francis, Day and Hunter, 1896); reprinted in *Sixty Old-Time Variety Songs,* 1–3.

120. Words and music by Harry King (London: Francis and Day, 1888); reprinted in Davison, *Songs of the British Music Hall.*

121. Words and music by Albert Chevalier [Charles Ingle] (London: Reynolds, 1892).

122. Words and music by A. J. Mills and Frank W. Carter (London: Feldman, 1910); reprinted in Peter Gammond, ed., *The Good Old Days Songbook* (London: EMI, 1983),144–46.

123. *Popular Music in England, 1840–1914* (Manchester: Manchester University Press, 1987), 96; Russell discusses music and morals at 17–59.

124. Words and music by George Ware (London: Hopwood and Crew, 1885); reprinted in Garrett, *Sixty Years of British Music Hall,* n.p.

125. Words by Fred Murray and Fred W. Leigh, music by George Le Brunn (London: Francis, Day and Hunter).

126. "Conspiracies of Meaning," 150, and *Popular Culture and Performance in the Victorian City,* 136.

127. *Minutes of Evidence Taken before the Select Committee on Theatres and Places of Entertainment,* 23 May 1892, 330.

128. Quoted in Sterling Mackinlay, *Origin and Development of Light Opera* (London: Hutchinson, 1927), 227.

129. Alexandra Carter questions the evidence for the immorality of these dancers, in *Dance and Dancers in the Victorian and Edwardian Music Hall Ballet* (Aldershot, England: Ashgate, 2005), 112–21.

130. Bracebridge Hemyng, "Prostitution in London," in Henry Mayhew, *London Labour and the London Poor* (London: Frank Cass, 1967; originally published London: Griffin, Bohn, 1862), 4:210–72, 243. Hemyng mentions the brothels of St. James's at 246–47.

131. Jane W. Stedman, *W. S. Gilbert: A Classic Victorian and His Theatre* (New York: Oxford University Press, 1996).

132. See Reginald Allen, *The Life and Work of Sir Arthur Sullivan: Composer for Victorian England* (New York: Pierpont Morgan Library, 1975), 33–35.

133. Sullivan, "About Music," reprinted in Arthur Lawrence, *Sir Arthur Sullivan: Life Story, Letters, and Reminiscences* (London: James Bowden, 1899), 261–87; quotation from 285. John Ruskin was more cautious, arguing that music in her "health" was a teacher of "perfect order" but in her "depravity" was also the teacher of "perfect disorder and disobedience, and the *Gloria in Excelsis* becomes the *Marseillaise*." "Queen of the Air" (1869), quoted in Meirion Hughes and Robert Stradling, *The English Musical Renaissance, 1840–1940: Constructing a National Music*, 2nd ed. (Manchester: Manchester University Press, 2001; originally published 1993), 4.

134. Words by E. Newton, music by Arthur F. Tate (London: J. H. Larway).

135. Words by Samuel Mitchell, music by Charles Pratt.

Chapter 4

1. Herbert J. Gans, *Popular Culture and High Culture: An Analysis and Evaluation of Taste* (New York: Basic Books, 1974), 115.

2. Bourdieu continually refined his idea of the habitus. For his later thoughts, see *The Field of Cultural Production* (Cambridge: Polity Press, 1993), 67–73 (the first essay, trans. Richard Nice, 1983, has the same title as the book).

3. Hans Georg Gadamer, *Wahrheit und Methode: Grundzüge einer philosophischen Hermeneutik*, 2nd ed. (1960; reprint, Tübingen: Mohr, 1965), 33; trans. William Glen-Doepel, rev. Joel Weinsheimer and Donald G. Marshall as *Truth and Method* (New York: Continuum, 2004), 36.

4. Pierre Bourdieu, *Distinction: A Social Critique of the Judgement of Taste*, trans. Richard Nice (London: Routledge, 1989; originally published as *La Distinction. Critique sociale du jugement* [Paris: Editions de Minuit, 1979]), 7.

5. See William Weber, *Music and the Middle Class: The Social Structure of Concert Life in London, Paris and Vienna between 1830 and 1848*, 2nd ed. (Aldershot, England: Ashgate, 2004; originally published London: Croom Helm, 1975), 25–26.

6. See Lawrence Levine, *Highbrow/Lowbrow: The Emergence of Cultural Hierarchy in America* (Cambridge, Mass.: Harvard University Press, 1988), 221.

7. Carl Dahlhaus, *Nineteenth-Century Music*, trans. J. Bradford Robinson (Berkeley: University of California Press, 1989; originally published as *Die Musik des 19. Jahrhunderts* [Wiesbaden: Athenaion, 1980]), 311.

8. Ibid., 314.

9. Ibid., 314–15.

10. Ibid., 314.

11. Ibid., 317.

12. Percy M. Young, *The Concert Tradition: From the Middle Ages to the Twentieth Century* (London: Routledge and Kegan Paul, 1965), 155.

13. Ibid., 188.

14. Lunn voices his distaste for "artists letting themselves out for hire" without concern for the degradation to art in "The London Musical Season," *Musical Times and Singing Class Circular* 12, no. 283, 1 Sep. 1866, 363–65, 364.

15. "The Music Hall of the Future," *Musical Times and Singing-Class Circular* 35, no. 620, 1 Oct. 1894, 657–58, 657.

16. The writer of an article in 1864 is concerned to demonstrate the inappropriateness of the "light" and "heavy" opposition, and is at pains to avoid characterizing all "good" music as solemn. "'Light' and 'Heavy,'" *Dwight's Journal of Music* 24, no. 13, Sep. 1864, 310.

17. "Ein gerechter Unwille muß jeden ergreifen, der, wenn Strauß spielt, die Namen 'Kunst und Künstler' solcherart frivol entweihen hört." Cited in Max Schönherr and Karl Rienhöhl, *Johann Strauss Vater: Ein Werkverzeichnis* (Vienna: Universal, 1954), 100, and in Andreas Ballstaedt, "Die Walzer von Johann Strauss (Sohn)—Gebrauchtmusik oder Werk?" in Ludwig Finscher and Albrecht Riethmüller, eds., *Johann Strauss: Zwischen Kunstanspruch und Volksvergnügen* (Darmstadt: Wissenschaftliche Buchgesellschaft, 1995), 76–96, 80.

18. Tia DeNora traces the origins of serious music ideology to certain aristocratic salons in Vienna, and discusses how it was based around particular "learned" compositions of Haydn, Mozart, and Beethoven, in *Beethoven and the Construction of Genius: Musical Politics in Vienna, 1792–1803* (Berkeley: University of California Press, 1995), 11–36.

19. Norbert Linke, *Musik erobert die Welt: Wie die Wiener Familie Strauss die "Unterhaltungsmusik" revolutionierte* (Vienna: Herold, 1987), 105.

20. Schumann writing in *Neue Zeitschrift für Musik,* 1838, quoted in ibid., 105.

21. *From Max Weber: Essays in Sociology,* trans. and ed. H. H. Gerth and C. Wright Mills (New York: Oxford University Press, 1946), 191; original source is *Wirtschaft und Gesellschaft* (1922), pt. 3, chap. 4.

22. "Specimen of a Leader for a Music Journal," from an anonymous correspondent, *Musical Examiner* 95, 24 Aug. 1844, 749.

23. Vol. 14, no. 339, 28 Jan. 1871, 37–38.

24. All the quotations are from ibid., 37.

25. Ibid., 38

26. "Nichts ist der Kompositionsweise von Johann Strauss angemessener als das Leichte . . . Wer jedoch das Leichte von vornherein im Verdacht hat, künstlerischer Ausarbeitung nicht zugänglich zu sein . . . oder es nur als das Seichte wahrnehmen kann . . . der wird sich mit 'leichter Musik' unumgänglich schwertun." Albrecht Riethmüller, "Johann Strauss und der Makel der Popularität," in Finscher and Riethmüller, *Johann Strauss*, 1–17, 8–9.

27. *Die neue freie Presse,* no. 3113, 24 Apr. 1873, *Das Morgenblatt,* 7, cited in Clemens Hellsberg, "Die wiener Philharmoniker spielen Strauss," in *Wiener Philharmoniker Johann Strauss Jubiläums-Edition 1999,* book accompanying, compact disc set, Deutsche Grammophon 459734-2 (1999), 6–8, 6.

28. Sydney Northcote, *The Ballad in Music* (London: Oxford University Press, 1942), 91.

29. *Strand Musical Magazine* 4, Jul. 1892, 83–89.

30. "Classical v. Popular Music," from a correspondent ("A Wellwisher"), *Musical World* 40, no. 37, 13 Sep. 1862, 587.

31. Quoted in Henry Schnitzler, "'Gay Vienna'(Myth and Reality," *Journal of the History of Ideas* 15, no. 1 (Jan. 1954), 100. I am grateful to Roy Prendergast for this reference.

32. Eduard Hanslick, *Vienna's Golden Years of Music 1850–1900,* trans. Henry Pleasants (London: Victor Gollancz, 1951), 326.

33. *The Civilizing Process* (Oxford: Blackwell, 1994; originally published as *Über den Prozess der Zivilisation* [Basel: Haus zum Falken, 1939]), 30.

34. It can be heard on *J. Strauss, Jr. Edition,* compact disc set with notes, 51 vols., Slovak State Philharmonic Orchestra, conductor Christian Pollack, vol. 42, Marco Polo 8.223242 (1992), track 2.

35. The term Lawrence Levine uses in *Highbrow/Lowbrow.*

36. J. B. Macdonnell, "Classical Music and British Musical Taste," *Macmillan's* 1 (1860), 383–89, 384.

37. Quoted in Reginald Allen, *The First Night Gilbert and Sullivan,* rev. ed. (London: Chappell, 1976; originally published New York: Limited Editions Club, 1958), 49, and in Arthur Jacobs, *Arthur Sullivan: A Victorian Musician* (Oxford: Oxford University Press, 1984), 112.

38. Quoted in Arthur Jacobs, "Sullivan, Gilbert and the Victorians," *Music Review* 12 (1951), 122–32, 123, and in E. D. Mackerness, *A Social History of English Music* (London: Routledge and Kegan Paul, 1964), 191.

39. See Jacobs, *Arthur Sullivan,* 119.

40. Howard Becker, *Art Worlds* (Berkeley: University of California Press, 1982), 30.

41. James D. Brown, *Biographical Dictionary of Musicians* (Paisley, Scotland: Alexander Gardner, 1886; reprint, Hildesheim: Georg Olms, 1970), 51.

42. Gans, *Popular Culture and High Culture,* 23.

43. Samuel Smiles, *Self-Help* (London: John Murray, 1859), 35–67.

44. "The Educational Value of Dance Music," *Musical Times* 26, no. 507, 1 May 1885, 253–55, 254.

45. Bernard Gendron, *Between Montmartre and the Mudd Club: Popular Music and the Avant-Garde* (Chicago: University of Chicago Press, 2002), 5.

46. London: J. Curwen, 492–97. See the discussion of Davey's antiurban utopianism in Bennett Zon, "'Loathsome London': Henry Davey's *History of English Music* (1895) and the Anti-urban Socialist Utopianism of Ruskin and Morris," forthcoming.

47. William Weber, "The Intellectual Origins of Musical Canon in Eighteenth-Century England," *Journal of the American Musicological Society* 47 (1994), 488–520, 512, citing Charles Avison, *Essay on Musical Expression* (London: Davis, 1752).

48. William Weber, "Canon and the Traditions of Musical Culture," in Jan Gorak, ed., *Canon vs. Culture: Reflections on the Current Debate* (New York: Garland, 2001), 135–50, 142.

49. Jürgen Habermas, *The Structural Transformation of the Public Sphere: An Inquiry into a Category of Bourgeois Society,* trans. Thomas Burger, with the assistance of Frederick Lawrence, 2nd ed. (Cambridge: Polity Press, 1989; originally published as *Struckturwandel der Öffentlicheit* [Darmstadt: Luchterhand, 1962]), 22–23. The expressions "public opinion," "opinion publique," and "öffentliche

Meinung" all arose in the second half of the eighteenth century (26). Coffeehouses, *salons,* and *Tischgesellschaften* were important to this development (32–37).

50. *Beethoven and the Construction of Genius,* 179–82.

51. *Art Worlds,* 137.

52. Ibid., 157.

53. Camille Crittenden, *Johann Strauss and Vienna: Operetta and the Politics of Popular Culture* (Cambridge: Cambridge University Press, 2000), 97.

54. *Art Worlds,* 162; discussion of the institutional theory of aesthetics, 145–62.

55. Ibid., 341.

56. Peter L. Berger and Thomas Luckmann, *The Social Construction of Reality: A Treatise in the Sociology of Knowledge* (New York: Anchor Books, 1967; originally published New York: Doubleday, 1966), 118.

57. *Art Worlds,* 222.

58. Becker discusses arts and crafts in chap. 9 of *Art Worlds,* 272–99. Crafts, briefly, involve "the skill to make useful objects" or, in the case of music, "the ability to play music that can be danced to" (273).

59. Gans, *Popular Culture and High Culture,* 28. For an example, see my essay "The Impact of African-American Music Making on the European Classical Tradition in the 1920s," in *From the Erotic to the Demonic: On Critical Musicology* (New York: Oxford University Press, 2003), 179–201.

60. *Art Worlds,* 360.

61. "'Light' and 'Heavy,'" 310.

62. Ibid., 310.

63. Ibid.

64. "Music for the People," *Musical Times and Singing Class Circular* 26, no. 512, 1 Oct. 1885, 579–81, 579.

65. *Music Criticism in Vienna 1896–1897: Critically Moving Forms* (Oxford: Clarendon Press, 1996), 111.

66. Levine, *Highbrow/Lowbrow,* 90.

67. Philip Hone, quoted in Julius Mattfield, *A Hundred Years of Grand Opera in New York, 1825–1925* (New York: New York Public Library, 1927), 34; cited in Charles Hamm, *Music in the New World* (New York: Norton, 1983), 201.

68. G. W. Curtis, "Editor's Easy Chair," *Harper's* 64, February 1882, 467–78, quoted in Levine, *Highbrow/Lowbrow,* 135. Showing similar disapproval to those American critics who decried Patti's choice of concert material, Henry Lunn was arguing for a change in the works performed for the general public in London, claiming the times when the "people" knew nothing of great orchestral works had passed away. "Popular Music," *Musical Times and Singing Class Circular* 19, no. 430, 1 Dec. 1878, 660–61, 661.

69. Quoted in Robert C. Toll, *On with the Show: The First Century of Show Business in America* (New York: Oxford University Press, 1976), 21.

70. Ibid., 41.

71. Nathaniel Parker Willis, *Memoranda of the Life of Jenny Lind* (Philadelphia: Robert E. Peterson, 1851), 144–45, quoted in Levine, *Highbrow/Lowbrow,* 97.

72. Quoted in Nicholas Tawa, *The Way to Tin Pan Alley: American Popular Song, 1866–1910* (New York: Schirmer Books, 1990), 7–8.

73. Boston: Oliver Ditson, 1841.

74. Words and music by Jacob Ahlström (New York: Samuel C. Jolie, 1850).

75. Tim Wise, "Yodelling in American Popular Music" (Ph.D. Diss. University of Liverpool, 2004); see 96–105.

76. Mat. WAX 5113, Columbia PX 2; reissued on *Dame Clara Butt,* compact disc, Pavilion Records GEMM CD 9301 (1988), track 2.

77. *Modernity and Ambivalence* (Cambridge: Polity Press, 1991), 15.

78. *La Belle Hélène,* conducted by Michel Plasson, compact disc set, EMI Classics CDS 7 47157 8 (1984), disc 2, track 10.

79. Renée Doria, soprano, and Tasso Janopoulo, piano, *Les Introuvables du chant français,* compact disc set, EMI 7243 5 85828 2 6 (2004), disc 8, track 23; transferred from Cecilia (1953), matrix number unknown.

80. "Er aber war selbst mitgerissen, und während stets unruhig sein rechter Fuss charakteristisch den Takt stampste, tanzte seine ganze Gestalt, seine Seele mit." "Strauss," obituary, *Ost-Deutsche Post,* Friday, 28 Sep. 1849, 1.

81. Georg Simmel, "The Metropolis and Mental Life," in Kurt H. Wolff, trans. and ed., *The Sociology of Georg Simmel* (New York: Free Press, 1950), 409–24, 416; originally published as "Die Grossstädte und das Geistesleben," *Die Grossstädte: Vorträge und Aufsätze* 9 (1902–3), 185–206.

82. *Truth and Method,* 36, points out that the true opposite of good taste is not bad taste but no taste.

83. "Popular Music," *Musical Times and Singing Class Circular* 19, 430, 1 Dec. 1878, 660–61, 661.

84. Paula Gillett, "Entrepreneurial Women in Britain," in William Weber, ed., *The Musician as Entrepreneur, 1700–1914: Managers, Charlatans, and Idealists* (Bloomington: Indiana University Press, 2004), 198–220, 208.

85. Lunn, "The London Musical Season," 363.

86. "A Monument to Beethoven," *Musical Times and Singing Class Circular* 21, no. 448, 1 Jun. 1880, 281.

87. Johann Seidl sees it as a reproach to the bourgeosie's "hostility to culture" (Kulturfeindlichkeit). *Musik und Austromarxismus: Zur Musikrezeption der österreichischen Arbeiterbewegung im späten Kaiserreich und in der Ersten Republik* (Vienna: Böhlau, 1989), 21.

88. Rev. ed. (Leipzig: Rudolph Weigel, 1858).

89. Meirion Hughes and Robert Stradling, *The English Musical Renaissance, 1840–1940: Constructing a National Music,* 2nd ed. (1993; reprint, Manchester: Manchester University Press, 2001), 22. The authors identify John Alexander Fuller Maitland as the person who brought the English Musical Renaissance "into the mainstream of musical discourse" (45) in his *English Music in the Nineteenth Century* (London: Grant Richards, 1902).

90. Walter Pater, *The Renaissance: Studies in Art and Poetry* (Oxford: Oxford University Press, 1986; originally published as *Studies in the History of the Renaissance* [London: Macmillan, 1873] [title changed for the 2nd ed. of 1877]), 86, 88.

91. "Macht sich zuletzt die subjektive Willkür mit ihren Einfallen, Kapricen, Unterbrechungen, geistreichen Neckereien, täuschenden Spannungen, überraschenden Wendungen, Sprüngen und Blitzen, Wunderlichkeiten und ungehörten Effekten." Georg W. F. Hegel, *Vorlesungen über die Ästhetik* (1835–38), vol. 3, *Das System der einzelnen Künste,* sec. 3, "Die romantischen Künste," chap. 2, "Die Musik," 3b; complete text, <www.textlog.de/3421.html>.

92. "Popular Appreciation of Music," *Musical Times and Singing-Class Circular* 21, no. 449, 1 Jul. 1880, 360.

93. Frederick Corder, "The Music of the People," *Musical Times and Singing-Class Circular* 26, no. 503, 1 Jan. 1885, 9–11, 9.

94. *Der Fall Wagner. Ein Musikanten-Problem* (Leipzig: C. G. Naumann, 1888), 2.

95. "The Parsifal Sickness," reprinted in Charles Reid, *The Music Monster: A Biography of James William Davison, Music Critic of the "Times" of London, 1846–78, with Excerpts from His Critical Writings* (London: Quartet Books, 1984), 215–17.

96. "The Music Hall of the Future," *Pall Mall Gazette*, 13 Apr. 1892, quoted in "The Music Hall Mania," *Musical Times and Singing-Class Circular* 33, no. 591, 1 May 1892, 265–66, 265.

97. "The Pedigree of the Music Hall," *Contemporary Review* 63 (April 1893), 575, quoted in Barry J. Faulk, *Music Hall and Modernity: The Late-Victorian Discovery of Popular Culture* (Athens: Ohio University Press, 2004), 29.

98. "The Music Hall of the Future," 657.

99. See *Music Hall and Modernity*, 34–36, 53–74.

100. While cautioning that it oversimplifies matters, Weber describes classes as "stratified according to their relations to the production and acquisition of goods," and status groups as "stratified according to the principles of their *consumption* of goods as represented by special 'styles of life.'" *From Max Weber*, 193; original source is *Wirtschaft und Gesellschaft* (1922), pt. 3, chap. 4. A status group is united by its adherence to a specific lifestyle and may be willing to form an alliance with the "wrong" class in defense of its interests.

101. *La Chanson à Montmartre* (Paris: Editions de la Table Ronde, 1967), 270.

102. *Cabaret, Cabarets: Origines et décadence* (Paris: Plon, 1991), 85.

103. *Laughter: An Essay on the Meaning of the Comic*, trans. Cloudesley Brereton and Fred Rothwell (London: Macmillan, 1911; reprint, New York: Dover, 2005; originally published as *Le Rire: Essai sur la signification du comique* [Paris: Félix Alcan, 1900], reprinted from three articles in the *Revue de Paris*), 62.

104. "When the thought 'this is only a dream' occurs during a dream, it has the same purpose in view as when the words are pronounced on the stage by *la belle Hélène* in Offenbach's comic opera of that name: it is aimed at reducing the importance of what has just been experienced and at making it possible to tolerate what is to follow. It serves to lull a particular agency to sleep which would have every reason at that moment to bestir itself and forbid the continuance of the dream—or the scene in the opera." *The Interpretation of Dreams*, trans. James Strachey (1953) (Harmondsworth, England: Penguin, 1976; originally published as *Die Traumdeutung* [Leipzig: Deuticke, 1900]), 628–29.

105. Donald Davidson, "Communication and Convention," *Synthese* 59 (1984), 3–17, reprinted in *Inquiries into Truth and Interpretation* (Oxford: Clarendon Press, 2001), 265–80, 274.

106. Walter Benjamin, "The Author as Producer" ("Der Autor als Produzent," 1934), in *Reflections: Essays, Aphorisms, Autobiographical Writings*, ed. Peter Demetz (New York: Schocken Books 1978), 235.

107. "A Tenor, All Singers Above," act 2, *Utopia Limited* (1893). In explaining the mechanics of what is needed at this point of the drama—instead of singing an expected love song to the heroine—it is similar in effect to "The Song That Goes Like This," a song in the musical *Spamalot* (Eric Idle and John Du

Prez, 2005) that substitutes an explanation of the workings of the "show-stopper" for the thing itself.

108. Robert Elkin, *Royal Philharmonic: The Annals of the Royal Philharmonic Society* (London: Rider, 1946), 67.

109. Joseph Bennett, "Observations on Music in America: III.—Orchestral and Choral Music," *Musical Times and Singing Class Circular* 26, no. 507, 1 May 1885, 255–57, 255.

110. "Music for the People," 580.

111. Hughes and Stradling, *The English Musical Renaissance,* 78. Engel's work had, in fact, reached a wide public with the serialization of his book *The Literature of National Music* in the *Musical Times,* 1878–89 (published as a book in 1879 by Novello).

112. Philip V. Bohlman, *World Music: A Very Short Introduction* (Oxford: Oxford University Press, 2002), 102.

113. Jane Fulcher, "The Popular Chanson of the Second Empire: 'Music of the Peasants' in France," *Acta Musicologica* 52, no. 1 (1980), 27–37, 27. This article shows how differing political interpretations may be made of the same material.

114. For information concerning Ritson and a thoughtful evaluation of Chappell's collection see E. David Gregory, *Victorian Songhunters: The Recovery and Editing of English Vernacular Ballads and Folk Lyrics, 1820–1883* (Lanham, Md.: Scarecrow Press, 2006).

115. "Popular Music of the Olden Time," *Musical World* 37, no. 51 (17 Dec. 1859), 805–6. In the 1860s and 1870s it was home to the respectable entertainers Albert and Priscilla German Reed. John Parry and Corney Grain also performed there.

116. *Popular Music of the Olden Time* (London: Chappell, 1859), 2:735.

117. Parry's speech of 2 Feb. 1899 is excerpted in Reginald Nettel, *A Social History of Traditional Song* (London: Phoenix House, 1969; originally published as *Sing a Song of England* [London: Phoenix House, 1954]), 238.

118. Cecil J. Sharp, *English Folk-Song: Some Conclusions,* 2nd ed. (1907; reprint, London: Novello, 1936), 137.

119. Ibid., x–xi, 2–5.

120. Ibid., x, 32. Sharp is not alone in being caught up in the fiction of race; see my "In Search of Genetically Modified Music: Race and Musical Style in the Nineteenth Century," *Nineteenth-Century Music* 3, no. 1 (2006), 3–23.

121. *Beethoven and the Construction of Genius,* 49.

122. *Music and the Middle Class,* xx.

123. Judith Tick, *American Women Composers before 1870* (Rochester, N.Y.: University of Rochester Press, 1979), 95, taking issue with Nicholas Tawa, *Sweet Songs for Gentle Americans: The Parlor Song in America, 1790–1860* (Bowling Green, Ohio: Bowling Green University Popular Press, 1980), 5–7.

124. I discuss this idea, apropos of drawing room ballads, in *The Singing Bourgeois: Songs of the Victorian Drawing Room and Parlour,* 2nd ed. (Aldershot, England: Ashgate, 2001; originally published Milton Keynes, England: Open University Press, 1989), 134–68.

125. Editorial ["The Ratcatcher's Daughter"], *Musical World* 33, no. 44, 3 Nov. 1855, 710.

126. "Some Kinds of Music," *Musical Times and Singing Class Circular* 30, no. 553, 1 Mar. 1889, 143–44, 144.

127. Oliver Burkeman, "How Many Hits?" *Guardian Weekend*, 11 Nov. 2006, 55–61, 57.

128. *Die Zeit*, 9 Oct 1897, 26, quoted in McColl, *Music Criticism in Vienna 1896–1897*, 83.

129. Hanslick, *Vienna's Golden Years of Music*, 325–26. Looking back on the days of Lanner and Strauss, while admiring their talents, he remarks: "it can readily be understood that this sweetly intoxicating three-quarter time, to which heads as well as feet were abandoned, combined with Italian opera and the cult of virtuosity, rendered listeners steadily less capable of intellectual effort" (6).

130. Quoted in Reginald Allen, ed. and comp., *The Life and Work of Sir Arthur Sullivan: Composer for Victorian England* (New York: Pierpont Morgan Library,), xxii.

131. Henry J. Wood, *My Life of Music* (London: Victor Gollancz, 1938), 92, quoted in Simon Mcveigh, "An Audience for High Class Music," in Weber, *The Musician as Entrepreneur*, 162–82, 179.

132. Wood, *My Life of Music*, 96.

133. From a correspondent, *Musical Times*, 21, no. 449, 1 Jul. 1880, 360.

134. William Pole, "The London Concert Season," *Macmillan's* 4 (1861), 449.

135. See Levine, *Highbrow/Lowbrow*, 165–66.

136. Herbert Gans, who prefers to speak of "taste cultures," provided one of the earliest and most comprehensive critiques of the theory of mass culture in *Popular Culture and High Culture*, 19–64.

137. In the 1970s some musicians succeeded in arguing that they were creating "high entertainment" music (*gehobene Unterhaltungsmusik*), comparable to the "progressive rock" of that time. See Edward Larkey, *Pungent Sounds: Constructing Identity with Popular Music in Austria* (New York: Peter Lang, 1993), 41.

Chapter 5

1. Hans Fantel, *Johann Strauss: Father and Son and Their Era* (Newton Abbot, England: David and Charles, 1971), Joseph Wechsberg, *The Waltz Emperors: The Life and Times and Music of the Strauss Family* (London: Weidenfeld and Nicolson, 1973), Norbert Linke, *Johann Strauss* (Reinbek bei Hamburg: Rowohlt, 1996). This is not the case with Linke's *Musik erobert die Welt: Wie die Wiener Familie Strauss die "Unterhaltungsmusik" revolutionierte* (Vienna: Herold, 1987).

2. See Eduard Reeser, *The History of the Waltz*, trans. W. A. G. Doyle-Davidson (Stockholm: Continental Book, 1949, originally published as *De Geschiedenis van de wals* [Amsterdam, 1947]), 10–12. For the many edicts against rotating dances in German cities in the eighteenth century, see also Heinrich Eduard Jacob, *Johann Strauss: A Century of Light Music*, trans. Marguerite Wolff (London: Hutchinson, 1940; originally published as *Johann Strauss und das neunzehnte Jahrhundert. Die Geschichte einer musikalischen Weltherrschaft, 1819–1917* [Amsterdam: Querido-Verlag, 1937]), 21.

3. "There can be no doubt that it was more particularly the Dreher which on account of its coarse morals was opposed by the ministers of religion." Reeser, *The History of the Waltz*, 9. Jacob holds that the waltz was the direct offspring of the Dreher, see *Johann Strauss*, 24.

4. The map of the Danube today must not be taken as a reliable guide, since its course was altered radically to prevent flooding in the 1890s. The whole of Leopodstadt is, today, a virtual island, and the Donaukanal is closer to the site of Strauss Sr.'s father's inn than the "new" Danube (and Donauinsel is even further away). I am grateful to Eduard Strauss of the Wiener Institut für Strauss-Forschung for alerting me to this.

5. "Gentlemen are not permitted to enter the Ball Room in boots." Thomas Wilson, *A Companion to the Ball Room* (London: Button, Whittaker, 1816), excerpted in Elizabeth Aldrich, *From the Ballroom to Hell: Grace and Folly in Nineteenth-Century Dance* (Evanston, Ill.: Northwestern University Press, 1991), 220 (and elsewhere).

6. Quoted in Reeser, *The History of the Waltz,* 19.

7. *A Description of the Correct Method of Waltzing* (London, 1816). Wilson was the dancing master at the King's Theatre.

8. "From My Study," *Musical Times* 36, no. 627, 1 May 1895, 297–301, 297.

9. I repeat the warning in my introduction that "popular" must not automatically be translated into the French "populaire" or the German "populär," both of which retained different nuances of meaning. Likewise, "musique légère" and "light music" began as translations of "leichte Musik" but acquired different nuances because of the way the words "léger" and "light" function in the French and English languages.

10. See Franz Schubert, *Sämtliche Tänze für Klavier* (Vienna: Wiener Urtext Edition, 1973), 2:120.

11. They both use it in their compositions labeled Opus 1, but Lanner's *Neue Wiener,* op. 1, consists of *Ländler,* unlike Strauss Sr.'s *Täuberln-Walzer,* op. 1. We should, however, bear in mind that Norbert Linke has revealed that it would be mistaken to regard this waltz as Strauss's first composition; *Musik erobert die Welt,* 59–60, and 63.

12. *Music erobert die Welt,* 88–89. Linke remarks that the new design is often falsely attributed to Lanner.

13. Strauss reveals a familiarity with a broad range of musical styles: for example, his Op. 10 medley (1827) contains an old German *Polstertanz,* but his next opus (1828) is *Walzer à la Paganini.*

14. "Das Volk erkannte in diesen Tanzweisen seine eigenen Züge." Quoted by Franz Mailer, notes to *Johann Strauss I Edition,* compact disc set, Marco Polo 8.225281 (2003), vol. 5.

15. A piano score can be found in Johann Strauss [Sr.], *Sämtliche Werke in Wiedergabe der Originaldrucke,* ed. Ernst Hilmar, 5 vols. (Tutzing: Hans Schneider, 1987), 1:1–7. The full score of *Täuberln-Walzer* is in Hans Gál, ed., *Johann Strauss Vater: Acht Walzer, Denkmäler der Tonkunst in Österreich* (Graz: Akademische Druck- u. Verlaganstalt, 1960), 68:1–6. Waltz 5 from the piano score is missing. This is an A major waltz, the only waltz not in the tonic. No explanation is given in Gál's *Revisionsbericht.* Thus, the oddly syncopated waltz is here 6b, but in the piano score it is 7b. For the explanation for the new fifth waltz in the piano version and the reason this waltz is incorrectly labeled as Strauss's Opus 1, see Linke, *Musik erobert die Welt,* 63.

16. Waltzes 5a and 6a in the piano version. Andrew Lamb says incorrectly that the waltzes are made up of two eight-measure sections until the final sixteen-measure section. "Waltz," in Stanley Sadie, ed., *The New Grove Dictionary of Music and Musicians* (London: Macmillan, 2001), 27:72–78, 74.

17. It continues today, as may be heard on *Wiener Tänze,* Ensemble Wien (two violins, viola, and double bass), compact disc, ORF, VMS 134 (2004).

18. Quoted in Jacob, *Johann Strauss,* 72–73.

19. Quoted in ibid., 73, Wechsberg, *The Waltz Emperors,* 45, Fantel, *Johann Strauss,* 43–44, and elsewhere without any precise citing of the source, which is in Laube's *Reise durch das Biedermeyer* (Hamburg: Hoffmann und Campe 1965; originally published as *Reisenovellen* [Mannheim: H. Hoff., 1834–37]), 248–50.

20. *Mein Leben* (1880), vol. 1. English translation, www.gutenberg.org/dirs/etext04/wglf110.txt.

21. Jacob, *Johann Strauss,* 74.

22. Ibid., 163.

23. "The True Waltz Tempo—Strauss in New York," *Weekly Review,* 13 Jul. 1872, reprinted in *Dwight's Journal of Music* 32, no. 9, Jul. 1872, 276.

24. The third timpani stroke in this example is given as a D in the autograph score (in Strauss Sr.'s own hand), but it would appear to be an error; the harmony is the dominant seventh. In the piano arrangement of this waltz, published by Tobias Haslinger, a conventional "um-pah-pah" accompaniment is provided.

25. Max Schönherr, "Modelle der Walzerkomposition: Grundlagen zu einer Theorie des Walzers," *Österreichische Musikzeitschrift* 30 (1975), 273–86; see table, 275.

26. *Music erobert die Welt,* 95–96.

27. Ibid., 231–39. Linke also discusses Strauss Jr.'s orchestration in *"Es mußte einem was einfallen": Untersuchungen zur kompositorischen Arbeitsweise der "Naturalisten"* (Tutzing: Hans Schneider, 1992), 179–85.

28. I do not intend to suggest that antecedent–consequent phrasing is never found; it is present, for example, in Strauss Sr.'s *Einzugs-Galopp,* op. 35 (1830).

29. Peter Van der Merwe, *Origins of the Popular Style: The Antecedents of Twentieth-Century Popular Music* (Oxford: Oxford University Press, 1989), 230.

30. Ibid., 256.

31. *Musik erobert die Welt,* 89–90. Linke maintains that the "frech hinzugefügte Sexte" (cheeky added sixth) is the real marker of the *Wiener Ton;* he cites as an early example waltz 5a of *Der Frohsinn, mein Ziel,* op. 63 (1833). There were, however, antecedents paving the way to this use of the sixth, as de Merwe shows; *Origins of the Popular Style,* 225–56.

32. It is this regular hypermeter that, despite some erroneous assumptions about other musical features, enables the successful computer-generated form recognition in the tests detailed in Dan Liu, Nai-Yao Zhang, and Han-Cheng Zhu, "Form Recognition for Johann Strauss's Waltz Centos Based on Musical Features," *Proceedings of the First International Conference on Machine Learning and Cybernetics* (Beijing: Institute of Electrical and Electronics Engineers, 2002), 2:800–804. (The term "cento" is more commonly employed to refer to a patchwork literary composition.) There are exceptions to Strauss Sr.'s use of a regular four-measure hypermeter—for instance, waltz theme 4b of *Gute Meinung für die Tanzlust.*

33. Letter from Carson City, 12 Dec. 1862, *Virginia City* (Nev.) *Territorial Enterprise,* <www.twainquotes.com/18621212t.html>. As for figure dances, here is Twain, in the same letter, commenting on one of the figures of the

"plain" quadrille: "The next order is, 'Ladies change.' This is an exceedingly difficult figure, and requires great presence of mind; because, on account of shaking hands with the lobby members so much, and from the force of human nature also, you are morally certain to offer your right, when the chances are that your left hand is wanted."

34. "Strauß ist der populärste Musiker der Erde. Seine Walzer entzücken die Amerikaner, sie klingen über die chinesische Mauer, sie jubeln im afrikanischen Bivouak und eine mir befreundete Wienerin schrieb unlängst, wie tief es sie gerührt habe, als sie den Boden Australiens betrat, und ein Bettler mit einem Strauß'schen Walzer um Almosen bat. In Europa verbreitete er persönlich die dreimal süße Lehre vom göttlichen Leichtsinn des Alt-Wienerthums." "Strauss," obituary *Ost-Deutsche Post,* Friday, 28 Sep. 1849, 1.

35. Strauss Sr.'s grandparents on his father's side were Jewish, a fact the Nazis made strenuous efforts to cover up; see Fantel, *Johann Strauss,* 219–20, and Peter Kemp, *The Strauss Family: A Portrait of a Musical Dynasty* (Tunbridge Wells, England: Baton Press, 1985), 15–16.

36. A myth has built up concerning a bad-tempered rift between Lanner and Strauss in 1825, but this has been disputed by Peter Kemp, "Strauss," in Sadie, *New Grove II,* 24:474–96, 475. Linke contests the traditional explanation of Lanner's *Trennungs-Walzer,* op. 19, as an attempt to mend fences; *Musik erobert die Welt,* 53–54.

37. "War Lanner melodisch schmelzend, weich und sentimental, so war Strauß feurig, stürmisch, erobernd, er elektrisirte die Beine und machte die Herzen und die Pulse fliegen" (If Lanner was melodically melting, soft, and sentimental, then Strauss was fiery, stormy, conquering; he elecrtified the legs and made hearts and pulses fly). "Strauss," obituary.

38. Norbert Rubey, *"Des Verfassers beste Laune": Johann Strauss (Vater) und das Musik-Business im Biedermeier,* exhibition catalogue (Vienna: Wiener Stadt- und Landesbibliothek, 2004).

39. Puzzlingly, Jacob tells us there were twenty-eight musicians, but later quotes Berlioz's enumeration of the orchestral forces, which adds up to twenty-six. Jacob, *Johann Strauss,* 94. Incidentally, Strauss now has eight violins but still no viola; and he has two double basses but only one cello.

40. Review of 18 Apr. 1838, quoted in Kemp, *The Strauss Family,* 29. Details of Strauss Sr.'s English tour are given in Rudolf Kleinecke, *Johann Strauss: Ein Lebensbild* (Leipzig: Internationale Verlags- und Kunstanstalt, 1894), 20–26.

41. Editorial, *Musical World* 13, no. 192, new ser. 5, no. 109, 21 Nov. 1839, 461–62, 461.

42. Ibid.

43. It is a tribute to virtuoso violinist Heinrich Ernst, whose *Carnaval de Venise,* op.18, like Strauss's fantasia, is a set of variations on a tune already exploited by Paganini.

44. Linke, *Musik erobert die Welt,* 121.

45. His electric energy is commented on in the *Ost-Deutsche Post* obituary: "er elektrisirte die Beine." "Strauss," obituary.

46. "Voll jener elektrischen Schwunghaftigkeit." Review, 15 Jan. 1846, quoted by Franz Mailer, notes to *J. Strauss, Sr.: Orchestral Works,* compact disc set, Marco Polo 8.223617 (1994), 23.

47. Details given in Jacob, *Johann Strauss,* 111 n.; also given in briefer form in Wechsberg, *The Waltz Emperors,* 77.

48. "Denn unter den Vorgaben eines sich entfaltenden kapitalistischen Warenmarktes, der natürlich auch vor dem Musikleben nicht halt machte, war mit diesem gebrauchsmusikalischen Aspekt im 19. Jahrhundert weit mehr gemeint: Die Musik sollte nicht nur ihren Zweck erfüllen, sondern dies auch mit dem größtmöglischen ökonomischen Erfolg. . . . So finden sich dann auch bei den Kompositionen von Strauß Vater und Sohn alle äußeren Anzeichen für eine maximale ökonomische Verwetbarkeit." Andreas Ballstaedt, "Die Walzer von Johann Strauss (Sohn)—Gebrauchtmusik oder Werk?" in Ludwig Finscher and Albrecht Riethmüller, eds., *Johann Strauss: Zwischen Kunstanspruch und Volksvergnügen* (Darmstadt: Wissenschaftliche Buchgesellschaft, 1995), 76–96, 77.

49. Metternich wielded great power because of the "hands off" policies of both Franz I and Ferdinand II. Vienna had a long history of power being placed in the hands of appointed civil servants; it was a major factor in ensuring the docility of the middle class during the Biedermeyer period.

50. Linke, *Musik erobert die Welt*, 115.

51. See Max Schönherr's centenary celebration article "An der schönen blauen Donau: Marginalien zur 100. Wiederkeh des Tages der Urauffürung," *Österreichische Musikzeitschrift* 22 (1967), 3–15, and Schönherr's extensive bibliography for this much-discussed waltz, 38–40. The original manuscript is in the Archiv des Wiener Männergesang-Verein.

52. The success of Strauss's performances at the Cercle International owed much to the publicity provided by Jean Villemessant, owner of *Le Figaro*. It helped Strauss's cause that he spoke French fluently. Offenbach was, of course, the composer who was all the rage in Paris at this time. It should be pointed out that the *Blue Danube* had been performed as an orchestral composition prior to this in Vienna's Volksgarten, and had proved an enormous success.

53. Norbert Linke calls it "die erste Schlager der Welt" ("the first world hit"). *Johann Strauss* (Reinbek bei Hamburg: Rowohlt, 1996), 76. For its impact on twentieth-century popular culture, see http://en.wikipedia.org/wiki/The_Blue_Danube.

54. Linke, *Musik erobert die Welt*, 207.

55. The Viennese were renowned for their hearty appetites; see Fantel, *Johann Strauss*, 17–18.

56. Reproduced in Linke, *Johann Strauss*, 78, from Erich Wilhelm Engel, *Johann Strauss und seine Zeit* (Vienna: Verlag der k.u.k. Hof-Verlags-Buchandlung Emil M. Engel, 1911), 114.

57. It appeared in the *Wanderer,* and is quoted in Ludwig Eisenberg, *Johann Strauss: Ein Lebensbild* (Leipzig: Breitkopf und Härtel, 1894), 59, and a host of other places since.

58. Eisenberg, *Johann Strauss*, 81.

59. Jacob, *Johann Strauss*, 152. Howard Becker notes that free-lancing teaches artists to devote all their attention to "what is immediately at hand." *Art Worlds* (Berkeley: University of California Press, 1982), 89.

60. Wechsberg, *The Waltz Emperors*, 17. On the necessity to the functioning of an art world of a network of organized activities and an extensive division of labor, see Becker, *Art Worlds*, 2–14.

61. Wechsberg, *The Waltz Emperors*, 176.

62. "A Talk with Mr. Strauss," *New York Sun*, 13 Jul. 1872, reprinted in *Dwight's Journal of Music* 32, no. 9, Jul. 1872, 276–77. The reporter conducted the interview in German, since Strauss spoke no English.

63. Georg Simmel, "The Metropolis and Mental Life," in Kurt H. Wolff, trans. and ed., *The Sociology of Georg Simmel* (New York: Free Press, 1950) 409–24; originally published as "Die Grossstädte und das Geistesleben," *Die Grossstädte: Vorträge und Aufsätze* 9 (1902–3), 185–206.

64. Ibid., 422.

65. "Ein Viertel Frühling, ein Viertel Liebe, ein Viertel Wein." Quoted by Jürgen Glauert in "Robert Stolz," notes to *Wiener Musik,* compact disc, RCA Red Seal (2005), 23–27, 23.

66. See Derek B. Scott, *From the Erotic to the Demonic: On Critical Musicology* (New York: Oxford University Press, 2003), 159–60, 166–67.

67. Eduard Strauss's *Wiener Welt-Ausstellungs-Marsch,* op. 107, marks the occasion.

68. Jacob, *Johann Strauss,* 181.

69. Strauss Jr., foreword to keyboard edition of Strauss Sr., *Gesamtausgabe* (1887–89), cited in Kleinecke, *Johann Strauss,* 41.

70. Philipp Fahrbach commented, "die Tanzmusik nicht allein existire, um eben nur nach dem dreiviertel Takt sich belustigen und tanzen zu koennen, sondern daß man auch etwas gethan habe, um das Gehoer eben wie die Fueße zu electrisiren." "Geschichte der Tanzmusik seit 25 Jahren," *Wiener Allgemeine Musik-Zeitung* 7 (1847), 138; see Ballstaedt, "Die Walzer von Johann Strauss (Sohn)," 84. It could also be argued that the symphonic style of waltz can be seen emerging in Strauss Sr.'s *Loreley-Rhein-Klänge.*

71. John Cale, for instance, spoke of an opportunity "to do something symphonic" with the music of the Velvet Underground. Joe Harvard, *The Velvet Underground and Nico* (New York: Continuum, 2004), 67, quoted in Carys Wyn Jones, "Is There a Canon in Rock Music? Canonical Values, Terms and Mechanisms in the Reception of Rock Albums" (Ph.D. diss., University of Cardiff; 2006), 85.

72. Hanslick, *Vienna's Golden Years of Music,* 325. He also, like Brahms, admired Strauss Jr.'s orchestration; see 328.

73. See Peter Kemp, notes to *J. Strauss, Jr. Edition,* compact disc set, 51 vols., vol. 36, Marco Polo 8.223236 (1993), 14.

74. *Fremden-Blatt,* 28 Jan. 1858; Kemp, notes to *J. Strauss, Jr. Edition,* 13, 30.

Chapter 6

1. Don B. Wilmeth, *Variety Entertainment and Outdoor Amusements: A Reference Guide* (Westport, Conn.: Greenwood Press, 1982), 119. The origins of the song "Jim Crow" have often been discussed; for a short account quoting primary source material, see Charles Hamm, *Yesterdays: Popular Song in America* (New York: Norton, 1979), 118–21.

2. Charles Hamm, *Music in the New World* (New York: Norton, 1983), 183.

3. Quoted in Robert C. Toll, *On with the Show: The First Century of Show Business in America* (New York: Oxford University Press, 1976), 91.

4. Stuttgart: Cotta, 1854.

5. See Denja J. Epstein, *Sinful Tunes and Spirituals: Black Folk Music to the Civil War* (Urbana: University of Illinois Press, 1977), 242.

6. One of his innovative "voice quadrilles" is reproduced in Eileen Southern, ed., *Readings in Black American Music,* 2nd ed. (1971; reprint, New York: Norton, 1983), 127–34.

7. Mary Wollstonecroft, *A Vindication of the Rights of Men* (Oxford: Oxford University Press, 1999; originally published London: Joseph Johnson, 1790), 13.

8. Quoted in the *Spirit of the Times,* 7 Jan. 1837, and in Dale Cockrell, *Demons of Disorder: Early Blackface Minstrels and Their World* (Cambridge: Cambridge University Press, 1997), 68. For an account of Rice's reception in Britain, see Michael Pickering, *Blackface Minstrelsy in Britain* (Aldershot, England: Ashgate, forthcoming).

9. See Hamm, *Yesterdays,* 150–52.

10. On the subject of the blackface mask in British minstrelsy, see Michael Pickering, "White Skin, Black Masks," in Jacqueline Bratton, ed., *Music Hall: Performance and Style* (Milton Keynes, England: Open University Press, 1986), 70–91, 78–80, and chap. 4 of Pickering, *Blackface Minstrelsy in Britain.*

11. See Christine Bolt, "Race and the Victorians," in C. C. Eldridge, ed., *British Imperialism in the Nineteenth Century* (London: Macmillan, 1984), 126–47, 127–28.

12. They did not sing in harmony; see Hans Nathan, *Dan Emmett and the Rise of Early Negro Minstrelsy* (Norman: University of Oklahoma Press, 1962), 129 n. 14.

13. *Manchester Guardian,* 7 Jun. 1843, quoted in Grahame Shrubsole, "'Jim Crow,' Old Dan Tucker and Miss Lucy Long: The Early Years of Negro Minstrelsy in Manchester," *Manchester Sounds* 3 (2002), 23–53, 33.

14. 3 Jun. 1846, quoted in Shrubsole, "Jim Crow," 36.

15. Words and music by James Sanford (Philadelphia: A. Fiot, [1844?]). Eric Lott, while noting the juxtaposition of "dubious racial feeling" with anti-slavery views among British journalists, cites a *Daily News* review of the Ethiopian Serenaders claiming that their performances "raise feelings which may at no distant period produce results that every friend of negro emancipation would hail with satisfaction." Press notices were included in a pamphlet issued in the year of their English tour, *Ethiopian Serenaders* (1846), and are quoted in Lott, *Love and Theft: Blackface Minstrelsy and the American Working Class* (New York: Oxford University Press, 1993), 269.

16. 17 May 1847, quoted in Shrubsole, "Jim Crow," 44.

17. 15 Mar. 1848, quoted in Shrubsole, "Jim Crow," 46.

18. 7 Apr. 1847, quoted in Shrubsole, "Jim Crow," 45.

19. See Eileen Southern and Josephine Wright, *Images: Iconography of Music in African-American Culture (1770s–1920s)* (New York: Garland, 2000), 71–73.

20. This was a "duett" with chorus written in 1843 by Anthony Winnemore for his troupe, the Boston Minstrels. I am grateful to Dee Gallo for this reference.

21. Dan Emmett's manuscripts are in the collection MSS 355 Daniel D. Emmett Papers, c. 1840–1880, Archives/Library of the Ohio Historical Society. Columbus, OH, but this dance is reproduced in Nathan, *Dan Emmett and the Rise of Early Negro Minstrelsy,* 204.

22. Gunther Schuller refers to the novelty of the long-short, rather than short-long, type of syncopation in ragtime, in "Jazz and Musical Exoticism," in Jonathan Bellman, ed., *The Exotic in Western Music* (Boston: Northeastern University Press, 1998), 281–91, at 284–85; but one can see that developing, too, in the "come out tonight" of "Buffalo Gals" or "Get out de way" of "Old Dan Tucker."

23. Quotation from William Pole, *The Philosophy of Music,* lectures at the Royal Institution (1877), 4th ed. (1879; reprint, London: Kegan Paul, Trench, Trübner, 1910), 165.

24. See Samuel A. Floyd, Jr., "Ring Shout! Literary Studies, Historical Studies, and Black Music Inquiry," *Black Music Research Journal* 11, no. 2 (1991), 265–88, reprinted in Gena Dagel Caponi, ed., *Signifyin(g), Sanctifyin', and Slam Dunking: A Reader in African American Expressive Culture* (Amherst: University of Massachusetts Press, 1999), 135–56, at 142 and 155.

25. Nathan, *Dan Emmett and the Rise of Early Negro Minstrelsy,* 176–77.

26. Derek B. Scott, *The Singing Bourgeois: Songs of the Victorian Parlour and Drawing Room,* 2nd ed. (Aldershot, England: Ashgate, 2001; originally published Milton Keynes, England: Open University Press, 1989), 85.

27. William J. Mahar, *Behind the Burnt Cork Mask: Early Blackface Minstrelsy and Antebellum American Popular Culture* (Urbana: University of Illinois Press, 1999), 304. It often depends on the city (New York, for example, rather than Philadelphia), since the songs were varied to suit different audiences.

28. Frank W. Sweet, *A History of the Minstrel Show* (Palm Coast, Fla.: Backintyme, 2000), 8.

29. "Dixie's Land" was published by Firth, Pond, New York, 1860. Emmett's MS. (MSS 355 Daniel D. Emmett Papers, 1859) is reproduced in Nathan, *Dan Emmett and the Rise of Early Negro Minstrelsy,* 359–61. "Dashing White Sergeant," with words by General Bargoyn, was published in England in 1826. It began to circulate in America after its New York publication in 1829; see 256.

30. Songs referred to here are Stephen Foster's "Gwine to Run All Night" (1850), and Frederick Buckley's "I'd Choose to Be a Daisy" (1860) sung by the Buckley Serenaders.

31. Advertisement in "Driven from Home" (words and music by Will S. Hays, 1871), back cover.

32. Bernard Shaw, *The Irrational Knot* (1880; reprint, London: Constable, 1914), 236. I am grateful to Phyllis Weliver for drawing my attention to the music scenes of this novel.

33. Advertisement in "Ten Little Niggers" (words by Frank Green, music by Mark Mason, 1869), back cover. The words and music of "Annie Lisle" are by H. S. Thompson (Boston: Oliver Ditson, 1860). Its melody was adopted for the Cornell University song "Far above Cayuga's Waters" (Archibald Weeks and Wilmot Smith, 1870).

34. Hugh R. Haweis, *Music and Morals,* 17th ed. (London: Allen, 1893; originally published London: Statham, 1871), 551.

35. An advertisement in the *Illustrated London News,* 15 Feb. 1868, announces an upcoming program "of unusual excellence" that "will afford families who reside in the suburban districts an excellent opportunity of visiting the great entertainment of London."

36. Harry Reynolds, *Minstrel Memories: The Story of Burnt Cork Minstrelsy in Great Britain from 1836 to 1927* (London: Alston Rivers, 1928), 104. Harold Scott comments on the longstanding moral wholesomeness of the London minstrels in *The Early Doors: Origins of the Music Hall* (New York: Oxford University Press, 1946), 185.

37. Charles Dodd, *Tour Notes 1878,* MS in the possession of Sara M. Dodd.

38. "The Moore & Burgess Minstrels," *Strand Musical Magazine* 4, Jul.–Dec. 1896, 78–79, 79.

39. They became the Moore and Burgess Minstrels in 1869 (though Reynolds says, in *Minstrel Memories,* that it was in 1871, the sheet music of "The Grecian Bend" of 1869 clearly says Moore and Burgess on the title page). They seem to have dropped the name Christy Minstrels around two years later.

40. He recorded the melancholy ballad "She Wore a Wreath of Roses" (words by T. Bayly, music by J. Knight, c. 1840) as a "Japanese Fiddle Solo," phonographic cylinder, Edison Bell 6869, in 1906. It is on *Gone Where They Don't Play Billiards,* compact disc, Old Bean 501 (2001), track 8.

41. Songs making fun of this fashion were many; see Lester S. Levy, *Grace Notes in American History: Popular Sheet Music from 1820 to 1900* (Norman: University of Oklahoma Press, 1967), 76–77.

42. Information on the Mohawk Minstrels is given in Reynolds, *Minstrel Memories,* 139–59.

43. '"Because He Was a Nob" (Hunter), included in *505 Mohawk Minstrels' Songs and Ballads* (Francis, Day and Hunter, 1891).

44. Frederick Corder, "The Music of the People," *Musical Times and Singing-Class Circular* 26, no. 503, 1 Jan. 1885, 9–11, 10–11.

45. See Marian Hannah Winter, "Juba and American Minstrelsy," in Annemarie Bean, James V. Hatch, and Brooks McNamara, eds., *Inside the Minstrel Mask: Readings in Nineteenth-Century Blackface Minstrelsy* (Hanover, N.H.: Wesleyan University Press, 1996), 223–41.

46. Quoted in Toll, *On with the Show,* 112.

47. *American Notes for General Circulation* (London: Chapman and Hall, 1842), excerpted in Bean, *Inside the Minstrel Mask,* 48–49.

48. 5 Aug. 1848, excerpted in Bean, *Inside the Minstrel Mask,* 49–50.

49. The group he toured with was the Ethiopian Minstrels; see Winter, "Juba and American Minstrelsy," 226.

50. Reynolds, *Minstrel Memories,* 164.

51. Information on Hague in England is given in ibid., 163–7.

52. For information on Billy Kersands, see Tom Fletcher, *100 Years of the Negro in Show Business* (New York: Da Capo Press, 1984; originally published New York: Burge, 1954), 61–65.

53. See Eileen Southern, "The Georgia Minstrels: The Early Years," in Bean, *Inside the Minstrel Mask,* 163–75; details of exceptional performers among Callender's Georgia Minstrels, 168–71. For information on Sam Lucas, see Fletcher, *100 Years of the Negro in Show Business,* 67–77.

54. Toll, *On with the Show,* 106.

55. Ibid., 107.

56. Scott, *The Singing Bourgeois,* 116–18.

57. J. B. T. Marsh, *The Story of the Jubilee Singers* (London: Hodder and Stoughton, 1899), 73. Gilroy, *The Black Atlantic: Modernity and Double Consciousness* (London: Verso, 1993), 90–93.

58. It was published as no. 2 in *Songs of the Freedmen of Port Royal* (Philadelphia); this version is reproduced in Epstein, *Sinful Tunes and Spirituals,* 267–69.

59. Stratton can be heard singing "Little Dolly Daydream (Pride of Idaho)" (Leslie Stuart, 1897), recorded 1904, Mat. 4649b, Gramophone Company 3–2008, on *The Glory of the Music Hall,* compact disc set, Pearl GEMM CD 9475 (1991), vol. 1, track 12. Hampton can be heard singing a British "coon song," "The Shrimp and Winkle Man" (unknown authorship), recorded 1906, Edison

Bell 6588, on *Gone Where They Don't Play Billiards,* compact disc, Old Bean 501 (2001), track 14.

60. See Michael J. Budds, ed., *Jazz and the Germans* (New York: Pendragon Press, 2002), 9.

61. See Sigmund Spaeth, *A History of Popular Music in America* (New York: Random House, 1948), 245; and James Fuld, *The Book of World-Famous Music: Classical, Popular and Folk* (New York: Crown, 1966), 463.

62. A topic discussed in James Deaville, "African-American Entertainers in *Jahrhundertwende* Vienna: Austrian Identity, Viennese Modernism and Black Success," *Nineteenth-Century Music* 3, no. 2 (2006), 89–112.

63. It is Fleece's sermon to the sharks.

64. On Irishness and the minstrels, see Seymour Stark, *Men in Blackface: True Stories of the Minstrel Show* (Philadelphia: Xlibris, 2000), 27–50.

65. Quoted in Epstein, *Sinful Tunes and Spirituals,* 34.

66. John Dixon Long, *Pictures of Slavery in Church and State* (Philadelphia: John Dixon Long, 1857), 18, quoted in Southern and Wright, *Images,* 71.

67. Karen Linn, *That Half-Barbaric Twang: The Banjo in American Culture* (Urbana: University of Illinois Press, 1991), 30.

68. Eric Lott, *Love and Theft,* 113. Lott discusses blackface minstrelsy and desire for the Other, 148.

69. Ibid., 41.

70. Newton Abbot, England: David and Charles.

71. See survey published in Boston in 1878 by African-American author Richard M. Trotter, *Music and Some Highly Musical People,* excerpted in Southern, *Readings in Black American Music,* 142–48.

72. Mikhail Bakhtin, *Rabelais and His World,* trans. Hélène Iswolsky (Bloomington: Indiana University Press, 1984; originally published Cambridge, Mass.: MIT Press, 1968).

73. See Mahar, *Behind the Burnt Cork Mask,* 350–53.

74. Sweet, *A History of the Minstrel Show,* 16.

75. W. T. Lhamon Jr., *Raising Cain: Blackface Performance from Jim Crow to Hip Hop* (Cambridge, Mass.: Harvard University Press, 1998), 218–26.

76. W. T. Lhamon Jr., "Ebery Time I Weel About I Jump Jim Crow: Cycles of Minstrel Transgression from Cool White to Vanilla Ice," in Bean, *Inside the Minstrel Mask,* 275–84, 282–83.

Chapter 7

1. See, for example, Peter Bailey, ed., *Music Hall: The Business of Pleasure* (Milton Keynes, England: Open University Press, 1986), and Dagmar Kift, *The Victorian Music Hall: Culture, Class and Conflict,* trans. Roy Kift (Cambridge: Cambridge University Press, 1996; originally published as *Arbeitkultur im gesellschaftlichen Konflikt: Die englische Music Hall im 19. Jahrhundert* [Essen: Klartext Verlag, 1991]).

2. See the collection of essays edited by Jacqueline Bratton, *Music Hall: Performance and Style* (Milton Keynes, England: Open University Press, 1986).

3. The ideas of "imagined real" and "replicant" are indebted to the work of Jean Baudrillard, as will become evident later; see notes 32–34 here.

4. Bernard Darwin, introduction to *The Posthumous Papers of The Pickwick Club,* by Charles Dickens (Oxford: Oxford University Press, 1948), v–vi.

5. Charles Dickens, *Pickwick Papers* (1836), chap. 10.

6. Henry Mayhew, *London Labour and the London Poor* (London: Charles Griffin, 1861), 1:23–24.

7. *A Few Odd Characters out of the London Streets, as Represented in Mr. Henry Mayhew's Curious Conversazione* (London: R. S. Francis, 1857), 7.

8. "Confusion between [w] and [v] is often thought of as one of the most important characteristics of the London dialect, but it may be that this view is due in large measure to the popularity of the novels of Dickens, who makes very free use of words illustrating this confusion." G. L. Brook, *The Language of Dickens* (London: Andre Deutsch, 1970), 223. Although in the preceding quotation and elsewhere in this article there is a reference to Cockney as a dialect, it should be noted that the Dialect Society, founded in 1873, refused to recognize it as a dialect; "proper" dialects were to be found in rural rather than urban environments. See Robert Colls and Philip Dodd, *Englishness: Politics and Culture 1880–1920* (London: Croom Helm, 1986), 16.

9. Editorial ["The Ratcatcher's Daughter"], *Musical World* 33, no. 44, 3 Nov. 1855, 709–10, 709.

10. Ibid., 709.

11. His verse was published in 1842 (London: James Bohn); the earliest surviving music sheets are from the 1850s, when the song had three publishers: John Shepherd, Davidson, and Charles Sheard. I am citing from the latter, an arrangement by E. J. Westrop, published as no. 797 of the Musical Bouquet series in 1855. Bradley wrote under the pseudonym "Cuthbert Bede" and was a contributor to *Punch*, among other periodicals.

12. Renton Nicholson contends that Cowell revived an eighteenth-century song for use as "The Ratcatcher's Daughter," but offers no evidence; see John L. Bradley, ed., *Rogue's Progress: The Autobiography of "Lord Chief Baron" Nicholson*, reprint of the autobiography published in 1865 (Boston: Houghton Mifflin, 1965), 40. The correspondent to the *Musical World* (3 Nov. 1855) cited earlier claims that the tune was based on a serenade by Augustus Wade.

13. See Peter Gammond, *The Oxford Companion to Popular Music* (Oxford: Oxford University Press, 1991), 135–36.

14. Words and music to the complete song can be found in Aline Waites and Robin Hunter, *The Illustrated Victorian Songbook* (London: Michael Joseph, 1984), 70–71.

15. The theatre fronted Wych Street, a street that disappeared in the Aldwych and Kingsway development of 1900–1905; see Andrew Goodman, *Gilbert and Sullivan's London* (London: Faber, 2000; originally published Tunbridge Wells, England: Spellmount, 1988), 33, 36.

16. It was published as a song in London in 1854, and the next year as no. 452 of the *Musical Bouquet*. It also gave its title to a "tragico-comico burlesque" in one act by F. C. Burnand, performed at the A. D. C. Rooms, Cambridge, in 1855.

17. See Roy Palmer, *The Sound of History: Songs and Social Comment* (Oxford: Oxford University Press, 1988), 4, 122–24.

18. Also spelled "Cider Cellars" on some posters and for the publication *The Cider Cellar Songster: A Collection of Spreeish Chants and Nobby Songs* (London: Henry Smith, [between 1840 and 1857]).

19. J. E. Ritchie, "The Costermongers' Free and Easy," from *The Night Side of London* (London: William Tweedie, 1857), 200–203. George R. Sims found that the Free and Easy (usually held weekly on a Saturday or Monday) was

dying out in the 1880s, as cheaper music halls and gaffs multiplied in poorer areas; see *How the Poor Live* (New York: Garland, 1984; originally published London: Chatto and Windus, 1889), 79, 84.

20. Mayhew in John Canning, ed., *The Illustrated Mayhew's London* (London: Weidenfeld and Nicolson, 1986), 47.

21. The publication of 1865 says that the song was written and composed by Harry Clifton and arranged by J. Candy. Michael Kilgariff asserts that it is based on a traditional air, "Nightingales Sing," but gives no source or evidence, and I have been able to find none myself; see *Sing Us One of the Old Songs: A Guide to Popular Song 1860–1920* (Oxford: Oxford University Press, 1998), 75, 414.

22. See Arthur Roberts, *Fifty Years of Spoof* (London: Bodley Head, 1926), 163.

23. This comic song should not be confused with the socially committed play of the same name and similar date (1863) by Tom Taylor.

24. See Canning, *The Illustrated Mayhew's London*, 181.

25. This figure is deduced from the information provided by E. H. Hunt, *British Labour History 1815–1914* (London: Weidenfeld and Nicolson, 1981), 176–77.

26. *Minutes of Evidence Taken before the Select Committee on Theatres and Places of Entertainment*, 1892 (London: Eyre and Spottiswoode for HMSO, 1892), app. 9, 450. There was also a Hebrew Dramatic Club in nearby Spitalfields.

27. *Life and Labour of the People in London*, first series, *Poverty*, vol. 2 (1891; reprint, London: Macmillan, 1902), app., table 3.

28. Though Yiddish would be expected rather than Hebrew, Oskar Schmitz, "Die Juden in Whitechapel," remarks on the Hebrew seen at several shops ("An vielen Läden sieht man hebräische Inschriften"), in *Das Land ohne Musik: Englische Gesellschaftsprobleme* (Munich: Georg Müller, 1914), 236. However, it is difficult to know whether this would have been the case fifty years earlier.

29. Matrix Lx 44; Fr. Odéon 32364; *The Glory of the Music Hall*, compact disc set, Pearl, GEMM CD 9475 (Pavilion Records, 1991), vol. 1, track 4. His real name was Colin McCallum, born in Mile End. He took his stage name from Coborn Road, Bow; see Gammond, *The Oxford Companion to Popular Music*, 122.

30. D. A. DeSola, untitled essay, in *The Ancient Melodies of the Liturgy of the Spanish and Portuguese Jews*, harmonized by Emanuel Aguilar (London: Wessel, 1857), 39, no. 42.

31. On *Itzhak Perlman, Klezmer: In the Fiddler's House*, compact disc, EMI Classics 7243 5 55555 2 6 (1996), track 11.

32. Jean Baudrillard, *Simulations* (1983), excerpted in Antony Easthope and Kate McGowan, *A Critical and Cultural Theory Reader* (Buckingham, England: Open University Press, 1992), 203–5, 204. Baudrillard's three orders of simulation are related to the history of commodities and proceed from counterfeit to industrial production in the nineteenth century to generation by models in the twentieth century (a recent and controversial example of the latter would, I suppose, be genetically modified crops).

33. Ibid., 203.

34. "Symbolic Exchange and Death," in *Selected Writings*, ed. Mark Poster (Cambridge: Polity Press, 1988), 119–48, 147.

35. The published music to Bellwood's song gives "What cheer," but she would undoubtedly have sung the first word without aspirating it (which is the point of the spelling "wot" in the other songs). As long ago as 1791, in John

Walker's *Pronouncing Dictionary,* it was noted that Cockneys pronounced *wh* as *w.* See William Matthews, *Cockney Past and Present: A Short History of the Dialect of London* (London: Routledge and Kegan Paul, 1972; originally published London: Routledge, 1938), 36–37. This is a point easily lost nowadays, when so few people aspirate words beginning with *wh.*

36. See John M. Garrett, *Sixty Years of British Music Hall* (London: Chappell, 1976), sect. 4. Interval, n.p.

37. Popular music began to recognize the amount of ethnic mixing in urban communities in the late nineteenth and early twentieth centuries in songs like "There's a Little Bit of Irish in Sadie Cohen," words by Alfred Brian, music by Jack Stern (New York: Remick, 1916). See William H. A. Williams, *'Twas Only an Irishman's Dream: The Image of Ireland and the Irish in American Popular Song Lyrics, 1800–1920* (Urbana: University of Illinois Press, 1996), 195.

38. This does not mean that Jewish elements cannot be identified: Jeffrey Magee reveals their presence in hit songs of the 1920s and 1930s in "'The Sweetest Sounds': Jewish Resonance in American Popular Song," paper presented at the *American Musicological Society* conference "Musical Intersections," Toronto, 5 Nov. 2000, session 5–7. On black-Jewish relations, see Jeffrey Melnick, *A Right to Sing the Blues: African Americans, Jews, and American Popular Song* (Cambridge, Mass.: Harvard University Press, 1999).

39. E. R. Shrosberry and H. Boden, arranged by E. Forman (London: Francis and Day, 1884).

40. Words and music by Edwin V. Page (London: Willey, 1882). Jacqueline Bratton has written on Hill's career in "Jenny Hill: Sex and Sexism in the Victorian Music Hall," in *Music Hall: Performance and Style,* 92–110.

41. Bernard Shaw, quoted on jacket of *Pygmalion: A Romance in Five Acts,* definitive text under the supervision of Dan H. Laurence (Harmondsworth, England: Penguin, n.d.).

42. *Times* (London), 10 Oct. 1874, cited in Dagmar Höher, "The Composition of Music Hall Audiences, 1850–1900," in Bailey, *Music Hall: The Business of Pleasure,* 73–92, 74.

43. At the end of the century, Booth found no greater respect for the institution of marriage among the "lowest classes" of the East End, for whom "pre-marital relations" were very common; *Life and Labour of the People in London,* third series, *Religious Influences,* vol. 1 (1902), 55.

44. Quoted in Edward Lee, *Folksong and Music Hall* (London: Routledge, 1982), 104. For more information on Mrs. Ormiston Chant, see Kift, *The Victorian Music Hall,* 162–64, and Barry J. Faulk, *Music Hall and Modernity: The Late-Victorian Discovery of Popular Culture* (Athens: Ohio University Press, 2004), 75–110.

45. Hubert Parry, *Style in Musical Art* (1911), quoted in Peter van der Merwe, *Origins of the Popular Style: The Antecedents of Twentieth-Century Popular Music* (Oxford: Oxford University Press, 1989), 223.

46. "It's a Great Big Shame! Or, I'm Blowed If 'E Can Call 'Isself 'Is Own," words by Edgar Bateman, music by George Le Brunn (London: Francis, Day and Hunter, 1895), Pathetone 96, 1932. This is one of four Pathé shorts documenting Elen's performances of music hall songs. The song is reprinted in *Sixty Old-Time Variety Songs* (London: EMI, 1977), 1–3.

47. See Adrian New, *Times* (London), 19 Dec. 1970, reprinted in Benny Green, *The Last Empires: A Music Hall Companion* (London: Pavilion Books, 1986), 119–23.

48. Elen, "Business Make-Ups," notebook, quoted in Green, *The Last Empires*, 122.

49. Words by Edgar Bateman, music by George Le Brunn (London: Francis, Day and Hunter), reprinted in *Sixty Old-Time Variety Songs*, 72–74.

50. See Matthews, *Cockney Past and Present*, 62–65.

51. In the first scene of *Pygmalion*, Liza claims that Freddy ruined her flowers and "ran awy athaht pyin" (ran away without paying); see Shaw, *Pygmalion*, ed. Laurence, 16.

52. Elen "presents a plain, ungarnished portrayal of the coster as he really is, as he would be found at his work or in his home," according to the *Nottingham Daily Express*, quoted in the *Era*, 16 Sep. 1899. When Elen toured the United States, the *New York Times* (10 Sep. 1907) commented on his providing "true pictures" rather than "merely pictorial representations." It is significant that Elen's coster was recognizable as true to life by those living outside of London and unfamiliar with coster communities. These quotations are taken from Frank M. Scheide, *South London, English Music Hall, and the Early Films of Charlie Chaplin* (Oxford: Oxford University Press, forthcoming).

53. "Heyday of the Cockney Comedian," *Times* (London), 9 Jan.1958, quoted in Ulrich Schneider, *Die Londoner Music Hall und ihre Songs 1850–1920* (Tübingen: Niemeyer, 1984), 157. Colin MacInnes refers to Elen as a "genuine coster singer" and "everything Albert Chevalier wanted to be, and was not: a dyed-in-the-wool Cockney" in *Sweet Saturday Night: Pop Song 1840–1920* (London: MacGibbon and Kee, 1967), 30, 36.

54. *Travels in Hyperreality* (London: Pan, 1987; originally published London: Secker and Warburg, 1986), 7.

55. *Music and Society since 1875* (London: Barrie and Jenkins, 1976), 154.

56. Consider the remarks of Laura Ormiston Chant already cited, and the reference to the singing of sentimental ballads in Sims, *How the Poor Live*, 79.

57. *Uses of Literacy* (Harmondsworth, England: Penguin, 1958), 15; cited in Peter Bailey, introduction to Bailey, *Music Hall*, xiv.

58. Matthews, *Cockney Past and Present*, 98.

59. Regal Zonophone T. 897 ab15398e, 23 Jul. 1912.

60. Regal G. 7076 29672, c. May 1912.

61. Regal Zonophone T. 897 ab15399e, 23 Jul. 1912.

62. Matthews remarked on the noticeable contribution of music halls to "the Cockney dialect as it is spoken in the streets." *Cockney Past and Present*, 82.

63. Althusser's theory of interpellation is expounded in his essay "Ideology and the State," in *Lenin and Philosophy and Other Essays*, trans. B. Brewster (London: New Left Books, 1977), 136–69; see, especially, 160–64.

64. Words by Billy O'Brien, music by Billy O'Brien and Jack Martin.

65. Words and music by Lonnie Donegan, Peter Buchanan, and Beverly Thorn.

66. Paul Hoggart, "Kids, Kidnappers and Carry-on Cockneys," *Times* (London), Friday, 13 Mar. 1998, 51.

Chapter 8

1. Bernard Gendron, *Between Montmartre and the Mudd Club: Popular Music and the Avant-Garde* (Chicago: University of Chicago Press, 2002); Steven Whiting, *Satie the Bohemian: From Cabaret to Concert Hall* (Oxford: Clarendon Press,

1998). François Lesure discusses the Chat Noir's influence on Debussy in "Debussy et Le Chat Noir," *Cahiers Debussy* 23 (1999), 35–43. Mention should also be made of Mary Ellen Poole, "Chansonnier and Chanson in Parisian *Cabarets artistiques,* 1881–1914" (PhD diss., University of Illinois, 1994).

2. Interpreting the meaning of the gothic illustrates how necessary it is to understand signification in cultural context. In England, owing to the Gothic Revival architects, it was regarded as a serious, morally wholesome style. David Wright, for instance, describes the Gothic façade of Royal College of Music (opened 1894) as denoting "a public building intended for a serious professional purpose." "The South Kensington Music Schools," *Journal of the Royal Musical Association* 130, no. 2 (2005), 236–82, 262. John Ruskin emphasizes the moral elements of Gothic style in "The Nature of Gothic," in *The Stones of Venice,* 3 vols. (London: Smith, Elder, 1851–53). For Ruskin, the very presence of imperfection and "savageness" in gothic buildings makes them an index of the Christian religious principle that recognizes the individual value of every soul while confessing its imperfection.

3. See Mariel Oberthür, *Cafés and Cabarets of Montmartre* (Layton, Utah: Gibbs M. Smith, 1984), 21.

4. Mariel Oberthür claims that there was no surveillance of cabaret chansons until 6 April 1897 in *Le Chat Noir 1881–1897* (Paris: Réunion des musées nationaux, 1992), 18. However, this contradicts the information given in note 68 below.

5. See Peter Hawkins, *Chanson: The French Singer-Songwriter from Bruant to the Present Day* (Aldershot, England: Ashgate, 2000).

6. They were embraced by opposing political camps, since they offered a picture of a unified French culture. Some prized them for their naïveté, while others admired their shrewdness. See Jane Fulcher, "The Popular Chanson of the Second Empire: 'Music of the Peasants' in France," *Acta Musicologica* 52, no. 1 (1980), 27–37.

7. See Pierre d'Anjou, *Au Temps du Chat Noir* (Paris: Henri Lemoine, 1943), 15–20.

8. See Patrick Biau, *Jules Jouy 1855–1897: Le "poète chourineur"* (Paris: Editions Fortin, 1997), 43, and Harold B. Segel, *Turn-of-the-Century Cabaret* (New York: Columbia University Press, 1987), 6–7. Further information on the club of the Hydropathes can be found in Michael Herbert, *La Chanson à Montmartre* (Paris: Éditions de la Table Ronde, 1967), 15–52.

9. Maurice Donnay, *Mes Débuts à Paris* (Paris: Libraire Anthème Fayard, 1937), quoted in Segel, *Turn-of-the-Century Cabaret,* 36.

10. Phillip Dennis Cate, "The Spirit of Montmartre," in Phillip Dennis Cate and Mary Shaw, eds., *The Spirit of Montmartre: Cabarets, Humor, and the Avant-Garde, 1875–1905,* exhibition catalogue (New Brunswick, N.J.: Jane Voorhees Zimmerli Art Museum, Rutgers University, 1996), 1–93, 25.

11. Georges Fragerolle, *Le Fumisme,* quoted in Cate, "The Spirit of Montmartre," 89 n. 19.

12. Whiting, *Satie the Bohemian,* 45.

13. Allais later published it in his *Album Primo-Avrilesque* (Paris: Ollendorf, 1897), 25, and it is reprinted in Guy Schraenen, *Erratum Musical* (Bremen: Institut Français, 1994).

14. "La blague est la seule arme à employer contre la solennité," quoted on "Histoire de Paris" notice at 84 boulevard de Rochechouart. Further infor-

mation on the founding of the Chat Noir and its journal is in Herbert, *La Chanson à Montmartre*, 53–70.

15. Sylvie Buisson and Christian Parisot, *Paris Montmartre: A Mecca of Modern Art 1860–1920* (Paris: Editions Terrail, 1996), 61.

16. For an account of Allais's invitation (in the guise of Sarcey), and his warning of the jealous, maniacal servant, see Herbert, *La Chanson à Montmartre*, 156–57 (and in other sources).

17. Erik Satie, "Les Musiciens de Montmartre" (1900), in *Ecrits*, ed. Ornella Volta (Paris: Champ Libre, 1990), 47.

18. See Robert Orledge, *Satie Remembered* (London: Faber, 1995), 38, and Whiting, *Satie the Bohemian*, 68–97, and 561–62.

19. "Cessant d'écrire des chansonnettes badines ou entraînantes, il s'était révélé le magistral 'barde du pavé.'" Herbert, *La Chanson à Montmartre*, 116.

20. Toulouse-Lautrec did not restrict himself to posters; he designed more that thirty song-sheet covers, as did other well-known artists. For a selection of reproductions, see *Au Temps du Chat Noir: 8 Chansons illustrées par Toulouse Lautrec, Steinlen, Willette* (Paris: Editions Fortin, 1991). Bruant's chansons also inspired some of his paintings (for example, *A Grenelle*).

21. Francis Carco finds a past model for Bruant in the fifteenth-century outlaw poet François Villon. See *La Belle Epoque au temps de Bruant* (Paris: Éditions Gallimard, 1954), 41, 77, 158.

22. At the second Chat Noir (on three floors) in rue Laval (now rue Victor Massé), Salis made a determined effort to attract high society. He introduced the shadow theatre as a new attraction.

23. See Lisa Appignanesi, *Cabaret: The First Hundred Years* (London: Methuen, 1984; originally published Studio Vista, 1975), 27.

24. Oberthür, *Cafés and Cabarets of Montmartre*, 81–82.

25. Appignanesi, *Cabaret*, 27.

26. Aristide Bruant, *Quelques souvenirs pour servir de préface*, in *Dans la rue: Poèmes et chansons choisis*, new ed. (Paris: Eugène Rey, 1924), i–xv, vii.

27. Hawkins, *Chanson*, 71.

28. Henri Marc, *Aristide Bruant: Le maître de la rue* (Paris: Editions France-Empire, 1989), 84–85.

29. A performance recorded c. 1913 can be heard on *Aristide Bruant "A Montmerte," enregistrements originaux 1905–1914*, 2 compact discs, EPM 983302 (1994).

30. My translation; translated with the aid of Oliver Leroy, *A Glossary of French Slang* (London: Harrap, 1922). I also thank Mireille Ribière for her help.

31. Contemporary quotation from Arthur Symons, *Colour Studies in Paris* (New York: Dutton, 1918), 67–68, quoted in Segel, *Turn-of-the-Century Cabaret*, 63.

32. Carco, *La Belle Epoque au temps de Bruant*, 77, my translation. "Les belles dames frissonnaient d'horreur sans se douter que Bruant, après les avoir troublées, devait en rire."

33. Hawkins, *Chanson*, 71–2.

34. *Frame Analysis: An Essay on the Organization of Experience* (Boston: Northeastern University Press, 1986; originally published 1974), 394. To "flood out" is to lose control of an existing frame, or one that is assumed to exist.

35. My translation.

36. A performance by Bruant himself, recorded around 1913, can be

heard on *Aristide Bruant "A Montmerte," enregistrements originaux 1905–1914*, 2 compact discs, EPM 983302 (1994), disc 1, track 1.

37. Bruant self-published many of his chansons without music in the collection *Dans la rue*, 2 vols., piano accompaniment available separately (Paris: Editions d'aujourd'hui, 1976; originally published Paris: A. Bruant, 1889 and 1895). A third volume of *Dans la rue* appeared in 1897 (Paris: Flammarion).

38. These chansons are reproduced in Segel, *Turn-of-the-Century Cabaret*, 37–39. Clément's song was set to music and sung by Antoine Renard at the *Eldorado* in 1868. Clément became an elected member of the Commune.

39. The refrain runs: "Mourons ensemble / Pour être heureux; / La mort rassemble / Les amoureux!" The chanson can be found in Maurice Mac-Nab, *Nouvelles Chansons du Chat Noir, musique nouvelle de Roland Kohr* (Paris: Heugel, [1894?]), 113–16.

40. "Le chef de file de tous les chansonniers actuels." *La Chanson à Montmartre*, 109. For the texts of "Les Fœtus," "L'Expulsion," and "Suicide en partie double" see André Velter, *Les Poètes du Chat Noir* (Paris: Éditions Gallimard, 1996), 335–37, 341–44.

41. Anonymous introduction to *Chansons du Chat Noir, musique nouvelle ou harmonisée par Camille Baron*, by Maurice Mac-Nab, (Paris: Heugel, 1888), 9: "Mac-Nab possédait la voix la plus rauque et la plus fausse qu'il soit possible d'imaginer; on croyait entendre un phoque enrhumé. Mais cela l'inquiétait peu. Il chantait tout de Même, sans se préoccuper des gestes désespérés d'Albert Tinchant, son accompagnateur ordinaire." My translation.

42. My translation.

43. See Donald Mac-Nab, preface to Mac-Nab, *Nouvelles Chansons du Chat Noir*, 7–22, 17. The text of this chanson-*cum*-advertisement, "Les Poêles mobiles," can be found in Velter, *Les Poètes du Chat Noir*, 331–32. Advertisers themselves, of course, make use of lyrical language. By coincidence, shortly after writing this passage I was sent an advertisement by email (23 Mar. 2006) about a portable heater: "the 1.5KW Freedom Gas Heater offers warmth in an instant, combining radiant heat with soothing far infrared rays." Yet an advertisement seldom avoids more concrete product specification: "it's the only truly-portable gas heater to meet the tough, new European safety standards." Mac-Nab satirizes the incongruous mixture of romance and materialism in the business world.

44. *Au Temps du Chat Noir*, 54.

45. Herbert, *La Chanson à Montmartre*, 216.

46. *La Chanson à Montmartre*, 214. Three different performances of this chanson, recorded in 1909, 1933, and 1949, can be heard on *Paul Delmet: Ses chansons, ses interprètes 1901–1949*, 2 compact discs, EPM 980032 (2000).

47. My translation.

48. Emile Goudeau, preface to Paul Delmet, *Chansons du Quartier Latin* (Paris: Enoch, 1897), i–iv. There is no space to discuss other important performers at the Chat Noir, such as Maurice Rollinat, Arthur Marcel-Legay, or Georges Fragerolle.

49. Marie Oberthür claims Salis invited Guilbert to sing one evening at the Chat Noir in 1890, in "Yvette Guilbert et la chanson Montmartroise" in *Yvette Guilbert diseuse fin-de-siècle* (Musées d'Aix-en-Provence – Musée Toulouse-Lautrec, Albi, Paris, 1994), 35–39, 36. However, the Chat Noir is not listed among

any of Guilbert's documented appearances during the nineteenth century on pages 75–76. I could find no reference to her singing at the Chat Noir in her autobiography *La Chanson de ma vie* or in *Struggles and Victories*. However, in *Autres Chants, Autres Temps* (Paris: Laffont, 1946), 59–60, Guilbert writes that "par exception à sa règle" the Chat Noir invited her to perform there in 1892 in grateful acknowledgment of her having been the first to propagate *la verve chatnoiresque* elsewhere in Paris. I am grateful to Jacqueline Waeber for putting this last source my way.

50. Cited without date, but c. 1891, in Yvette Guilbert and Harold Simpson, *Yvette Guilbert: Struggles and Victories* (London: Mills and Boon, 1910), 199.

51. She can be heard on *Yvette Guilbert, 47 enregistrements originaux de 1897 à 1934,* 2 compact discs, EPM 982442 (1992).

52. Biau, *Jules Jouy,* 215.

53. Guilbert and Simpson, *Struggles and Victories,* 317.

54. Henry Bauer, quoted in Guilbert and Simpson, *Struggles and Victories,* 206–7. Xanrof made his début at the Mirliton but achieved success when he moved to the new Chat Noir.

55. Guilbert and Simpson, *Yvette Guilbert: Struggles and Victories,* 116–17; Yvette Guilbert's autobiography, *Luttes et victoires de ma vie,* is printed side by side with an English translation, 1–163.

56. "Je suis pocharde!" (recorded in 1897) is on *Yvette Guilbert, 47 enregistrements originaux de 1897 à 1934,* 2 compact discs, EPM 982442 (1992), disc 2, track 13.

57. Yvette Guilbert, *La Chanson de ma Vie (Mes Memoires)* (Paris: Bernard Grasset, 1927), 93.

58. Quoted without source in Carco, *La Belle Epoque,* 155.

59. See Guilbert and Simpson, *Yvette Guilbert,* 207.

60. Oberthür, curator of the Musée de Montmartre, provides many precise locations in her *Cafés and Cabarets of Montmartre.*

61. Quoted without source in Carco, *La Belle Epoque,* 136.

62. Ibid., 129.

63. It reopened for a few months in 1898 as the Cabaret du Pacha Noir, then in 1899–1901 became the chansonnier Henry Fursy's Boîte à Fursy. The building lost its eccentric rustic façade in 1951, and it is now a dentist's surgery.

64. Emile Goudeau, preface to *Guide de l'étranger à Montmartre,* by Victor Meusy and Edmond Depas (Paris: Strauss, 1900), quoted in Cate, "The Spirit of Montmartre," 39.

65. After years of silence, he made a single comeback, in his seventies, at the Empire *music-hall* in Paris in 1924.

66. Maurice Boukay, preface to *Chansons de Montmartre,* by Paul Delmet (Paris: Enoch, 1898), 1–3. An example of a Boukay and Delmet romance is "Baiser d'amants" (1896).

67. *La Belle Epoque au temps de Bruant,* 83.

68. See *Annexes,* in Lionel Richard, *Cabaret, Cabarets: Origines et décadence* (Paris: Plon, 1991), 257–60. Richard gives as a source Georges d'Avenel, "*Le Mécanisme de la vie moderne,* Le Théâtre, III, Auteurs, public et directeurs," *Revue des Deux Mondes,* 1 Jan. 1902, 54–57. The reader should be advised that I cannot find these cited details in the place Richard specifies, nor in the book that d'Avenel published as *Le Mécanisme de la vie moderne* (Paris: A. Colin, 1902).

69. Herbert, *La Chanson à Montmartre*, 338.

70. Whiting, *Satie the Bohemian*, 34.

71. Preface to Delmet, *Chansons de Montmartre*, 1.

72. Richard describes the motivations of the new cabaret entrepreneurs thus: "l'espoir d'une réussite commerciale avec un incestissement minime." *Cabaret, Cabarets*, 125.

73. Appignanesi, *Cabaret*, 19.

74. Armond Fields, *Le Chat Noir: A Montmartre Cabaret and Its Artists in Turn-of-the-Century Paris* (Santa Barbara, Calif.: Santa Barbara Museum of Art, 1993), 11. The stress, however, has to be on the locals of Montmartre. Although Bruant sang of Belleville and Ménilmontant, there was little chance of the working-class residents of those places paying a visit. See Richard, *Cabaret, Cabarets*, 130.

75. Carco, *La Belle Epoque*, 53.

76. Bessière, *Autour de la Butte: Chansons de Montmartre et d'ailleurs* (Paris: Joubert, 1899), v.

77. The whole chanson is in ibid., 243–25.

78. The name is a pun on its sign, painted by André Gill (*lapin à Gill*).

79. Fields, *Le Chat Noir*, 37.

80. For the spread of cabaret outside of France, see Segel, *Turn-of-the-Century Cabaret*; Appignanesi, *Cabaret*; Richard, *Cabaret, Cabarets*; and Gendron, *Between Montmartre and the Mudd Club*, 70–79.

81. Henri de Saint-Simon, *Opinions litteraires, philosophes et industrielles* (1825), excerpted in Steve Edwards, *Art and Its Histories: A Reader* (New Haven, Conn.: Yale University Press, 1999), 188–90.

82. The lines "He turns revolt into a style, prolongs / The impulse to a habit of the time" are from Thom Gunn's poem "Elvis Presley." They inspired the title of George Melly's book *Revolt into Style: The Pop Arts* (Oxford: Oxford University Press, 1989; originally published London: Allen Lane, 1970). Paul Wood argues that Manet retains the tensions of the term "avant-garde" in his work. See "The Avant-Garde and the Paris Commune," in Paul Wood, ed., *The Challenge of the Avant-Garde* (New Haven, Conn.: Yale University Press, 1999), 113–36, 128–9.

83. See Clement Greenberg, "Avant-Garde and Kitsch," *Partisan Review* 6, no. 5 (1939), reprinted in Charles Harrison and Paul Wood, eds., *Art in Theory 1900–1990: An Anthology of Changing ideas* (Oxford: Blackwell, 1992), 529–41.

84. Gretel Adorno and Rolf Tiedemann, eds., and Robert Hullot-Kentor, trans. (London: Continuum, 2004; originally published as *Ästhetische Theorie* [Frankfurt am Main: Suhrkamp, 1970]).

85. *Between Montmartre and the Mudd Club*, 3, 54–55.

86. *Dada Manifesto* (1918), quoted in Wood, *The Challenge of the Avant-Garde*, 230.

87. Peter Bürger, *Theory of the Avant-Garde*, trans. Michael Shaw (Minneapolis: University of Minnesota Press, 1984; originally published as *Theorie der Avantgarde* [Frankfurt: Suhrkamp Verlag, 1974]), 47.

88. Carco, *La Belle Epoque*, 123. Again, it may be necessary to remind the reader that "populaire" carries a stronger sense of someone or something being "of the people" than does the English word "popular."

89. Andreas Huyssen, *After the Great Divide: Modernism, Mass Culture, Postmodernism* (London: Macmillan, 1986), vii.

90. While Max Paddison has seen Zappa as abandoning the popular to join the "serious avant garde," Arved Ashby has argued that "popular topoi remained vital to Zappa's 'serious' concert music." See Paddison, *Adorno, Modernism and Mass Culture: Essays in Critical Theory and Music* (London: Kahn and Averill, 1995), 104, and Arved Ashby, "Frank Zappa and the Anti-fetishist Orchestra," *Musical Quarterly* 83:4 (1999), 557–606, 559.

Bibliography

For reasons of space, this bibliography is confined to material cited in the text.

Adorno, Theodor W. *Theodor W. Adorno: Über Walter Benjamin* (1962). Ed. Rolf Tiedemann. Frankfurt: Suhrkamp Verlag, 1970.

———. *Aesthetic Theory* (1970). Ed. Gretel Adorno and Rolf Tiedemann. Trans. Robert Hullot-Kentor. London: Continuum, 2004.

———. *Dissonanzen. Musik in der verwalteten Welt* (1956). In *Gesammelte Schriften*, vol. 14. Frankfurt: Suhrkamp Verlag, 1973.

———. *Einleitung in die Musiksoziologie*. Frankfurt: Suhrkamp Verlag, 1962.

———. *Introduction to the Sociology of Music* (1962). Trans. E. B. Ashton. New York: Continuum, 1989.

———. *Philosophie der neuen Musik*. Frankfurt: Europäische Verlaganstalt, 1958.

———. *Philosophy of Modern Music* (1958). Trans. Anne G. Mitchell and Wesley V. Blomster. New York: Seabury Press, 1973.

Aldrich, Elizabeth. *From the Ballroom to Hell: Grace and Folly in Nineteenth-Century Dance*. Evanston, Ill.: Northwestern University Press, 1991.

Allen, Francis William, Charles Pickard Ware, and Lucy McKim Garrison. *Slave Songs of the United States* (1867). New York: Oak, 1965.

Allen, Reginald, ed. and comp. *The First Night Gilbert and Sullivan* (1958). 2nd ed. London: Chappell, 1976.

———. *The Life and Work of Sir Arthur Sullivan: Composer for Victorian England*. New York: Pierpont Morgan Library, 1975.

Althusser, Louis. *Lenin and Philosophy and Other Essays*. Trans. B. Brewster. London: New Left Books, 1977.

The Ancient Melodies of the Liturgy of the Spanish and Portuguese Jews. Harmonized by Emanuel Aguilar. With an essay by D. A. DeSola. London: Wessel, 1857.

Appignanesi, Lisa. *The Cabaret* (1975). 2nd ed. New Haven, Conn.: Yale University Press, 2004.

Ashby, Arved. "Frank Zappa and the Anti-fetishist Orchestra." *Musical Quarterly* 83.4 (1999): 557–606.

Atlas, Allan W. *The Wheatstone English Concertina in Victorian England*. Oxford: Clarendon Press, 1996.

Attali, Jacques. *Noise: The Political Economy of Music* (1977). Trans. Brian Massumi. Manchester: Manchester University Press, 1985.

Austin, William W. *"Susanna," "Jeanie," and "The Old Folks at Home": The Songs of Stephen C. Foster from His Time to Ours*. London: Macmillan, 1975.

Avison, Charles. *Essay on Musical Expression*. London: Davis, 1752.

Bailey, Peter, ed. "Champagne Charlie: Performance and Ideology in the Music Hall Swell Song." In Bratton, *Music Hall*, 49–69.

———. "A Community of Friends: Business and Good Fellowship in London Music Hall Management c. 1860–1885." In Bailey, *Music Hall*, 33–52.

———. "Conspiracies of Meaning: Music-Hall and the Knowingness of Popular Culture." *Past and Present* 144 (Aug. 1994): 138–70.

———. *Leisure and Class in Victorian England: Rational Recreation and the Contest for Control, 1830–1885* (1978). London: Methuen, 1987.

———. *Music Hall: The Business of Pleasure*. Milton Keynes, England: Open University Press, 1986.

———. *Popular Culture and Performance in the Victorian City*. Cambridge: Cambridge University Press, 1998.

Baily, Leslie. *The Gilbert and Sullivan Book* (1952, rev. ed. 1956). London: Spring Books, 1966.

Bakhtin, Mikhail. *Rabelais and His World* (1968). Trans. Hélène Iswolsky. Bloomington: Indiana University Press, 1984.

Ballstaedt, Andreas. "Die Walzer von Johann Strauss (Sohn)—Gebrauchtmusik oder Werk?" In Finscher and Riethmüller, *Johann Strauss*, 76–96.

Ballstaedt, Andreas, and Tobias Widmaier. *Salonmusik: Zur Geschichte und Funktion einer bürgerlichen Musikpraxis*. Stuttgart: Steiner Verlag, 1989.

Bashford, Christina, and Leanne Langley, eds. *Music and British Culture, 1785–1914: Essays in Honour of Cyril Ehrlich*. Oxford: Oxford University Press, 2000.

Bass, Michael T. *Street Music in the Metropolis*. London: John Murray, 1864.

Baudrillard, Jean. *Simulations* (1983). Excerpted in Antony Easthope and Kate McGowan, *A Critical and Cultural Theory Reader*, 203–5. Buckingham, England: Open University Press, 1992.

———. "Symbolic Exchange and Death." In Mark Poster, ed., *Selected Writings*, 119–48. Cambridge: Polity Press, 1988.

Bauman, Zygmunt. *Modernity and Ambivalence*. Cambridge: Polity Press, 1991.

Bean, Annemarie, James V. Hatch, and Brooks McNamara, eds. *Inside the Minstrel Mask: Readings in Nineteenth-Century Blackface Minstrelsy*. Hanover, N.H.: Wesleyan University Press, 1996.

Becker, Howard. *Art Worlds*. Berkeley: University of California Press, 1982.

Benjamin, Walter. "The Author as Producer" (1934). In Peter Demetz, ed., *Reflections: Essays, Aphorisms, Autobiographical Writings*. New York: Schocken Books, 1978.

———. "Paris: Capital of the Nineteenth Century." *Perspecta* 12 (1969): 163–72. Extracted from the incomplete *Arcades Project* [*Passagen-Werk*], 1927–40.

Bennett, Joseph. "Observations on Music in America: III.—Orchestral and Choral Music." *Musical Times and Singing Class Circular* 26.507 (1 May 1885): 255–57.

———. *A Story of Ten Hundred Concerts, 1859–87.* London: Chappell, 1887.

Berger, Peter L., and Thomas Luckmann. *The Social Construction of Reality: A Treatise in the Sociology of Knowledge* (1966). New York: Anchor Books, 1967.

Bergson, Henri. *Laughter: An Essay on the Meaning of the Comic* (1900). Trans. Cloudesley Brereton and Fred Rothwell (1911). New York: Dover, 2005.

Berlin, Edward A. *King of Ragtime: Scott Joplin and His Era.* New York: Oxford University Press, 1994.

Bessière, Emile. *Autour de la Butte: Chansons de Montmartre et d'ailleurs.* Paris: Joubert, 1899.

Best, Geoffrey. *Mid-Victorian Britain 1851–75* (1971). London: Fontana, 1979.

"The Black Opera." *New York Tribune,* 30 Jun. 1855. Reprinted in *Musical World* 36.32 (7 Aug. 1858): 502–3.

Biau, Patrick. *Jules Jouy 1855–1897: Le "poète chourineur."* Paris: Editions Fortin, 1997.

Bledsoe, Robert Terrell. *Henry Fothergill Chorley: Victorian Journalist.* Aldershot, England: Ashgate, 1998.

"The Blue Danube." http://en.wikipedia.org/wiki/The_Blue_Danube.

Bohlman, Philip V. *World Music: A Very Short Introduction.* Oxford: Oxford University Press, 2002.

Bolt, Christine. "Race and the Victorians." In C. C. Eldridge, ed., *British Imperialism in the Nineteenth Century,* 126–47. London: Macmillan, 1984.

Boon, Brindley. *Play the Music, Play! The Story of Salvation Army Bands* (London: Salvationist, 1966.

Boosey, William. *Fifty Years of Music.* London: Ernest Benn, 1931.

Booth, Charles. *Life and Labour of the People in London* (1891). 9 vols. London: Macmillan, 1902.

Boukay, Maurice. Preface to *Chansons de Montmartre,* by Paul Delmet. Paris: Enoch, 1898.

Bourdieu, Pierre. *La Distinction. Critique sociale du jugement.* Paris: Editions de Minuit, 1979.

———. *Distinction: A Social Critique of the Judgement of Taste* (1979). Trans. Richard Nice. London: Routledge, 1989.

———. *The Field of Cultural Production.* Ed. Randal Johnson. Trans. Richard Nice et al. Cambridge: Polity Press, 1993.

Bradley, John L., ed. *Rogue's Progress: The Autobiography of "Lord Chief Baron" Nicholson.* Reprint of the autobiography published in 1865. Boston: Houghton Mifflin, 1965.

Bratton, Jacqueline S. "Jenny Hill: Sex and Sexism in the Victorian Music Hall." In Bratton, *Music Hall,* 92–110.

———, ed. *Music Hall: Performance and Style.* Milton Keynes, England: Open University Press, 1986.

———. *The Victorian Popular Ballad.* London: Macmillan, 1975.

Brécy, Robert. *La Chanson de la Commune: Chansons et poèmes inspirés par la Commune de 1871.* Paris: Éditions Ouvrières, 1991.

Broadwood, Lucy, and J. A. Fuller Maitland. *English Country Songs.* London: Leadenhall Press, 1893.

Brook, G. L. *The Language of Dickens.* London: Andre Deutsch, 1970.

Brown, James D. *Biographical Dictionary of Musicians* (1886). Hildesheim: Georg Olms, 1970.

Bruant, Aristide. *Dans la rue* (1889 and 1895). 2 vols. Paris: Editions d'aujour-d'hui, 1976.

———. *Dans la rue*. Vol. 3. Paris: Flammarion, 1897.

———. *Dans la rue: Poèmes et chansons choisis*. New ed. Paris: Eugène Rey, 1924.

Budds, Michael J., ed. *Jazz and the Germans*. New York: Pendragon Press, 2002.

Buisson, Sylvie, and Christian Parisot. *Paris Montmartre: A Mecca of Modern Art 1860–1920*. Paris: Editions Terrail, 1996.

Burd, Van Akin, ed. *The Winnington Letters*. London: Allen and Unwin, 1969.

Bürger, Peter. *Theory of the Avant-Garde* (1974). Trans. Michael Shaw. Minneapolis: University of Minnesota Press, 1984.

Burkeman, Oliver. "How Many Hits?" *Guardian Weekend*, 11 Nov. 2006, 55–61.

Busch, Moritz, comp. *Wanderungen zwischen Hudson und Mississippi, 1851 und 1852*. Stuttgart: Cotta, 1854.

Byron, George [Horace Hornem, pseud.]. *The Waltz: An Apostrophic Hymn* (n.p., 1813). London: John Murray, 1816.

Canning, John, ed. *The Illustrated Mayhew's London*. London: Weidenfeld and Nicolson, 1986.

Caponi, Gena Dagel, ed. *Signifyin(g), Sanctifyin', and Slam Dunking: A Reader in African American Expressive Culture*. Amherst: University of Massachusetts Press, 1999.

Caradec, François, and Alain Weill. *Le Café-concert*. Paris: Hachette, 1980.

Carco, Francis. *La Belle Epoque au temps de Bruant*. Paris: Editions Gallimard, 1954.

Carter, Alexandra. *Dance and Dancers in the Victorian and Edwardian Music Hall Ballet*. Aldershot, England: Ashgate, 2005.

Cate, Phillip Dennis, and Mary Shaw, eds. *The Spirit of Montmartre: Cabarets, Humor, and the Avant-Garde, 1875–1905*. Exhibition catalogue. New Brunswick, N.J.: Jane Voorhees Zimmerli Art Museum, Rutgers University, 1996.

A Century and a Half in Soho: A Short History of the Firm of Novello. London: Novello, 1961.

Chappell, William. *Popular Music of the Olden Time*. 2 vols. London: Chappell, 1855–59.

Chorley, Henry Fothergill. "Depths and Heights of Modern Opera." *All the Year Round* 9 Oct. 1869: 450–54.

"Chronique—Le Café-concert." *Le Réveil*, 29 Sep. 1886.

The Cider Cellar Songster: A Collection of Spreeish Chants and Nobby Songs (London: Henry Smith, [between 1840 and 1857]).

Clark, Timothy J. *The Painting of Modern Life: Paris in the Art of Manet and His Followers*. London: Thames and Hudson, 1985.

"Classical v. Popular Music." *Musical World* 40.37 (13 Sep. 1862): 587.

Cockrell, Dale. *Demons of Disorder: Early Blackface Minstrels and Their World*. Cambridge: Cambridge University Press, 1997.

———. "Nineteenth-Century Popular Music." In David Nicholls, ed., *The Cambridge History of American Music*, 158–85. Cambridge: Cambridge University Press, 1998.

Colls, Robert, and Philip Dodd. *Englishness: Politics and Culture 1880–1920*. London: Croom Helm, 1986.

Condemi, Concetta. *Les Cafés-concerts: Histoire d'un divertissement (1849–1914)*. Paris: Quai Voltaire, 1992.

Cook, Will Marion. "Clorindy, the Origin of the Cakewalk" (1947). In *Theater Arts Anthology*, ed. Rosamond Gilder et al. New York: Theater Arts Books, 1950.

Cooper, Victoria L. *The House of Novello: Practice and Policy of a Victorian Music Publisher, 1829–1866*. Aldershot, England: Ashgate, 2003.

Coover, James, comp. *Music Publishing, Copyright and Piracy in Victorian England*. London: Mansell, 1985.

Corder, Frederick. "The Music of the People." *Musical Times and Singing-Class Circular* 26.503 (1 Jan. 1885): 9–11.

———. "Some Kinds of Music." *Musical Times and Singing Class Circular* 30.553 (1 Mar. 1889): 143–44.

Coulonges, Georges. *La Commune en chantant*. Paris: Messidor, 1970.

Crittenden, Camille. *Johann Strauss and Vienna: Operetta and the Politics of Popular Culture*. Cambridge: Cambridge University Press, 2000.

Crocker, Richard L. *A History of Musical Style*. New York: McGraw-Hill, 1966.

Csáky, Moritz. "Der soziale und kulturelle Kontext der Wiener Operette." In Finscher and Riethmüller, *Johann Strauss*, 28–65.

Curtis, G. W. "Editor's Easy Chair." *Harper's* 64 (February 1882): 467–78.

Dahlhaus, Carl. *Esthetics of Music* (1967). Trans. William Austin. Cambridge: Cambridge University Press, 1982.

———. *Nineteenth-Century Music* (1980). Trans. J. Bradford Robinson. Berkeley: University of California Press, 1989.

d'Anjou, Pierre. *Au Temps du Chat Noir*. Paris: Henri Lemoine, 1943.

Darwin, Bernard. Introduction to *The Posthumous Papers of The Pickwick Club*, by Charles Dickens, v–vi. Oxford: Oxford University Press, 1948.

d'Avenel, Georges. *Le Mécanisme de la vie moderne*. Paris: A. Colin, 1902.

Davey, Henry. *History of English Music*. London: J. Curwen, 1895.

Davidson, Donald. *Inquiries into Truth and Interpretation*. Oxford: Clarendon Press, 2001.

Davison, James. "The Parsifal Sickness" (1883). Reprinted in Charles Reid, *The Music Monster: A Biography of James William Davison, Music Critic of The Times of London, 1846–78, with Excerpts from His Critical Writings*, 215–17. London: Quartet Books, 1984.

Davison, Peter, comp. and ed. *Songs of the British Music Hall*. Jerry Silverman, music ed. New York: Oak, 1971.

Deaville, James. "African-American Entertainers in *Jahrhundertwende* Vienna: Austrian Identity, Viennese Modernism and Black Success." *Nineteenth-Century Music* 3.2 (2006): 89–112.

Delmet, Paul. *Chansons de Montmartre*. Paris: Enoch, 1898.

———. *Chansons du Quartier Latin*. Paris: Enoch, 1897.

DeNora, Tia. *Beethoven and the Construction of Genius: Musical Politics in Vienna, 1792–1803*. Berkeley: University of California Press, 1995.

Dickens, Charles. *American Notes for General Circulation* (1842). Excerpted in Bean, Hatch, and McNamara, *Inside the Minstrel Mask*, 48–49.

———. *Pickwick Papers* (1836). London: Penguin, 2000.

Dobson, Henry C., and G. Clifton Dobson. *Dobson's Universal Banjo Instructor*. Boston: Oliver Ditson, 1882.

Dodd, Charles. *Tour Notes 1878*. Manuscript in the Wrexham Library, Wales.

Donnay, Maurice. *Mes Débuts à Paris*. Paris: Libraire Anthème Fayard, 1937.

Earl, John. "Building the Halls." In Bailey, *Music Hall*, 1–32.

Eco, Umberto. *Travels in Hyperreality* (1986). London: Pan, 1987.

Editorial. *Musical World* 13.192, new ser., 5.109 (21 Nov. 1839): 461–62.

Editorial ["The Ratcatcher's Daughter"]. *Musical World* 33.44 (3 Nov. 1855): 710.

"The Educational Value of Dance Music." *Musical Times* 26.507 (1 May 1885): 253–55.

Ehrlich, Cyril. *Harmonious Alliance: A History of the Performing Right Society*. Oxford: Oxford University Press, 1989.

———. *The Music Profession in Britain since the Eighteenth Century: A Social History*. Oxford: Clarendon Press, 1985.

———. *The Piano: A History*. London: Dent, 1976.

Ehrlich, Cyril, Simon McVeigh, and Michael Musgrave. "London." In "Concert Life: 1850–1900," sec. 6.2.2 in *New Grove II*, 141–44.

Eisenberg, Ludwig. *Johann Strauss: Ein Lebensbild*. Leipzig: Breitkopf und Härtel, 1894.

Elias, Norbert. *The Civilizing Process* (1939). Oxford: Blackwell, 1994.

Elkin, Robert. *Royal Philharmonic: The Annals of the Royal Philharmonic Society*. London: Rider, 1946.

Ellis, Katharine. *Music Criticism in Nineteenth-Century France: La Revue et Gazette musicale de Paris, 1836–1880*. Cambridge: Cambridge University Press, 1995.

Emerson, Ken. *Doo-dah! Stephen Foster and the Rise of American Popular Culture*. New York: Simon and Schuster, 1997.

Engel, Carl. *The Literature of National Music* (1878–79). London: Novello, 1879.

Engel, Erich Wilhelm. *Johann Strauss und seine Zeit*. Vienna: Verlag der k.u.k. Hof-Verlags-Buchandlung Emil M. Engel, 1911.

Epstein, Dena J. *Sinful Tunes and Spirituals: Black Folk Music to the Civil War*. Urbana: University of Illinois Press, 1977.

Erskine, John. *The Philharmonic Society of New York: Its First Hundred Years*. New York: Macmillan, 1943.

Ewen, David. *All the Years of American Popular Music*. Englewood Cliffs, N.J.: Prentice Hall, 1977.

———. *American Popular Song*. New York: Random House, 1966.

Fantel, Hans. *Johann Strauss: Father and Son and Their Era*. Newton Abbot, England: David and Charles, 1971.

Faulk, Barry J. *Music Hall and Modernity: The Late-Victorian Discovery of Popular Culture*. Athens: Ohio University Press, 2004.

Fields, Armond. *Le Chat Noir: A Montmartre Cabaret and Its Artists in Turn-of-the-Century Paris*. Santa Barbara, Calif.: Santa Barbara Museum of Art, 1993.

Finscher, Ludwig, and Albrecht Riethmüller, eds. *Johann Strauss: Zwischen Kunstanspruch und Volksvergnügen*. Darmstadt: Wissenschaftliche Buchgesellschaft, 1995.

505 Mohawk Minstrels' Songs and Ballads. London: Francis, Day and Hunter, 1891.

Fletcher, Tom. *100 Years of the Negro in Show Business* (1954). New York: Da Capo Press, 1984.

Flaubert, Gustave. *Madame Bovary* (1856). Paris: Classiques universels, 2000.

Floyd, Samuel A., Jr. "Ring Shout! Literary Studies, Historical Studies, and Black Music Inquiry." *Black Music Research Journal* 11.2 (1991): 265–88.

Foner, Philip S. *American Labor Songs of the Nineteenth Century.* Urbana: University of Illinois Press, 1975.

Foucault, Michel. *Surveiller et punir: Naissance de la prison.* Paris: Gallimard, 1975.

Foucault, Michel, and Pierre Boulez. "Contemporary Music and the Public." Trans. John Rahn, *Perspectives of New Music* (fall–winter 1985): 6–12. Excerpted as "On Music and Its Reception," in Derek B. Scott, ed., *Music, Culture, and Society: A Reader,* 164–67. Oxford: Oxford University Press, 2000.

Freud, Sigmund. *The Interpretation of Dreams* (1899). Trans. James Strachey (1953). Harmondsworth, England: Penguin, 1976.

Frith, Simon. *Performing Rites: On the Value of Popular Music.* New York: Oxford University Press, 1996.

"From My Study." *Musical Times* 36.627 (1 May 1895): 297–301.

Fulcher, Jane. "The Orphéon Societies: Music for the Workers in Second-Empire France." *International Review of the Aesthetics and Sociology of Music* 10 (1979): 47–56.

———. "The Popular Chanson of the Second Empire: 'Music of the Peasants' in France." *Acta Musicologica* 52.1 (1980): 27–37.

Fuld, James. *The Book of World-Famous Music: Classical, Popular and Folk.* New York: Crown, 1966.

Fuller Maitland, John Alexander. *English Music in the Nineteenth Century.* London: Grant Richards, 1902.

Gadamer, Hans Georg. *Truth and Method* (1965). Trans. William Glen-Doepel. Rev. Joel Weinsheimer and Donald G. Marshall. New York: Continuum, 2004.

———. *Wahrheit und Methode: Grundzüge einer philosophischen Hermeneutik* (1960). 2nd ed. Tübingen: Mohr, 1965.

Gál, Hans, ed. *Johann Strauss Vater: Acht Walzer, Denkmäler der Tonkunst in Österreich* 68. Graz: Akademische Druck- u. Verlaganstalt, 1960.

Gammond, Peter, ed. *The Good Old Days Songbook.* London: EMI, 1983.

———. *The Oxford Companion to Popular Music.* Oxford: Oxford University Press, 1991.

Gans, Herbert J. *Popular Culture and High Culture: An Analysis and Evaluation of Taste.* New York: Basic Books, 1974.

"The Garde Republicaine Band." *Dwight's Journal of Music* 32.9 (Jul. 1872): 277.

Garrett, John M. *Sixty Years of British Music Hall.* London: Chappell, 1976.

Gendron, Bernard. *Between Montmartre and the Mudd Club: Popular Music and the Avant-Garde.* Chicago: University of Chicago Press, 2002.

Genouillac, H. Gourdon de, comp. *Les Refrains de la rue de 1830 à 1870.* Paris: E. Dentu, 1879.

Giddens, Anthony. *New Rules of Sociological Method: A Positive Critique of Interpretative Sociologies* (1976). 2nd ed. Cambridge: Polity Press, 1993.

Gilbert, Douglas. *American Vaudeville: Its Life and Times.* New York: McGraw-Hill, 1940.

Gillett, Paula. "Entrepreneurial Women in Britain." In Weber, *The Musician as Entrepreneur,* 198–220.

———. *Musical Women in England, 1870–1914.* London: Macmillan, 2000.

Gilroy, Paul. *The Black Atlantic: Modernity and Double Consciousness.* London: Verso, 1993.

Glauert, Jürgen. "Robert Stolz." Notes to *Wiener Musik,* compact disc, 23–27. RCA Red Seal 82876–67890–2 (2005),

Goffman, Erving. *Frame Analysis: An Essay on the Organization of Experience* (1974). Boston: Northeastern University Press, 1986.

Goncourt, Jules de and Edmond de. *Journal: Mémoires de la vie littéraire.* Ed. Robert Laffont. 22 vols. [1887–96; journal founded 1851 but publication began only in 1887]. Monaco: Fasquelle and Flammarion, 1956.

Goodman, Andrew. *Gilbert and Sullivan's London* (1988). London: Faber, 2000.

Goudeau, Emile. Preface to *Chansons du Quartier Latin,* by Paul Delmet. Paris: Enoch, 1897.

Gramit, David. "Selling the Serious." In Weber, *The Musician as Entrepreneur,* 81–100.

Gramsci, Antonio. *Selections from the Prison Notebooks.* Ed. and trans. Quintin Hoare and Geoffrey N. Smith. London: Lawrence and Wishart, 1971.

Green, Benny. *The Last Empires: A Music Hall Companion.* London: Pavilion Books, 1986.

Greenberg, Clement. "Avant-Garde and Kitsch" (1939). In Charles Harrison and Paul Wood, eds., *Art in Theory 1900–1990: An Anthology of Changing Ideas,* 529–41. Oxford: Blackwell, 1992.

Gregory, E. David. *Victorian Songhunters: The Recovery and Editing of English Vernacular Ballads and Folk Lyrics, 1820–1883.* Lanham, Md.: Scarecrow Press, 2006.

Guilbert, Yvette. *La Chanson de ma Vie (Mes Memoires).* Paris: Bernard Grasset, 1927.

Guilbert, Yvette, and H. Simpson. *Yvette Guilbert: Struggles and Victories.* London: Mills and Boon, 1910.

Habermas, Jürgen. *The Structural Transformation of the Public Sphere: An Inquiry into a Category of Bourgeois Society* (1962). Trans. Thomas Burger, with the assistance of Frederick Lawrence. 2nd ed. Cambridge: Polity Press, 1989.

Halker, Clark D. *For Democracy, Workers, and God: Labor Song-Poems and Labor Protest, 1865–95.* Urbana: University of Illinois Press, 1991.

Hamm, Charles. *Music in the New World.* New York: Norton, 1983.

———. *Yesterdays: Popular Song in America.* New York: Norton, 1979.

Hanslick, Eduard. *Geschichte des Concertwesens in Wien* (1869–70). 2 vols. Hildesheim: Georg Olms, 1979.

———. *Vienna's Golden Years of Music 1850–1900.* Trans. Henry Pleasants. London: Victor Gollancz, 1951.

———. *Vom musikalisch-Schönen* (1854). 2nd ed. Leipzig: Rudolph Weigel, 1858.

Hanson, Alice M. *Musical Life in Biedermeier Vienna.* Cambridge: Cambridge University Press, 1985.

Harding, Rosamond E. M. *The Piano-Forte: Its History Traced to the Great Exhibition of 1851.* Cambridge: Cambridge University Press, 1933.

Harker, Dave. *Fakesong: The Manufacture of British "Folksong" 1700 to the Present Day.* Milton Keynes, England: Open University Press, 1985.

Haweis, Hugh Reginald. *Music and Morals.* 1871. Reprint, London: Longmans, Green, 1912.

Hawkins, Peter. *Chanson: The French Singer-Songwriter from Bruant to the Present Day.* Aldershot, England: Ashgate, 2000.

Hegel, Georg W. F.. *Vorlesungen über die Ästhetik* [1835–38]. Vol. 3, *Das System der einzelnen Künste.* Ed. Eva Moldenhauer. Werke in 20 Bänden und Register, Bd.15. Frankfurt: Suhrkamp Verlag, 1986.

Hellsberg, Clemens. "Die wiener Philharmoniker spielen Strauss." In *Wiener Philharmoniker Johann Strauss Jubiläums-Edition 1999*, book accompanying, compact disc set, 6–8. Deutsche Grammophon 459734–2 (1999).

Hemyng, Bracebridge. "Prostitution in London" (1862). In Henry Mayhew, *London Labour and the London Poor*, 4:210–72. London: Frank Cass, 1967.

Herbert, Michel. *La Chanson à Montmartre*. Paris: Editions de la Table Ronde, 1967.

Hillery, David. *The Théâtre des Variétés in 1852*. Durham: University of Durham Modern Languages Series, 1996.

Hogarth, George. *Musical History, Biography, and Criticism* (1838). New York: Da Capo, 1969.

Hoggart, Paul. "Kids, Kidnappers and Carry-on Cockneys." *Times* (London), Friday, 13 Mar. 1998, 51.

Hoggart, Richard. *Uses of Literacy*. Harmondsworth, England: Penguin, 1958.

Höher, Dagmar. "The Composition of Music Hall Audiences 1850–1900." In Bailey, *Music Hall*, 73–92.

Howard, John Tasker. *Stephen Foster: America's Troubadour* (1934). 2nd ed. New York: Crowell, 1953.

Hughes, Meirion, and Robert Stradling. *The English Musical Renaissance, 1840–1940: Constructing a National Music* (1993). 2nd ed. Manchester: Manchester University Press, 2001.

Hunt, E. H. *British Labour History 1815–1914*. London: Weidenfeld and Nicolson, 1981.

Huyssen, Andreas. *After the Great Divide: Modernism, Mass Culture, Postmodernism*. London: Macmillan, 1986.

Ivanoff, Vladimir. "From the Danube to the Bosporus: The Ecstasy of the Waltz and the Mysticism of the Dervishes." Notes to *The Waltz—Ecstasy and Mysticism*, compact disc, 9–11. Archiv Produktion, 00289 477 5420 (2005).

Jacob, Heinrich Eduard. *Johann Strauss: A Century of Light Music* (1937). Trans. Marguerite Wolff. London: Hutchinson, 1940.

———. *Johann Strauss und das neunzehnte Jahrhundert. Die Geschichte einer musikalischen Weltherrschaft, 1819–1917*. Amsterdam: Querido-Verlag, 1937.

Jacobs, Arthur. *Arthur Sullivan: A Victorian Musician*. Oxford: Oxford University Press, 1984.

———. "Sullivan, Gilbert and the Victorians." *Music Review* 12 (1951): 122–32.

James, Henry. *Portrait of a Lady* (1881). Oxford: Oxford University Press, 1999.

Johann Strauss, Jr. Edition. Compact disc set with notes. 51 vols. Marco Polo 8.223201–47, 8.233249, 8.233275–76, 8.233279 (1989–96).

Johnson, James H. *Listening in Paris: A Cultural History*. Berkeley : University of California Press, 1995.

Johnston, William M. *The Austrian Mind: An Intellectual and Social History 1848–1938*. Berkeley: University of California Press, 1972.

"Jullien's Concerts." *Musical Examiner* 110 [wrongly published as 109] (7 Dec. 1844): 70–71.

Kahn, E. J., Jr. *The Merry Partners: The Age of Harrigan and Hart*. New York: Random House, 1955.

Kasson, John F. *Rudeness and Civility: Manners in Nineteenth-Century Urban America*. New York: Hill and Wang, 1990.

Kemp, Peter. Notes to *Johann Strauss, Jr. Edition*. Compact disc set. 51 vols. Marco Polo 8.223236 (1993).

————. *The Strauss Family: A Portrait of a Musical Dynasty* (1985). London: Omnibus, 1989.

————. "Strauss." In *New Grove II*, 24:474–96.

Kift, Dagmar. *The Victorian Music Hall: Culture, Class and Conflict* (1991). Trans. Roy Kift. Cambridge: Cambridge University Press, 1996.

Kilgariff, Michael. *Sing Us One of the Old Songs: A Guide to Popular Song 1860–1920.* Oxford: Oxford University Press, 1998.

King, A. Hyatt. *Four Hundred Years of Music Printing.* London: British Museum, 1964.

Kleinecke, Rudolf. *Johann Strauss: Ein Lebensbild.* Leipzig: Internationale Verlags- und Kunstanstalt, 1894.

Kolodin, Irving, Francis D. Perkins, and Susan Thielmann Sommer. "New York." In *New Grove II*, 17:171–89. London: Macmillan, 2001.

Kracauer, Siegfried. *Offenbach and the Paris of His Time* (1937). Trans. Gwenda David and Eric Mosbacher. London: Constable, 1937.

Lamb, Andrew. "Music of the Popular Theatre." In Nicholas Temperley, ed., *The Romantic Age 1800–1914*, vol. 5 of *The Blackwell History of Music in Britain* (1981), 92–108. Oxford: Blackwell, 1988.

————. "Waltz." In *New Grove II*, 27:72–78.

Langley, Leanne. "The Musical Press in Nineteenth-Century England." *Notes*, 2nd ser., 46.3 (Mar. 1990): 583–92.

Larkey, Edward. *Pungent Sounds: Constructing Identity with Popular Music in Austria.* New York: Peter Lang, 1993.

Laube, Heinrich. *Reise durch das Biedermeyer* (1834–37). Hamburg: Hoffmann und Campe, 1965. (Originally entitled *Reisenovellen.*)

Lawrence, Arthur. *Sir Arthur Sullivan: Life Story, Letters, and Reminiscences.* London: James Bowden, 1899.

Lee, Edward. *Folksong and Music Hall.* London: Routledge, 1982.

Leneberg, Hans, ed. and trans. *Breitkopf and Härtel in Paris: The Letters of Their Agent Heinrich Probst between 1833 and 1840.* Stuyvesant, N.Y.: Pendragon Press, 1990.

Leppert, Richard. *The Sight of Sound: Music, Representation, and the History of the Body.* Berkeley: University of California Press, 1993.

Leroy, Oliver. *A Glossary of French Slang.* London: Harrap, 1922.

Lesure, François. "Debussy et Le Chat Noir." *Cahiers Debussy* 23 (1999): 35–43.

Levine, Lawrence. *Highbrow/Lowbrow: The Emergence of Cultural Hierarchy in America.* Cambridge, Mass.: Harvard University Press, 1988.

Levy, Lester S. *Grace Notes in American History: Popular Sheet Music from 1820 to 1900.* Norman: University of Oklahoma Press, 1967.

Lhamon, W. T., Jr. "Ebery Time I Weel About I Jump Jim Crow: Cycles of Minstrel Transgression from Cool White to Vanilla Ice." In Bean, Hatch, and McNamara, *Inside the Minstrel Mask*, 275–84.

————. *Raising Cain: Blackface Performance from Jim Crow to Hip Hop.* Cambridge, Mass.: Harvard University Press, 1998.

"'Light' and 'Heavy.'" *Dwight's Journal of Music* 24.13 (Sep. 1864): 310.

Lindert, Peter H., and Jeffrey G. Williamson. "English Workers' Living Standards During the Industrial Revolution: A New Look." *Economic History Review* 36 (1983): 1–25.

Linke, Norbert. *"Es mußte einem was einfallen": Untersuchungen zur kompositorischen Arbeitsweise der "Naturalisten."* Tutzing: Hans Schneider, 1992.

————. *Johann Strauss*. Reinbek bei Hamburg: Rowohlt, 1996.

————. *Musik erobert die Welt: Wie die Wiener Familie Strauss die "Unterhaltungsmusik" revolutionierte*. Vienna: Herold, 1987.

Linn, Karen. *That Half-Barbaric Twang: The Banjo in American Culture*. Urbana: University of Illinois Press, 1991.

Liu, Dan, Nai-Yao Zhang, and Han-Cheng Zhu. "Form Recognition for Johann Strauss's Waltz Centos Based on Musical Features." In *Proceedings of the First International Conference on Machine Learning and Cybernetics*, 2 vols., 2:800–804. Beijing, Institute of Electrical and Electronics Engineers, 2002.

Lloyd, Albert L. *Come All Ye Bold Miners: Ballads and Songs of the Coalfields* (1952). 2nd ed. London: Lawrence and Wishart, 1978.

Locke, Ralph P. *Music, Musicians and the Saint-Simonians*. Chicago: University of Chicago Press, 1986.

————. "The Music of the French Chanson, 1810–1850." In Peter Bloom, ed., *Music in Paris in the Eighteen-Thirties*, 431–56. Stuyvesant, N.Y.: Pendragon Press, 1987).

Loesser, Arthur. *Men, Women and Pianos: A Social History*. New York: Simon and Schuster, 1954.

Long, John Dixon. *Pictures of Slavery in Church and State*. Philadelphia: John Dixon Long, 1857.

Lott, Eric. *Love and Theft: Blackface Minstrelsy and the American Working Class*. New York: Oxford University Press, 1993.

Lunn, Henry C. "The London Musical Season." *Musical Times and Singing Class Circular* 12.283 (1 Sep. 1866): 363–65.

————. "Popular Music." *Musical Times and Singing Class Circular* 19.430 (1 Dec. 1878): 660–61.

Macdonnell, J. B. "Classical Music and British Musical Taste." *Macmillan's* 1 (1860): 383–89.

MacInnes, Colin. *Sweet Saturday Night: Pop Song 1840–1920*. London: MacGibbon and Kee, 1967.

[MacKay, Charles]. "Modern Cynicism." *Blackwood's Edinburgh Magazine* 103.627 (Jan. 1868): 62–70.

Mackerness, E. D. *A Social History of English Music*. London: Routledge and Kegan Paul, 1964.

Mackinlay, Sterling. *Origin and Development of Light Opera*. London: Hutchinson, 1927.

Mac-Nab, Donald. Preface to *Nouvelles Chansons du Chat Noir, musique nouvelle de Roland Kohr*, by Maurice Mac-Nab. Paris: Heugel, [1894?], 7–22.

Mac-Nab, Maurice. *Chansons du Chat Noir, musique nouvelle ou harmonisée par Camille Baron*. Paris: Heugel, 1888.

————. *Nouvelles Chansons du Chat Noir, musique nouvelle de Roland Kohr*. Paris: Heugel, [1894?].

Magee, Jeffrey. "'The Sweetest Sounds': Jewish Resonance in American Popular Song." Paper presented at the *American Musicological Society* conference "Musical Intersections," Toronto, 5 Nov. 2000.

Mahar, William J. *Behind the Burnt Cork Mask: Early Blackface Minstrelsy and Antebellum American Popular Culture*. Urbana: University of Illinois Press, 1999.

Mailer, Franz. Notes to *Johann Strauss I Edition 5*. Compact disc. Marco Polo 8.225281 (2003).

————. Notes to *J. Strauss, Sr.: Orchestral Works.* Compact disc. Marco Polo 8.223617 (1994).

Marc, Henri. *Aristide Bruant: Le maître de la rue.* Paris: Editions France-Empire, 1989.

Maretzek, M. *Revelations of an Opera Manager in Nineteenth-Century America* (1855). New York: Dover, 1968.

Marsh, J. B. T. *The Story of the Jubilee Singers with Their Songs* (1875). New ed. with a supplement by F. J. Loudin. Mineola, N.Y.: Dover, 2003.

Marston, William M., and John H. Fuller. *F. F. Proctor Vaudeville Pioneer.* New York: Richard R. Smith, 1943.

Marx, Karl. "The Chartists." *New York Daily Tribune,* 25 Aug. 1852. In *Karl Marx: Selected Writings in Sociology and Social Philosophy,* ed. T. B. Bottomore and M. Rubel, 2nd ed., 204–7. Harmondsworth, England: Penguin, 1961.

————. *Das Kapital. Kritik der politischen Oekonomie* (1867). Paderborn: Voltmedia, 2004.

Marx, Karl, and Friedrich Engels. *Die deutsche Ideologie* (1845–46). Full text based on the original manuscript in Marx-Engels-Lenin Institute, Moscow, www.mlwerke.de/me/me03/me03_009.htm.

Mattfield, Julius. *A Hundred Years of Grand Opera in New York, 1825–1925.* New York: New York Public Library, 1927.

Matthews, William. *Cockney Past and Present: A Short History of the Dialect of London* (1938). London: Routledge and Kegan Paul, 1972.

Mayhew, Henry. *A Few Odd Characters out of the London Streets, as Represented in Mr. Henry Mayhew's Curious Conversazione.* London: R. S. Francis, 1857.

————. *London Labour and the London Poor.* Vol. 1. London: Charles Griffin, 1861.

McColl, Sandra. *Music Criticism in Vienna 1896–1897: Critically Moving Forms.* Oxford: Clarendon Press, 1996.

McFarlane, Gavin. *Copyright: The Development and Exercise of the Performing Right.* Eastbourne, England: Offord, 1980.

McVeigh, Simon. "An Audience for High Class Music." In Weber, *The Musician as Entrepreneur,* 162–82.

————. "The Society of British Musicians (1834–1865) and the Campaign for Native Talent." In Christina Bashford and Leanne Langley, eds., *Music and British Culture, 1785–1914: Essays in Honour of Cyril Ehrlich,* 145–68. Oxford: Oxford University Press, 2000.

Melnick, Jeffrey. *A Right to Sing the Blues: African Americans, Jews, and American Popular Song.* Cambridge, Mass.: Harvard University Press, 1999.

Melville, Herman. *Moby-Dick* (1851). Mineola, N.Y.: Dover, 2003.

Meusy, Victor, and Edmond Depas. *Guide de l'étranger à Montmartre.* Paris: Strauss, 1900.

Meyer, Leonard B. *Style and Music: Theory, History, and Ideology* (1989). Chicago: University of Chicago Press, 1996.

Middleton, Richard. "Popular Music." In *New Grove II,* 20:128–30. London: Macmillan, 2001.

Mill, John Stuart. *On Liberty and Other Essays.* Oxford: Oxford University Press, 1991.

————. *Principles of Political Economy.* [With Harriet Taylor]. 2 vols. 3rd ed. London: John W. Parker, 1852.

Mills, C. Wright. *The Sociological Imagination.* New York: Oxford University Press, 1959.

Minutes of Evidence Taken before the Select Committee on Theatres and Places of Entertainment. London: Eyre and Spottiswoode for HMS0, 1892.

Mittag, Erwin. *The Vienna Philharmonic.* Trans. J. R. L. Orange and G. Morice. Vienna: Gerlach and Wiedling, 1950.

"A Monument to Beethoven." *Musical Times and Singing Class Circular* 21.448 (1 Jun. 1880): 281.

"The Moore & Burgess Minstrels." *Strand Musical Magazine* 4 (Jul.–December 1896): 78–79.

Morris, George P. *The Deserted Bride and Other Poems.* New York, 1838.

"Mrs. Hunt's Orchestra." *Strand Musical Magazine* 5 (May 1897(: 268–69, 268.

"The Musical 'Cheap Jack.'" Editorial. *Musical Standard* (17 Mar. 1871): 117–18.

"Music for the People." *Musical Times and Singing Class Circular* 26.512 (1 Oct. 1885): 579–81.

"The Music Hall Mania." *Musical Times and Singing-Class Circular* 33.591 (1 May 1892): 265–66.

"The Music Hall of the Future." *Musical Times and Singing-Class Circular* 35.620 (1 Oct. 1894): 657–58.

"The Music Hall of the Future." *Pall Mall Gazette,* 13 Apr. 1892.

Myers, Margaret. "Searching for Data about Ladies' Orchestras." In Pirkko Moisala and Beverley Diamond, eds., *Music and Gender,* 189–213. Urbana: University of Illinois Press, 2000.

Nathan, Hans. *Dan Emmett and the Rise of Early Negro Minstrelsy.* Norman: University of Oklahoma Press, 1962.

Nettel, Reginald. *The Orchestra in England: A Social History.* London: Jonathan Cape, 1946.

———. *A Social History of Traditional Song* (1954). London: Phoenix House, 1969.

Newsome, Roy. *Brass Roots: A Hundred Years of Brass Bands and Their Music, 1836–1936.* Aldershot, England: Ashgate, 1998.

Nicholls, David, ed. *The Cambridge History of American Music.* Cambridge: Cambridge University Press, 1998.

Niecks, Frederick. "Popular Appreciation of Music." *Musical Times and Singing-Class Circular* 21.449 (1 Jul. 1880): 360.

Nietzsche, Friedrich. *Der Fall Wagner. Ein Musikanten-Problem.* Leipzig: C. G. Naumann, 1888.

Northcote, Sydney. *The Ballad in Music.* London: Oxford University Press, 1942.

Oberthür, Mariel. *Cafés and Cabarets of Montmartre.* Layton, Utah: Gibbs M. Smith, 1984.

———. *Le Chat Noir 1881–1897.* Paris: Réunion des musées nationaux, 1992.

Odell, George C. D. *Annals of the New York Stage* (1927–49). 15 vols. New York: AMS Press, 1970.

Offenbach, Jacques. *Orpheus in America* (1877). Trans. Lander MacClintock. Bloomington: Indiana University Press, 1957.

Orledge, Robert. *Satie Remembered.* London: Faber, 1995.

Paddison, Max. *Adorno, Modernism and Mass Culture: Essays in Critical Theory and Music.* London: Kahn and Averill, 1995.

Palmer, Roy. *A Ballad History of England.* London: Batsford, 1979.

———. *The Sound of History: Songs and Social Comment.* Oxford: Oxford University Press, 1988.

Parry, Charles Hubert. *Style in Musical Art.* London: Macmillan, 1911.

Parsons, Talcott. *The Social System*. London: Routledge and Kegan Paul, 1951.

Pater, Walter. *The Renaissance: Studies in Art and Poetry* (1877). 2nd ed. Oxford: Oxford University Press, 1986.

Paulus. *Trente Ans de café-concert: Souvenirs recueillis par Octave Pradels*. Paris: Société d'édition, 1927.

Pearsall, Ronald. *Victorian Popular Music*. Newton Abbot, England: David and Charles, 1973.

Peiss, Kathy. *Cheap Amusements: Working Women and Leisure in Turn-of-the-Century New York*. Philadelphia: Temple University Press, 1986.

Pénet, Martin. *Mémoire de la chanson: 1100 chansons du Moyen-Age à 1919*. Paris: Omnibus, 1998.

Pennybacker, Susan. "'It Was Not What She Said, but the Way in Which She Said It': The London County Council and the Music Hall." In Bailey, *Music Hall*, 118–40.

"The Pianoforte Virtuoso." Paris, 25 Mar. 1843. Excerpt (via a translation in *Dwight's Journal of Music*). *Musical World* 36.32 (7 Aug. 1858): 500–501.

Pickering, Michael. *Blackface Minstrelsy in Britain*. Aldershot, England: Ashgate, 2008.

———. "White Skin, Black Masks." In Bratton, *Music Hall*, 70–91.

Pike, G. D. *The Jubilee Singers and Their Campaign for Twenty Thousand Dollars*. Boston: Lee and Shepard, 1874.

Poe, Edgar Allan. "George P. Morris." In Rufus Wilmot Griswold, ed., *The Works of the Late Edgar Allan Poe*, vol. 3, *The Literati: Some Honest Opinions about Autorial Merits and Demerits*, 255–56. New York: Redfield, 1850.

Pole, William. "The London Concert Season." *Macmillan's* 4 (1861): 449.

———. *The Philosophy of Music* (1879). London: Kegan Paul, Trench, Trübner, 1910.

"Popular Composers." *Strand Magazine* 4 (Jul. 1892): 83–89.

"Popular Music." *St. James's Magazine* (June 1868). Excerpted in *Musical Standard* 8.203 (20 Jun. 1868): 246–47.

"Popular Music." *Musical Times and Singing Class Circular* 19.430 (1 Dec. 1878): 660–61.

"Popular Music of the Olden Time." *Musical World* 37.51 (17 Dec. 1859): 805–6.

Rainbow, Bernarr. *The Land without Music: Musical Education in England 1800–1860 and Its Continental Antecedents*. London: Novello, 1967.

"The Ratcatcher's Daughter." Correspondence. *Musical World* 33.44 (3 Nov. 1855): 709–10.

Raynor, Henry. *Music and Society since 1815*. London: Barrie and Jenkins, 1976.

Reeser, Eduard. *The History of the Waltz* (1947). Trans. W. A. G. Doyle-Davidson. Stockholm: Continental Book, 1949.

Reid, Charles. *The Music Monster: A Biography of James William Davison, Music Critic of the "Times" of London, 1846–78, with Excerpts from His Critical Writings*. London: Quartet Books, 1984.

Reynolds, Harry. *Minstrel Memories: The Story of Burnt Cork Minstrelsy in Great Britain from 1836 to 1927*. London: Alston Rivers, 1928.

Richard, Lionel. *Cabaret, Cabarets: Origines et decadence*. Paris: Plon, 1991.

Richards, Denis. *Offspring of the Vic: A History of Morley College*. London: Routledge and Kegan Paul, 1958.

Riethmüller, Albrecht. "Johann Strauss und der Makel der Popularität." In Finscher and Riethmüller, *Johann Strauss*, 1–17.

Riis, Thomas L. "'Bob' Cole: His Life and His Legacy to Black Musical Theater." *Black Perspective in Music* 13.2 (autumn 1985): 135–50.

———. *Just before Jazz: Black Musical Theater in New York, 1890 to 1915.* Washington, D.C.: Smithsonian Institution Press, 1989.

Ritchie, J. E. *The Night Side of London.* London: William Tweedie, 1857.

Roberts, Arthur. *Fifty Years of Spoof.* London: Bodley Head, 1926.

Rodenburg, M. de. *Journal d'un voyage à Londres.* Translation from *La Revue et Gazette Musicale. Musical World* 36.30 (24 Jul. 1858): 467.

Rodgers, C., and J. Black, eds. *The Gathering of the Forces, by Walt Whitman.* New York: Knickerbocker Press, 1920.

Rubey, Norbert. *"Des Verfassers beste Laune": Johann Strauss (Vater) und das Musik-Business im Biedermeier.* Vienna: Wiener Stadt- und Landesbibliothek, 2004.

Ruskin, John. *The Stones of Venice.* 3 vols. London: Smith, Elder, 1851–53.

Russell, David. *Popular Music in England, 1840–1914* (1987). 2nd ed. Manchester: Manchester University Press, 1997.

Russell, Henry. *Cheer, Boys, Cheer!* London: John Macqueen, 1895.

Rutherford, Lois. "'Managers in a Small Way': The Professionalization of Variety Artistes, 1860–1914." In Bailey, *Music Hall,* 93–117.

Sachs, Curt. *World History of the Dance* (1933). Trans. Bessie Schönberg. New York: Norton, 1937.

Sadie, Stanley, ed. *The New Grove Dictionary of Music and Musicians.* Executive ed. John Tyrrell. 2nd ed. 29 vols. London: Macmillan, 2001. Referred to elsewhere in this bibliography as *New Grove II.*

Said, Edward W. *Culture and Imperialism* (1993). New York: Vintage, 1994.

Saint-Simon, Henri de. *Opinions litteraires, philosophes et industrielles* (1825). Excerpted in Steve Edwards, *Art and Its Histories: A Reader,* 188–90. New Haven, Conn.: Yale University Press, 1999.

Sampson, Henry T. *Blacks in Blackface: A Source Book on Early Black Musical Shows* (1980). 2nd ed. Lanham, Md.: Scarecrow Press, 1995.

Sanjek, Russell. *American Popular Music and Its Business: The First Four Hundred Years.* Vol. 2. *From 1790 to 1909.* New York: Oxford University Press, 1988.

Satie, Erik. "Les Musiciens de Montmartre" (1900). In Ornella Volta, ed., *Ecrits,* 47. Paris: Champ Libre, 1990.

Scheide, Frank M. *South London, English Music Hall, and the Early Films of Charlie Chaplin.* Oxford: Oxford University Press, forthcoming.

Schmitz, Oskar. *Das Land ohne Musik: Englische Gesellschaftsprobleme.* 8th ed. Munich: Georg Müller, 1914.

Schneider, Ulrich. *Die Londoner Music Hall und ihre Songs 1850–1920.* Tübingen: Niemeyer, 1984.

Schnitzler, Henry. "'Gay Vienna'—Myth and Reality." *Journal of the History of Ideas* 15.1 (Jan. 1954): 94–118.

Scholes, Percy A. *The Mirror of Music 1844–1944: A Century of Musical Life in Britain as Reflected in the Pages of the "Musical Times."* 2 vols. London: Novello, 1947.

Schönherr, Max. "An der schönen blauen Donau: Marginalien zur 100. Wiederkeh des Tages der Urauffürung." *Österreichische Musikzeitschrift* 22 (1967): 3–15.

———. "Modelle der Walzerkomposition: Grundlagen zu einer Theorie des Walzers." *Österreichische Musikzeitschrift* 30 (1975): 273–86.

Schönherr, Max, and Karl Rienhöhl. *Johann Strauss Vater: Ein Werkverzeichnis.* Vienna: Universal, 1954.

Schraenen, Guy. *Erratum Musical.* Bremen: Institut Français, 1994.

Schubert, Franz. *Sämtliche Tänze für Klavier.* Vol. 2. Vienna: Wiener Urtext Edition, 1973.

Schuller, Gunther. "Jazz and Musical Exoticism." In Jonathan Bellman, ed., *The Exotic in Western Music,* 281–91. Boston: Northeastern University Press, 1998.

Scott, Derek B. *From the Erotic to the Demonic: On Critical Musicology.* New York: Oxford University Press, 2003.

———. "In Search of Genetically Modified Music: Race and Musical Style in the Nineteenth Century." *Nineteenth-Century Music* 3.1 (2006): 3–23.

———. *The Singing Bourgeois: Songs of the Victorian Drawing Room and Parlour* (1989). 2nd ed. Aldershot, England: Ashgate, 2001.

Scott, Harold. *The Early Doors: Origins of the Music Hall.* London: Nicholson and Watson, 1946.

Segel, Harold B. *Turn-of-the-Century Cabaret.* New York: Columbia University Press, 1987.

Seidl, Johann W. *Musik und Austromarxismus: Zur Musikrezeption der österreichischen Arbeiterbewegung im späten Kaiserreich und in der Ersten Republik.* Vienna: Böhlau, 1989.

Senelick, Laurence, ed. *Tavern Singing in Early Victorian London: The Diaries of Charles Rice for 1840 and 1850.* London: Society for Theatre Research, 1997.

Sharp, Cecil J. *English Folk-Song: Some Conclusions* (1907). 2nd ed. London: Novello, 1936.

Shaw, George Bernard. *The Irrational Knot* (1880). London: Constable, 1914.

———. *Pygmalion: A Romance in Five Acts.* Ed. Dan H. Laurence. Harmondsworth, England: Penguin, 2000.

———. *Shaw's Music.* Ed. Dan H. Laurence. 3 vols. London: Bodley Head, 1981.

A Short History of Cheap Music. London: Novello, Ewer, 1887.

Shrubsole, Grahame. "'Jim Crow,' Old Dan Tucker and Miss Lucy Long: The Early Years of Negro Minstrelsy in Manchester." *Manchester Sounds* 3 (2002): 23–53.

Simmel, Georg. "The Metropolis and Mental Life" (1902–3). In Kurt H. Wolff, trans. and ed., *The Sociology of Georg Simmel,* 409–24. New York: Free Press, 1950.

Simpson, Harold. *A Century of Ballads 1810–1910: Their Composers and Singers.* London: Mills and Boon, 1910.

Sims, George R. *How the Poor Live* (1889). New York: Garland, 1984.

Sixty Old-Time Variety Songs. London: EMI, 1977.

Smiles, Samuel. *Life and Labour.* London: John Murray, 1887.

———. *Self-Help* (1859). London: John Murray, 1936.

Solie, Ruth A. *Music in Other Words: Victorian Conversations.* Berkeley: University of California Press, 2004.

Southern, Eileen. "The Georgia Minstrels: The Early Years." In Bean, Hatch, and McNamara, eds., *Inside the Minstrel Mask,* 163–75.

———. *The Music of Black Americans: A History* (1983). 2nd ed. New York: Norton, 1971.

———, ed. *Readings in Black American Music* (1971). 2nd ed. New York: Norton, 1983.

Southern, Eileen, and Josephine Wright. *Images: Iconography of Music in African-American Culture (1770s–1920s).* New York: Garland, 2000.

Spaeth, Sigmund. *A History of Popular Music in America.* New York: Random House, 1948.

"Specimen of a Leader for a Music Journal." *Musical Examiner* 95 (24 Aug. 1844): 749.

Stark, Seymour. *Men in Blackface: True Stories of the Minstrel Show.* Philadelphia: Xlibris, 2000.

Stedman, Jane W. *W. S. Gilbert: A Classic Victorian and His Theatre.* New York: Oxford University Press, 1996.

"Strauss." Obituary. *Ost-Deutsche Post,* Friday, 28 Sep. 1849, 1.

Strauss, Johann [Sr.]. *Sämtliche Werke in Wiedergabe der Originaldrucke.* Ed. Ernst Hilmar. 5 vols. Tutzing: Hans Schneider, 1987.

Strauss, Johann [Jr.]. Foreword to Johann Strauss [Sr.], *Gesamtausgabe,* keyboard edition (1887–89).

Sullivan, Arthur. "About Music" (1888). In Arthur Lawrence, *Sir Arthur Sullivan: Life Story, Letters, and Reminiscences,* 261–87. London: James Bowden, 1899.

Sweet, Frank W. *A History of the Minstrel Show* (Palm Coast, Fla.: Backintyme, 2000.

Symons, Arthur. *Colour Studies in Paris.* New York: Dutton, 1918.

"A Talk with Mr. Strauss." *New York Sun,* 13 Jul. 1872. Reprinted in *Dwight's Journal of Music* 32.9 (Jul. 1872): 276–77.

Tawa, Nicholas. *A Music for the Millions: Antebellum Democratic Attitudes and the Birth of American Popular Music.* New York: Pendragon Press, 1984.

———. *Sweet Songs for Gentle Americans: The Parlor Song in America, 1790–1860.* Bowling Green, Ohio: Bowling Green University Popular Press, 1980.

———. *The Way to Tin Pan Alley: American Popular Song, 1866–1910.* New York: Schirmer Books, 1990.

Thérésa [Emma Valadon]. *Mémoires de Thérésa écrits par elle-même.* [With Victorien Monnier]. Paris: E. Dentu, 1865.

Tick, Judith. *American Women Composers before 1870.* Rochester, N.Y.: University of Rochester Press, 1979.

Toll, Robert C. *On with the Show: The First Century of Show Business in America.* New York: Oxford University Press, 1976.

Traubner, Richard. *Operetta: A Theatrical History* (1983). New York: Oxford University Press, 1989.

Tressell, Robert. *The Ragged Trousered Philanthropists* (1955). London: Grafton Books, 1965.

Trollope, Frances. *Vienna and the Austrians.* Paris: Galignani, 1838.

Trotter, Richard M. *Music and Some Highly Musical People* (1878). Excerpted in Southern, *Readings in Black American Music,* 142–48.

"The True Waltz Tempo—Strauss in New York." *Weekly Review,* 13 Jul. 1872. Reprinted in *Dwight's Journal of Music* 32.9 (Jul. 1872): 276.

Tunley, David. *Salons, Singers and Songs: A Background to Romantic French Song 1830–1870.* Aldershot, England: Ashgate, 2002.

Turner, Michael R., and Antony Miall, eds. *Just a Song at Twilight: The Second Parlour Song Book.* London: Michael Joseph, 1975.

———. *The Parlour Song Book: A Casquet of Vocal Gems* (1972). London: Pan, 1974.

Twain, Mark [Samuel Clemens]. Letter from Carson City. Virginia City (Nev.) *Territorial Enterprise,* 12 Dec. 1862. www.twainquotes.com/18621212t .html.

Twyman, Michael. *Early Lithographed Music.* London: Farrand Press, 1996.

Van Akin Burd, ed. *The Winnington Letters.* London: Allen and Unwin, 1969.

Van der Merwe, Peter. *Origins of the Popular Style: The Antecedents of Twentieth-Century Popular Music.* Oxford: Clarendon Press, 1989.

Velter, André, ed. *Les Poètes du Chat Noir.* Paris: Editions Gallimard, 1996.

Wagner, Richard. *Mein Leben* (1880). Vol. 1. English translation, www .gutenberg.org/dirs/etext04/wglf110.txt.

———. *Wagner Writes from Paris: Stories, Essays, and Articles by the Young Composer.* Ed. and trans. Robert L. Jacobs and Geoffrey Skelton. London: George Allen and Unwin, 1973.

Waites, Aline, and Robin Hunter. *The Illustrated Victorian Songbook.* London: Michael Joseph, 1984.

Waring, Dennis G. *Manufacturing the Muse: Estey Organs and Consumer Culture in Victorian America.* Middletown, Conn.: Wesleyan University Press, 2002.

Weber, Max. *The Protestant Ethic and the Spirit of Capitalism* (1904–5). Trans. Talcott Parsons. New York: Routledge, 1992. Full text in German, http://de.wikisource.org/wiki/Die_protestantische_Ethik_und_der_Geist_des_Kapitalismus.

———. *Economy and Society* [*Wirtschaft und Gesellschaft*, 1922]. Ed. Günther Roth and Claus Wittich. Trans. Ephraim Fischoff, et al. 2 vols. Berkeley: University of California Press, 1978. Full text in German http://www.textlog.de/weber_wirtschaft.html

———. *From Max Weber: Essays in Sociology.* Trans. and ed. H. H. Gerth and C. Wright Mills. New York: Oxford University Press, 1946.

Weber, William. "Canon and the Traditions of Musical Culture." In Jan Gorak, ed., *Canon vs. Culture: Reflections on the Current Debate*, 135–50. New York: Garland, 2001.

———. "From the Self-Managing Musician to the Independent Concert Agent." In Weber, *The Musician as Entrepreneur*, 105–29.

———. *The Great Transformation of Musical Taste: Concert Programming from Haydn to Brahms.* Cambridge: Cambridge University Press, forthcoming.

———. "The Intellectual Origins of Musical Canon in Eighteenth-Century England." *Journal of the American Musicological Society* 47 (1994): 488–520.

———. "The Muddle of the Middle Classes." *Nineteenth-Century Music* 3 (1979): 175–85.

———. *Music and the Middle Class: The Social Structure of Concert Life in London, Paris and Vienna between 1830 and 1848* (1975). 2nd ed. Aldershot, England: Ashgate, 2003.

———, ed. *The Musician as Entrepreneur, 1700–1914: Managers, Charlatans, and Idealists.* Bloomington: Indiana University Press, 2004.

Wechsberg, Joseph. *The Waltz Emperors: The Life and Times and Music of the Strauss Family.* London: Weidenfeld and Nicolson, 1973.

Weiss, Jeffrey S. "Picasso, Collage, and the Music Hall." In Kirk Varnedoe and Adam Gopnik, eds., *Modern Art and Popular Culture: Readings in High and Low*, 83–115. New York: Abrams, 1990.

Whitcomb, Ian. *After the Ball: Pop Music from Rag to Rock* (1972). New York: Limelight Editions, 1986.

Whiting, Steven. *Satie the Bohemian: From Cabaret to Concert Hall.* Oxford: Clarendon Press, 1998.

Williams, Raymond. *Culture.* London: Faber, 1981.

————. *Culture and Society 1780–1950* (1958). Harmondsworth, England: Penguin, 1961.

————. *Keywords.* London: Fontana, 1976.

————. *The Long Revolution* (1961). Harmondsworth, England: Penguin, 1965.

Williams, William H. A. *'Twas Only an Irishman's Dream: The Image of Ireland and the Irish in American Popular Song Lyrics, 1800–1920.* Urbana: University of Illinois Press, 1996.

Willis, Nathaniel Parker. *Memoranda of the Life of Jenny Lind.* Philadelphia: Robert E. Peterson, 1851.

Wilmeth, Don B. *Variety Entertainment and Outdoor Amusements: A Reference Guide.* Westport, Conn.: Greenwood Press, 1982.

Wilson, Thomas. *A Companion to the Ball Room.* London: Button, Whittaker, 1816.

————. *A Description of the Correct Method of Waltzing.* London: Sherwood, Neely, and Jones, 1816.

Winter, Marian Hannah. "Juba and American Minstrelsy." In Bean, Hatch, and McNamara, *Inside the Minstrel Mask,* 223–41.

Wise, Tim. "Yodelling in American Popular Music." Ph.D. diss., University of Liverpool, 2004.

Wittke, Carl. *Tambo and Bones: A History of the American Minstrel Stage* (1930). New York: Greenwood Press, 1968.

Woll, Allen. *Black Musical Theatre—From Coontown to Dreamgirls* (1989). New York: Da Capo Press, 1991.

Wollstonecroft, Mary. *A Vindication of the Rights of Men* (1790). Oxford: Oxford University Press, 1999.

Wood, Henry J. *My Life of Music.* London: Victor Gollancz, 1938.

Wood, Paul. "The Avant-Garde and the Paris Commune." In Paul Wood, ed., *The Challenge of the Avant-Garde,* 113–36. New Haven, Conn.: Yale University Press, 1999.

Workman, James. "Home, Sweet Home." *Strand Musical Magazine* 2 (1895): 252–56.

Wright, David. "The South Kensington Music Schools." *Journal of the Royal Musical Association* 130.2 (2005): 236–82.

Wyndham, Henry Saxe. *August Manns and the Saturday Concerts: A Memoir and a Retrospect.* London: Walter Scott, 1909.

Wyn Jones, Carys. "Is There a Canon in Rock Music? Canonical Values, Terms and Mechanisms in the Reception of Rock Albums." Ph.D. diss., University of Cardiff, 2006.

Yaraman, Sevin H. *Revolving Embrace: The Waltz as Sex, Steps, and Sound.* New York: Pendragon Press, 2002.

Young, Percy M. *The Concert Tradition: From the Middle Ages to the Twentieth Century.* London: Routledge and Kegan Paul, 1965.

Zon, Bennett. "'Loathsome London': Henry Davey's *History of English Music* (1895) and the Anti-urban Socialist Utopianism of Ruskin and Morris." Forthcoming.

Index

copyright and performing right, 25,
31–34, 156
Corder, Frederick, 99, 111, 162–63
Costa, Michael, 40
couplets, 55
Covent Garden, 48, 174
Theatre Royal, 40, 42
Royal Italian Opera House (from
1847), 16, 46, 56, 136
Cowell, Sam, 174
"Bacon and Greens," 176
"The Ratcatcher's Daughter," 111,
174–76, 178
"Villikins and His Dinah," 176–77
Crystal Palace, 17–18, 23, 35, 62
Cuffey, William, 145
Curwen, John, 27, 61
Czerny, Carl, 28

Dada, 217
Dahlhaus, Carl, 6, 86, 117
D'Albert, George, 161
dance halls, 44–45
dandy, 21, 52, 69–70, 154, 171, 182,
184–85
d'Anjou, Pierre, 210
Davey, Henry, 92
Davidson (publishing house), 26,
156
Musical Treasury, 156
Davidson, Donald, 106
Davison, James, 99
Degas, Edgar, *Au Café-concert, le chan-
son du chien*, 76
Delmet, Paul, 210–11, 214
"Les Petits Pavés," 210
DeNora, Tia, 41, 93, 110
Devereaux, L., "The Swiss Herds-
man," 96
Dianabad-Saal, 134
Dickens, Charles, 163, 172–74
Hard Times, 174
Oliver Twist, 174
Pickwick Papers, 172–73
Dibdin, Charles, "Peggy Perkins," 153
diseuse, 211
Ditson, Oliver, 25
Dixon, George, "Zip Coon," 52, 154
Dobson, Henry, 47, 149
Dockstader, Lew, 165

Dodd, Charles, 157
Dommayer's Casino, 135–36, 142
Donizetti, Gaetano, 88
La Favorite, 101
Donnay, Maurice, 198
Doors, The, 218
D'Oyly Carte, Richard, 56
drawing-room ballads, 65–69, 83–84,
86
Dreher, 11, 118, 248 n. 3
Drury Lane (Theatre Royal), 40–41
Duchamp, Marcel, *Fountain*, 217
Duclerc, Marguerite, 166
Dufresne, Louis, 42
Duke of York's Theatre, 213
Dumba, Nicolaus, 98, 139
Dundee Ladies' String Orchestra, 22
Dupont, Pierre, "Le Chant des
paysans," 73
Durand, Claude, "Le Chant des vi-
gnerons," 73
Dylan, Bob, 7, 149
"Desolation Row," 218

"Early One Morning," 109
Eco, Umberto, 190–91
Eden-Concert, 54, 69, 212
education, 10, 16, 25, 53, 60–61,
108, 156
Edward, Prince of Wales (later, King
Edward VII), 164, 168, 213
Ehrlich, Cyril, 16, 30
Elen, Gus, 35, 65, 187, 189–92, 194
"Down the Road," 192
"If It Wasn't for the 'Ouses in
Between," 189–91
"I'm Very Unkind to My Wife," 192
"It's a Great Big Shame," 79, 189,
191–92
Elias, Norbert, 90
Elisabeth, Empress, 109
Ella, John, 86
Elliot, G. H., 169
Elysée-Montmartre, 51
Emmett, Dan, 168
"Dixie's Land," 152, 154–55
Genuine Negro Jig, 150
My First Jig, 152
"Old Dan Tucker," 145, 149–52,
170